IMPORTANT.

HERE IS YOUR REGISTRATION CODE TO ACCESS
YOUR PREMIUM McGRAW-HILL ONLINE RESOURCES.

W9-BQV-448

For key premium online resources you need THIS CODE to gain access. Once the code is entered, you will be able to use the Web resources for the length of your course.

If your course is using **WebCT** or **Blackboard**, you'll be able to use this code to access the McGraw-Hill content within your instructor's online course.

Access is provided if you have purchased a new book. If the registration code is missing from this book, the registration screen on our Website, and within your WebCT or Blackboard course, will tell you how to obtain your new code.

Registering for McGraw-Hill Online Resources

TO gain access to your McGraw-Hill web resources simply follow the steps below:

1. USE YOUR WEB BROWSER TO GO TO: **http://www.mhhe.com/huff**

2. CLICK ON **FIRST TIME USER**.

3. ENTER THE REGISTRATION CODE* PRINTED ON THE TEAR-OFF BOOKMARK ON THE RIGHT.

4. AFTER YOU HAVE ENTERED YOUR REGISTRATION CODE, CLICK **REGISTER**.

5. FOLLOW THE INSTRUCTIONS TO SET-UP YOUR PERSONAL UserID AND PASSWORD.

6. WRITE YOUR UserID AND PASSWORD DOWN FOR FUTURE REFERENCE. KEEP IT IN A SAFE PLACE.

TO GAIN ACCESS to the McGraw-Hill content in your instructor's **WebCT** or **Blackboard** course simply log in to the course with the UserID and Password provided by your instructor. Enter the registration code exactly as it appears in the box to the right when prompted by the system. You will only need to use the code the first time you click on McGraw-Hill content.

Thank you, and welcome to your McGraw-Hill online Resources!

ONLINE RESOURCES

REGISTRATION CODE

5U7K-7NF9-W899-W5V5-KI0G

Mc Graw Hill Higher Education

0-07-297828-7 T/A HUFF: RELIGION, 1E

RELIGION
A SEARCH FOR MEANING

Margaret C. Huff

Northeastern University

Ann K. Wetherilt

Emmanuel College

McGraw
Hill

Boston   Burr Ridge, IL   Dubuque, IA   Madison, WI   New York
San Francisco   St. Louis   Bangkok   Bogotá   Caracas   Kuala Lumpur
Lisbon   London   Madrid   Mexico City   Milan   Montreal   New Delhi
Santiago   Seoul   Singapore   Sydney   Taipei   Toronto

Higher Education

RELIGION: A SEARCH FOR MEANING

Published by McGraw-Hill, a business unit of The McGraw-Hill Companies, Inc., 1221 Avenue of the Americas, New York, NY, 10020. Copyright © 2005, by The McGraw-Hill Companies, Inc. All rights reserved. No part of this publication may be reproduced or distributed in any form or by any means, or stored in a database or retrieval system, without the prior written consent of The McGraw-Hill Companies, Inc., including, but not limited to, in any network or other electronic storage or transmission, or broadcast for distance learning.

Some ancillaries, including electronic and print components, may not be available to customers outside the United States.

This book is printed on acid-free paper.

1 2 3 4 5 6 7 8 9 0 FGR/FGR 0 9 8 7 6 5 4

ISBN 0-07-286217-3

Publisher: *Christopher Freitag*
Sponsoring editor: *Jon-David Hague*
Editorial assistant: *Allison Rona*
Senior marketing manager: *Zina Craft*
Media producer: *Lance Gerhart*
Project manager: *Destiny Rynne Hadley*
Production supervisor: *Janean A. Utley*
Senior designer and interior design: *Kim Menning*
Associate supplement producer: *Meghan Durko*
Photo research coordinator: *Nora Agbayani*
Art editor: *Cristin Yancey*
Photo researcher: *Inge King*
Cover design: *Jeanne Calabrese*
Cover credit: Paul Klee, Tempelgärten (Temple Gardens), 1920, 186; 18.4 × 26.7 cm; watercolor on paper; The Metropolitan Museum of Art, New York; © 2004 Artists Rights Society (ARS), New York/VG Bild-Kunst, Bonn.
Typeface: *10/13 Palatino*
Compositor: *Precision Graphics*
Printer: *Quebecor World Fairfield Inc.*

Library of Congress Cataloging-in-Publication Data
Huff, Margaret Craddock.
    Religion : a search for meaning / Margaret C. Huff, Ann K. Wetherilt.
        p. cm.
    ISBN 0-07-286217-3 (pbk. : alk. paper)
    1. Religion. I. Wetherilt, Ann Kirkus. II. Title.
BL48.H75 2005
200—dc22

                                                2004040164

www.mhhe.com

We dedicate this book to the memory of our parents:

Jane Bland Craddock and French H. Craddock, Jr.
and
Molly Kirkus Wetherilt and James E. Wetherilt

⌐ Brief Contents ¬

⌈ CONTENTS ⌋

CHAPTER EIGHT

INTERPRETING THE CANON: COMMUNICATING SACRED TRUTH   190

CHAPTER NINE

WHO SAYS SO? TRADITIONS, AUTHORITY, AND POWER   222

DIVERSION THREE

NEW CANONS, NEW AUTHORITIES?   242

PART IV   SEEKING ULTIMACY, SEEKING HOPE:
EXPERIENCING THE SACRED

CHAPTER TEN

IS THE SENSORY WORLD ALL THERE IS? UNDERSTANDINGS OF
THE SACRED   248

⌈ PREFACE ⌉

Everyone who writes a textbook does so, we expect, because they have not found a text that provides what they want to teach. So we have, with the assistance of many students and others, written the text we have wanted to teach.

In our experience at both of our institutions, and regardless of their initial religious practices or lack of same, our students are engaged in a search for meaning. For all those students, we hope we have created the text we had not been able to find—namely, one which is about learning meaningful questions, not just about learning the answers that have been meaningful for others. Our goal is to invite and to enable students to bring their own search for meaning into dialogue with the explorations experienced and expressed through multiple religious traditions. In this way, we hope that they will gain a deeper understanding of and appreciation for both their own traditions and those of other people and places. While we are both from Christian backgrounds, we are not advocating a particular religion, but we are advocating an empathetic approach to all particular religions and to the phenomenon of religion. We believe that part of the goal of any educational experience is to engage students in such a way that they will continue to think about and further explore the issues raised after the course is over, in the future. This is nowhere more potentially significant than in religion understood as the "search for meaning," a life-long endeavor.

One characteristic of this text is that it is written in a relatively informal style so as to attract student interest. We want to engage in a conversation with our readers, and we ask them lots of questions. This informal writing style, along with our use of several genres of writing, means that an instructor can point out the different styles—everything from protest songs to formal scientific pieces—as a tool in teaching writing across the curriculum. And, of course, engaging in conversation with students means that we are not being didactic in an authoritarian way. Students often open up and participate more significantly when the text, as well as the teacher, shows a real respect for what they have to say. We hope both the style and the substance of our text do just that.

We provide a multitude of questions but not many answers. If we, the authors, and the teachers who use this book, ask the right questions, our students will supply answers that they internalize, because those answers come from their own experiences. As they read the essays, short stories, excerpts from novels and news articles, songs, excerpts from plays, biographies, and academic works, the readers can compare their lives with those of fictional and real characters, fictional and real situations, contemporary and historical eras. This process reflects our pedagogical orientation, one that privileges an interactive learning style. The news stories will help to show the relevance of religion, even in our technological age. We have used excerpts that reflect the multiplicity of ethnic, racial, and religious backgrounds that our students live, demonstrating a belief that knowledge about all ways of living is important to us.

An important feature throughout the text is the activity boxes. These boxed activities are suggestions meant to be numerous enough that something will appeal to everyone, though not all will appeal to everyone. These boxes reflect our commitment to experiential learning, as the activities usually involve students *doing* something, rather than merely reading the text.

We want to stress that this text emphasizes inductive learning. We think that the fundamental crux of the search for meaning exemplified by religion is best internalized if someone discerns it for himself or herself. The inductive format also makes it possible for students from diverse backgrounds, ethnicities, races, religions, and sexual orientations to bring their particularities to bear on the topic under discussion.

The structure of this book has undergone many revisions, primarily because in our understandings of religion, all topics are interrelated; thus divisions become quite arbitrary. Apart from the conventional chapter structure, the main divisions that we have in the text are really noted only by the fact that a "Diversion" follows each. Thus teachers may choose to alter the order in which the first three parts of the book are presented, or to refer backward and forward to readings in other parts of the text, or even to begin with the Sacred and return to its components. All the same, except for cross-references to texts in other parts of the book, we do recommend the order in which the materials are presented now, because the students with whom we have tested the book seem to find it "natural."

Within each main part, we begin with what seem to us the key ingredients of that portion of the text and end with what we call a "Diversion"—not a detour or an amusement, but material that draws together the learning of the preceding chapters and yet also turns away from it to new and more imaginative manifestations of the topics.

We started with the essential ingredients for a religion—an individual who is part of a community of believers who communicate with one another through symbols and rituals. After three chapters devoted to these matters, we included as the "Diversion" a section that dealt with identity, symbol, and ritual—and the nonhuman animal. We came to this diversion from some of the books of speculative fiction we had read that included non-human protagonists and from philosophy texts one of us had used that dealt with the narrowing gaps between human and nonhuman animals. This kind of question, wholly new to some of the students, obviously led to ethical issues.

The ethical stance of a religion and its proponents is tied into the use of symbols and rituals—communication in general—and is essential for a self, a community, and their interrelationship. In the second part of the book, therefore, we included chapters on evil and suffering, ethics, and justice. These chapters deal with responsibility to self and others. Here, for the Diversion, we have included a piece from a medical ethics text. The excerpt is an example from that text; the other material is informed by that and other medical ethics texts and articles generally discussing IVF (In Vitro Fertilization). Although many of the cutting-edge issues in ethics are in the field of medical ethics, this one seemed particularly appropriate, dealing as it does with questions of good and evil, personal and group ethics, and justice.

The third part of our text has to do with epistemology. Chapters 7, 8, and 9 deal with different ways of knowing generally, standards of knowledge, ways of knowing and communicating sacred truth, and finally looking at the authorities that determine what counts as knowledge. Scriptures are handled in this section, so for the Diversion, we chose an article about a different Old Testament, one which would "stand beside" the usual Hebrew Scripture, at least in Christianity.

Finally, having laid the framework of the ideas, concepts, and tools necessary for understanding, we turn explicitly to the Sacred. In Part Four, in addition to ideas of what is meant by the Sacred, we look at notions from many sources of what constitutes wholeness, in life and death. Our final Diversion comes from a magazine article about a new, or rather a readopted and readapted, method of easing the dying process in the West.

In material we have quoted, we have neither corrected sexist language nor have we used *sic* to show that we are aware of the language. In some cases, such changes would have been minimal; in others, the changes would have been so numerous as to interfere with the author's point. Some of these could be teaching opportunities—for instance, does an author mean to include women in her or his article?

Similarly, we have not "sanitized" colloquial language. As bell hooks has so clearly shown, the richness of the English language is dependent on the enrichment it receives from nonstandard English. Some terms will fade as poor replacements; others, however, will become part of the language. Likewise, we decided to leave "G-d" in pieces we excerpted from Jewish authors. None of our students has found it confusing, although some have asked their Jewish classmates why this is done.

As an accompaniment to this text, we have developed a website, hosted by McGraw-Hill: www.mhhe.com/huff. Among the items on the website are pictures, links to other sites, and suggestion for further reading and music for listening. The website will be updated periodically with new material, including new illustrative material, to supplement that already in the text. Through a "contact the authors" link, we invite your own suggestions as to how we can continually improve our material.

Many have contributed to this book in innumerable ways. We have taught various versions of "Search" with introductory classes in religion at Emmanuel College and Northeastern University. This text is considerably better than it would otherwise have been because of student and colleague comments and suggestions. To all of our students who persevered with multiple drafts, photocopies, and incomplete manuscripts, our grateful thanks. One outgrowth of student comments is the "Note to Students," which follows, which explains a bit about the process of the book. We have found it helpful for *all* to read this Note to Students.

We have had the incalculable benefit of having had the entire manuscript read, twice, by Patricia B. Craddock, Distinguished Professor of English, University of Florida. We feel a confidence in our book which would have not been possible without her assistance.

Our team at McGraw-Hill has been helpful and encouraging throughout. A special thanks to Ken King, who suggested an introductory text to us many years ago. Jon-David Hague, our editor, has from the beginning seen and supported what we have tried to do, offering suggestions and encouragement through his inexhaustible ability to find the "silver lining." Alison Rona, assistant editor, has provided great persistence and competence for getting the nitty-gritty materials and support we needed. Destiny Rynne Hadley, our project manager, has overseen the final processes with humor and patience, and great competence. Our copy editor, Peter de Lissovoy, has been extraordinary with his meticulous work and helpful observations and suggestions.

We thank also all our reviewers. Edward John Hughes (California State University, Long Beach), Martin S. Jaffee (University of Washington), Eve Mullen (Mississippi State University), and Richard Pilgrim (Syracuse University) read our proposal and first chapters and gave invaluable feedback as we continued to develop our text. Julia Fleming (Creighton University) and Dan Spencer (Drake University) read the entire penultimate draft and provided both encouragement and constructive suggestions that were invaluable. The final reponsibility for the content, of course, is ours.

More personal thanks go to a series of Great Pyrenees dogs who have shared life with us through the years, and who have helped us maintain our sense of humor and thus our sanity. Sugar, Shelley, Paddington, Ivy Rose, Tori, and Blair, like others of their breed, put aside their dignity to clown when we needed laughter, insisted on walks in the arboretum when we needed a break, and continue to challenge us beyond anthropocentric ways of thinking and being. Tori and Blair will see the end of this manuscript, but the paw prints of all are present (on all the good parts, they say).

Margaret especially thanks, in addition to her sister, Patricia B. Craddock, her children, David Huff and Patricia Alvarado; her grandchildren, Tatiana and Mayan Alvarado; and her daughter-in-law, the Rev. Carolyn T. Huff, for all their contributions, with special thanks to Carolyn, for explaining an idosyncrasy of clerical garb.

Ann particularly thanks Emmanuel colleagues Mary E. Hines and Michael Hartwig, who have class-tested multiple incarnations of this manuscript and have given invaluable feedback. She is deeply grateful to Emmanuel College for a sabbatical leave that enabled this manuscript to take shape and for funding her two splendid research assistants Paula Kolek and Anne Webber. A special word of gratitude is due Professor Emeritus Richard Beauchesne whose approach to and love for the study of religion has enriched Ann's teaching, and thus her contributions to this text.

Margaret C. Huff
Ann K. Wetherilt

A Note to Students

The academic study of religion is as complex as religion itself. In this text we are inviting you to a particular way of learning and investigation. While the book provides a great deal of diverse information, it is not supposed to give you simple answers to complex questions. We believe that, given the appropriate data, having asked some appropriate questions, and asking questions of your own, you can determine responses for yourselves. We think our job, and that of your instructors, is to facilitate your finding these answers, not to give them to you. From our own experience, we remember things better, and appreciate them more, if we figure them out for ourselves. We hope that is your experience as well, and we invite you into the world of questions that constitute this book. Some questions will resonate with you better than others. We do not expect everyone to be engaged by every question; choose your questions and wrestle with them!

One of the limitations of a printed text is that it must be designed in linear form. This means that we have had to make what might seem arbitrary decisions as to the order of chapters and of material within those chapters. You will notice that many themes and issues come up in more than one place. All of the topics included in this text are interrelated; we have chosen the current format and grouping to provide coherence within the main parts, not to imply a neat linear progression. In the text as a whole and within each chapter, we begin by inviting you to reflect on your own experience of the topic being addressed. Our assumption is that, whether or not you consider yourself "religious," you are engaged in the human search for meaning in some way. Having considered the ways in which you seek meaning in your life, you will more effectively engage the other voices you encounter in the text. These voices include representatives of many traditions and cultures.

In addition to examples from many religious and cultural traditions there are selections from various genres: poetry, song, fiction, autobiography, news stories, as well as more conventional texts. Our intention is to invite you into the process of exploring the ways in which humankind seeks meaning, particularly through the medium of religion. You will get the most out of this process if you enter dialogue with those whose words you will encounter. We hope that our informal writing style invites you into this dialogue.

We do not give you definitions in this text; rather, we hope that you, in dialogue with the authors we present here, will arrive at your own description of the terms discussed. You can then test your perceptions against the definitions others have derived. You may decide that your description needs some clarification, or that it is fine as it stands. Either way, you will be engaging in the critical scholarly endeavor of analysis. We hope that we are inviting you to do so in a (relatively) painless way!

At the end of a recent course in which a draft of this book was used, a student wrote:

> "*Search for Meaning* has not just been about a certain type of religion or faith. This book has shown all the different parts that, when combined, compose the true meaning of religion. Religion, with all of its traditions, symbols, rituals, and sacred truths, is swirled all together to create meaning and a purpose for people's lives. . . . Religion is not simply worshipping an all-powerful being, but is about everything combined that can give people a sense of wholeness, or purpose in life."*

---

* Elizabeth A. Reed
  Emmanuel College
  (Used with permission)

I

Seeking Community, Seeking Self, Seeking the Sacred: Experiencing Be-ing

CHAPTER ONE

WHO AM I, WHO ARE WE?
THE SEARCH FOR IDENTITY

In this book, we are interested in the human search for meaning and in the phenomenon of religion as one way in which individuals and communities engage in that search. But who are those individuals and communities who ask such questions? What defines them, shapes them, encourages them or discourages them from inquiring into and grappling with issues that have kept philosophers and religious thinkers occupied through the ages? Before we engage some of the wider issues that are usually associated with the study of religion, we need to look closer to home, to be somewhat self-reflective. In short, we have to develop at least a working response to the question, "Who am I?"

SETTING THE STAGE: HOW DO WE KNOW WHO WE ARE?

Have you ever really thought about this question and its significance in your life? In his autobiography, *Lame Deer: Seeker of Visions,* John Fire Lame Deer recounts his experience of the vision quest, the rite of passage to adulthood for young Lakota boys. Coming-of-age rituals such as the vision quest are common in many cultures and are associated with the transition from childhood to the increasing responsibilities of adulthood. Imagine yourself at sixteen years of age, left alone in the wilderness for four days and nights with only the sparse comforts with which Lame Deer's community has provided him. What effect would such an experience have had on you? How does this experience shape the young Lame Deer's self-understanding, and his relationship with his community? Is there any evidence in this narrative of anything we might call "religion," or the sacred dimension of life?

Members of the Lakota Sioux still hold sacred the Black Hills region of South Dakota.

I was all alone on the hilltop. I sat there in the vision pit, a hole dug into the hill, my arms hugging my knees as I watched old man Chest, the medicine man who had brought me there, disappear far down in the valley. He was just a moving black dot among the pines, and soon he was gone altogether.

Now I was all by myself, left on the hilltop for four days and nights without food or water until he came back for me. You know, we Indians are not like some white folks—a man and a wife, two children, and one baby sitter who watches the TV set while the parents are out visiting somewhere.

Indian children are never alone. They are always surrounded by grandparents, uncles, cousins, relatives of all kinds, who fondle the kids, sing to them, tell them stories. If the parents go someplace, the kids go along.

But here I was, crouched in my vision pit, left alone by myself for the first time in my life. I was sixteen then, still had my boy's name and, let me tell you, I was scared. I was shivering and not only from the cold. The nearest human being was many miles away, and four days and nights is a long, long time. Of course, when it was all over, I would no longer be a boy, but a man. I would have had my vision. I would be given a man's name.

Sioux men are not afraid to endure hunger, thirst and loneliness, and I was only ninety-six hours away from being a man. The thought was comforting. Comforting, too, was the warmth of the star blanket which old man Chest had wrapped around me to cover my nakedness. My grandmother had made it especially for this, my first *hanblechia,* my first vision-seeking. . . . If Wakan Tanka, the Great Spirit, would give me the vision and the power, I would become a medicine man and perform many ceremonies wrapped in that quilt. I am an old man now and many times a grandfather, but I still have that star blanket my grandmother made for me. I treasure it; some day I shall be buried in it.

The medicine man had also left a peace pipe with me, together with a bag of *kinnickinnick*—our kind of tobacco made of red willow bark. This pipe was even more of a friend to me than my star blanket. To us the pipe is like an open Bible. White people need a church house, a preacher and a pipe organ to get into a praying mood. . . . For us Indians there is just the pipe, the earth we sit on and the open sky. . . . That smoke from the peace pipe, it goes straight up to the spirit world. But this is a two-way thing. Power flows down to us through that smoke, through the pipe stem. . . . Smoking this pipe would make me feel good and help me to get rid of my fears. . . . As I fingered the pipe, touched it, felt its smoothness that came from long use, I sensed that my forefathers who had once smoked this pipe were with me on the hill, right in the vision pit. I was no longer alone.

Besides the pipe the medicine man had also given me a gourd. In it were forty small squares of flesh which my grandmother had cut from her arm with a razor blade. I had seen her do it. Blood had been streaming down from her shoulder to her elbow as she carefully put down each piece of skin on a hand-kerchief, anxious not to lose a single one. . . . Someone dear to me had under-gone pain, given me something of herself, part of her body, to help me pray and make me stronghearted. How could I be afraid with so many people—living and dead—helping me? . . .

Night was coming on. I was still lightheaded and dizzy from my first sweat bath in which I had purified myself before going up the hill. . . . The sweat bath had prepared me for my vision-seeking. Even now, an hour later, my skin still tingled. But it seemed to have made my brains empty. Maybe that was good, plenty of room for new insights.

Darkness had fallen upon the hill. I knew that *hanhepiwi* had risen, the night sun, which is what we call the moon. Huddled in my narrow cave, I did not see it. Blackness was wrapped around me like a velvet cloth. It seemed to cut me off from the outside world, even from my own body. It made me listen to the voices within me. I thought of my forefathers who had crouched on this hill before me, because the medicine men in my family had chosen this spot for a place of meditation and vision-seeking ever since the day they had crossed the Missouri to hunt for buffalo in the White River country some two hundred years ago. I thought that I could sense their presence right through the earth I was leaning against. I could feel them entering my body, feel them stirring in my mind and heart.

Sounds came to me through the darkness: the cries of the wind, the whis-per of the trees, the voices of nature, animal sounds, the hooting of an owl. Sud-denly I felt an overwhelming presence. Down there with me in my cramped hole was a big bird. The pit was only as wide as myself, and I was a skinny boy, but that huge bird was flying around me as if he had the whole sky to himself. I could hear his cries, sometimes near and sometimes far, far away. I felt feathers or a wing touching my back and head. This feeling was so overwhelming that it was just too much for me. I trembled and my bones turned to ice. I grasped the rattle with the forty pieces of my grandmother's flesh. It also had many little stones in it, tiny fossils picked up from an ant heap. Ants collect them. Nobody knows why. These little stones are supposed to have a power in them. I shook the rattle and it made a soothing sound, like rain falling on rock. It was talking to me, but it did not calm my fears. I took the sacred pipe in my other hand and began to sing and pray: "Tunkashila, grandfather spirit, help me." But this did not help. I don't know what got into me, but I was no longer myself. I started to cry. Crying, even my voice was different. I sounded like an older man. I couldn't even recognize this strange voice. I used long-ago words in my prayer, words no longer used nowadays. I tried to wipe away my tears, but they wouldn't stop. In the end I just pulled that quilt over me, rolled myself up in it. Still I felt the bird wings touching me.

Slowly I perceived that a voice was trying to tell me something. It was a bird cry, but I tell you, I began to understand some of it. That happens sometimes. I know a lady who had a butterfly sitting on her shoulder. That butterfly told her things. This made her become a great medicine woman.

I heard a human voice too, strange and high-pitched, a voice which could not come from an ordinary, living being. All at once I was way up there with the birds. The hill with the vision pit was way above everything. I could look down even on the stars, and the moon was close to my left side. It seemed as though the earth and the stars were moving below me. A voice said, "You are sacrificing yourself here to be a medicine man. In time you will be one. You will teach other medicine men. We are the fowl people, the winged ones, the eagles and the owls. We are a nation and you shall be our brother. You will never kill or harm any one of us. You are going to understand us whenever you come to seek a vision here on this hill. You will learn about herbs and roots, and you will heal people. You will ask them for nothing in return. A man's life is short. Make yours a worthy one."

I felt that these voices were good, and slowly my fear left me. I had lost all sense of time. I did not know whether it was day or night. I was asleep, yet wide awake. Then I saw a shape before me. It rose from the darkness and the swirling fog which penetrated my earth hole. I saw that this was my great-grandfather, Tahca Ushte, Lame Deer, old man chief of the Minneconjou. I could see the blood dripping from my great-grandfather's chest where a white soldier had shot him. I understood that my great-grandfather wished me to take his name. This made me glad beyond words.

We Sioux believe that there is something within us that controls us, something like a second person almost. We call it *nagi*, what other people might call soul, spirit or essence. One can't see it, feel it or taste it, but that time on the hill—and only that once—I knew it was there inside of me. Then I felt the power surge through me like a flood. I cannot describe it, but it filled all of me. Now I knew for sure that I would become a *wicasa wakan*, a medicine man. Again I wept, this time with happiness.

> I didn't know how long I had been up there on that hill—one minute or a lifetime. I felt a hand on my shoulder gently shaking me. It was old man Chest, who had come for me. He told me that I had been in the vision pit four days and four nights and that it was time to come down. He would give me something to eat and water to drink and then I was to tell him everything that had happened to me during my *hanblechia*. He would interpret my visions for me. He told me that the vision pit had changed me in a way that I would not be able to understand at that time. He told me also that I was no longer a boy, that I was a man now. I was Lame Deer. [1]

In Western cultures, we acknowledge that many factors contribute to our sense of self, yet we still often think of identity as a rather personal thing. Many other cultural traditions place great emphasis on the community as contributing to—or even defining—one's identity. You may also have noticed the extent to which the boundaries became blurred for Lame Deer between his concrete present surroundings and the spiritual realm. How do you think Lame Deer would respond if asked to describe himself without reference to his community, or to the sacred dimensions of life? Would these questions even make sense to him?

WHAT DO YOU THINK? PERSONAL IDENTITY

You have probably been in many situations in which you have had to give at least a brief response to the question, "Tell us/me about yourself." How do you introduce yourself to a person you've just met at a party and to whom you are somewhat attracted? What about a new roommate? A co-worker? A prospective employer? How do you process, even censor, your response according to the context? Do you construct your answer to meet what you think are the expectations of the person or persons? In any of these instances, do you convey to the other person just exactly who you are? Who are you, anyway?

The tension of having others perceive him differently from the way in which he perceives himself is at the heart of a poem written by German theologian Dietrich Bonhoeffer. Bonhoeffer was imprisoned in Nazi Germany because of his involvement in a plot to assassinate Adolf Hitler. Although you have probably never been in a situation comparable to that of Bonhoeffer's, you may have asked yourself some of the same questions that occupied him during his incarceration.

> Who am I? They often tell me
> I stepped from my cell's confinement
> calmly, cheerfully, firmly,
> like a Squire from his country house.
>
> Who am I? They often tell me
> I used to speak to my warders

freely and friendly and clearly,
as though it were mine to command.

Who am I? They also tell me
I bore the days of misfortune
equably, smilingly, proudly,
like one accustomed to win.

Am I then really that which other men tell of?
Or am I only what I myself know of myself?
Restless and longing and sick, like a bird in a cage,
struggling for breath, as though hands were compressing my throat,
yearning for colours, for flowers, for the voices of birds,
thirsting for words of kindness, for neighbourliness,
tossing in expectation of great events,
powerlessly trembling for friends at an infinite distance,
weary and empty at praying, at thinking, at making,
faint, and ready to say farewell to it all.

Who am I? This or the Other?
Am I one person today and tomorrow another?
Am I both at once? A hypocrite before others,
and before myself a contemptible woebegone weakling ?
Or is something within me still like a beaten army
fleeing in disorder from victory already achieved?

Who am I ? They mock me, these lonely questions of mine.
      Whoever I am, Thou knowest, O God, I am thine![2]

Where does Bonhoeffer experience the most dissonance between his own sense of himself and the perception of himself by others? Why might Bonhoeffer's particular circumstances—imprisoned and unlikely to escape with his life—provoke him to this kind of introspection? Note particularly Bonhoeffer's conclusion. What do you think he means? Has he answered his own question? What are some of the factors that might lead to others' seeing Bonhoeffer differently from the way he sees himself? How might the Nazis have described this man who was plotting to assassinate their leader? How might a resistance worker have described him? Who would be "right"? And to what extent do factors outside ourselves influence the persons we become?

Take a piece of paper and tell yourself who you are. What are those elements of your personality that are most important in defining who you are? What are the most significant characteristics of you that others, or at least most others, don't know about? What do you most want the world to see? Would one of your parents describe you in the same way? Your closest friend? Would any of these descriptions really capture the complexity of the person you are? And are you the same person today that you were five years ago, or that you will be five years from now?

CULTURAL AND SOCIAL INFLUENCES ON IDENTITY

As the passages from John Fire Lame Deer and Dietrich Bonhoeffer illustrate, our most basic sense of self is deeply influenced by the culture and society in which we are raised as well as by our immediate family.

IDENTITY AND SOCIAL CONTEXT

However we perceive ourselves at any given point in our lives, our early experiences have a lasting impact on us. What are your earliest memories of yourself in the context of your family or community? Are those memories ones you cherish and remember with joy and gratitude or are they hard to think about, reminiscent of times you'd prefer to forget? The following passage is from a Yiddish folksong once sung by little Jewish girls in Eastern Europe.

> *Sheyn bin ich, sheyn,*
> *sheyn iz mayn Nomen.*
> (Beautiful am I, beautiful,
> beautiful is my name.)
> A pretty girl am I,
> red socks I wear,
> money in our pockets,
> wine in our bottles,
> milk in our jugs,
> babies in our cradles,
> all of them cry: beautiful,
> beautiful am I, beautiful.[3]

How would you describe the child in the song? In particular, how would you describe the way she feels about herself? What kind of identity, self-perception, has she developed? What is it like to grow up in her community, her family? By way of contrast, consider this poem, written by a 17-year-old student in Harlem, a young man who uses the pen name "Clorox."

> WHAT AM I?
> I have no manhood—What am I?
> You made my woman head of the house—What am I?
> You have oriented me so that I hate and distrust
> my brothers and sisters—What am I?
> You misprounce [sic] my name and say I have no
> self-respect—What am I?
> You give me a dilapidated education system and
> expect me to compete with you—What am I?
> You say I have no dignity, and then deprive me
> of my culture—What am I?
> You call me a boy, dirty lowdown slut—
> What am I?

> Now I'm a victim of the welfare system—What am I?
> You tell me to wait for change to come, but 400
> years
> have passed and change ain't come—What am I?
> I am all of your sins
> I am the skeleton in your closets
> I am the unwanted sons and daughters in-laws, and
> rejected babies
> I may be your destruction, but above all I am, as
> you so crudely put it, your nigger.[4]

What might you deduce about Clorox's life from this poem? What are the major differences between the two examples above? What are some of the elements that shape the perception of identity held by the writers of the two poems/songs? Which of these, if either, is closer to your own experience?

These examples raise questions about the extent to which we are responsible for the shaping of our own identities, and the extent to which our families and surrounding cultural and social contexts influence both the persons we become and the ways in which we perceive ourselves. Look back at what you wrote in response to the "who am I?" question, and consider any influences that affected the ways in which you see yourself. Do you, for example, remember specific instances when you were affirmed for a particular action or talent? Do you recall other instances when you were put down for something you contributed or tried? And are there ways in which you have felt judged by factors that have nothing to do with your own actions or abilities? How important are such messages in the development of identity? German poet and theologian Dorothee Sölle suggests that the experiences we have as children are highly formative. We are affected most intimately, of course, by our immediate family, but the wider society, with all its religious, cultural, political and economic structures and institutions, participates in this shaping of identity and self-perception. Sölle claims that, for the Jewish child chanting the happy Yiddish song above, "life has said a great 'Yes' to me, affirmed my existence."[5] She asks,

> What does it mean for a child to grow up in a world where a song like this is sung? What does it mean to learn and sing such a song? Who I am is not determined by me alone but also by the interpretation the world around me puts on me. Were my parents eager to have me, or was I an unwanted child? Am I the prime object of their love and protection, or do I come far behind the car? And with this interpretation that is already given, I do not mean just the one that my parents and those closest to me give to me but also the one that society puts on me. The institutions and customs of a society convey a message, an interpretation of its life, to every child. They can tell the child: You are important. You are something extra special. Or they can say: You are superfluous. There is no room for you. Parking lots are more important than playgrounds for you. The sidewalk is not there for you to play hopscotch on. The arms industry is much

more important than your school. For many children it has been determined
long before they were even born that they do not need any place for
themselves, that they have nothing to say, and that they should be as quiet and
unobtrusive as possible.

In our song, things are quite different. The child has a place in the world of
a comfortably functioning economy—money in our pockets, wine in our
bottles. Life is worth living; happiness is possible; the self is beautiful. God said
on the seventh day of creation that everything was very good. This song
concurs with that. It expresses what a happy childhood gives a person for life:
trust in the reliability of the world. Tomorrow will be as yesterday was. There
will be wine in the bottles, milk in the jugs. Everything tells me I am beautiful,
beautiful. That will not always be true for me, but that it was once true can
never be taken away from me. . . . This interpretation from outside forms and
determines my own interpretation of myself. [6]

Not only is this "beautiful" child secure in her own person, she also seems confident that her surrounding culture has the capacity to continue to nurture her
and to provide her with the good things of life. How does this differ from the
messages "Clorox" received about his worth and value, and about the trust-
worthiness of the world around him? How did the outside world function in
relation to developing Clorox's sense of himself? What are some of the factors
that placed him at odds with what society considers normative?

To a great extent, appearance often determines our first evaluation of others. Whether we are talking about racial/ethnic characteristics, sex, age, general appearance or the presence of physical handicaps, we often make assumptions about others (and ourselves) based upon stereotypes that may have
nothing to do with the essence of who the person is. In this opening passage
from a mystery novel, we encounter an example of the ways in which our self-
perception is shaped by our physical reality.

If I were a self-help book, I would be *The Big-Boned Syndrome: Hardy Women
Who Can't Leave Well Enough Alone.* If we had a twelve-step program I would be
the first to stand, and I would say, *My name is Nora Lumsey, and I am a big-boned
woman and my intentions are good but I keep fucking up.*

I was made too big. I am built like the proverbial brick shithouse, and this
awful outsized quality I have—of never being sure of where I begin and end—
has sent me teetering through the world, bumping hard into people, smashing
things as I go.

Clumsy Lumsey.

This is a story about blundering in.[7]

How much do our physical characteristics affect our self-perceptions? And are
these just our own personal perceptions or does society send us messages about
how we should perceive people who are taller or shorter than the average,
weigh more or less than some arbitrary norm, or have lighter or darker skin?

Spend a few minutes browsing through a contemporary magazine, or watch MTV, or a favorite music video, noting the physical characteristics of the people presented in the program or advertisements. Choose the one you think most nearly fits your culture's definition of the "ideal" person—the one everyone should aspire to be like. How many "real people" do you know who come close to this "ideal"? What about you? List the ways in which you "fail" to measure up, as well as those areas where you come close. What do these discrepancies say about who you are as a person? Do they define your identity in any way? Would others say they do? How important are these images?

THE SELF IN COMMUNITY

In the dominant European culture of the United States, ultimate significance is often placed on the individual, on personal rights and freedoms, sometimes even to the extent that the relationship of the individual with the social groups to which he or she belongs gets overlooked. Many other cultural traditions reverse this emphasis. In Lame Deer's account of his vision quest, for example, we saw the importance of his community in shaping the experience he went through. Think about your own understandings of the relationship between your individual identity and the communities to which you belong: your family, religious and/or cultural groups, your closest friends, a sports team, and so on. What is lost and what is gained when the focus shifts more to an emphasis on the individual rather than the community? Some would say that the development of strong individuals is essential in building strong and effective communities. Others claim that we cannot really *have* a meaningful identity outside of community or communities. Freda McDonald felt this so strongly that she had the sense of her very identity being stripped from her because of a particular application of Canadian law:

> The bottom of my world dropped out when I was handed the card reading, "Not deemed to be an Indian within the law or any other statute" because I had married a non-Native. The stigma of this life sentence entered my soul. This tore the last vestiges of my being into shreds, spiritually and mentally. By law, I could not live or be with my people anymore. I stood alone, once more, but this time naked—stripped of my identity and banished into a world of alienation and discrimination. My roots were severed. I was spiritually wounded. I entered a pit of burning, all-consuming rage! I unknowingly carried this into my marriage. I was sixteen years old. Too young to understand this devastation, I shut myself off and wrapped myself in a cocoon of deadly silence that I thought would protect me.
>
> I walked my road of emptiness, loneliness, and complete isolation. I longed for my parents! I yearned for their love! I missed my brothers and sisters! I wanted my home back. I wanted my community back. I thought of the affection

I received from my people. I remembered how beautiful my life had been on my *shkonigun.* Poor, yes! but full of love—all a person needs to survive. I wept secretly, feeling this great void of nothing. I searched for brown faces on the streets of the towns where I lived in order to assure myself that my people were still around. I longed to run up to them and tell them, "I'm Indian, too!" I was a lost soul, once again a victim of the government's one-sided history and the broken treaties.

When I agreed to set this story on paper, I thought I would sail through it. It would be a breeze, I told myself! How wrong I was! I struggle and weep revisiting my pain. It has become a giant step in my own healing. Truth purges my soul. I hear the words of my grandparents once again, "*Waybeenun!*" "Throw it away!" My spirit is free.

To my people out there, I love you! Have courage. [8]

Is there a community to which you belong where the kind of "excommunication" that McDonald experienced would have such an effect on you?

Whatever our communities of origin, we are all raised with certain sets of expectations, some coming from our immediate families, some from the wider social context. Many of these expectations, values, and cultural norms get passed on from one generation to another and have a profound influence on our self-understanding. In the following excerpt Mencius, a student of the Chinese philosopher Confucius, discusses his understanding of human identity:

Mencius said: "When the harvest is good, the younger people are for the most part amenable, but when the harvest is lean, they are obstreperous. Their reacting differently under these differing circumstances is not due to the nature with which Heaven has endowed them but to those who create these overwhelming conditions. Sow the barley and cover it with soil. Providing that the ground is uniform and the barley is sown at one time, it will spring to life, and in due time all the barley will ripen. However, differing circumstances do arise; some ground is rich, some is poor; some well watered, some not; not all is equally well-tended. Even so, things of a kind resemble each other. And can we doubt that human beings are any different? The Sages and we ourselves are things of a kind. Lung Tzu said, 'The sandal-maker may not know beforehand the size of his customer's feet, but we can be sure that he will not make the sandals the size of baskets.' Sandals resemble each other; men's feet are things of a kind. All men relish flavourings in their food. But it took an Yi Ya first to discover those flavourings. Suppose: Yi Ya's nature differed in kind from those of other men, just as the nature of horses and hounds differs from that of a man. How could it have happened that, whatever flavourings humans like, all derive from Yi Ya? As far as flavorings are concerned, the world is indebted to Yi Ya, but this could only happen because all men's palates are similar.

"This, too, is true of the ear. For music, the world is indebted to K'uang the Music Master. But this could only happen because all men's ears are similar. This, too, is true of the eyes. No one would deny that Tzu-tu was handsome, unless he was blind.

"Therefore, the human mouth enjoys its flavorings, the ear its music, the eye its beauty. These things are all alike. And is this not true of the things of the heart? What are those things that all hearts have in common? I say, 'the underlying principle, the essential Justice.'

"The Sages (differ from us only) in being the first to discover those things which all hearts have in common. The underlying principle and the essential Justice evoke joy in our hearts just as rich meat delights our palate."[9]

Many cultures pass on values and information from one generation to another through storytelling, sometimes through the telling of *parables*—stories that use common, everyday symbols and experiences to get a deeper point across. Mencius uses the metaphor of barley and the growing of crops to illustrate his point about human nature or identity. Is this effective? Do you think it would have been effective in China at the time in which he was writing? You are probably familiar with the ancient Greek writer Aesop's *fables,* another kind of teaching stories that have instructed many generations of listeners and readers.

What are some of the particular stories that get told within your family and culture that pass on values and traditions? How do these affect your sense of who you are, both individually and as a member of the group?

The sense of being part of a community is intimately connected with the religious beliefs of individuals in some groups. In thinking about the selections you have read so far, you may have noticed that no distinction is made in most of them between "culture" and "religion." In many indigenous traditions, there is no word for "religion" in the language, because the concepts and practices that we call "religious" were always understood to be an inherent part of the culture and day-to-day life of the group. In addition, to speak of community in such cultures is to include the ancestors, those who have gone before. Christianity picks up this same theme with the idea of the "communion of saints," belief that those who have died are still present in some real and eternal way. Thus engagement with the community, those living now, those who have gone before, and those yet to come, is an essential part of an individual's own identity.

Dr. Martin Luther King, Jr. was one who understood himself to be inherently connected to the communities of which he was a part. Shortly before Dr. King was assassinated, he spoke to a group of fellow clergy. Frequently, his own colleagues were among those who criticized King's actions most, telling him that he should stay away from controversial issues and activities, be patient, and focus on his spiritual responsibilities. But King repeatedly refused such a dichotomy between the "religious" and the "secular," urging other clergy to speak up on behalf of their people. In this instance, sanitation workers were striking *for* better pay and working conditions and *against* the racism and segregation they encountered on a daily basis. In a strangely prophetic speech, King talked about his awareness that he might very well meet a violent death. Yet this possibility did not deter him, did not even seem to bother him much. As you read the following short excerpt, ask yourself just what factors enabled King to hold his own earthly life—his individual self—so relatively lightly. (Note: King is referring in this passage to the parable in the Christian scriptures about the Good Samaritan. If you are not familiar with this parable, you may read it in the appendix at the end of this chapter before you attempt to understand the following reading.)

> And you know, it's possible that the priest and the Levite looked over that man on the ground and wondered if the robbers were still around. Or it's possible that they felt that the man on the ground was merely faking. And he was acting like he had been robbed and hurt, in order to seize them over there, lure them there for quick and easy seizure. And so the first question that the Levite asked was, "If I stop to help this man, what will happen to me?" But then the good Samaritan came by. And he reversed the question: "If I do not stop to help this man, what will happen to him?"
>
> That's the question before you tonight. Not, "If I stop to help the sanitation workers, what will happen to all of the hours that I usually spend in my office every day and every week as a pastor?" The question is not, "If I stop to help this man in need, what will happen to me?" "If I do not stop to help the sanitation workers, what will happen to them?" That's the question . . .
>
> Well, I don't know what will happen now. We've got some difficult days ahead. But it doesn't matter with me now. Because I've been to the mountaintop. And I don't mind. Like anybody, I would like to live a long life. Longevity has its place. But I'm not concerned about that now. I just want to do God's will. And He's allowed me to go up to the mountain. And I've looked over. And I've seen the promised land. I may not get there with you. But I want you to know tonight, that we, as a people will get to the promised land. And I'm happy, tonight. I'm not worried about anything. I'm not fearing any man. Mine eyes have seen the glory of the coming of the Lord.[10]

What motivates a person to a life of self-giving, even to the point of giving life itself? What kind of understanding of "self" might such a person have? What difference do you think it makes that King's culture is one that sees membership in the community as an essential dimension of full personhood?

Archbishop Oscar Romero of San Salvador was appointed to his position at a time when his nation was ruled by a repressive military regime that was responsible for widespread killing and the impoverishment of great numbers of Salvadoran people. Considered by the church authorities to be a safe choice who would not disturb the relatively benign relationship between the official church and the affluent ruling elite, Romero became increasingly active and outspoken on behalf of the ordinary Salvadoran people as he witnessed first-hand the effects of the violence and oppression. In a radio broadcast, just days before he was assassinated while celebrating Mass in the cathedral in San Salvador, Romero noted, "If they kill me, I shall rise up in the Salvadoran people." Both Romero and King inherited a legacy of religious faith that led them into a lifelong, and ultimately fatal, struggle for civil rights. Both had many, though somewhat different, cultural forces playing roles in their identity formation (as do we all). Think about how their statements, their beliefs, apply to the relationship between individual identity and community identity, particularly in the context of religious faith. Are there comparable beliefs about this relationship within your own family or community?

> *What kind of influence does membership in a community have on someone's identity? Is it always positive, even when the community has a religious basis? Survey a recent newspaper or news magazine and locate articles that relate to individuals and their membership in groups. Which articles reflect a positive influence on individuals by their membership in the group? Do any indicate a negative influence? Would everyone agree with your assessment? Why or why not? What is your own experience of the effect of communities on developing a sense of identity in members?*

IDENTITY AND RELIGION

Much of what we have explored so far in this chapter may not seem to have much to do with religion. Yet religions play a large role in cultural understandings of identity, whether religion is seen as a separate phenomenon or as an integral part of daily life. Eastern understandings of the self are often difficult to comprehend for those of us raised in Western cultures where a concept of individuality is of prime importance. In a section from the *Chandogya Upanishad*, a religious text from Hindu tradition, a father talks to his son, Svetaketu, about his tradition's understanding of the "self": Just what point is the father making in each of his examples?

> "If someone were to strike once at the root of this large tree, it would bleed, but live. If he were to strike at its stem, it would bleed, but live. If he were to strike at the top, it would bleed, but live. Pervaded by the living Self, this tree stands firm, and takes its food; but if the Self were to depart from one of its branches, that branch would wither; if it were to depart from a second, that would wither; if it were to depart from a third, that would wither. If it were to depart from the whole tree, the whole tree would wither.
>
> "Likewise, my son, know this: The body dies when the Self leaves it—but the Self dies not.
>
> "All that is has its self in him alone. He is the truth. He is the subtle essence of all. He is the Self. And that, Svetaketu, THAT ART THOU."
>
> "Please, sir, tell me more about this Self. . . ."

"Be it so. Put this salt in water, and come to me tomorrow morning."

Svetaketu did as he was bidden. The next morning his father asked him to bring the salt which he had put in the water. But he could not, for it had dissolved. Then said Uddalaka:

"Sip the water, and tell me how it tastes."

"It is salty, sir."

"In the same way," continued Uddalaka, "though you do not see Brahman in this body, he is indeed here. That which is the subtle essence—in that have all things their existence. That is the truth. That is the Self. And that, Svetaketu, THAT ART THOU."

"Please, sir, tell me more about this Self," said the youth again. [11]

Why do you think the son keeps asking for more? Does each new illustration add to his understanding?

Although not identical, Hindu and Buddhist understandings of the self share certain characteristics with each other and with other Eastern traditions. Vietnamese Buddhist monk Thich Nhat Hanh portrays the Buddha (Gautama) engaged in conversation with a disciple. Kassapa, the disciple, is seeking a deeper understanding of the meaning of the Buddha's teachings and insights. What challenges does the Buddha present to Kassapa? What challenges does he present to you, in terms of your understanding of "self"?

"Gautama, water cannot really help one attain liberation. Water naturally flows down. Only fire rises. When we die, our body rises in smoke thanks to fire."

"Master Kassapa, that is not accurate. The white clouds floating above are also a form of water. Thus, water rises too. Indeed, smoke itself is no more than evaporated water. Both clouds and smoke will eventually return to a liquid state. All things, as I'm sure you know, move in cycles."

"But all things share one fundamental essence and all things return to that one essence."

"Master Kassapa, all things depend on all other things for their existence. Take, for example, this leaf in my hand. Earth, water, heat, seed, tree, clouds, sun, time, space—all these elements have enabled this leaf to come into existence. If just one of these elements was missing, the leaf could not exist. All beings, organic and inorganic, rely on the law of dependent co-arising. The source of one thing is all things. Please consider this carefully. Don't you see that this leaf I am now holding in my hand is only here thanks to the interpenetration of all the phenomena in the universe, including your own awareness? . . ."

[The next day] they sat by the lotus pond and conversed. Kassapa said, "Yesterday you said that the presence of a leaf resulted from the coming together of many different conditions. You said that humans, too, exist only because of the coming together of many other conditions. But when all these conditions cease to be, where does the self go?"

The Buddha answered, "For a long time humans have been trapped by the concept of *atman*, the concept of a separate and eternal self. We have believed that when our body dies, this self continues to exist and seeks union with its

Buddhist monk at his studies.

source, which is Brahma. But, friend Kassapa, that is a fundamental misunderstanding which has caused countless generations to go astray.

"You should know, friend Kassapa, that all things exist because of interdependence and all things cease to be because of interdependence. This is because that is. This is not because that is not. This is born because that is born. This dies because that dies. This is the wonderful law of dependent co-arising which I have discovered in my meditation. In truth, there is nothing which is separate and eternal. There is no self, whether a higher or a lower self. Kassapa, have you ever meditated on your body, feelings, perceptions, mental formations, and consciousness? A person is made up of these five aggregates. They are continuously changing rivers in which one cannot find even one permanent element."

Uruvela Kassapa remained silent for a long moment. Then he asked, "Could one say then that you teach the doctrine of non-being?"

The Buddha smiled and shook his head. "No. The concept of non-being is one narrow view among a whole forest of narrow views. The concept of non-being is just as false as the concept of a separate, permanent self. Kassapa, look at the surface of this lotus pond. I do not say that the water and lotus do not exist. I only say that the water and the lotus arise thanks to the presence and interpenetration of all other elements, none of which are separate or permanent."

Kassapa lifted his head and looked into the Buddha's eyes. "If there is no self, no atman, why should one practice a spiritual path in order to attain liberation? Who will be liberated?"

> The Buddha looked deeply into the eyes of his brahmana friend. His gaze was as radiant as the sun and as gentle as the soft moonlight. He smiled and said, "Kassapa, look for the answer within yourself." [12]

What is the parallel that Gautama draws between the leaf and the human person? And what do you think the Buddha means when he tells Kassapa to "look for the answer within" himself?

The understanding of the human self's relative position within a wider realm of life and being is not particular to Buddhism. Think back, for instance, to Lame Deer's descriptions of the elements of the natural world that are so much a part of his own sense of himself and his community. Chinese writer Chiang Yee refers to the ways in which much Chinese art reflects his culture's sense of self.

> We love natural truth; our philosophers were convinced that human desire has grown beyond bounds; man's eagerness to grasp the object of his desire gives rise to much unnatural and untruthful behaviour. Man, we think, is no higher in the scale of things than any other kind of matter that comes into being; rather, he has tended to falsify his original nature, and for that reason we prefer those things that live by instinct or natural compulsion; they are at least true to the purpose for which they were created. We paint figures occasionally, but not so much as you do in the West. [13]

What similarities do you see in the perspectives presented by Chiang Yee and those in the passages from the *Upanishad* and from Thich Nhat Hanh? Now compare these ideas with Psalm 8 from the Hebrew Scriptures. What views of humanity and the self emerge in this particular passage?

> O Lord, our Lord
> > How majestic is Your name throughout the earth,
> > You who have covered the heaven with your splendor!
> From the mouths of infants and sucklings
> > You have founded strength on account of Your foes,
> > You put an end to enemy and avenger.
> When I behold Your heavens, the work of Your fingers,
> > the moon and stars that You set in place,
> > what is man that You have been mindful of him,
> > mortal man that You have taken note of him,
> > that You have made him little less than divine,
> > and adorned him with glory and majesty;
> > You have made him master over Your handiwork,
> > laying the world at his feet,
> > sheep and oxen, all of them,
> > and wild beasts too;
> > the birds of the heavens, the fish of the sea,
> > whatever travels the paths of the seas.
> O Lord, our Lord, how majestic is Your name throughout the earth! [14]

What views do the Eastern traditions and this Hebrew psalm convey of creation and, in particular, of the place of the human within that creation? And in what ways do these religious understandings of humanity and its place in creation influence understandings of the self?

Visit your local art museum, or check out some of the excellent art websites that are available. Try to locate some art works from both Western and Eastern perspectives that illustrate the relative positions that these different cultural perspectives give to human beings and the rest of the world.

Some Questions about Identity

As we have encountered a variety of expressions of identity and ideas about how our personal and communal identities are formed and shaped, any one particular definition might seem less plausible to you than it did at the beginning of the chapter. All the more so, issues of identity are central to our explorations of the ways in which humans search for meaning in their world. Our identities are shaped by every experience and interaction we have—and by our responses to those experiences and interactions. Yet we are not only the sum of what other people, other groups, our society or community tells us we are. Especially, like Clorox, many of us retain the ability to question the negative messages that we may receive, to reflect on them, and to reject them. If we are fortunate, there will be some one or ones in our lives who encourage us to move beyond the limits that might be placed upon us.

Some religious traditions emphasize the extent to which we develop as members of a community; some tribal African traditions proclaim that "I am because we are, and we are because I am." Think about the implications of such a statement, both for the individual and for the community.

Eastern traditions tend to deemphasize the importance of the individual in favor of a sense of connectedness with ultimate being, with all that is. Thus the importance of the individual lies in her or his acceptance of this interrelatedness. In the earliest Christian communities, those who died were buried in common graves because it was understood that the Resurrection would be for the community of believers together. Is this concept contrary to belief in the individual as personally created and loved by a divine being?

Perhaps human identity is something we recognize when we see it but can never fully define. Is identity, like so many other human characteristics, relative, complex, fluid? Does our identity change in significant ways over the course of our lives? Is there a central core that remains, even when we go through major crises or transformations? Can we really change our identity? Our way of experiencing our world is continually dependent upon our individual and communal identities, while at the same time those identities shape the ways in which we perceive our activities and experiences. We are social creatures, with an extended dependency on others in infancy and beyond for meeting our basic physical and emotional needs. Who we are, and who we are becoming, is of central importance to the ways in which we find meaning in our lives.

What Some Others Have Said about Identity

Questions about human identity have probably been around for as long as there have been humans to wonder about such things. Certainly scholars in fields as varied as philosophy, anthropology, sociology, psychology, and religion have grappled with the complexity of the human person. So far, we have looked at some specific expressions of personal identity and the ways in which persons experience their identity as being influenced by social, cultural, and religious factors. In this context, we have asked you to come up with some of your own understandings of just what makes up the human person and how our identity is shaped. Now we invite you to bring those emerging understandings into dialogue with other perspectives.

Auschwitz survivor and psychiatrist Viktor Frankl picks up on many of the psychoanalytic theories developed by Sigmund Freud and Carl Jung and extends them to what he calls "existential analysis"—paying careful attention to what clients describe as their own experiences, particularly what is happening *now* to them rather than what has happened in the past. In his book *Man's Search for Ultimate Meaning,* Frankl uses the term "logotherapy" for his own particular form of psychotherapy. Frankl suggests that for the human to be considered "responsible," she or he must be thought of as neither totally rational nor totally irrational and instinctual. Read the following and think about how his proposition of a "spiritual unconscious" enables him to avoid this dichotomy. What are the main points Frankl makes, particularly as regards human agency: our freedom to choose what we do, including the kinds of persons we become?

> Existential analysis . . . is a psychotherapeutic method because it is . . . intended to bring man . . . to an awareness of his responsibleness. . . . In existential analysis man becomes conscious of something. But whereas in psychoanalysis it is the instinctual of which he becomes conscious, in existential analysis . . . he becomes conscious of the spiritual, or existential. For it is only from the viewpoint of man's spirituality, or existentiality, that being human can be described in terms of being responsible. What comes to consciousness in existential analysis, then, is not drive or instinct, neither id drives nor ego drives, but self. Here it is not the ego that becomes conscious of the id but rather the self that becomes conscious of itself. . . .
>
> With the discovery of the spiritual unconscious, existential analysis eluded the peril to which psychoanalysis had succumbed, namely, of id-ifying the unconscious. With the concept of the spiritual unconscious, existential analytic

logotherapy also avoided any one-sided intellectualism and rationalism in its theory of man. Logos is deeper than logic. Thus the fact that man can no longer be considered as a totally rational being has been recognized by logotherapy without falling prey to the *other* extreme, i.e., idolizing the irrational and the instinctual, as did psychoanalysis.[15]

Do you agree with Frankl that there is such a thing as a "spiritual unconscious" in all humans? Frankl suggests that there is not only a spiritual unconscious, but also an "unconscious religiousness":

> Now, in its third stage of development, existential analysis has uncovered—within the spiritual unconscious—unconscious religiousness. This unconscious religiousness, revealed by our phenomenological analysis, is to be understood as a latent relation to transcendence inherent in man. If one prefers, he might conceive of this relation in terms of a relationship between the immanent self and a transcendent Thou. . . .
>
> It cannot be emphasized strongly enough that not only is the unconscious neither divine nor omniscient, but above all man's unconscious relation to God is profoundly personal. The "unconscious God" must not be mistaken as an impersonal force operant in man. This misunderstanding was the great mistake to which C. G. Jung fell prey. Jung must be credited with having discovered distinctly religious elements within the unconscious. Yet he misplaced this unconscious religiousness of man, failing to locate the unconscious God in the personal and existential region. Instead, he allotted it to the region of drives and instincts, where unconscious religiousness no longer remained a matter of choice and decision. According to Jung, something within me is religious, but it is not I who then is religious; something within me drives me to God, but it is not I who makes the choice and takes the responsibility.
>
> For Jung, unconscious religiousness was bound up with religious archetypes belonging to the collective unconscious. For him, unconscious religiousness has scarcely anything to do with a personal decision, but becomes an essentially impersonal, collective, "typical" (i.e., archetypical) process occurring in man. However, it is our contention that religiousness could emerge least of all from a collective unconscious, precisely because religion involves the most personal decisions man makes, even if only on an unconscious level. But there is no possibility of leaving such decisions to some processes merely taking place in me.[16]

What major distinctions does Frankl make between his own development of this idea of "unconscious religiousness" as a universal human characteristic and Jung's idea of the unconscious? In what way does he suggest that his own framework makes more sense? Do you agree? Frankl continues by spelling out some of the implications of this particular understanding, especially as it relates to the human search for identity and a sense of meaning and self:

> Thus, human existence—at least as long as it has not been neurotically distorted—is always directed to something, or someone, other than itself—be it

a meaning to fulfill or another human being to encounter lovingly. I have termed this constitutive characteristic of human existence "self-transcendence." What is called "self-actualization" is ultimately an effect, the unintentional by-product, of self-transcendence. So it turns out that Pindar's imperative that one should become what he is—in other words, that man should actualize his potentialities—is valid only if we add what Karl Jaspers once said: "What one is, he has become through that cause which he has made his own." Or, as Abraham H. Maslow put it, the "business of self-actualization" can best be carried out "via a commitment to an important job."

Just as self-actualization can be obtained only through a detour, through the fulfillment of meaning, so identity is available only through responsibility, through being responsible for the fulfillment of meaning. . . .

Therefore man is originally characterized by his "search for meaning" rather than his "search for himself." The more he forgets himself—giving himself to a cause or another person—the more *human* he is. And the more he is immersed and absorbed in something or someone other than himself the more he really becomes *himself*. Just consider a child who, absorbed in play, forgets himself—this is the moment to take a snapshot; when you wait until he notices that you are taking a picture, his face congeals and freezes, showing his unnatural self-consciousness rather than his natural graciousness. Why do most people have that stereotyped expression on their faces whenever they are photographed? This expression stems from their concern with the impression they are going to leave on the onlooker. It is "cheese" that makes them so ugly. Forgetting themselves, the photographer, and the future onlooker would make them beautiful.[17]

Is Frankl right that there is a "religiousness"—broadly defined—at the heart of human be-ing? And is he right that we only find ourselves as humans by engaging in a "search for meaning" that takes us beyond ourselves? How might someone who did not subscribe to a specific set of religious beliefs respond to Frankl's suggestions? And how do you think Frankl would respond to someone who claimed no "religiousness"?

✦ APPENDIX

THE PARABLE OF THE GOOD SAMARITAN

Just then a lawyer stood up to test Jesus. "Teacher," he said, "what must I do to inherit eternal life?" He said to him, "What is written in the law? What do you read there?" He answered, "You shall love the Lord your God with all your heart, and with all your soul, and with all your strength, and with all your mind; and your neighbor as yourself." And he said to him, "You have given the right answer; do this, and you will live." But wanting to justify himself, he asked Jesus, "And who is my neighbor?" Jesus replied, "A man was going down from Jerusalem to Jericho, and fell into the hands of robbers, who stripped him, beat him, and went away, leaving him half dead. Now by chance a priest was going down that road; and when he saw him, he passed by on the other side. So likewise a Levite, when he came to the place and saw him, passed by on the other side. But a Samaritan while traveling came near him; and when he saw him, he was moved with pity. He went to him and bandaged his wounds, having poured oil and wine on them. Then he put him on his own animal, brought him to an inn, and took care of him. The next day he took out two denarii, gave them to the innkeeper, and said, 'Take care of him; and when I come back, I will repay you whatever more you spend.' Which of these three, do you think, was a neighbor to the man who fell into the hands of the robbers?" He said, "The one who showed him mercy." Jesus said to him, "Go and do likewise."

(Luke 10: 29–37, New Revised Standard Version)

CHAPTER TWO

How Do We Communicate? Symbols and Human Identity

Think of the last time you wanted to communicate something of very deep significance to someone you really care about. How did you go about conveying to the person just what you wanted to say? Did you use certain words? A card? Flowers? E-mail? An invitation to a special meal? If, as we suggested in Chapter 1, humans are inherently social creatures whose identities are developed in the context of communities (as well as in other ways), then we are constantly in the process of figuring out just how to communicate best those values and ideals that shape the persons we are in the process of becoming, and so we frequently have great difficulty expressing just exactly what it is we want to say. What are we to do?

Setting the Stage: The Power of Symbols

We met John Fire Lame Deer in Chapter 1. He was born in a cabin between the Pine Ridge and Rosebud Indian reservations in 1903. His was a world of tensions between his Lakota Sioux heritage and the "white man's ways." Lame Deer discusses the profound significance of symbols in the life of his people and makes some observations about the relationship he perceives between the "white man," symbols, and the natural world. Are there symbols that are particularly important for you personally, in your family, as a part of your culture? If so, how do they differ from Lame Deer's? If not, can you imagine how your life might be different if it were more rooted in symbolic meaning?

What do you see here, my friend? Just an ordinary old cooking pot, black with soot and full of dents.

It is standing on the fire on top of that old wood stove, and the water bubbles, and moves the lid as the white steam rises to the ceiling. Inside the pot is boiling water, chunks of meat with bone and fat, plenty of potatoes.

It doesn't seem to have a message, that old pot, and I guess you didn't give it a thought. Except the soup smells good and reminds you that you are hungry. Maybe you are worried that this is dog stew. Well, don't worry. It's just beef— no fat puppy for a special ceremony. It's just an ordinary, everyday meal.

But I'm an Indian. I think about ordinary, common things like this pot. The bubbling water comes from the rain cloud. It represents the sky. The fire comes from the sun which warms us all—men, animals, trees. The meat stands for the four-legged creatures, our animal brothers, who gave of themselves so that we should live. The steam is living breath. It was water; now it goes up to the sky, becomes a cloud again. These things are sacred. Looking at that pot full of good soup, I am thinking how, in this simple manner, Wakan Tanka takes care of me. We Sioux spend a lot of time thinking about everyday things, which in our mind are mixed up with the spiritual. We see in the world around us many symbols that teach us the meaning of life. We have a saying that the white man sees so little, he must see with only one eye. We see a lot that you no longer notice. You could notice if you wanted to, but you are usually too busy. We Indians live in a world of symbols and images where the spiritual and the commonplace are one. To you symbols are just words, spoken or written in a book. To us they are part of nature, part of ourselves—the earth, the sun, the wind and the rain, stones, trees, animals, even little insects like ants and grasshoppers. We try to understand them not with the head but with the heart, and we need no more than a hint to give us the meaning. . . .

To our way of thinking, the Indians' symbol is the circle, the hoop. Nature wants things to be round. The bodies of human beings and animals have no corners. With us the circle stands for the togetherness of people who sit with one another around the campfire, relatives and friends united in peace while the pipe passes from hand to hand. The camp in which every tipi had its place was also a ring. The tipi was a ring in which people sat in a circle and all the families in the village were in turn circles within a larger circle, part of the larger hoop which was the seven campfires of the Sioux, representing one nation. The nation was only a part of the universe, in itself circular and made of the earth, which is round, of the sun, which is round, of the stars, which are round. The moon, the horizon, the rainbow—circles within circles within circles, with no beginning and no end.

To us, this is beautiful and fitting, symbol and reality at the same time, expressing the harmony of life and nature. Our circle is timeless, flowing; it is new life emerging from death—life winning out over death.

From birth to death we Indians are enfolded in symbols as in a blanket. An infant's cradle board is covered with designs to ensure a happy, healthy life for the child. The moccasins of the dead have their soles beaded in a certain way to ease the journey to the hereafter. For the same reason, most of us have tattoos on our wrists—not like the tattoos of your sailors—daggers, hearts and nude girls—but just a name, a few letters or designs. The Owl Woman who guards the road to the spirit lodges looks at these tattoos and lets us pass. They are like a passport. Many Indians believe that if you don't have these signs on your body, that Ghost Woman won't let you through but will throw you over a cliff. In that case you don't have to roam the earth endlessly as a *wanagi*—a ghost. All you can do then is frighten people and whistle. Maybe it's not so bad being a *wanagi*. It could even be fun. I don't know. But, as you see, I have my arms tattooed.

Every day in my life I see symbols in the shape of certain roots or branches. I read messages in the stones. I pay special attention to them, because I am a Yuwipi man and that is my work. But I am not the only one. Many Indians do this.

Inyan—the rocks—are holy. Every man needs a stone to help him. There are two kinds of pebbles that make good medicine. One is white like ice. The other is like ordinary stone, but it makes you pick it up and recognize it by its special shape. You ask stones for aid to find things which are lost or missing. Stones can give warning of an enemy, of approaching misfortune. The winds are symbolized by a raven and a small black stone the size of an egg. . . .

Words, too, are symbols and convey great powers, especially names. Not Charles, Dick and George. There's not much power in those. But Red Cloud, Black Elk, Whirlwind, Two Moons, Lame Deer—these names have a relationship to the Great Spirit. Each Indian name has a story behind it, a vision, a quest for dreams. We receive great gifts from the source of a name; it links us to nature, to the animal nations. It gives power. You can lean on a name, get strength from it. It is a special name for you and you alone—not a Dick, George, Charles kind of thing.

Each Indian name tells a story that remains hidden to outsiders unless it is explained to them. Take our famous chief Man-Afraid-of-His-Horse. It sounds funny in English. Man-Afraid once led the warriors in battle against the enemy who fled before him. The medicine men wanted to honor him and so they bestowed this name on him, which really means: He is so brave, so feared, that his enemies run away when merely seeing his horse, even if he is not on it. That is a powerful name. He had to live up to it. . . . To a white man, symbols are just that: pleasant things to speculate about, to toy with in your mind. To us, they are much, much more. Life to us is a symbol to be lived.[1]

In cultures like Lame Deer's, a child's permanent and most significant name is not bestowed for years, until it becomes clear just who this new member of the community is. How much have you thought about the importance of your name? Do you know why and how you were named as you were? Lame Deer suggests that for most Americans of European origin, symbols are merely "pleasant things to speculate about." Is he right? Or does even such an apparently simple symbol as our own name have some deeper significance?

Begin a list of symbols that are important to you personally. Think about what makes each one significant. Does it have to do with how you acquired it? A particular event in your life? Is it associated with an individual or group with whom you have or had a significant relationship? Are there symbols that are important to groups you belong to, such as family, religious group, sports team, or other social entity? How does your own relationship with these symbols relate to Lame Deer's description of the role of symbols in his community? The next time you are near a commercial area of any kind, or just reading the newspaper or watching TV, make a second list of the signs and symbols that you see over a period of an hour or so. Do the two lists overlap at all?

WHAT DO YOU THINK? PERSONAL EXPERIENCES OF SYMBOLS

Take a moment to notice what you are wearing. How did you decide what to put on when you last dressed or changed your clothes? When you leave the privacy of your room or home, do you change anything? If your best friend comes by? If you have an important interview or meeting with someone? Why do you choose particular items for going on a job interview, others for going to a club, still others for attending a sporting event? Do certain kinds of clothes make you feel a particular way? Are there specific items in your wardrobe that carry special importance? What is the significance of what you wear? Here is a passage from a *Boston Globe* article about a familiar recent trend related to the symbol of dressing for business:

> Andy Pike, 29, a Boston investment banker, wants it every morning, but it's now a sort of forbidden pleasure. He didn't even realize how much he liked it, that feeling of power it bestowed, until he had to stop doing it just to fit in around the office. Pike wants to wear a suit.
>
> "It's a uniform," said Pike, whose firm approved "casual days" this summer for the first time. "You just get up in the morning and grab a suit. When you're in a meeting with older men, the suit makes you feel more like an equal . . ."
>
> Men have clearly struggled more with casual day than women, who have never stuck to a corporate uniform and who have a wider selection when it comes to choosing attire. Psychologists say many men, to some degree, see casual day as yet another arena where they have to compete. Indeed the jungle of casual fashion requires a mix-and-match ability and a fashion sense that many men say they don't possess.
>
> "When everyone wears the same suit, there's less competition," said clinical psychologist Jerrold Lee Shapiro, adding that men's suits can be thought of like competition-reducing school uniforms.
>
> Some employers and workers say they don't like the way dress-down day has turned into leisure day, affecting not only attire but behavior. They aren't

surprised by a national study this year showing that 44 percent of firms that allow casual dress at least one day a week saw an increase in tardiness and absenteeism among staff. Flirtatious behavior went up 30 percent at these firms, according to the study by Jackson Lewis, a New York employment law firm. . . .

As casual clothes have spread from Fridays to all days and summers-only to year-round, some people complain of a new fashion fascism. Donning a suit—when you aren't seeing a client or attending a formal meeting—can project the image of being stuck in the past or shamelessly seeking the approval of the firm's old-liners.

"There's some internal pressure to conform and not wear a suit," said a Hale & Dorr law associate in his 30s who asked that his name not be revealed. "If you wear a suit, people ask, 'Did you go to court today?' or 'What did you do that was so important? . . .'"

What to wear to work carries a particular significance for minority professionals, said Monroe "Bud" Moseley, vice president of a Boston executive-search firm. While informal dress can lead to a less stratified work environment, a plus for many minorities, it can also be "an additional opportunity" to diminish the status of minority professionals, he said.

Carolyn Golden Hebsgaard, executive director of the Boston Law Firm Group, which advocates for more minority recruitment at law firms, said, "Casual day standards may not be the same" for minority workers. She advises young minority attorneys to stay on the conservative side of "business casual," which means well-pressed slacks and collared shirts.

A 34-year-old lawyer at one of Boston's largest firms, who is African-American, gave the sobering observation that even when he's dressed in a suit, he is often mistaken for working as a paralegal or a member of the support staff.

"They think, 'He's black, he can't be a lawyer,'" said the lawyer, who asked to remain anonymous. Boston College sociologist Charles Derber said he thinks anxiety about casual business dress also reflects a persistent insecurity among today's workers, even in a good economy, about just where they stand.

"Even in this boom period, workers are struggling with the rapidly changing work environment," he said. "Maybe people are looking for some trappings of order."

Boston venture capitalist Bill Collatos predicted that the end of the boom, a recession, will ultimately be what rains on the dress-down day parade. Though he enjoys the benefits of casual attire, he remembers his father's telling him: "A tie is the cheapest form of dignity."[2]

The clothing we wear is in some way symbolic. Whether or not we are currently employed in a position where issues of dress code affect our life significantly, few of us use clothes simply to provide protection against the elements or against the possibility of arrest for "indecent exposure." Our choice of clothes is a dimension of our *identity*, who we say we are. Consider the different reactions various individuals in the article have to similar items of clothing. The specific meaning of the symbol varies according to a host of factors, including stereotypes. An African American in casual dress must have come to fix the

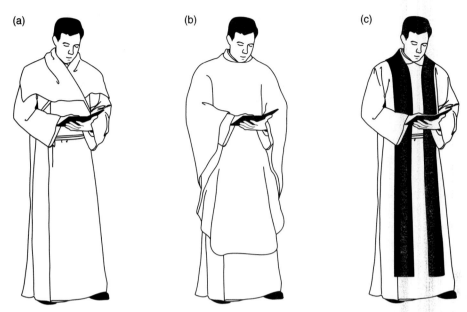

(a) A priest wearing alb, amice, and cinture. (b) The chasable is worn over the amice, alb, and cinture. (c) Just the stole is added to alb, amice, and cinture before the Eucharist.

copy machine; a woman in a lab coat must be a research or pharmacy assistant. When persons have been systematically excluded from a particular context or occupation on the basis of their race, sex, ethnicity, all symbols that indicate that they have arrived, that they have a right to be there, become increasingly important. Dress that symbolizes success within one's chosen occupation means reducing the likelihood of being stereotyped according to past expectations.

If clothing can have profound symbolic significance in our everyday lives, or in the corporate world, it is still more the case when clothing is associated with the fundamental and life-shaping beliefs of individuals and communities. Religious traditions also have their own particular styles and patterns of clothing that are considered appropriate, or that have deep symbolic meaning. For Christians in previous generations, the concept of "Sunday dress" meant that church attendance required special attentiveness to what one wore, to honor the God who would be worshipped. The simple white robes worn by all Muslims making their pilgrimage to Mecca symbolize purity and the central Islamic belief that all people are equal before Allah. The turban or veil and bracelet that Sikhs wear denote them as members of a particular religion with a specific set of practices. Traditional Jewish men come to prayer with their *talit*—prayer shawl—the fringe of which symbolizes and reminds them of the commandments given to them by their God.

The simple black robes worn by many Protestant ministers, derived from academic robes, which in turn symbolized their education, indicate a concern that elaborate dress and decoration detract from the seriousness of worship. On the other hand, the elaborate vestments worn by priests in some other Christian denominations symbolize the royal sovereignty of God. Churches such as the Roman Catholic, Eastern Orthodox, Anglican, and Lutheran feature many symbolic vestments, both in the "dressing" of the church with hangings in seasonally appropriate colors and in the attire that the clergy wear. The liturgical colors help set the tone of the worship—white, red, green, purple and, occasionally, black.

Consider the colors and vestments used in the Episcopal Church of the United States. Black signifies death and is seldom used except occasionally on Good Friday, the Christian remembrance of the day of the crucifixion of Jesus. While black used to be worn for burial offices and Requiems, the Christian emphasis now is more often on the resurrection faith, symbolized by white. An Episcopal priest wrote, in the letter planning his own funeral, that he wanted black used in the church for the requiem, but he wanted to be vested in white in his coffin. In this way, he symbolized the Christian belief that death is followed by resurrection with his choices of liturgical colors.

Red symbolizes the descent of the Holy Spirit at Pentecost. The Holy Spirit is depicted as descending in the form of "tongues of fire," giving the disciples the gift of tongues, the ability to teach in the languages of the world. Red is also the color for ordinations. Technically, the red for martyrs is supposed to be the crimson of blood, but many congregations use one set of red vestments for both.

Purple is the penitential color, used in Advent and Lent, the seasons of penitence and preparation. White, symbolizing purity, is used for Easter, Christmas, and the days in these seasons that do not need other colors. Green, the most used color, symbolizes life, and its usage covers the time between Pentecost and Lent. Each item of apparel worn by the clergy can emphasize aspects of Christianity to those who know the symbols. These items of clothing say something not only about the identity of the wearers as individuals, but also about their identity in relationship to their traditions and communities.

> Look up some of the terms for Eucharistic vestments either on the Web or in an unabridged dictionary, the Oxford English Dictionary, for example. What were the original meanings of chasuble, cassock, alb, amice, maniple, and stole? What do the different vestments symbolize? Look at the terms for the sacramental attire used in other religions. What are they, and what are the origins of the terms?

CULTURAL AND SOCIAL UNDERSTANDINGS OF SYMBOLS

We turn now to the relationship between the symbols that are an integral part of our lives and our individual and community identities. Symbols have much to do with how we acquire a sense of self, or a sense of belonging. The stories

A civil rights rally in Selma, Alabama in 1965.

Separate but equal?

we inherit in our families and cultures—incorporating our symbol world—shape our being in both conscious and unconscious, intentional and unintentional ways. We *are* our "collective pasts" with their symbols, as well as our present and future.

In this poem by African American poet Mari Evans, note the references to events and symbols that lie deep in the author's cultural history. Why might these symbolic events, many of them occurring years before her own lifetime, continue to hold such power for Evans?

    i
Have Arrived
i am the
    New Negro
    i
am the result of
President Lincoln
World War I
and Paris
the Red Ball Express
white drinking fountains
sitdowns and
sit-ins
Federal Troops
Marches on Washington
    and
prayer meetings . . .

today
They hired me
it
is a status
job . . .
along
with my papers
They
gave me my
Status Symbol
the key
to the
White . . . Locked . . .
John[3]

If you have studied the period of the Civil Rights Movement of the 1960s and
beyond, you will know what Evans means with her references to white drinking fountains, sitdowns, marches, and prayer meetings, and the "white locked
john." These are symbols of the racist segregation that limited the lives of
Evans's people. What do the symbols of Lincoln, World War I, Paris, and the
Red Ball Express suggest to you? When Evans refers to herself as "the new
Negro," she is acknowledging as integral parts of her identity both these historical memories of oppressive cultural and social patterns and also the "freedom" of now having the use of the same bathroom as everyone else. Evans's
individual identity is forever influenced by the identity of her culture, her community, her people.

*How does Evans's experience of her people's past relate to your own symbolic
cultural history? Are there stories in your own family and community that have
functioned as "symbol" to at least partially shape the ways in which you see
yourself, individually and as a member of that family and community? Ask a senior
member of your own family or community to tell you something of their past, some
particularly life-shaping event that they will never forget that affected not just
them personally, but their family and/or community. Are there ways in which your
own life experience has been touched by this symbolic event? Would you be a
somewhat different person had you grown up in a different social context?*

SYMBOLS AND SIGNS

Before we can begin to address the question of the relationship between symbols and communication, we need to identify just what can count as a "symbol."
We are accustomed to thinking of the more formal symbols with which we
are familiar: the flag that might represent citizens' love of their homeland; the
rings exchanged by a couple vowing commitment to each other; the cross on

a Christian church, the Jewish Star of David, or the minarets and dome on a mosque; the logo of a company or organization. We might be tempted to confine our definition of the word "symbol" to such formalized images.

Symbols, however, are much broader than that—a smile or gesture, certain language, every detail of the elaborate religious ceremonies performed regularly by members of religious traditions, all the small day-to-day rituals we engage in. What are some of the specific "symbols" that you use when you want to convey thoughts and feelings to another person? Are they different for different people in your life? Do you use the same language when you write an e-mail to a friend as you do when you write a term paper? How do you go about selecting a card for someone's birthday or for some other special occasion? How does the way you greet a dear friend on the street differ from the way you greet someone you recognize but don't know well? Your body language, your facial and vocal expressions, your words, will all participate in "symbolizing" your feelings.

It is important here to distinguish between signs and symbols. A *sign* is a simple representation of the object, action, idea to which it refers. An example might be a stop sign, whose meaning is clear, demanding a particular action—to stop. The relationship between the sign and the action has been determined by convention: nations around the world, recognizing the importance of having a standard set of road signs to ensure safety, agreed that this particular sign would signal a particular requirement for drivers. Whether or not you can read the word on the sign, you know what it signifies.

An example of a different kind of sign is the black clouds gathering in the sky that warn of an upcoming rainstorm, or at least the probability of one. This time, it is our observation of the natural world rather than human convention that determines the relationship between the clouds and the rain to come. Both the stop sign and the rain clouds are signs. There is a clear and agreed-upon relationship between the object and that which it signifies, a relationship obvious by simple observation of the sign itself. Signs do not generally point beyond this obvious meaning to some deeper reality.

Symbols, on the other hand, are more open to interpretation and evoke levels of meaning that go far beyond the engagement of our five senses or our conscious memory. Think back to some of the comments quoted by the author of the article on "casual Fridays," or to Lame Deer's description of the symbolism of fire, water, the cooking pot. While the importance and meaning of symbols may be largely determined by the conventions of a particular human community, this is a long process with levels of meaning deepening and expanding over time. Such meanings cannot simply be changed at will. Some of the symbols you listed earlier might be items that continue to gain deeper, maybe even different, significance as time passes; others might have started out as simple signs, but gained meaning enough that you now consider them symbols.

Even such apparently simple signs as the stop sign and the rain cloud can take on symbolic qualities. What extra meaning might you give to a stop sign, for example, if you have been involved in an accident caused by your or another driver's failure to stop at such a sign? Your reaction to stop signs is likely to be different in the future. Yes, you will probably take greater care, maybe not even assume you will be granted the right of way. But the sign itself may well symbolize for you a whole range of life and death emotions that are related to the particular circumstances surrounding your accident. The same is true with the rain clouds. If you are a farmer who has acres of hay cut and drying and needs another couple of clear, warm days before the field is ready for baling, your response will be different from that of a person in sub-Saharan Africa, who hasn't seen rain in several years and for whom water is a rapidly disappearing commodity. In both of these situations, those dark clouds building to the west symbolize far more than rain. In the first instance, they may imply a significant loss of revenue, insufficient food for stock and humans during the upcoming winter, potential tragedy. In the second situation, the clouds hold the promise of a last-minute reprieve from deadly drought, a blessing. Simple signs can thus take on symbolic importance when they point beyond themselves to other factors that represent deep value in people's lives.

SYMBOLS AND HUMAN COMMUNICATION

Because we humans have an immense capacity for feeling deeply, for imaginative and creative expression, for reflection and questioning and speculating, we have never been satisfied with symbolism that operates only on the level of the stop sign. Even our spoken language, complex as it is, always seems to fall short of fully expressing what it is we want to communicate. Regardless of our efforts to create new words to express new realities, or to capture old realities more adequately, we have always needed our artists to help us express our rich and complex experiences. Experiences are never adequately communicated through our limited abilities to recount the facts. We are constantly engaged in the process of interpretation.

Consider how differently two persons will describe the same specific event, often to the point that a listener or reader will not realize that it *is* the same event! And think about the difficulty of describing a powerful experience to someone who was not present. It's not too hard to relate the specific events that occurred, although even here we usually edit our accounts according to what we experienced as most significant. But what about the deeper emotional impact of the experience? If you are a visual artist, a poet, a dancer, or musician, you may attempt to put into the medium of your own greatest creativity something of the power you felt; you use your own most powerful system of symbols.

When people are attempting to give expression to experiences that transcend explanation and definition through our five physical senses, the use of symbol becomes increasingly essential and central. The word "symbol" itself is derived from the Greek *sun* (with) and *ballein* (to throw). What is being "thrown or brought together"? We use symbols to bring together, or at least to bring as close as possible, the reality or experience itself with our attempt to convey our interpretation of it to another and even to ourselves. Our means of expression are always limited both by the media available to us, and also by that which is being expressed. We are, then, always and everywhere, interpreting our experiences, and using the symbolic means of our culture, our religious tradition, our artistic disciplines to attempt to make accessible to others those experiences that are most important to us.

The following passage is excerpted from *The Star Dancers,* a novel of speculative fiction by Spider and Jeanne Robinson. The chief protagonists are a dance troupe, recruited for their particular expressive skills and creativity. Their task is to attempt to communicate with a group of aliens who resemble fireflies, and who are seen by some as posing a threat to space travelers, and perhaps to earth itself. The major challenge is that these creatures appear to have no physical or verbal characteristics or abilities in common with humans. Before you read this passage, try to imagine yourself in a situation in which words and traditional body language are no longer effective means of communication. How would you approach the challenge of conveying complex information and experiences to someone with whom you share no common language, no cultural understandings, no common physical characteristics? Are there media you might use that do not require the use of traditional language? How would you approach the "aliens" if your desire was for genuine mutual communication?

> We danced. The mechanical structure of that dance, the "steps" and their interrelation, are forever unknowable to you, and I won't try to describe them. It began slowly, tentatively; as Shara had, we began by defining terms. And so we ourselves gave the choreography less than half our attention.
>
> Perhaps a third. A part of our minds was busy framing computer themes in artistic terms, but an equally large part was straining for any signs of feedback from the aliens, reaching out with eyes ears skin mind for any kind of response, sensitizing to any conceivable touch. And with as large a part of our minds, we felt for each other, strove to connect our awareness across meters of black vacuum, to see as the aliens saw, through many eyes at once.
>
> And something began to happen. . . .
>
> It began slowly, subtly, in imperceptible stages. After a year of study, I simply found myself understanding, and accepting the understanding without surprise or wonder. At first I thought the aliens had slowed their speed—but then I noted, again without wonder, that my pulse and everyone's respiration had slowed an equal amount. I was on accelerated time, extracting the maximum of information from each second of life, being with the whole of my being. Experimentally I accelerated my time sense another increment, saw the aliens' frenzy slow to a speed that anyone could encompass. I was aware that I could make

time stop altogether, but I didn't want to yet. I studied them at infinite leisure, and understanding grew. It was clear now that there was a tangible if invisible energy that held them in their tight mutual orbits, as electromagnetism holds electrons in theirs. But this energy boiled furiously at their will and they surfed its currents like wood chips that magically never collided. They created a never-ending roller coaster before themselves. Slowly, slowly I began to realize that their energy was *more than* analogous to the energy that bound me to my family. What they were surfing on was their mutual awareness of each other, and of the Universe around them.

My own awareness of my family jumped a quantum level. I heard Norrey breathing, could see out her eyes, felt Tom's sprained calf tug at me, felt Linda's baby stir in my womb, watched us all and swore under Harry's breath with him, raced down Raoul's arm to his fingers and back into my own ears. I was a six-brained Snowflake, existing simultaneously in space and time and thought and music and dance and color and something I could not yet name, and all of these things strove toward harmony.

At no point was there any sensation of leaving or losing my *self*; my unique individual identity. It was right there in my body and brain where I had left it, could not be elsewhere, existed as before. It was as though a part of it had always existed independent of brain and body, as though my brain had always known this level but had been unable to *record* the information. Had we six been this close all along, all unawares, like six lonely blind men in the same volume of space? In a way I had always yearned to without knowing it, I touched my selves, and loved them. We understood entirely that we were being shown this level by the aliens, that they had led us patiently up invisible psychic stairs to this new plane. If any energy detectable by Man had passed between them and us, Bill Cox would have been heating up his laser cannon and screaming for a report, but he was still on conference circuit with the diplomats, letting us dance without distraction.

But communication took place, on levels that even physical instruments could perceive. At first the aliens only echoed portions of our dance, to indicate an emotional or informational connotation they understood, and when they did so we *knew* without question that they had fully grasped whatever nuance we were trying to express. After a time they began more complex responses, began subtly altering the patterns they returned to us, offering variations on a theme, then counterstatements, alternate suggestions. Each time they did so we came to know them better, to grasp the rudiments of their "language" and hence their nature. They agreed with our concept of sphericity, politely disagreed with our concept of mortality, strongly agreed with the notions of pain and joy. When we knew enough words to construct a "sentence," we did so. [4]

If you have ever been profoundly moved by creative expression of any kind, as performer or audience, you will understand a little of what the dancers in the text are attempting, experiencing, and achieving. They have spent long hours studying videotapes of an initial encounter between the aliens and a single dancer, yet none of this has given them the kind of insight necessary for communication. But as the dancers in the narrative pour their own self-expression into their dance, and simultaneously focus deep attention on the movements of the aliens, engagement begins to happen, deepens, until mutual communication is achieved. Words are useless in this context, and another symbolic form of expression has been found that can convey meaning to both parties.

There has been a heavy emphasis, particularly in Western cultural history, on spoken and written language, sometimes at the expense of multiple other modes of expression that, in many situations, empower communication better across the boundaries of time and space, personhood and identity, culture, and even species. This is not to deny that words remain powerful symbols within most of our cultural contexts. Perhaps we remember the childhood poem, "sticks and stones will break my bones, but names will never hurt me." Most of us know well that names and other words have the power both to wound deeply, and also to lift us up, give hope, make us laugh, bring us closer to a loved one. Yet words are still limited in their capacity to fully communicate complex human concepts and understandings. Poets, musicians, visual artists, writers in all genres, assist in the attempt to put into accessible form that which can never be fully communicated through our limited human capacities.

Our symbols do not merely help us to communicate. They enable us to convey our individuality, our sense of who we are and what we value, and our relationship with our loved ones, our world in general. For many, this includes communication with, or at least some articulation of, a sacred reality believed to lie beyond our ordinary human capacity to understand. A group's symbols and rituals—the organized patterns of symbolic action—help it to communicate and celebrate shared meanings and values and to nourish those dimensions of life it holds dear. These complex symbol systems also distinguish one group from another—help to establish individual and communal identity, as well as to convey a particular worldview. Indeed, a group's symbol system is, to a large extent, what makes it a cohesive and identifiable group. You would not read John Fire Lame Deer's autobiography, for example, and think that you were reading an account from a Christian monastery in France or a Buddhist center in Tibet. Even if Lame Deer made no reference to his own historical background or geographical location, the symbols he uses would help you to identify his location.

When we define "symbol" broadly, to include the multiple media that people use to convey their thoughts and feelings, we can conclude that there is no culture we know about that does not have a symbol system. For one thing, the absence of such would mean that we would have no way of knowing about the group! Imagine having no set of pictorial or linguistic symbols, no music or artwork, no spoken or body language. Without any of these tools, members of a group would have no way to communicate with one another, and no means to leave behind any data that would enable historians, archaeologists, and anthropologists to study and attempt to understand their lives and times.

SYMBOLS AND THEIR CULTURAL AND HISTORICAL CONTEXT

Consider this very simple basic image:

What is it? A letter "t," a plus sign, a Christian cross? If you assume that it is a cross, symbolic of Christianity, what are your reactions to it? Some of you may even be wearing some kind of symbolic representation of this item. If you

An Indonesian garden sculpture with ancient religious symbols.

travel in a non-Christian country, where you don't speak the language and you find the cultural traditions very different from your own, locating such a symbol on top of a building might give you a point of connection, a sense of familiarity, a reminder of "home" in a moment of loneliness.

But consider a different situation. Imagine that you are an African American living in Birmingham, Alabama, during the 1950s and 60s. You are awakened in the middle of the night by some kind of commotion. You look out of your window and see one of these objects in the middle of your front yard. As you watch, a group of white-robed individuals sets it on fire. The feelings invoked will be vastly different from those described above. Even if you are a devout Christian, this fundamental symbol, subverted by the Ku Klux Klan, is now being used in a way that conveys feelings of bigotry, hatred, violence, and threat, rather than comfort and hope.

Look carefully at the image in the photograph. With what do you associate this symbol? What is your immediate reaction to it? For most of us, the swastika depicted here is a reminder of the rise of Nazism in the 20th century. The swastika of the Nazis was actually reversed from the original, as is this Indonesian sculpture. We are familiar with its continuing use as an object of hatred or contempt, evidence of anti-Semitism and/or racism, when painted on the wall of a synagogue or Black church, or a stone in a Jewish cemetery. But the symbol dates to the 8th century BCE, long before the swastika became associated in our minds with Hitler and his followers.[5] A walk through almost any museum will demonstrate that this symbol is found on artifacts from many cultures. The word "swastika" itself is derived from the Sanskrit term, *swasti*, which means "well-being," or "good luck." As such, the symbol has a very different meaning within Hinduism, for example, from that associated with it in contemporary Western European cultures.

We are dependent on the symbols of our own culture and the meanings and interpretations that our personal and social histories give to those symbols. How does this apply to our efforts to communicate our experiences of the transcendent, of that which is beyond our five senses? Do the metaphors, analogies, and symbols of our religious traditions also depend on their cultural and historical context? The following passage is from the *Popol Vuh,* an ancient Mayan text. Take note, as you read, of the symbols that are especially related to the specific location of the peoples for whom the text contains deep and continuing significance.

> And here is the beginning of the conceptions of humans, and of the search for the ingredients of the human body. So they spoke, the Bearer, Begetter, the Makers, the Modelers named Sovereign Plumed Serpent:
> "The dawn has approached, preparations have been made, and morning has come for the provider, nurturer, born in the light, begotten in the light. Morning has come for humankind, for the people of the face of the earth,"

they said. It all came together as they went on thinking in the darkness, in the night, as they searched and they sifted, they thought and they wondered.

And here their thoughts came out in clear light. They sought and discovered what was needed for human flesh. It was only a short while before the sun, moon, and stars were to appear above the Makers and Modelers. Split Place, Bitter Water Place is the name: the yellow corn, white corn came from there.

And these are the names of the animals who brought the food: fox, coyote, parrot, crow. There were four animals who brought the news of the ears of yellow corn and white corn. They were coming from over there at Split Place, they showed the way to the split.

And this was when they found the staple foods.

And these were the ingredients for the flesh of the human work, the human design, and the water was for the blood. It became human blood, and corn was also used by the Bearer, Begetter.

And so they were happy over the provisions of the good mountain, filled with sweet things, thick with yellow corn, white corn, and thick with pataxte and cacao, countless zapotes, anonas, jocotes, nances, matasanos, sweets—the rich foods filling up the citadel named Split Place, Bitter Water Place. All the edible fruits were there: small staples, great staples, small plants, great plants. The way was shown by the animals.

And then the yellow corn and white corn were ground, and Xmucane did the grinding nine times. Food was used, along with the water she rinsed her hands with, for the creation of grease; it became human fat when it was worked by the Bearer, Begetter, Sovereign Plumed Serpent, as they are called.

After that, they put it into words:
the making, the modeling of our first mother-father,
with yellow corn, white corn alone for the flesh,
food alone for the human legs and arms,
for our first fathers, the four human works.
It was staples alone that made up their flesh.[6]

What are the items in the Mayan story that demonstrate the connections between symbols and everyday life? For example, corn is a common feature in the religious narratives of these people. Why is such a basic foodstuff so laden with symbolic meaning? For the Maasai people of Eastern Africa, cattle perform this same function. For Plains Indians of the United States it was the buffalo, for peoples of the Pacific Northwest, the salmon.

The symbol system of a people reflects, in some deep and abiding way, those items and objects that form the very stuff of their life, their survival. Like many peoples and traditions, most of the significant sacred symbols of the Mayan people have their roots in particular relationships with elements of the natural world. For peoples who lived prior to the development of large urban settlements and industrial and technological revolutions, the natural world was much more than simply a matter of physical beauty or a resource for raw materials. Their livelihood and indeed their very survival depended upon their ability to live in relationship with their environment. The sun and the rains coming at the right—or wrong—times determined the success or failure of crops, the hunt, and seasonal migration between summer and winter camps. It should come as no surprise that the symbols of greatest importance to such peoples reflected this dependence on nature, or that such images were often central in how people depicted sacred reality.

The most obvious need for symbolic language and imagery within religious traditions is when people attempt to describe the transcendent reality they experience in various ways. Whether or not you are a religious believer, you have something in mind when you hear the term, "the Sacred." That is to say, you have some idea about what it is that you either do or do not believe in. If your idea is of a sacred "being," what are some of the characteristics you attribute—or you think others attribute—to that being? To what extent is your response to this question influenced by time and culture, by your own experiences of social location?

Social location includes those factors of our identity over which we have little or no control yet that influence the ways in which we perceive and are perceived by our broader cultural context. Such factors include, but are not limited to, sex, age, race, ethnicity, culture, sexual orientation, economic status, level of education, and so on. You can undoubtedly add to this list. Whether we like it or not, our society frequently makes judgments about us on the basis of one or more of these factors of our identity, and this in turn affects the ways in which we both perceive ourselves and act within that society. And our location within our society affects our understandings of its symbolic structures.

> *Choose a specific religion and do a Web search to identify several websites related to the tradition. Use the Web address to locate sites in different countries. Compare and contrast some of the images and symbols you find. What are some of the factors that you think might contribute to any differences you see? Are there some similarities that you would not have expected to find in culturally diverse groups?*

THE DYNAMIC NATURE OF SYMBOLS

Do you and your parents always speak the same language? In one of our course evaluations, a student said, "Professor X's course rocks." What does this mean? We choose to assume it's a compliment! Rock, as a verb, means to move back and forth, as a rocking chair moves, or to shake on its base, as a building rocks in an earthquake. It seems that from this idea of movement comes the application in popular music—rock and roll. And, possibly, from this connection to the student's comment about the class. Of course, the student could have been making the connection with the earthquake: the class was a disaster!

Such vernacular language, often called slang, is a way of communicating in words that sometimes are clearly derived from, but sometimes seem to have no connection with, the dictionary definition of the words. In 2003, the expression "wicked bad" continues to mean something that is excellent, superb. On the other hand, you may never have heard the depression era U.S. slang term "twenty-two, skiddoo" which has no meaning today; its only point of reference is a brand of snowmobile.

Today's vernacular language seems, in part, to be based on using words to mean the opposite of their traditional meaning, depending on context to convey meaning. U.S. slang from the 1930s seems to have depended on newly manufactured words, like "twenty-two, skiddoo" and the nonsense song "Mares Eat Oats," which used deliberate distortion of language. The Cockneys of London have a famous rhyming vernacular in which the word that is used rhymes with the word meant. And, of course, there's the famous "supercalifragilisticexpialidocious" from "Mary Poppins." What do these changing practices show about the English language? Can you think of terms, slang or other, that have recently entered the English language? Think of the number of terms that have been introduced in our own time because of scientific or technological development. Bytes and gigabytes, black holes, in vitro fertilization, micromanagement, bipolar disorder, quantum physics, and chaos theory: all these terms would have been meaningless just a generation or two ago.

When King James II of England first saw Christopher Wren's magnificent new structure, St. Paul's Cathedral, he described it as "amusing, awful, and artificial." You might imagine he was being insulting. Of course, what the monarch meant was that the structure was "pleasing, awe-inspiring, and skillfully achieved."[7] Over time, word meanings can become so different as to create major misunderstandings. If you have ever tried to read a tract in Middle English, or even to read a selection from a more recent historical document such as a journal or record from the 17th or 18th century, you will know the difficulty of contending with changing word meanings and differences between language systems.

In the early years of the development of the United States of America, the goal was to achieve a "melting pot"—for all inhabitants of this country to leave behind their cultures of origin and become "American." For many years, immigrants who came to these shores from whatever part of the world were encouraged to leave behind as quickly as possible the cultures (especially the languages) from which they emerged. Of course, this applied less to those who came from white, English-speaking European areas. Their language, culture, and religious ideologies would come to define to a large extent what "American" meant. In more recent times, however, descendants of the indigenous peoples who were already in this land, as well as immigrants, those who came by choice and those forced from their homelands, are recognizing the value of retaining, or reclaiming, traditional cultural practices and beliefs. Many today

'Twas brillig, and the slithy toves
Did gyre and gimble in the wabe.
All mimsy were the borogoves,
And the mome raths outgrabe.

Lewis Carroll's "Jabberwocky" draws
on our ability to infer meaning and
mood from creative nonsense.

see cultural diversity, including language, religious/spiritual practice, art forms and so forth, as a deep value. "Salad bowl" may be a more accurate metaphor for the United States than the "melting pot."

This shift in perspective illustrates the tension between the need for continuity and the need for change in our symbol systems. Those from cultures other than the dominant white Anglo-Saxon Protestant one recognize that a certain sense of community identity has been lost in the "melting pot" ideology and are often increasingly insistent upon reclaiming and/or retaining the richness of their ancestral culture in a new context. They are at once acknowledging the need for continuity with their own history and moving both themselves and the rest of the nation into a redefinition of what it means to be "American."

Another area where symbols have changed dramatically over time is that of religious understandings of the sacred. Those from a Jewish, Christian, or Muslim background often tend to think of God as just God. Yet might not our ideas even of the sacred be shaped by time and culture, by experiences of social location? Westerners are generally familiar with the monotheistic deity referred to as Yhwh, God, or Allah. Yet religious persons even in the parts of the world where the major monotheistic religions emerged have not always understood the sacred in those terms. Have you ever considered what it would be like to think of sacred reality as female? Some contemporary scholars suggest that long before we had images of God the Father, there were powerful depictions of Goddesses, not only as "Mother," but sometimes as warrior, hunter, bearer of rage, or healer.

What happened to these female images of the divine? When and why did the images change? Scholars disagree on the source of the shift, but one reason often given is a limited understanding of biology. Knowledge of the male role in procreation is relatively recent in human history. In prehistoric cultures, a connection was not made between the process of a woman giving birth and the act of sexual intercourse that had occurred nine months previously. Women were thus held in awe as those who could not only produce both female and male children from their own bodies, but also nurture those children with sustenance from their breasts. In addition, women could bleed regularly without the dire results—usually death—which befell the hunter or warrior who bled so profusely. Given the attributes so often attached to deities—giver of life, nurturer, all-powerful, mysterious—it is not surprising that peoples of such a time would have imaged sacred reality in the form they deemed most powerful in their human experience: woman.

Over time, warrior gods are thought to have displaced the goddess as the central sacred figure in religious belief systems. Knowledge of the connection between intercourse and childbirth led eventually to women being seen as passive recipients of male sperm, which provided the spirit and soul of the child; at best, women provided only the lesser material substance. Great philosophers such as Aristotle, Aquinas, and many of their followers, referred to women as "misbegotten males." The "perfect" human child was male; only when something went awry was a female born. This imperfection was the fault of the female for supplying an imperfect matrix. How then could the deity, the supreme being who was the epitome of perfection, be other than male? The symbol had to change to reflect different cultural understandings and patterns of relationships.

Today many people, especially women, are questioning whether this exclusively male symbolism for sacred reality is adequate to contemporary understandings of gender roles and relationships. In addition, persons from different races and ethnicities question whether they are truly "made in the image" of a deity who is often pictured with blue eyes and blond hair. To what extent are our symbols and images, even those representing sacred reality itself, created in *our* image, through our own culture-bound creative powers and imaginings? These are questions we will revisit later when we focus more specifically on different understandings of transcendence and the sacred.

Within a given culture's language and symbol systems, then, both continuity and change seem to be necessary. Symbol systems, including language, are the way in which meaning and experiences are transmitted among people of a given place and time, and passed down through the generations as the historical record of the group. Without a certain degree of continuity, symbols lose their power to communicate. The value and usefulness of a given symbol is dependent on its location within a community that shares a relatively common understanding of its meaning. If you were to speak about something as commonplace to you as an apple to a person who has never had experience of either the word or the fruit it symbolizes, you would be greeted with a blank stare.

On the other hand, language and other symbols are continuously changing to reflect new realities and understandings. You will have experienced some of this yourself, as does each generation. Again, think of some of the words that are part of your life that your parents or other older family members or friends don't understand, or which have a totally different meaning in a different context. Symbol systems that do not retain a flexibility that allows them to incorporate new concepts, new physical realities, new experiences, quickly become irrelevant and ultimately die.

Visit a local art museum and explore art work from a particular culture or part of the world—Europe, the United States, China—through several time periods. Are there dimensions that have remained the same over time? Others that have changed? How does this relate to our discussion of symbols?

SOME QUESTIONS ABOUT SYMBOLS

Symbols, as we have learned, include the communication systems that humans have developed and called "languages," as well as all of the nonverbal ways we have devised to make sense of our own experiences and to share those experiences with others. We cannot do without symbols in our social and cultural groups, our families, our personal relationships. At the same time we cannot assume we understand the symbols of other cultures.

As we mentioned earlier, religions have symbol systems that are particular to them, and we frequently fail to recognize what these symbols are when we do not share the religious beliefs of others. This failure to recognize another faith's religious symbols has led to wars and terrorism. As another example, only recently have some of the skeletons of Native Americans been returned to their nations by the Smithsonian Institution and other museums. In our quest for scientific knowledge, our culture's symbolism, we have not understood the symbolism of an unburied ancestor to Native Americans. We co-opt symbols from other religions to wear as jewelry, or to use as designs in fabrics, wallpaper, and the like. This may be interpreted as an affront to the sacred symbols of others.

Think how you would feel if some foreign group co-opted the symbols of your religion, your country, or your family. Knowledge of the depth of feeling that people attach to such symbols as, for example, the flag that represents their country has prompted opponents to burn the flag of that country. What would your response be to the destruction or other violation of a symbol about which you felt deeply?

Religious phenomena are beyond the reach of our five physical senses, experiences that cannot be explained, related to, or defined through everyday language or scientific language or modes of analysis. Even people who do not have a religious orientation to life need symbols to signify and communicate experiences like love, sorrow, and excitement that defy ordinary human language.

Our symbol systems are infinitely complex and varied, limited only by the bounds of human imagination and creativity. Symbols are deeply significant expressions of a group's identity, including its history and culture, its many ways of understanding itself and its world. Indeed, the identity of the group or individual belonging to it is in many ways constituted by symbols and their interpretations within their social context. Our ability to make sense of our world is dependent on the strength of our symbol systems, on their capacity to retain enough flexibility to incorporate new realities and enough consistency to sustain the transmission of meaning from one individual to another, one age to another. Because of the deep-seated power of our most important symbols, any attempt to change them often evokes great resistance. Yet only by remaining open to new possibilities of meaning and interpretation do symbol systems, and symbols themselves, stay dynamic and retain their capacity to truly evoke and communicate the depths of human identity and meaning.

What Some Others Have Said About Symbols

Swiss psychologist Carl Jung (1875–1961) was particularly interested in the origins of symbols and the ways in which symbols presented themselves in dreams. For Jung, there was a clear distinction between symbols and signs, with the former containing meaning often largely unavailable to the conscious mind. Not only do real symbols tap into one's unconscious world, claims Jung, but they also evolve over time in a communal as well as individual sense. Thus, according to Jung, the meaning we sense in symbols in our own time has its origin in ancient mythology, and perhaps dates back even to prehuman experience. These selections from Jung's "Approaching the Unconscious" give a glimpse of his insights into human consciousness—and unconsciousness—as they relate to symbols.

A word or an image is symbolic when it implies something more than its obvious and immediate meaning. It has a wider "unconscious" aspect that is never precisely defined or fully explained. Nor can one hope to define or explain it. As the mind explores the symbol, it is led to ideas that lie beyond the grasp of reason. The wheel may lead our thoughts toward the concept of a "divine" sun, but at this point reason must admit its incompetence; man is unable to define a "divine" being. When, with all our intellectual limitations, we call something "divine," we have merely given it a name, which may be based on a creed, but never on factual evidence.

Jung goes on to explain why, in his view, people use symbols.

> Because there are innumerable things beyond the range of human understanding, we constantly use symbolic terms to represent concepts that we cannot define or fully comprehend. This is one reason why all religions employ symbolic language or images. But this conscious use of symbols is only one aspect of a psychological fact of great importance: Man also produces symbols unconsciously and spontaneously, in the form of dreams.
>
> It is not easy to grasp this point. But the point must be grasped if we are to know more about the ways in which the human mind works. Man, as we realize if we reflect for a moment, never perceives anything fully or comprehends anything completely. He can see, hear, touch, and taste; but how far he sees, how well he hears, what his touch tells him, and what he tastes depend upon the number and quality of his senses. These limit his perception of the world around him. By using scientific instruments he can partly compensate for the deficiencies of senses. For example, he can extend the range of his vision by binoculars or of his hearing by electrical amplification.
>
> But the most elaborate apparatus cannot do more than bring distant or small objects within range of his eyes, or make faint sounds more audible. No matter what instruments he uses, at some point he reaches the edge of certainty beyond which conscious knowledge cannot pass.
>
> There are, moreover, unconscious aspects of our perception of reality. The first is the fact that even when our senses react to real phenomena, sights, and sounds, they are somehow translated from the realm of reality into that of the mind. Within the mind they become psychic events, whose ultimate nature is unknowable (for the psyche cannot know its own psychical substance). Thus every experience contains an indefinite number of unknown factors not to speak of the fact that every concrete object is always unknown in certain respects, because we cannot know the ultimate nature of matter itself.
>
> Then there are certain events of which we have not consciously taken note; they have remained, so to speak, below the threshold of consciousness. They have happened, but they have been absorbed subliminally, without our conscious knowledge. We can become aware of such happenings only in a moment of intuition or by a process of profound thought that leads to a later realization that they must have happened; and though we may have originally ignored their emotional and vital importance, it later wells up from the unconscious as a sort of afterthought. . . .

Do you think that Jung makes it clear *why* there are some things we know that are beyond scientific evidence? Do you think that we will continue to confront such ineffable things, or do you think that science will eventually demystify everything?

> I began this essay by noting the difference between a sign and a symbol. The sign is always less than the concept it represents, while a symbol always stands for something more than its obvious and immediate meaning. Symbols, moreover, are natural and spontaneous products. No genius has ever sat down with a pen or a brush in his hand and said: "Now I am going to invent a symbol." No one can take a more or less rational thought, reached as a logical conclusion or by deliberate intent, and then give it "symbolic" form. No matter what fantastic trappings one may put upon an idea of this kind, it will still remain a sign, linked to the conscious thought behind it, not a symbol that hints at something not yet known. In dreams, symbols occur spontaneously, for dreams happen and are not invented; they are, therefore, the main source of all our knowledge about symbolism. . . .
>
> There are many symbols, however (among them the most important), that are not individual but *collective* in their nature and origin. These are chiefly religious images. The believer assumes that they are of divine origin—that they have been revealed to man. The skeptic says flatly that they have been invented. Both are wrong. It is true, as the skeptic notes, that religious symbols and concepts have for centuries been the object of careful and quite conscious elaboration. It is equally true, as the believer implies, that their origin is so far buried in the mystery of the past that they seem to have no human source. But they are in fact "collective representations," emanating from primeval dreams and creative fantasies. As such, these images are involuntary spontaneous manifestations and by no means intentional inventions.[8]

Jung claims that both the believer and the skeptic are wrong about the origins of humankind's most powerful symbols. Could we entertain the possibility that both may be right?

> *Get a group together to try to "intentionally" invent a symbol. Agree upon just what it is you want to symbolize, then draw on the elements of "symbol" we have discussed in this chapter to determine what best represents the concept you have identified. Is this easier or harder than inventing something like a color?*

We have already noted that race, class, and culture are important contexts of the understanding of symbols. Gender also matters a great deal in the understanding of symbols. As a very obvious example, look at the ways in which two friends greet each other. The particular ways will vary according to age and culture, but in the United States, there is often a great difference depending upon the gender of the people involved. For many males, the greeting has a component of touching, either simply shaking hands, or going through some sort of ritualistic bumping of fists or shoulders. The same males might greet a female friend quite differently. Two female friends greet each other differently from the way men greet each other, and from the way in which they would greet a male friend. In the United States, female friends are more inclined to hug than bump one another.

Gender plays a role in many ways in our understanding religious symbols and concepts. The next selections are from *Gender and Religion: On the Complexity of Symbols.* The book is a collection of essays that grew out of a program of the Comparative Religion faculty of the University of Washington that was investigating the questions that were emerging about religion and gender. The first essay in that collection, which also serves as an introduction to the volume as a whole, deals with the "Complexity of Symbols." In this chapter, Caroline Walker Bynum, the leader of the group and one of the editors of the book, explains the process they used in investigating the theme of religion and gender, and in the process discusses some of the earlier studies, what they have adapted from those studies, and what they have rejected, and why. See if you agree with Bynum and her collaborators, or if you, too, would further modify the points that you will accept as "givens."

> In exploring the relationship between gender and religion, the authors of this volume insist upon two fundamental insights. First, they insist upon the feminist insight that all human beings are "gendered"—that is, that there is no such thing as generic *homo religiosus*. No scholar studying religion, no participant in ritual, is ever neuter. Religious experience is the experience of men and women, and in no known society is this experience the same. Second, this volume assumes the phenomenological insight that religious symbols point men and women beyond their ordinary lives. As Paul Ricoeur explains it, there is no such thing as a religious symbol that is merely a sign of or statement about social structure. However religious symbols "mean," they never simply prescribe or transcribe social status. Rather they transmute it, even while referring to it. Religious symbols are, as the anthropologist Victor Turner puts it, "polysemic"; they have the quality of possessing manifold meanings. . . .
>
> Some examples may make our method clearer. . . . The Church of the Latter-day Saints, sometimes known as the Mormons, teaches that all spirits are created by a Heavenly Father and a Heavenly Mother and progress toward perfection in this life and beyond as members of human families. To Mormon adherents, the individual self has gender for all eternity, and this gender reflects a male/female division lodged at the heart of ultimate reality. To Christians in medieval Europe, on the other hand, God was sometimes seen as a bridegroom to whom all souls, no matter what sort of sexual body they inhabited, related as brides. But the "otherness" of God from creation meant that this God could also be seen as a whirlwind, a circle whose center is everywhere, or a nursing mother; it meant that all such epithets were finally valueless for evoking or explaining the essence of the divine. If we turn to the Chinese tradition, we find yet a third way in which gender symbols refer to the ultimately real. A beloved document of Confucianism says: "Heaven [Ch'ien] is my father and Earth [K'un] is my mother." But the Confucian tradition also teaches that wholeness

is a feminine image and that wholeness transcends diversity. The ultimate, to a Chinese philosopher, is clearly not father or masculine; but if it is feminine, it is so only with an expanded meaning of feminine that leaves its referent in social experience far behind. Self and cosmos are thus not male and female for a Chinese philosopher or a Christian mystic in the same sense in which they are male and female for a Mormon. But do they have gender at all? And, if so, what does it mean to attribute gender to that ultimate Wholeness or Oneness that is beyond distinction or definition?

These three cases raise questions about the meaning of religious symbols. How do such symbols refer to and make use of gender? But the questions we ought to ask do not stop here. For it is also unclear, in the three cases described above, *whose* meaning we are analyzing. Neo-Confucian theories, which may be understood as feminizing the cosmos, were produced by men. Male mystics in medieval Europe venerated the Virgin Mary and wrote of Jesus as mother. Mormon theologians (all male by theological prescription) prohibit the priesthood to women because fatherhood means leadership. But what is the significance of Chinese men elaborating the idea of wholeness as feminine? Do female mystics in Christian Europe see God as mother and mean by *mother* what their male counterparts mean? Do Mormon women experience in the same way as Mormon men their church's theories of male and female roles lasting for all eternity?[9]

Do the different understandings of male and female in the three religions make sense to you? What questions might you have for a male Christian mystic, a Mormon theologian, and/or a Neo-Confucian? Many people have suggested that we should reclaim some of the "feminine" symbols for the sacred that exist in diverse religious traditions. But Bynum seems to go a step further. What do you think of Bynum's suggestion that the gender of the person who encounters the symbol—or who describes it in the first place—makes a difference in the interpretation of that same symbol?

CHAPTER THREE

How Do We Communicate? Ritual and Human Identity

In the last chapter, we discussed the role of symbols in the human quest to give meaning to life and to communicate our personal and communal experiences with one another. Now we are turning our attention to symbolic *action,* or ritual. What do you think of when you hear the term "ritual"? You may have particular "rituals" that are important in your life. For example, what do you do when you move into a new living space to make it feel like "home"? You might simply haul in the practical items that you'll need to take care of day-to-day physical necessities, but perhaps there are other items or activities that are important, even essential, to help transform the new space, to make it "yours." What do you have to do to get going in the morning? Are there certain things that have to happen if your day is going to feel "right," to run smoothly? Do you have particular things that *must* happen on particular occasions or celebrations, or when you get together with a certain person? If you answered "yes" to any of these questions, you already have a sense of the importance of ritual, of how ritual is different from mere habit, and of how ritual is present throughout our lives.

Setting the Stage: The Power of Ritual

Ritual has always been profoundly important within religious traditions, both for individuals and for the community. The prayer ritual in Islam is one that may be performed individually or in a group. In non-Muslim countries, it is likely that in most circumstances an observant Muslim will perform her or his prayer rituals alone. Yet although often performed by one lone Muslim, perhaps even in a context where she or he is surrounded by persons of other faiths, the ritual carries with it a sense of community. Muslims, regardless of where they are, turn toward Mecca, the holy city of Islam, and pray five times a day. The following description outlines not only the ritual of prayer itself, but the preparations that must be made prior to engaging in prayer. Notice that this is the prayer demanded of all faithful Muslims, not a few "professionals" who devote their lives to a particularly intense following of their faith. Dr. Hassan Hathout, an Egyptian American physician, tries to explain the purpose and practice of *salah*, the ritual prayer of Islam, in terms that non-Muslims can understand. Why would people commit to a lifestyle that makes such a demand? What would you see as the positive or negative effects of this practice in our own contemporary world?

The ritual prayer of Islam is a distinct entity, somewhat different from prayer in its wider sense, that is, communicating your feelings to God at any time in any place and asking for His guidance, help and forgiveness, a practice that is ordained by the Quran and commendable in other religions. Ritual Islamic prayer takes a special form and content, in which both body and soul are harmoniously involved. It is performed five times a day: at early morning, early afternoon, late afternoon, after sunset and after dark.

The prayers may be performed at any clean place (home, mosque, park, the workplace, etcetera) by an individual or by a group, Muslim men and/or women, with one of the men leading the prayers as an *imam* (leader). The five prayers each take only a few minutes to perform. Only the noon prayer on Friday is mandated to be a collective (group) prayer, which is held at the mosque and preceded by a sermon *(khutba)*. The imam (prayer leader) is not a priest, nor does the same person have to lead each prayer, but considerations of scholarship and knowledge of the Quran and the religion are exercised in choosing him (business-people, blue-collar workers, doctors, teachers, and others, as well as religious scholars, commonly bear this responsibility).

In order to perform the prayer one has to be clean, having performed an ablution *(wudu)* entailing cleaning by water of the mouth, nostrils, face, forearms to the elbows, and feet, and wiping the head and ears with wet hands. An ablution may take one through several prayers but must be repeated if one falls asleep or passes urine, stools, or flatus. Sexual intercourse necessitates a full bath. Women are exempted from the ritual prayers during their menstrual (and puerperal) flow, and at its cessation, a bath is necessary, as it is for men after ejaculation. However, anyone may pray to God at any time, in personal supplication, with or without wudu.

Each prayer is practically an audience with God. Facing in the direction of the Kaaba (the first mosque, ever, built by patriarch Abraham and his son Ishmael for the worship of the One God, at the site which long later became the city of Makkah in Arabia). Only around the Kaaba mosque in Makkah do Muslims stand in concentric circles for their prayers (quite an impressive scene). All the world over they pray standing in straight lines, leaving no gaps, and facing Makkah. Women usually occupy the back lines, not necessarily a requirement of religion but an aesthetic preference, since women would feel uncomfortable with men behind them during the movements of bowing and prostration.

The prayer is opened by reciting the words *Allahu Akbar*, i.e., God is Greater (than all else), with which the worshipper practically turns his or her back to all the universe and addresses God. One necessary component of each of the prayers is the Opening Chapter of the Quran, which reads: *"Praise be to Allah, Lord of the worlds. The Compassionate, the Merciful, Master of the Day of Judgment. You alone do we worship and You alone we ask for help. Guide us to the straight path, the path of those on whom You have bestowed Your grace, those who are not deserving of Your wrath, and who go not astray"* (1:1–7). The rest of the prayer consists of reciting additional portions of the Quran, and of bowing down and prostrating oneself (to God), interjecting *"Glory to my Lord the Greatest," "Glory to my Lord the Highest," "Allah listens to those who thank Him,"* and what fills one's heart by way of supplication. The prayer is concluded in the sitting position by reiterating the affirmation of the faith (the shahadah), and seeking God's peace and blessings on prophets Muhammad and Abraham and their families and followers.

Prayer, both obligatory and spontaneous, is an immense spiritual treasure to be tapped. It inspires peace, purity and tranquility, and instills a continuous awareness of and feeling of closeness to God. It amazingly reduces the hustle-and-bustle of life to tame proportions. By their spacing of five times a day, including at the day's beginning, prayers tend to help worshippers maintain a therapeutic level of well-being and practically leave no room in their consciousness for mischievous thought or deed.[1]

What distinction does Hathout make between this ritual form of prayer, salah, and the spontaneous informal prayer that is also encouraged among Muslim believers? Hathout claims that performing this ritual five times a day leaves Muslims little "room in their consciousness for mischievous thought or deed." What are some of the other specific functions that rituals fulfill? What do you do, for example, if you have had a particularly stressful day and need to recenter yourself? Are there certain practices that help you to regain a sense of composure, a sense of well-being?

WHAT DO YOU THINK? PERSONAL EXPERIENCES OF RITUAL

We all have particular things that we do every day, or every week, as a matter of routine. Sometimes these activities become special, set apart, transformed. Think, for example, about eating. This is something that all of us who have access to the economic means that sustain a reasonable standard of living do several times a day. Think about your own last meal, or at least about the last food you ate, and the context in which you ate it. It might have been a rushed bagel that you grabbed on your way out the door, or a celebratory dinner shared with a special friend. Eating is one of those activities necessary to sustain life, but in many, if not most, cultures, eating can be far more than this. Even outside of the fact that many religious rituals involve eating (or refraining from eating—fasting), we ritualize this day-to-day activity on many occasions and in many ways. Consider occasions in your own personal life, your family, your wider community, when the simple and necessary "habit" of eating becomes more than merely a means of sustaining life. What are the components that make any particular meal special? Is the setting important? Are there particular items of food that it is essential to include? Who must be there? Is there a certain way in which the group must come together? Would it change the meaning and significance of the meal if any of these components were missing?

> *Identify one particular celebration that involves eating and that is important to you. It may involve just one other person (an anniversary dinner) or it may be a large event that includes your extended family or a larger community group. Write a brief response of your own to the questions we asked above, and then ask these same questions of at least one other person who is usually or always involved in the event. Compare your responses, particularly to the question as to how you would each feel if one or more of the usual components were missing. Which things are essential to both/all of you? Are there some that are more important to one than another? Why do you think this is?*

Often when we hear the term "ritual" we think of something a little more formal, more structured than our individual practices in preparing or renewing our living space. Tom Driver adds the terms "ritualizing" and "ritualization" to help make distinctions among the various kinds of symbolic behavior and practice in which humans (and other animals) engage. For Driver, much "ritualization" must take place before full-blown "ritual" is achieved, yet he insists that a relationship must continue between the two.

> Like art, ritualization involves both improvisation and the establishment of repeatable form. These two elements provide a way of distinguishing the words "ritualization" and "ritual" in reference to human activity. The former (ritualization) emphasizes the making of new forms through which expressive behavior can flow, while the latter (ritual) connotes an already known, richly symbolic pattern of behavior. . . .
> Without its ritualizing (new-making) component, ritual would be entirely repetitious and static. Without aiming at the condition of ritual, ritualizing would lack purpose and avoid form.[2]

Using Driver's distinctions, would you categorize some of the activities you have encountered already in this chapter as "ritualizations" or as "ritual"? You might have witnessed evidence of "ritual"—or at least ritualizing—as you've driven in your car, watched television, attended a sporting event, or visited with family or friends. Think about some of the most important events in your own life. For many people, at least in the contemporary United States as well as in many other countries, one of the most important "coming of age" events is getting one's driver's license. What was so important about that event? Was there some symbolic meaning attached to the achievement that made it so significant? For some of you, gaining your license was perhaps a "rite of passage," symbolizing your movement from childhood toward an adulthood where you take on (and are given) increasing amounts of freedom and its attendant responsibility. Was this occurrence ritual or ritualization? What specific characteristics of the experience make it one or the other? Is the "performance" of such rituals strictly an individual event, or does it affect a wider group—your family, your neighborhood, the broader community?

Many of you will sense a certain familiarity in the next reading in this chapter. Roadside shrines to mark places where people have died in traffic accidents or other tragedies have become a commonplace sight in many parts of the country, and indeed in many places around the world. What is it that moves people to construct such shrines? Why do people visit them, sometimes to simply quietly be there, and sometimes to perform ceremonies there? Should these occasions of "ritual" be encouraged or forbidden? Would an official marker erected by the state or municipality have the same effect as the spontaneous shrines constructed by those who mourn the person or persons killed there?

> Weeks after Shequita Griffin was struck and killed while strapping her infant into a car seat, family and friends each Saturday visit a makeshift shrine at the scene of her death, adding stuffed animals, silk scarves and cards. . . .
>
> But Griffin's relatives spruce up the memorial each week when they gather there for a prayer, much as others do when visiting the graves of loved ones. In the process, Griffin's family hopes to remind drivers that too many people die in senseless accidents. "We don't want her death to be in vain," family friend Rosemarie McDowell said of the 22-year-old Griffin.
>
> The phenomenon of makeshift memorials has grown dramatically in recent years, filling medians and curbsides with tributes and memorabilia. Roadside shrines are such a visible part of the American landscape that they have become a field of academic study and even parody, by the likes of the satirical newspaper *The Onion,* which described the memorials as "hackneyed." And while providing comfort to many, they increasingly pose an annoyance and a constitutional affront to others. . . .
>
> Although such memorials have become prevalent in recent years, [James] Green [senior lecturer in anthropology at the University of Washington] said, they date to the 1300s in Greece, where families placed monuments along roads to alert passers-by of a death.
>
> "The memorials generally contained some words of wisdom, and were mini-billboards for how that person viewed life," Green said. He credits the resurgence in makeshift memorials to the Vietnam Veterans Memorial in Washington, D.C. The Vietnam memorial and the elaborate memorial at the site of the Oklahoma City bombing have become high-profile grieving places where people leave memorabilia, from family pictures to teddy bears. . . .

The U.S. practice of roadside memorials probably has its roots in the Indian and Hispanic cultures of the Southwest, Nance and others said. Called *descansos*, Spanish for resting places, they began when pallbearers hand-carried bodies to burial. Each time they rested, they would pray, carve crosses into rocks and pile the rocks along the roadside. . . .

[Paul] Chizook [of Boston] wants Massachusetts to replace temporary, makeshift memorials with permanent signs that would be erected along highways and feature the names of car crash victims and the dates they were killed.

Government-sanctioned memorials have been tried in some states, such as Texas and Florida. In Ireland, the government marks the place of fatal accidents with a warning sign that has a black dot and the words "Traffic Black Spot."

But the idea of replacing colorful, personalized roadside memorials with signs probably would be met with strong resistance from the families of many traffic accident victims, said Green. "It could be considered very cold," he said.[3]

What would make you want to create such a shrine? Think of some events that have occurred in your city or state. How might you memorialize the event with a shrine? What would you put there? What would you do there? How would this help deal with the circumstances of the tragedy?

Cultural and Social Experiences of Ritual

As might be clear from the examples we have encountered already, even the most personal of rituals frequently has a social or communal dimension. As in the case with roadside shrines and the Muslim prayer, the culture and social context of the individuals for whom the rituals have meaning greatly influence the experience and significance of the rituals themselves. James Baldwin's novel *Go Tell it on the Mountain* is the story of a family in Harlem. In the following passage, the younger son, John, reflects on his experiences of Sunday church attendance when he was a child. Read this narrative and note all the events or elements that you might call "ritual." In which ways do John's culture and social location influence his experiences of church-going on Sunday mornings?

His earliest memories—which were, in a way, his only memories—were of the hurry and brightness of Sunday mornings. They all rose together on that day; his father, who did not have to go to work, and led them in prayer before breakfast; his mother, who dressed up on that day, and looked almost young, with her hair straightened, and on her head the close-fitting white cap that was the uniform of holy women; his younger brother, Roy, who was silent that day because his father was home. Sarah, who wore a red ribbon in her hair that day, and was fondled by her father. And the baby, Ruth, who was dressed in pink and white, and rode in her mother's arms to church. . . .

Artist Janice Huse depicts the importance of Sunday morning worship for the African American family.

The Sunday morning service began when Brother Elisha sat down at the piano and raised a song. This moment and this music had been with John, so it seemed, since he had first drawn breath. It seemed that there had never been a time when he had not known this moment of waiting while the packed church paused—the sisters in white, heads raised, the brothers in blue, heads back; the white caps of the women seeming to glow in the charged air like crowns, the kinky, gleaming heads of the men seeming to be lifted up—and the rustling and the whispering ceased and the children were quiet; perhaps someone coughed, or the sound of a car horn, or a curse from the streets came in; then Elisha hit the keys, beginning at once to sing, and everybody joined him, clapping their hands, and rising, and beating the tambourines.

The song might be: *Down at the cross where my Saviour died!*

Or: *Jesus, I'll never forget how you set me free!*

Or: *Lord, hold my hand while I run this race!*

They sang with all the strength that was in them, and clapped their hands for joy. There had never been a time when John had not sat watching the saints rejoice with terror in his heart, and wonder. Their singing caused him to believe in the presence of the Lord; indeed, it was no longer a question of belief, because they made that presence real. He did not feel it himself, the joy they felt, yet he could not doubt that it was, for them, the very bread of life—could not doubt it, that is, until it was too late to doubt. Something happened to their faces and their voices, the rhythm of their bodies, and to the air they breathed; it was as though wherever they might be became the upper room, and the Holy Ghost were riding on the air. His father's face, always awful, became more awful now; his father's daily anger was transformed into prophetic wrath. His mother, her eyes raised to heaven, hands arced before her, moving, made real for John that patience, that endurance, that long suffering, which he had read of in the Bible and found so hard to imagine.

On Sunday mornings the women all seemed patient, all the men seemed mighty. While John watched, the Power struck someone, a man or woman; they cried out, a long, wordless crying, and, arms outstretched like wings, they began the Shout. Someone moved a chair a little to give them room, the rhythm paused, the singing stopped, only the pounding feet and the clapping hands were heard; then another cry, another dancer; then the tambourines began again, and the voices rose again, and the music swept on again, like fire, or flood, or judgment. Then the church seemed to swell with the Power it held, and, like a planet rocking in space, the temple rocked with the Power of God. John watched, watched the faces, and the weightless bodies, and listened to the timeless cries. One day, so everyone said, this Power would possess him; he would sing and cry as they did now, and dance before his King.[4]

One of the functions of ritual is to make the ordinary special, set apart in some way. As we shall see, this can apply to events, to places, even to people. In this context, reread the first paragraph of Baldwin's narrative, where John briefly describes the preparations his family makes for their church attendance. How is Sunday made different from other days through these activities? How do such preparations make the family ready for the worship that will follow? Would you call these preparations "ritual" or are they only getting ready for ritual?

Compare the scene that Baldwin describes through his character John with worship services you may have attended. Have you ever felt drawn into some phenomenon beyond yourself as John was? Was it in a formalized setting such as the organized service of a religious organization, or did your experience occur in a different context? Even if you have not had such an experience your-self, have you heard others describe anything similar?

One type of ritual common to almost every culture and tradition is the rite of passage, an event designed to mark the passing of community members from one stage of life to another. You might have experienced such a rite your-self: baptism, confirmation, a bar or bat mitzvah, or some other similar religious ceremony. We encountered one example in the story of Lame Deer's vision quest in Chapter 1. In many cultures, comparable rituals occurred to celebrate the coming-to-adulthood of young women. In her fictional account of the story of the biblical character Dinah, Anita Diamant creates such a ceremony and describes it from the perspective of the young woman involved.

It was nearly dark, and my ceremony began almost before I realized what was happening. Inna brought a polished metal cup filled with fortified wine, so dark and sweet I barely tasted its power. But my head soon floated while my mothers prepared me with henna on the bottoms of my feet and on my palms. Unlike a bride, they painted a line of red from my feet up to my sex, and from my hands they made a pattern of spots that led to my navel.

They put kohl on my eyes ("So you will be far-seeing," said Leah) and perfumed my forehead and my armpits ("So you will walk among flowers," said Rachel). They removed my bracelets and took my robe from me. It must have been the wine that prevented me from asking why they took such care with paint and scent yet dressed me in the rough homespun gown used for women in childbirth and as a shroud for the afterbirth after the baby came.

They were so kind to me, so funny, so sweet. They would not let me feed myself but used their fingers to fill my mouth with the choicest morsels. They massaged my neck and back until I was as supple as a cat. They sang every song known among us. My mother kept my wine cup filled and brought it to my lips so often that soon I found it difficult to speak, and the voices around me melted into a loud happy hum.

Zebulun's wife, Ahavah, danced with her pregnant belly to the clapping of hands. I laughed until my sides ached. I smiled until my face hurt. It was good to be a woman!

Then Rachel brought out the teraphim, and everyone fell silent. The household gods had remained hidden until that moment. Although I had been a little girl when I'd seen them last, I remembered them like old friends: the pregnant mother, the goddess wearing snakes in her hair, the one that was both male and female, the stern little ram. Rachel laid them out carefully and chose the goddess wearing the shape of a grinning frog. Her wide mouth held her own eggs for safekeeping, while her legs were splayed in a dagger-shaped triangle, ready to lay a thousand more. Rachel rubbed the obsidian figure with oil until the creature gleamed and dripped in the light of the lamps. I stared at the frog's silly face and giggled, but no one laughed with me.

In the next moment, I found myself outside with my mother and my aunts. We were in the wheat patch in the heart of the garden—a hidden place where grain dedicated to sacrifice was grown. The soil had been tilled in preparation for planting after the moon's return, and I was naked, lying face-down on the cool soil. I shivered. My mother put my cheek to the ground and loosened my hair around me. She arranged my arms wide, "to embrace the earth," she whispered. She bent my knees and pulled the soles of my feet together until they touched, "to give the first blood back to the land," said Leah. I could feel the night air on my sex, and it was strange and wonderful to be so open under the sky.

My mothers gathered around: Leah above me, Bilhah at my left hand, Zilpah's hand on the back of my legs. I was grinning like the frog, half asleep, in love with them all. Rachel's voice behind me broke the silence. "Mother! Innana! Queen of the Night! Accept the blood offering of your daughter, in her mother's name, in your name. In her blood may she live, in her blood may she give life."

It did not hurt. The oil eased the entry, and the narrow triangle fit perfectly as it entered me. I faced the west while the little goddess faced east as she broke the lock on my womb. When I cried out, it was not so much pain but surprise and perhaps even pleasure, for it seemed to me that the Queen herself was lying on top of me, with Dumuzi her consort beneath me. I was like a slip of cloth, caught between their lovemaking, warmed by the great passion.

My mothers moaned softly in sympathy. If I could have spoken I would have reassured them that I was perfectly happy. For all the stars of the night sky had entered my womb behind the legs of the smiling little frog goddess. On the softest, wildest night since the separation of land and water, earth and sky, I lay panting like a dog and felt myself spinning through the heavens. And when I began to fall, I had no fear.

The sky was pink when I opened my eyes. Inna was crouched beside me, watching my face. I was lying on my back, my arms and legs wide like the spokes of the wheel, my nakedness covered by my mother's best blanket. The midwife helped me to my feet and led me back to a soft corner in the red tent, where the other women still slept. "Did you dream?" she asked me. When I nodded that I had, she drew close and said, "What shape did she take?"

Oddly, I knew what she wanted to know, but I didn't know what to call the creature that had smiled at me. I had never seen anything like her—huge, black, a toothy grin, skin like leather. I tried to describe the animal to Inna, who seemed puzzled. Then she asked, "Was she in the water?"

I said yes and Inna smiled. "I told you that water was your destiny. That is a very old one, Taweret, an Egyptian goddess who lives in the river and laughs with a great mouth. She gives mothers their milk and protects all children." My old friend kissed my cheeks and then pinched them gently. "That is all I know of Taweret, but in all my years, I never knew a woman who dreamed of her. It must be a sign of luck, little one. Now sleep."

My eyes did not open until evening, and I dreamed all day about a golden moon growing between my legs. And in the morning, I was given the honor of being the first one outside, to greet the first daylight of the new moon. . . .

With every new moon, I took my place in the red tent and learned from my mothers how to keep my feet from touching the bare earth and how to sit comfortably on a rag over straw. My days took shape in relation to the waxing and waning of the moon. Time wrapped itself around the gathering within my body, the swelling of my breasts, the aching anticipation of release, the three quiet days of separation and pause. [5]

While this ritual is an imaginative creation of the author, many elements, including references to the goddess Inanna, suggest connections with ancient religious thoughts and ideas. What attitudes toward maturing sexuality does this narrative convey, particularly as they relate to young women? How different are these ideas from the attitudes you are aware of in your own culture? What difference would it make for a young woman to have the experience Diamant creates and describes?

An ordinary, everyday kind of event like eating or getting dressed to go out can take on ritual dimensions in the right context, and more formalized rituals can become central in a community's self-understanding. But can even the most formal and valued "ritual" degenerate into mere habit? You may have had the experience of participating in a ritual event because it's expected of you. People sometimes talk about the ways in which their attendance at religious worship services has become mere habit, something they may do only when visiting parents or grandparents, or on special occasions such as weddings or funerals, but which has no particular meaning for them any more. If this has ever been true of your experience, what are some of the factors that cause ritual to lose its meaningful qualities? Are there things that would help to keep it more engaging, more relevant? If you think back to our discussion of symbols, you will recall that we discussed the ways in which symbols must be dynamic. They must retain enough stability over time that they continue to communicate meaningfully from one generation to the next, but they must also retain a certain flexibility, a capacity to change. Each new generation brings a new range of experiences to symbols that must be incorporated in some way. Is this also true of ritual?

> *Identify some of the rituals that are most central to your own cultural or religious group. Should these, too, have the potential to incorporate new insights and experiences or are they fixed and unchanging? Have you ever encountered discussions, even arguments, over this in your community or family?*

INDIVIDUALS, COMMUNITIES, AND RITUAL

Although individuals often perform rituals alone (as in the case of Muslim prayer, perhaps), there is almost always a communal dimension to authentic ritual. Even if the specific ritual involves only a single individual, there are ways in which the very observance of the rite connects the person with a wider community, including those who have gone before. One of the significant distinctions between a religion and a cult is that religions have a past, a history, whereas cults generally fade out with the death of their original leader. Cultures, religions, even families usually have stories and happenings, traditions and rituals, that are so important that they must be communicated to each new generation. A major source of ritual in both religious and secular traditions is the mythology, or the stories, that have been passed down from the past.

Both Christians and Jews designate a specific day of the week as sacred. For most Christians, Sunday is selected as representing the day on which Jesus is believed to have risen from the dead. For most Jews, the sabbath, or *shabbat*, is celebrated from sundown on Friday to sundown on Saturday. In Orthodox Judaism, this is a day of rest on which no work of any kind is undertaken. This symbolizes the original biblical account of God's creation of the world where God is reported to have labored for six days to create the world, and to have rested on the seventh. That traditions such as this have lasted over such long periods of time is testimony to the fact that they continue to have relevance for the communities who practice them. Our next selection describes the importance of the Jewish observance of shabbat. Partly because of the dispersion of Jewish peoples around the world, in contexts where they were frequently persecuted for their faith, much Jewish ritual occurs within the home. Yet although these rituals are often performed by small groups or even individuals, the relationship with the wider community remains important. As you read, ask yourself about the value of keeping shabbat as it is described in the narrative. What are your feelings about such faithfulness?

> All the week we have worked. All the week we have lived in the illusion that power over the world is in our own hands. This has been a veil hiding from our eyes the truth that G-d is the source of all power.
>
> On Shabbat we have ceased from work. We have given up *melacha,* down to the last detail. As a result, the veil has been lifted. Now we can glimpse in all its glory that truth which lies behind our purpose in the world.
>
> This is a moment which must fill us with wonder and joy. It must awaken our hearts towards that spiritual contentment which is the secret of Shabbat rest. This is *Menuchah*—the blessing of Shabbat experienced to the full, in the ways the Torah has shown us. . . .
>
> Throughout the thousands of years of its history, Shabbat has always been a day of song and gladness in the Jewish home. Its coming is an eagerly awaited event for which the family begins preparing days in advance. In fact, the Shabbat casts its radiant glow over the whole week. The days themselves are named in Hebrew in relation to the Shabbat: "the first day to Shabbat," "the second day to Shabbat," etc.
>
> Everything looks forward to Shabbat. Business and social arrangements are made in such a way that they will not interfere with the Shabbat. Little luxuries bought during the week are stored up for the Shabbat. When Friday comes, the tempo increases. Every member of the household plays his or her part in the preparations.[6]

In an Orthodox community work of any kind, the use of electricity, automobiles, and so forth, are forbidden during shabbat observance. What would it be like to live in such a neighborhood? What would happen in mainstream contemporary Western communities if everyone were to keep the sabbath in such a way? How might our lives be richer or poorer for it?

A Hindu girl brings fresh flowers to perform her puja.

Hinduism is another tradition in which individual performance of rituals is very important. The next passage is from the autobiography of a young Hindu woman who was raised in a household with a mother who took very seriously the traditions of her faith and culture and a father who had adopted many Western ways. In this selection, Shudha Mazumdar talks about some of the rituals that were a part of her life from a very young age. It's important to remember that Hinduism is a very diverse tradition and is practiced very differently by different people, but think about the focus of Mazumdar's rituals and pay particular attention to the rich use of symbols.

> The existence of *Atman,* the Godhead or divinity within men and women, is accepted as a fact by all those who are of the Hindu faith, and it is believed that the highest good is the realization and the expression of that divinity. To achieve this, various spiritual disciplines and techniques were recommended by the sages and seers of ancient times. . . .
>
> The daily routine of the vast majority of Hindus (women in particular) is governed by rules that are in fact connected with those rules of discipline preliminary to yoga. First, there is the visit to the toilet followed by a bath. Then, dressed in clean clothes, comes prayers or meditation, and only after this is it possible to eat. This became my morning routine at the age of eight and I have not deviated from it.

One of the most popular *bratas* in Bengal for the unmarried girls is Shiva *puja* [worship]. The great Shiva is the ideal male, and a maiden is blessed with the words: "May you be granted a husband like Shiva." He is well known for his deep devotion to his beloved wife, Durga, and for the havoc he wrought throughout heaven and earth in his wild paroxysm of grief when he lost her. As old as the hills, the beautiful legend has still the power to thrill many a girl of the Hindu faith and make her long for a husband, not as resplendent as Indra, King of the Gods, but as great as Shiva. For the great yogi [a person who practices yoga] cared nothing for earthly riches and dearly loved his wife. Mothers initiated their daughters in this *brata,* for it was believed that the benediction of Shiva could bring the devotee a husband as greathearted and loving as he.

Bysakh, the first month of the Bengali year, is considered to be an auspicious time to commence any *brata niyama.* So, on 14 April (New Year's Day in Bengal), Mother made me undertake my first *brata,* the Shiva *puja.* I was then eight years old and learned to perform the little ritual every morning before I went to school. For this, the first *niyama* was observed; that is, I had to have a good bath and wear a crimson silk *cheli* sari, the correct dress for the occasion, and not allow a single morsel of food or drink of any kind to touch my lips before the conclusion of the ceremony.

Rising early in the morning, I first bathed and changed, and then I ran to the garden to pick some flowers and fresh young blades of *durva* grass with which to perform the *puja.* The ritual had to be finished before I could have breakfast, dress, and run, in frock and pigtails, to be ready at the gate where I waited breathlessly for a school bus that arrived unfailingly at 8:30 A.M. . . .

In an earthen pot in a corner of the *puja* room was kept some soft mud from the Ganges, and with a fistful of this substance I would mold my symbol of Shiva. I never could make this in a proper manner and was often in despair, for my Shiva would insist on being a crooked one, which boded no good for me. In a flat dish, I put my Shiva on a sprig of *bael,* then lit a little lamp and placed the food offering and the flower plate on either side, sitting on a small carpet to perform my ritual.

First I gave my Shiva a bath by gently sprinkling a little Ganges water from the tiny, copper shell-shaped vessel over him three times. Every time I did so I murmured, "I salute thee Shiva." Then, dipping a few flowers and leaves in the sandalwood paste and holding them in my joined palms, I said a little prayer before making my offering. Briefly, some of the attributes of Shiva were mentioned, and it ended something like this:

> Lord I am so small a maid
> That hymns of praise I know not
> Aconda flower, leaves of bael and water from the Ganga
> Be content with these my offerings,
> O Bhola Maheshwara.

Bhola is the name of Shiva meaning "oblivious one," for unlike other gods he is said to be oblivious to formal ritual and is content with a wild flower or a leaf if it is offered with love and devotion. Maheshwara is another name of Shiva, and it means "great god."

This offering too was made three times. Generally I closed my eyes, trying to visualize Shiva with the patch of deep blue on his fair throat, the third eye of wisdom on his forehead, and matted locks piled high on his head. There was such a picture of Shiva on the wall, with a slim crescent moon shining from above and a sweet little face peeping out from behind the moon. . . .

Every year for four years I regularly performed my Shiva *puja* throughout the month of Bysakh. I had been told that I must not think of anything else while I performed my *puja,* but it was a difficult order to follow. Once, I had devoutly closed my eyes as usual when offering flowers and, on opening them, found to my surprise and awe that a full-blown flower had covered my Shiva like a cap. I ran to inform Mother and dragged her in to see the miracle; she smiled and said perhaps I had said my prayer with "one mind" and that was the sign that the great god was pleased with me. [7]

Again, can you identify the ways in which the rituals described by Mazumdar and her mother were strictly individual, and the ways in which these rituals connect individuals with the history and traditions of their people? Mazumdar's rituals were particularly clearly defined, both in terms of their purpose and the ways in which they must be performed.

Think of an activity that you had to perform as a child or teenager that you would consider a ritual. Did you ever reach a stage where you questioned the continued performance of the ritual? If so, what made you raise such questions? How do you feel about the ritual now? Do you still do any part of it?

THE DEVELOPMENT OF RITUAL

In our chapter on symbols, we discussed the ways in which symbols need both to retain a certain consistency over time and also to develop and change at least sufficiently to retain relevance and meaning within changing social contexts. The same is true of rituals. People have different attitudes and opinions about changing something as fundamental to human meaning as foundational symbols and rituals. Yet most of us recognize that the rituals in which we participate have themselves evolved from their earliest expressions in ways that enable us today, in our own place and time, to participate in them in meaningful ways.

In addition to weekly Sabbath observation, there are annual celebrations within Judaism, as within most traditions, that commemorate events in the past, stories and traditions that have been handed down. Christians celebrate the Eucharist, or Holy Communion, as a reenactment of the Last Supper that Jesus shared with his disciples. And the Jewish celebration of Passover celebrates the liberation of the Hebrew people from slavery in Egypt. A glimpse into some contemporary celebrations of Passover illustrates the ways in which both continuity and change shape the preservation and continuing relevance of the ritual actions themselves.

According to *Tanakh*, the Hebrew scriptures, God has chosen the young Moses to go to the Pharaoh, ruler of the Egyptians, and seek release of the Hebrew people from their bondage in Egypt. Each time the Pharaoh refuses, God sends a yet more dire plague on the Egyptian people. Finally, God threatens the death of the first-born sons of each Egyptian household if Pharaoh will not let the people go. When Pharaoh still refuses, God provides the plan that will both prevent any of the Hebrew children being slain as well and enable the Hebrews to be ready to leave their captivity and set out for freedom at a moment's notice. Contemporary Jews around the world continue to commemorate this event so long in the past.

The night before Passover (Pesach) begins, the children of the family hunt any food made with leaven. Traditionally, a piece of bread is left for them to "find" and take away, thus making sure that the family obeys the injunction from Exodus that no leaven should be eaten on the day of the remembrance of the escape from bondage. The actual Seder is preceded by the lighting of candles, the symbol in Judaism of the transition from secular time to sacred time on the Sabbath.

The actual Seder is a splendid example of a ritual of remembrance. Each person is to experience it as if s/he is actually one of those who escapes the Pharaoh. There are six foods at the Passover meal—a roasted shank bone, reminding of the offering at the temple in Jerusalem; a boiled egg, symbolic of new life, which comes in the spring; a bitter herb, reminding of the slavery period; charoset, a mixture of wine, nuts, and pulp that represents the mortar that the Jews used building the cities of Egypt; another green vegetable that again is reminiscent of spring; and, finally, another bitter herb in a sandwich, recalling the teaching of the Rabbi Hillel, who sought to remind the Jews that their ancestors ate a bitter herb with matzah.

Wine is blessed at the beginning of the Seder, and it is drunk four times, representing God's four promises to Israel—freedom, deliverance, redemption and being the chosen people. The first cup is drunk to begin the Seder. The next action is the ceremonial washing of the hands, by the leader of the Seder. The first food eaten is the greens, which are dipped in salt water, in remembrance of the tears of the ancestors when they were not free, and in remembrance of any who are still enslaved.

Three pieces of matzot are uncovered. The leader breaks the middle one, replaces the smaller part in the "sandwich," and covers the other, larger, piece for later use. Then the leader takes a fourth matzah which is symbol of hope for those Jews in the world who are not free in any way. The matzah is also symbolic of the bread the Israelites ate in Egypt.

Probably the most symbolic part of the ceremony is the part in which the youngest person at the table asks the four questions. The questions are about why only unleavened bread, why only bitter herbs, why dip the herbs in salt

A contemporary couple jumps the broom.

have been like to have to literally reinvent culture, symbols, rituals, in a strange land with people who shared only skin color and the common experience of being brutally kidnapped and enslaved.

In America customs among people of color had to be re-created. When West Africans were brought forcibly to these shores some four hundred years ago they were stripped of much of what was theirs—their homeland, their community structure, their freedom, even, in some cases, their sometimes sexist ways. Not long after the beginning of slavery, Africans were also denied the right to marry in the eyes of the law.

Slaveholders apparently thought that their captives were not real people but were, instead, property to be bought and sold. As such, they had no rights. Further, if allowed formally to marry and live together, slaves might find strength in numbers that could lead to revolt. Adding to their trauma, these early friends to white settlers were quickly and brutally forbidden by law to marry their white counterparts—a situation that remains a sore spot for interracial couples today.

Yet the enslaved were spiritual people who had been taught rituals that began as early as childhood to prepare them for that big step into family life. How could they succumb to this denial? They could not. So they became inventive. Out of their creativity came the tradition of jumping the broom. The broom itself held spiritual significance for many African peoples, representing the beginning of homemaking for a couple. For the Kgatla people of southern Africa, it was customary, for example, on the day after the wedding for the bride to help the other women in the family to sweep the courtyard clean, thereby symbolizing her willingness and obligation to assist in housework at her in-laws' residence until the couple moved to their own home. During slavery, to the ever-present beat of the talking drum (until drums too were outlawed, since they were considered a dangerous means of communication), a couple would literally jump over a broom into the seat of matrimony. Today, this tradition and many others are finding their way back into the wedding ceremony. [9]

Why do you think that many contemporary African American couples are choosing to incorporate the "jumping the broom" ceremony into their wedding ceremonies now, when slavery is long over and there are no longer laws forbidding their marriage?

Are there customs associated with weddings in your own family that have been added or maintained to preserve a sense of identity, of community? Are there particular wedding customs that you might choose to either include or leave out if you were getting married? What would be your reasons for this decision?

THE SIGNIFICANCE OF RITUAL

Rituals seem to be an integral part of the human experience, particularly of the most significant events and occurrences in our lives. We tend to turn to rituals in times of crisis, to mark the significant passages of our lives, and to celebrate our most important moments. Think of the movement among lesbian and gay persons in these early years of the 21st century to have their commitments to one another celebrated through ceremonies similar to those that have long honored heterosexual unions. Certainly one component of this movement is to attempt to ensure some of the legal benefits and obligations that marriage confers, such as access to health insurance, ability to visit and to make decisions on behalf of a hospitalized partner, and so forth. But why have couples flocked from all over the country to Vermont, the first state to recognize and offer same-sex civil unions? None of the legal benefits will accrue to those from other states. And most of the couples taking advantage of Vermont's newly instituted law do not simply receive the short civil ceremony that recognizes their relationship; they include as well many of the trappings usually associated with traditional marriage. On the other hand, opposition to "same-sex marriage" is intense. "Defense of Marriage" legislation and initiatives have proliferated across the country on federal, state, and municipal levels. What do these two oppositional movements imply about the power of ritual?

One of the primary characteristics of ritual is its power to make connections. The simple ritual of "jumping the broom," along with all the multiple cultural and religious symbolism associated with celebrations of the connection, or relationship, between the two individuals, makes connections among all those who gather to celebrate with them, and with those who have gone before. Regardless of whether they share language and historical culture, all can come together and understand, through the symbolic action, what is taking place. The reclamation of this ritual in our own time links the contemporary African American community with its roots. And through their insistence on recognition of the authenticity and integrity of their relationships, lesbian and gay persons acknowledge the power of ritual and the violation that lack of access to ritual inflicts on the human spirit.

Of course, the power of ritual, like any kind of power, is not always a "good" power. You might be able to think of examples of ritual that you consider negative in their outcome. Sometimes this can occur even when the intentions of the participants are positive. There are, however, examples of ritual that most of us would consider negative in their intent, even if their participants would see it differently. The next selection is from Margaret Atwood's novel, *The Handmaid's Tale.* The story is set in a future time when the government has become a strict theocracy, that is, the political system is one that is ruled by a particular set of religious believers who believe that they are instituting God's rule and law. Of course, as in any theocracy, what is instituted is one particular interpretation of "God's law." At the time the novel takes place, ecological degradation has meant that fertility rates among humans have declined to the point where reproduction must be planned, indeed enforced. Those women of child-bearing age who are fertile—the "handmaids"—are assigned to an infertile couple from the group in power, to bear children for them. They are assigned names according to the commander to whom they "belong"—for example, the name "Offred," indicates that Fred is the commander who rules her life. As in most theocracies, imaginative like Atwood's or real like the former Taliban regime in Afghanistan, punishment for failing to perform according to one's assigned role brings swift and harsh judgment and punishment. In the scene that follows, the handmaids, along with the commanders and their wives, have been summoned to watch the ritual execution—"salvaging"—of three persons charged with various crimes which are not described to the group, allegedly because of the potential for "copycat" infractions. At the end of this execution, the handmaids are bidden by their supervisor, Aunt Lydia, to come forward and form a circle. As you read this account of what happens next, ask yourself what elements of ritual are present. In particular, how does the very power of ritual function in this instance to keep people in line and doing what they are told by the authorities?

> We are milling around now, on the grass space in front of the stage, some jockeying for position at the front, next to the center, many pushing just as hard to work their way to the middle where they will be shielded. It's a mistake to hang

back too obviously in any group like this; it stamps you as lukewarm, lacking in zeal. There's an energy building here, a murmur, a tremor of readiness and anger. The bodies tense, the eyes are brighter, as if aiming.

I don't want to be at the front, or at the back either. I'm not sure what's coming, though I sense it won't be anything I want to see up close. But Ofglen has hold of my arm, she tugs me with her, and now we're in the second line, with only a thin hedge of bodies in front of us. I don't want to see, yet I don't pull back either. I've heard rumors, which I only half believed. Despite everything I already know, I say to myself: they wouldn't go that far.

"You know the rules for a Particicution," Aunt Lydia says. "You will wait until I blow the whistle. After that, what you do is up to you, until I blow the whistle again. Understood?'

A noise comes from among us, a formless assent.

"Well then," says Aunt Lydia. She nods. Two Guardians, not the same ones that have taken away rope, come forward now from behind the stage. Between them they half carry, half drag a third man. He too is in a Guardian's uniform, but he has no hat on and the uniform is dirty and torn. His face is cut and bruised, deep reddish-brown bruises; the flesh is swollen and knobby, stubbled with unshaven beard. This doesn't look like a face but like an unknown vegetable, a mangled bulb or tuber, something that's grown wrong. Even from where I'm standing I can smell him: he smells of shit and vomit. His hair is blond and falls over his face, spiky with what? Dried sweat?

I stare at him with revulsion. He looks drunk. He looks like a drunk that's been in a fight. Why have they brought a drunk in here?

"This man," says Aunt Lydia, "has been convicted of rape." Her voice trembles with rage, and a kind of triumph. "He was once a Guardian. He has disgraced his uniform. He has abused his position of trust. His partner in viciousness has already been shot. The penalty for rape, as you know, is death. Deuteronomy 22:23–29. I might add that this crime involved two of you and took place at gunpoint. It was also brutal. I will not offend your ears with any details, except to say that one woman was pregnant and the baby died."

A sigh goes up from us; despite myself I feel my hands clench. It is too much, this violation. The baby too, after what we go through. It's true, there is a bloodlust; I want to tear, gouge, rend. We jostle forward, our heads turn from side to side, our nostrils flare, sniffing death, we look at one another, seeing the hatred. Shooting was too good. The man's head swivels groggily around: has he even heard her?

Aunt Lydia waits a moment; then she gives a little smile and raises her whistle to her lips. We hear it, shrill and silver, an echo from a volleyball game of long ago.

The two Guardians let go of the third man's arms and step back. He staggers—is he drugged?—and falls to his knees. His eyes are shriveled up inside the puffy flesh of his face, as if the light is too bright for him. They've kept him in darkness. He raises one hand to his cheek, as though to feel if he is still there. All of this happens quickly, but it seems to be slowly.

Nobody moves forward. The women are looking at him with horror, as if he's a half-dead rat dragging itself across a kitchen floor. He's squinting around at us, the circle of red women. One corner of his mouth moves up, incredible— a smile?

I try to look inside him, inside the trashed face, see what he must really look like. I think he's about thirty. It isn't Luke. But it could have been, I know that. It could be Nick. I know that whatever he's done I can't touch him.

He says something. It comes out thick, as if his throat is bruised, his tongue huge in his mouth, but I hear it anyway. He says, "I didn't . . ."

There's a surge forward, like a crowd at a rock concert in the former time, when the doors opened, that urgency coming like a wave through us. The air is bright with adrenaline, we are permitted anything and this is freedom, in my body also, I'm reeling, red spreads everywhere, but before that tide of cloth and bodies hits him. Ofglen is shoving through the women in front of us, propelling herself with her elbows, left, right, and running towards him. She pushes him down, sideways, then kicks his head viciously, one, two, three times, sharp painful jabs with the foot, well aimed. Now there are sounds, gasps, a low noise like growling, yells, and the red bodies tumble forward and I can no longer see, he's obscured by arms, fists, feet. A high scream comes from somewhere, like a horse in terror.

I keep back, try to stay on my feet. Something hits me from behind. I stagger. When I regain my balance and look around, I see the Wives and daughters leaning forward in their chairs, the Aunts on the platform gazing down with interest. They must have a better view from up there.

He has become an *it*.

Ofglen is back beside me. Her face is tight, expressionless. "I saw what you did," I say to her. Now I'm beginning to feel again: shock, outrage, nausea. Barbarism. "Why did you do that? You! I thought you . . ."

"Don't look at me," she says. "They're watching."

"I don't care," I say. My voice is rising, I can't help it.

"Get control of yourself," she says. She pretends to brush me off, my arm and shoulder, bringing her face close to my ear. "Don't be stupid. He wasn't a rapist at all, he was a political. He was one of ours. I knocked him out. Put him out of his misery. Don't you know what they're doing to him?"

One of ours, I think. A Guardian. It seems impossible.

Aunt Lydia blows her whistle again, but they don't stop at once. The two Guardians move in, pulling them off, from what's left. Some lie on the grass where they've been hit or kicked by accident. Some have fainted. They straggle away, in twos and threes or by themselves. They seem dazed. "You will find your partners and reform your line," Aunt Lydia says into the mike. [10]

What would make the handmaids act the way they do? Even Offred, the narrator, finds herself in some way caught up in the horror, although she is also sickened by it. Have you ever been part of a group where people begin to act in ways that they wouldn't ordinarily act? What are some of the factors that can cause this phenomenon? What about tearing down the goalposts after a football win? What about rioting at some sporting events or concerts? Can the power of ritual have anything to do with it?

SOME QUESTIONS ABOUT RITUAL

As we have looked at various examples of ritual, both religious and secular, we have raised a variety of questions regarding the occurrence of ritual in human life in general, the power of that ritual in the lives of both individuals and communities, and the ways in which ritual is used to express and celebrate our deepest longings and most profound feelings.

You might have noticed that the rituals we have examined fall into several categories. Some of them have to do with rites of passage, those moments in human life when the individual is moving from one stage of life to another. Naming, circumcision, and baptismal rites practiced by some groups fall into this category. So too do rites associated with puberty, the passage of a young person from childhood toward taking on the responsibilities of adulthood. Marriage and funeral rites are also rites of passage. Most human communities and civilizations have clearly defined rituals that acknowledge each of these realities. In religious and cultural contexts, the way in which such events are marked has to do with the particular worldview and set of beliefs of the group.

Another category of rituals includes those that might be called calendrical. Many of these tend to be more group than individually oriented, but celebrations of birthdays and anniversaries are examples of calendrical ritual. These rituals are characterized by their links with particular seasons of the year or times of day. For ancient peoples, as well as for less industrialized nations today, the rhythm of the seasons and of day and night were and are major factors in daily life. Fertility rites were often performed in the early spring to coincide with spring Equinox, to ensure that the gods would look favorably upon the crops being planted. Can you suggest why the Jewish commemoration of Passover and the Christian celebration of Easter, for example, occur in the early spring, at least in the northern hemisphere? What difference would it make to be a Christian or Jew in Australia, New Zealand, or Argentina?

We discussed at the beginning of the chapter the Muslim ritual of salah, formal prayer required of believers at five specified times during the day. In addition, Friday is set aside as a day when Muslims should, if at all possible, make their midday salah in the Mosque, just as Saturday and Sunday, respectively, are observed in a particular way by Jews and Christians. Marking off particular times of the day or year for special ritual observance ties tradition and cultural meaning in with the rhythms of the natural world.

Finally, there are rituals of crisis, when in response to a particular event in the community or in an individual's life ritual offers healing and empowerment. At the very least, when life appears to be at its most meaningless, participating in some form of ritual observance gives one the feeling of at least being able to do *something.* The roadside shrines described in the chapter might fall into this category. Although on one level these shrines mark the passage of an individual from this life into death, they generally commemorate sudden, often violent, and premature death, rather than the death that is a natural end to life. After the September 11, 2001, terrorist attacks on the World Trade Center in New York and the Pentagon in Washington, D.C., people in the United States and indeed around the world flocked to services in temples, mosques, and churches in unprecedented numbers. For many, this was the first time they had attended a religious service of any kind in many years, perhaps the first ever. In the face of helplessness, people turned to ritual to experience a connection with one another, to share grief and outrage, to know that they were not alone.

Although ritual functions to heal, to celebrate, and to promote what we might think of as the best impulses in the human spirit, so too it has the power to be abused, misused, in ways that can manipulate and distort that spirit. At its most benign, the abuse of ritual leads to loss of meaning, to mere habit replacing ritual significance and power. At its worst, ritual can lead a group into chaos and disaster. Our human responsibility is to participate in the construction of our own and one another's identity, in the development and appropriation of symbols that best reflect the wholeness of humanity, and in the development and practice of rituals that empower us and each other toward those good ends.

What Some Others Have Said about Ritual

Tom F. Driver, theology professor emeritus at Union Theological Seminary, has spent much of his professional life studying the human practice of ritual. In his many encounters with ritual in multiple cultures in different parts of the world, he has recognized, as the subtitle of his book declares, that humans have a "need for liberating rites that transform our lives and our communities." The following passage is from his chapter on rituals and community. The "liminality" to which Driver refers can be considered a condition that is "on the edge," betwixt and between two states of being.

> Rituals are inherently communal, while at the same time being imaginative and playful, even when most serious. They become bearers of communitas, which is a spirit of unity and mutual belonging that is frequently experienced in rituals of high energy, particularly those that are closer to the shamanic than to the priestly type of ritual pathway.
>
> In their liminality, rituals exist outside many of the rules and expectations society normally imposes upon behavior. Rituals partly substitute for society's codes of behavior special codes of their own (the understandings of what one is

supposed to do and not do during a particular ritual, and the tone or style of behavior that is appropriate), and partly they foster spontaneous performance and "inspired" words and actions. Much goes on in rituals that would not be tolerated at other times: Hand-clapping, ecstatic dancing, rhapsodic speech, cross-dressing, speech-song recitations, direct address to invisible beings, the treating of a statue or an entranced person as if it, she, or he were a god, public exchange of affection, mystical union with other participants, the telling of dreams, mind-altering music or drugs, the public sharing of sacred food, and more.

The liminality of rituals means that they are informed, on the one hand, by a greater than usual sense of order and, on the other, by a heightened sense of freedom and possibility. Being imaginative, rituals can experiment with both ideal order and ideal freedom, releasing feelings of love and participation in the process. Being playful, rituals can afford to fail. Freedom from the tyranny of having to succeed enhances, paradoxically, the likelihood of their achieving their goal.

In middle-class life in Western societies, it is difficult to find rituals that provide much experience of communitas. Here we keep our rituals close to the social shore, so to speak. We do not often let them head for high water, and this is our great loss. No doubt we dwellers in comfort in the privileged societies that consume most of the world's natural resources, leaving two-thirds of the world's population at starvation level, are fearful of losing what we have. Perhaps we do not want any strong reminder of a "generic human bond," lest it cause us to lose our heads and identify with those dying of hunger. Dream of a common humanity, especially when ritualized and therefore brought into experience, can threaten a socially privileged way of life.

It is different among the exploited and the marginalized. That is why, in order strongly to experience communitas manifest in ritual one must belong to or associate with groups of people who have little invested in the present social order. At carnival festivities attended by large numbers of the poor, at pilgrimages to which the common people flock, in very popular religions such as *vodou* in Haiti or Hinduism in southern India, in some types of evangelical Christianity not dominated by reactionary politics, in black American churches serving the urban and rural poor, in the churches of East Germany prior to the bloodless revolution of 1989, among women turning to ritual to help them find viable alternatives to patriarchy, and in some other settings, ritual is loved because it gives space for communitas to flow. There people can say that it is all dance, it is all song, it is all work, and it is all play.

When a spirit of rebellion against unjust social structures is rising, an understanding of ritual as an alternative order fostering freedom, creativity, and deliverance will take precedence over the idea that rituals enforce rigid notions of order. Community will come to mean something like Turner's idea of communitas. Ritual will be seen as the occasion for both symbolizing and experiencing relationships in which spontaneity, affection, and unity replace unwanted law and compelled obedience. Under these conditions, communities will put ritual in the service of personal and social transformation[.] [11]

Have you participated in a ritual that has the dimensions of "spontaneity, affection, and unity" that Driver describes? Are these dimensions present in most of the rituals you have encountered? Rituals and their use of symbols, particularly rituals of the kind that Driver has described, help both individuals and their communities develop and retain their sense of identity.

> *Participate in rituals from two religious traditions different from your own, and talk with at least two persons who are members of the community. To what extent do these rituals exemplify the dimensions Driver insists are central to authentic ritual? How about other characteristics that we have discussed in this chapter?*

IDENTITY AND OTHER-THAN-HUMAN ANIMALS

In the West, we tend to think of self-identity and personhood as characteristics limited to the human. Indigenous peoples do not hold this view, nor do many African and Eastern perspectives. These peoples tend to see humankind as intrinsically related to the rest of the natural world, as an animal species interdependent with other animals and with all the other elements of the "creation."

Concern for the other-than-human world is also very much present in other traditions. The Jewish Talmud, for example, is very explicit in terms of spelling out the ways in which animals must be treated. The way one treats animals indicates one's fitness for leadership of the people: "The Holy One, blessed be He, said, 'Let him who knows how to shepherd the flock, each according to its strength, come and lead My people.'" Instructions for how to kill animals for food are particularly explicit. Failure to follow the rules renders the animal "unclean" because it has suffered unnecessarily.[1] In many cultures today, often citing religious justification, animal rights groups protest the treatment of animals by humans—from the keeping of animals as domestic pets, to eating them as food, to the use of animals in scientific experimentation.

In this section, we ask particularly, what should be our human relationship with other animals? Should we care at all? As scientists suggest that we share as much as 97 percent of our DNA with nonhuman creatures, are there other shared attributes that we would do well to consider? The main characters in this section are first, fictitious camel-like creatures of a planet called Navohar, and second, Paddington, a Great Pyrenees dog.

We begin with a selection from a work of speculative fiction, *Navohar*, by Hilari Bell. In this novel, human DNA on earth has been altered to the extent that humans are susceptible to fatal genetic flaws. Irene Olsen, a scientist, is part of a mission to find colonies of humans who have DNA that has not been altered. Dr. Olsen has a personal interest in this; her nephew, Mark, has the fatal defect caused by the altered DNA.

The mission lands on one of the planets known to have been the target of colonists, and thus likely to have human inhabitants with unaltered DNA. Dr. Olsen and Mark become separated from the rest of the mission. They, separately, have been taken by camel-like animals, indigenous to the planet, to the camps of the colonists. Mark's genetic illness has been cured by immersion, at the instigation of the camels, into pools of water, called life pools by the colonists.

The colonists have concluded that the camels are intelligent. Olsen, with a typical Western perspective, refuses to grant intelligence to these animals without "scientific" proof. She devises an intelligence test that she thinks will show definitively whether or not the animals are intelligent. As you read, ask yourself how you would feel in a similar situation. Would you be skeptical, like Irene? And how effective and appropriate do you think the test is that she has developed, in terms of assessing the intellectual abilities of the "camels"?

["Cow" is the name Irene has given the camel who has "adopted" her. Maureen is a disgruntled colonist. Gus is the head of the colonists. Nola is the biologist of this group of colonists. Sondi is a young colonist, about the same age as Mark. "Goodnight" is Irene Olsen's nickname. The camels *love* turnips.]

> "This is a very simple test, Cow," said Irene clearly. She felt ridiculous, and the colonists who gathered in the vicinity, carefully pretending not to watch, only made it worse.
>
> Maureen wasn't among them; she'd been placed under twenty-four-hour watch, and forbidden to go near either Irene or Mark. Which made Irene wonder what *else* Maureen hadn't told her, but the other colonists' anger that Maureen had broken their pact was so deep, even among Irene's supporters, that she didn't dare challenge their decree. At least they didn't seem to blame her; Irene had enough to worry about.
>
> Cow's big, front eyes regarded her lazily. Her smug expression, as always, never changed—her teeth ground the bitter turnip root Irene had given her. It had taken the rest of the night before to dig up a plentiful supply and borrow three colorful, plastic tubs.
>
> Nola, amusement momentarily overpowering her anger, had assured Irene that the camels saw in color. Various families had donated the tubs, and Ravi provided cloth scraps of the same, or nearly the same, colors. Cicero had given her three opaque, airtight, plastic containers. It was a simple, sensible experiment. So why was everyone she spoke to struggling not to laugh?
>
> Even Mark bought into the idea of camel intelligence without requiring proof.
>
> "I've been wondering," was all he said, but glowing satisfaction transformed his thin face, and Irene hadn't had the heart to argue.
>
> "OK, Cow, here's the other half of the turnip root." She held it up, like a stage magician.
>
> Cow's ears swiveled forward.

"Good, watch closely. I'm putting it into one of these containers." The lid snapped down. "Now I'm going to mix them up, so you can't tell which is which."

Irene knelt with her back to Cow, not so much mixing them up—it wasn't a shell game—but handling each one, so her own scent on the container wouldn't give it away. She'd thought a lot about this while gathering the things she'd need. Cow's sense of smell would be her best way around this experiment; thwarting it was a secondary benefit of filling the tubs with water.

She stopped suddenly, realizing one of the draw-backs as well, and then went to the nearest tub and reopened the containers, dipping each one in, filling them so they wouldn't float.

Scattered chuckles rose from the crowd, who'd given up any pretense of not watching. A few curious camels had joined them. Let them laugh. Irene knew, even if they didn't, that all experiments had to be fine-tuned. They almost never worked smoothly the first time.

She closed the lids again and shuffled the containers. They were heavy in her arms when she turned back to Cow, and her shirt and sleeves were damp.

"Listen up, Cow; I'm going to put one of these in each tub. Only one has the root in it."

They splashed softly, and wobbled down to the bottom. That should thwart even the keenest sense of smell. Cow watched intently, nostrils widening with each breath, but she wasn't sniffing deep. Irene would have to watch for that, when she went to the tubs. If she went to the tubs.

"OK, this is it." Irene pulled the blue fabric scrap from her belt and held it out. The moons were bright enough to see the color—dimmer than in daylight, but clearly different from the other two. "The root is in the blue tub. The one that looks like this cloth. The same color. You can have it, if you just choose the right one. But only if you choose it. Come on, Cow, the blue tub. Blue. Like this."

Actually, Irene expected Cow to go and investigate all the tubs, but she was pretty certain she wouldn't dunk for the containers. That was the main reason she'd filled the tubs—and why she'd chosen big, deep ones. The only way for Cow to get the rest of the root was to single out the right tub, from Irene's color signal.

She was prepared to repeat the experiment several times, but if they really were intelligent it shouldn't take long for Cow to figure it out.

Cow swallowed the root she'd been chewing on and started forward. Irene's heart pounded, but Cow approached her, not the tubs.

"Blue, Cow. The tub that's the same color as this. Just go there and nudge it, and you get the root. Do you understand? The blue tub." She expected nothing, really, but hope . . . that was something else. You were never too old, it seemed, to wish for miracles.

Cow's nostrils widened and she sniffed the blue cloth. *No help there, my friend. Figure it out.* Her brown gaze fixed on Irene's, holding it. Were those eyes intelligent? Irene had to make an effort to release her breath. "The blue tub," she whispered. "Are you going to do this? Can you really—"

A soft nose brushed her neck and her shirt collar pulled tight, tugging her off-balance. Irene yelped and would have fallen, but for the grip of the strange camel who dragged her backward, staggering, away from Cow.

"What? Let me go, you demented animal! You're tearing my shirt. Let go!"

But it pulled her, an awkward, stumbling, backwards dance, across a dozen feet of sand, then lifted her half off her feet and released her.

Irene landed with a splash. The tubs weren't that deep, and it wasn't that cold, but she hadn't intended to wash her clothes. Or her hair. Or to listen to the whole damn camp whooping with laughter.

She tried to fight her way out of the tub, but one of her arms was down inside, and the leverage was bad.

Gus came up to her, holding out his hands. "Let me help you. I'm sorry. Really. I am." It would have been more convincing if he'd been able to stop laughing while he said it.

"Go to hell." Irene flung her weight to one side and the tub tipped, the wash of water sweeping her out onto the sand. She rose to her knees and scraped wet hair out of her eyes. She struggled to her feet and kicked the tub.

The blue tub. The blue tub, which had been the farthest from where she stood, so that fiend of a camel who'd . . . who'd *ambushed* her had to pass two others to reach it. Who'd ambushed her while she'd been distracted by . . .

"You bitch!" Irene yelled.

"Whouk, whouk, whouk." Cow's sides puffed in and out. Irene picked up the container and threw it at her, wildly, missing by feet. "You fink, you . . . you fiend. I'm going to make camel chops, do you hear me? Camel cho—"

A roar of laughter from the colonists interrupted her. Irene spun in the direction they were looking, just in time to see her ambusher trotting into the dunes, carrying the sack that held her whole supply of turnip roots. He was already too far away to chase, but his accomplice wasn't. She spun and ran at Cow, fists clenched.

The *whouking* camel pranced away, then turned and loped off. Irene couldn't possibly run her down.

She looked around. It was evidently the best joke in years. Mark laughed so hard he had to hold on to Sondi to stand, and Gus had fallen to his knees.

"Sorry," he gasped at her thunderous approach. "Don't kill me, I'm defenseless. Oh God, you should have seen your face when you saw it was the blue . . ." He doubled over, whooping.

Irene's lips twitched. Her belly quivered. She laughed so hard she ended up on the sand beside Gus, clutching her ribs, crying. It took her a long time to wind down and start thinking.

The blue tub.

Measure that, Goodnight.

"They are intelligent." Awe washed away the remnants of her laughter. *"They do communicate."*[2]

What lessons are to be learned from Irene's experience with the camels? And if the camels are intelligent, what are the implications for the colonists?

What are the implications for researchers if similar abilities are found in some actual animal species? And, from a religious perspective, if animals possess this kind of intelligence, can they be said to have "souls"? Why or why not?

The final example is an anecdote from our experience. It involves a dog named Paddington, and a child we will call Johnny. As you read this piece, think about the extent to which you see both the dog and the boy as having personalities and self-identity. Neither can communicate in words. Can they relate to one another? To others? Are they persons? Do they have distinct identities? If so, how are those identities formed?

At one time we, with our Great Pyrenees dog, Paddington, regularly visited a school for children with severe disabilities. Great Pyrenees are a large, fluffy breed who are excellent at therapy dog work because they are generally calm and gentle, especially when with children or ill persons. Paddington was very good at all the visits, letting all the children pet him (an easy task, because his head was even with the trays of their wheelchairs). We finally went into a classroom with some profoundly disabled children. Johnny was blind and deaf and had so little control of his body movements that he was strapped to a padded table-top. He had no discernible means of communicating with anyone and was dependent on others for all his needs. It was impossible to tell how old he was, perhaps about eight.

Paddington spotted Johnny as soon as we entered the room. He headed for the child, nuzzled him and gently licked his face. The child smiled, a broad grin that went from ear to ear, and his unseeing eyes sparkled.

Each day before we visited the hospital, we had to make certain preparations. One of us had to use an inhaler for asthma; we strapped on fanny packs containing treats for the children to give to Paddington; finally we put on his collar and leash, our own shoes and jackets. As time went on, Paddington became excited earlier and earlier in our preparation process. Initially, he didn't react until we reached for the collar. Then he began to dance around when we put on the fanny packs. Eventually, picking up the inhaler indicated to him that it was almost time to go. Was Paddington using symbols?

When we arrived at the hospital, we had to walk down a long hall to get to the rooms where the children were. On the way, we passed the office of the director of the facility; we'll call her Jill. She adored Paddington, and the feeling was mutual. If her door was closed, Paddington would sniff, maybe whimper a little, even bump the door. If the door was ajar, he would push it open and go on in. Jill would immediately stop whatever she was doing, sit on the floor, and Paddington, all 130 pounds of him, would sit in her lap for a few minutes while they engaged in mutual interaction. Once this "ritual" was concluded, Paddington would happily continue down the hall to visit the children.

We are not, of course, suggesting that the "camels" of Navohar, or Paddington, are human. But does this mean that they cannot have identity? In

Paddington, CGC, Th. D, Th. DX.

light of the particular attributes that they do exhibit, can we say that they are sentient, sapient beings? How about the disabled little boy Johnny, decidedly human? But can he "pass" any more of the usual criteria for personhood than these nonhuman animals can?

In our discussion of identity in Chapter 1, we talked about the importance of community in shaping individual identity and about the ways in which individuals in turn define and shape the communities to which they belong. If you have had the experience of adopting an animal from a shelter or other rescue organization or have observed animals in tight enclosures in a zoo or circus, you probably know something of the difference environment makes in the general emotional and physical well-being of any creature. In her autobiography, *Build Me an Ark: A Life with Animals,* author Brenda Peterson recounts in moving detail her encounter, as an adolescent, with Smokey the Bear in his enclosure in the National Zoo in Washington, D.C. Peterson's words suggest yet another way in which we might examine our relationship with animals, particularly in the context of our discussion of symbols:

> "Maybe they'll bring Smokey home when he gets too old to be on show like this," I ventured. "He can't even hibernate here during the winter." This was the cruelest of solitary confinement, I realized, to be alone and adored, stared at by millions who saw not a real bear, but a symbol.[3]

Peterson is particularly distressed by those who are disappointed in Smokey, in his failure to live up to their expectations of him, expectations developed through the propagation of images that bear no resemblance to the reality of the life of a bear removed from his natural surroundings and placed on display in inadequate and what we would now generally recognize as abusive conditions. Do animals like Smokey—like Paddington—demand some kind of respect from us, respect that requires us to see them in their own integrity and not simply as an extension of our own needs, as symbols?

What about the communication that passed between Paddington and Johnny? Neither of them was capable of speech or indeed of most of the other modes of communication that we generally recognize, yet none of the staff present in the room doubted that something profound had taken place between the two of them. Seldom had they seen Johnny smile so broadly. And why did Paddington head particularly for Johnny, rather than toward one of the other not so disabled children who were reaching out to him? If the use of symbols is indeed the only means we have of engaging in meaningful communication with each other, might we say that Paddington's gentle touch, soft tongue, indicated an intentional "use of symbols" in his interaction with Johnny?

Such a suggestion of the use of symbols and engagement in ritual by a four-legged creature such as Paddington is often dismissed as mere reflexive responses to a particular stimulus. A current spate of books and movies suggests that increasing numbers of individuals are dissatisfied with this explanation, one that does not account for their own experiences in relationships with nonhuman animals. Do we need to reexamine our position in the created world? In the words of the title of a children's book, "do dogs go to heaven"?

II

SEEKING THE RIGHT,
SEEKING GOOD:
EXPERIENCING RESPONSIBILITY

CHAPTER FOUR

Why Do Bad Things Happen? Questions of Evil and Suffering

In the first three chapters, we concerned ourselves with the identity of the human person, both individually and in the context of the many communities to which we all belong, and we looked at ways in which symbols have developed over time within human cultures, including religious traditions, affecting the development of our identities, our sense of ourselves in the world. We explored some of the actions—rituals—in which humans participate that help to establish their identity as members of their group and to mark significant events in their individual lives. Now we turn our attention to the variety of actions in which humans engage in their day-to-day lives in the world, particularly in their interactions with people in their own communities and people who may be radically different. We begin with consideration of the phenomenon of evil.

Setting the Stage: What Is Evil?

What comes to your mind when you hear the word "evil"? Although there is a tendency nowadays to apply the word rather loosely to anything we think is bad or wrong, we do make distinctions that characterize some actions as bad but not necessarily outright *evil*. You might think of things you have done yourself that you knew were not "right," or things you did not knowing what kind of consequences you were unleashing or things you did when you were somehow "not yourself." In retrospect, were these actions (and/or their consequences) evil, or merely bad? Is there a difference, and what makes the difference? Are people always responsible for their evil acts?

In June of 2001, Andrea Yates of Houston, Texas drowned her five children in a bathtub. Yates did not deny her action. In fact, immediately after killing the children, she called 911 to ask for police to come to the house, and then called her husband at his job and told him to come home. During the subsequent police interview, in her home, she described to the attending officer just how she had drowned each child. What is your initial reaction to hearing of this deed? In particular, do you define this action as "evil"? Is Andrea Yates evil?

As details of the Yates situation became known, we found out that Andrea Yates had suffered from postpartum psychosis—a severe and debilitating condition—after the birth of her fourth child. She had been hospitalized twice after suicide attempts, placed on medications, and advised by psychiatric personnel not to have more children. But Andrea and husband Russell (Rusty) decided that they would take whatever children God sent them, and soon Andrea was pregnant again with their fifth child.

At the time of the tragedy, with the fifth child now six months old, Andrea's condition seemed to be worsening. She had been taken by her husband to the hospital, but her psychiatrist refused to admit her, or to prescribe the medication that had seemed to help during her previous illness. Do any of these circumstances alter your perception of Yates' actions? Of Yates herself?

Yates and her husband did not attend a traditional Christian church, but they engaged in bible study at home, putting their own interpretation on what they encountered. Some have suggested that they were influenced by a former mentor of Russell Yates, Michael Woroniecki, a renegade minister whose writings blamed women for the faults and shortcomings of their children.[1] Yates spoke at various times of needing to "save" her children from their "bad" mother, and of needing to be punished herself for her failings.

At Yates' trial, her defense attorneys presented a "not guilty by reason of insanity" defense. This was supported by a succession of psychiatric experts who had spent time with Yates, one of whom described her as the "sickest person I have ever met." This was not compelling to the jury, however, who took only three hours to find Andrea Yates guilty of murder. The jury did, however, sentence Yates to life in prison rather than recommending the death penalty. What would you have done had you been a member of the jury? Would Yates' mental health have been a factor? Would particular religious influences in her life affect the way in which you would hold Yates accountable for her actions?

In January, 2004 a father in Massachusetts, James Martel, attacked his two young sons with a knife, killing the younger one and seriously injuring the other. After his father drove away, the older son, 11, called 911 and was able to tell aid workers that his father had injured him. Martel was stopped shortly afterwards and offered no resistance as police took him into custody. Martel's brother has told reporters that Martel suffered from bipolar disorder—a condition that can cause extreme mood swings—and that he was twice hospitalized against his will. There is speculation about whether Martel had discontinued the medications that kept his illness under control. At the time of writing, Martel is still undergoing psychiatric evaluation to determine, among other things, his fitness to stand trial. Is this case comparable to that of Andrea Yates? What might account for the fact that the Martel case is receiving very little press coverage compared to the national coverage given to the Yates case? Is James Martel evil? Andrea Yates?

You might find the concept of evil one about which you are tempted to say, "I don't know how to define it, but I know it when I see it." If so, you join generations of thinkers who have grappled with this issue. Some situations and circumstances seem to give a clear sense one way or the other. Few would suggest that "evil" is not an appropriate term to apply, for example, to Hitler's actions against the Jews, or to other instances of genocide. On the other hand, we are unlikely to consider minor acts of theft, selfishness, even actions that might cause some degree of pain and harm to another, as evil.

> *What is your own definition of evil, as you understand it right now? Write it down. What particular components, in your mind, define something as "evil" as opposed to just "bad"? Think of any examples you know of that seem to illustrate the difference. Throughout this chapter you will want to return to this initial definition you have written and add to it, clarify it, add more examples that make the distinction clearer. You may need to include unanswered, even unanswerable, questions as part of your definition.*

WHAT DO YOU THINK? THE DIFFERENCE BETWEEN "BAD" AND "EVIL"

In his autobiographical narrative *Night*, holocaust survivor Elie Wiesel recounts many of the horrors he witnessed and experienced both before and during his imprisonment. In the first chapter, he recalls the tales told by Moshe the Beadle in an attempt to warn the Jewish inhabitants of the upcoming peril they will face. After being expelled from his town of Sighet, Transylvania, along with all the other "foreigners," Moshe the Beadle almost miraculously escapes from his Nazi captors and returns to his village. There, he shares with all who will listen what happened after the trainload of villagers arrived at their destination:

> He told his story and that of his companions. The train full of deportees had crossed the Hungarian frontier and on Polish territory had been taken in charge by the Gestapo. There it had stopped. The Jews had to get out and climb into lorries. The lorries drove toward a forest. The Jews were made to get out. They were made to dig huge graves. And when they had finished their work, the Gestapo began theirs. Without passion, without haste, they slaughtered their prisoners. Each one had to go up to the hole and present his neck. Babies were thrown into the air and the machine gunners used them as targets. This was in the forest of Galicia, near Kolomaye. How had Moshe the Beadle escaped? Miraculously. He was wounded in the leg and taken for dead. [2]

In this narrative, as in the Yates account, children end up dead through the actions of others. Are these actions different only in terms of numbers—that is, the Gestapo killed more infants than did Andrea Yates? In our next selection Gregory Pence is introducing a chapter in a medical ethics textbook in which he will examine the variety of issues that contemporary health care and related technological advances present in the area of treatment of newborn infants. Very premature infants and those with profound medical complications can often survive today, usually through extensive medical intervention, in circumstances and situations which would have meant certain and rapid death only a generation ago. How do these different situations shed light on our efforts to identify the distinction between the merely bad and that which is truly evil? Compare the passages about Andrea Yates, the Nazis, the practices in ancient times, and current decisions that are made by parents and health care professionals about the fates of babies born less than "perfect." Which, if any, would you classify as evil?

> In ancient Sparta, a Cyclops baby would be left to die in a country field. Both the *Republic* of Plato and the *Politics* of Aristotle advocated killing defective newborns. Romans thought it proper to discard babies who looked grotesque. For most of two millennia, Bedouin tribes of Arabia, the Chinese, and much of India practiced female infanticide. Males stayed with the family and were considered assets, whereas females left the family and were considered liabilities. . . .
>
> Down syndrome, or trisomy 21, is a chromosomal abnormality discovered by Langdon Down in 1866, in which infants have 47 rather than 46 chromosomes in each cell, the extra chromosome being attached to chromosome 21. Down syndrome is a genetic condition always causing retardation and characteristic facial appearance; it is often accompanied by cardiac problems.
>
> In 1971, in a NICU (neonatal intensive care unit) at Johns Hopkins Hospital in Baltimore, some Down syndrome babies were born with defects incompatible with life. During this time, few NICUs existed and few defective infants were treated aggressively. The same baby born today in an NICU would be treated very differently.
>
> One mother in this case was a nurse who had worked previously with Down syndrome children; her 35-year-old husband was a lawyer. Her baby had duodenal atresia—a blockage between the higher duodenum and the lower stomach—which prevented passage of food and water. She was told that her baby had Down syndrome and that it would die if she did not consent to surgery to open the atresia. She immediately refused to sign, and the husband agreed. Pediatric surgeons and administrators honored the parents' refusal and did not go to court. . . .
>
> One mother was told at the time by a physician that the degree of mental retardation and IQ score could not be predicted at birth, but that Down syndrome people range in IQ "in the 50–80 range, and some times a little higher." She was also told that some rare Down syndrome adults score above IQ 65, but that the normal IQ range is between 25 and 60, with some severely

defective individuals below 25. The same physician told the parents that children with Down syndrome were "almost always trainable. They can hold simple jobs. And they're famous for being happy children. . . ."

In one case, the parents had two other children, in another case, five. One mother's reason for her decision was that "it would be unfair to the other children of the household to raise them with a mongoloid."

One baby took 11, and another 15, days to die. Such a death would normally take 4 days, but some staff members in sympathy with the baby surreptitiously hydrated the babies. The babies were allowed to die, and not just killed, because it was thought to be more morally acceptable and less likely to incur legal prosecution to do it that way.[3]

Deciding what is evil can be complicated. Just where does evil lie in these accounts? Who decides what is evil? And can we always identify evil adequately and accurately? What are some of the factors that determine whether a particular action is evil rather than merely "bad"?

Look back at the definition of evil you wrote down earlier. How would you change it in view of the Wiesel and Downs children readings? Does your definition of "evil" allow for the distinctions you want to make about these or other cases you know of? If not, revise it so that it does, or add questions to your definition.

CULTURAL AND SOCIAL UNDERSTANDINGS OF EVIL

We each have our own ideas about what constitutes evil and where we might draw the line between acts that are bad and wrong and those we would call evil; different cultures and traditions have their own understandings and determinations also. This does not imply that each individual within those cultures or traditions holds exactly the same definition, but nonetheless in many ways a communal understanding is necessary if persons are to live together in groups in a relatively harmonious way. Some of the issues involved are the relationship of suffering to evil, the origins of evil, how we recognize evil when we encounter it, and how we should respond to evil in the world.

IS ALL SUFFERING EVIL?

What are some of the most common instances of suffering that you can think of? Have you undergone experiences of suffering yourself? What were the circumstances surrounding your suffering or the suffering you witnessed in someone close to you? Instances of human suffering might range from discomfort or pain resulting from a necessary medical procedure, to the distress we might feel at a minor disappointment, to the profound grief we experience at the death of a loved one. So, does evil have to be present if humans suffer?

The following two short excerpts are newspaper accounts of the deaths of two individuals. One is taken from a news story and the other from an obituary. Presumably, both deaths caused grief and suffering to the families of the individuals, but as you read the two accounts, ask yourself what the major differences are. Do you feel differently about the two deaths?

Account 1: She lived in a big yellow house, with eight rooms and a "welcome" door-knocker, that sits high on a suburban patch of Wilmington just down a winding road from the town high school and local church.

Then she moved into a cold, dark, syringe-strewn, mattress-cushioned cave hidden in the girded catacombs beneath the Southeast Expressway in Boston. Through the years, she'd been on the run from the law; from her family; from a man who vowed to cut her into little pieces; and from a deep drug habit.

At 3:06 P.M. on Friday, Jan. 18, her time ran out.

A homeless girlfriend found her frigid body on a wedge of land where the Kneeland Street on-ramps to the Mass Pike and Expressway split, near the subterranean bunker the two shared with several others. Authorities are awaiting toxicology results but believe she overdosed on heroin in the cold.

Lisa Michelle Berube was 28. . . .

During a two-day jag in January, three others also died on the streets of a city where 6,000 are homeless: A 70-year-old man with a history of public drinking and two others who may also have had fatal heroin overdoses; a 56-year-old man who lived outside the lines for most of four decades and a military veteran in his 40s who died beside a Beacon Hill church. In the wake of their deaths, advocates for the homeless are trying to restrain state budget cuts and secure more services for heroin addicts, who sometimes have to wait months to get into longer-term recovery programs. This is just one of their stories.[4]

Account 2: John W. Gardner, the educator's educator, Cabinet secretary who helped launch Medicare, and the founder of Common Cause who preached grass-roots citizen participation in government and became known as "the father of campaign finance reform," died Saturday at his home in Palo Alto, Calif. He was 89. . . .

"When Americans attend open meetings or read their government's documents, or take part in our battered but resilient public finance system for presidential elections, there is a memorial to John Gardner," Scott Harshbarger, Common Cause president and former Massachusetts attorney general, told the Associated Press. "When we turn on public television, or when government ensures no senior or poor person goes without health care, we take part in programs John Gardner initiated."[5]

Reading these two accounts, it seems as if the only thing that Lisa Berube and John Gardner have in common is that both have died. Berube was young, only 28 years old, dead before she really had a chance to live. But the article implies that she was a homeless drug addict who overdosed on heroin. On the other hand, Gardner was 89. Although the obituary does not indicate a cause of death, we might assume that he perhaps died of natural causes at the end of a long and productive life. What were your reactions on reading these two accounts? In particular, think about the relationship of evil and suffering as they might relate to these two deaths. Does either death, or the circumstances surrounding it, have connotations of evil attached to it? Does either death require any response from us or from society in general?

Suffering can be intensely personal, even individual, and yet a whole community, even a nation, can share it. Sometimes even those not directly affected can feel the impact of intense suffering. Most of us can think of instances when an event or occurrence that has not affected us directly has caused us a degree of pain. This pain is not the same as for those more immediately involved, but nonetheless we do sometimes suffer vicariously, that is, second-hand. Many people who have read of the Holocaust, the institution of slavery, or genocide in any of its forms, will have had some deep feelings of unease that might be classified as suffering. This is especially true if you belong to a group that has been at some time targeted for elimination or humiliation. Think of the responses of people around the world after the events of September 11, 2001. The outpouring of grief was not only that of those who directly lost a loved one or even an acquaintance.

The Buddhist understanding of suffering is one that Westerners often find hard to grasp and understand, but it is a good example of acknowledging the reality of suffering as a fact of being human, being alive. For the Buddhist, such suffering is not the result of some force of evil, but is rather the result of our own attachments and expectations. In the next passage, the Buddha is sharing with some friends what he has discovered about suffering during his Enlightenment. As you read, note the particular examples he gives of human suffering. How does he account for these?

The Buddha's voice was filled with such spiritual authority that his five friends joined their palms and looked up at him. Kondanna spoke for them all, "Please, friend Gautama, show us compassion and teach us the Way."

The Buddha began serenely, "My brothers, there are two extremes that a person on the path should avoid. One is to plunge oneself into sensual pleasures, and the other is to practice austerities which deprive the body of its needs. Both of these extremes lead to failure. The path I have discovered is the Middle Way, which avoids both extremes and has the capacity to lead one to understanding, liberation, and peace. It is the Noble Eightfold Path of right understanding, right thought, right speech, right action, right livelihood, right effort, right mindfulness, and right concentration. I have followed this Noble Eightfold Path and have realized understanding, liberation, and peace.

"Brothers, why do I call this path the Right Path? I call it the Right Path because it does not avoid or deny suffering, but allows for a direct confrontation with suffering as the means to overcome it. The Noble Eightfold Path is the path of living in awareness. Mindfulness is the foundation. By practicing mindfulness, you can develop concentration which enables you to attain Understanding. Thanks to right concentration, you realize right awareness, thoughts, speech, action, livelihood, and effort. The Understanding which develops can liberate you from every shackle of suffering and give birth to true peace and joy.

"Brothers, there are four truths: the existence of suffering, the cause of suffering, the cessation of suffering, and the path which leads to the cessation of suffering. I call these the Four Noble Truths. The first is the existence of suffering. Birth, old age, sickness, and death are suffering. Sadness, anger, jealousy, worry, anxiety, fear, and despair are suffering. Separation from loved ones is suffering. Association with those you hate is suffering. Desire, attachment, and clinging to the five aggregates are suffering.

"Brothers, the second truth is the cause of suffering. Because of ignorance, people cannot see the truth about life, and they become caught in the flames of desire, anger, jealousy, grief, worry, fear, and despair.

"Brothers, the third truth is the cessation of suffering. Understanding the truth of life brings about the cessation of every grief and sorrow and gives rise to peace and joy.

"Brothers, the fourth truth is the path which leads to the cessation of suffering. It is the Noble Eightfold Path, which I have just explained. The Noble Eightfold Path is nourished by living mindfully. Mindfulness leads to concentration and understanding which liberates you from every pain and sorrow and leads to peace and joy. I will guide you along this path of realization."

While Siddhartha was explaining the Four Noble Truths, Kondanna suddenly felt a great light shining within his own heart. He could taste the liberation he had sought for so long. His face beamed with joy. The Buddha pointed at him and cried, "Kondanna! You've got it! You've got it!"[6]

What do you think about the Buddha's claim that by following the "Noble Eightfold Path," persons can be liberated from "every pain and sorrow"? How might this apply to Jews interned in the camps during the Holocaust? To Lisa Berube, the homeless drug addict who died on a Boston street, and to her family? Buddhism is considered by many to be the only religion that takes suffering seriously. In light of the kind of suffering mentioned in some of the excerpts we have read, how might the Buddha's suggestions "work"?

The Buddhist example indicates that we should make a distinction, perhaps, between the suffering that is an ordinary part of being human, being alive, and the suffering that is caused by the presence of "evil," or at least by some kind of action in the world. Perhaps not all suffering is evil, or caused by evil, but does all evil cause suffering? Other religious traditions also attempt different explanations to account for the reality of human suffering, both that which is a natural part of life and that which is caused by outside circumstances. In particular, most try to come up with some kind of account of where evil comes from and how it relates to human suffering.

> *Look at any newspaper or news magazine and make a list of the events you see reported that you think indicate a degree of suffering for someone. In each case, see if you can identify the immediate cause of suffering. In which examples do you see the presence of evil? Is suffering a part of your definition of the difference between the "bad" and the "evil"?*

WHERE DOES EVIL COME FROM?

Have you ever asked yourself this question? Think back to Chapter 1 where we discussed the concept of human identity and recall the psalmist who extolled the wonderful stature of the human, who was created by God to be little less than an angel. If this is the case, why do humans so often act in such nonangelic ways? How do you account for the violence and lack of consideration for one another of which humans are all too capable? We have only to listen to the nightly news or glance at the front page of a newspaper to know some of the devastation that humans are able to inflict on themselves, on one another, on other animals, and on the planet itself. The philosopher Thomas Hobbes suggested that human nature is naturally weak and base, that only through strongly enforced laws and regulations are we kept from annihilating each other. But if Hobbes is right, how do you account for acts of selfless generosity that humans often perform? Where do you stand on this?

"The devil made me do it." That phrase is sometimes used in a joking manner, often when someone has engaged in a relatively minor, often humorous activity. But for someone like Andrea Yates, this is no laughing matter. Do you believe the devil enters the picture? Historically, efforts to eliminate evil have often resulted in the personification of evil one way or another, as an identifiable enemy embodying Satan. The European witch hunts of the Middle Ages, as well as the witch trials in Salem, Massachusetts, exemplified the idea of the devil or Satan manifest in one or more individuals. The people on trial, often women, were suspected of having been possessed by the devil. Many religious traditions continue to believe in such a specific personification of evil, as suggested in the following account. This article is excerpted from an issue of "Sightings," an electronic newsletter that follows issues pertaining to religion in the public media.

> Mayor Carolyn Risher of Inglis, Florida . . . is the public official who, last Halloween night, used official stationery to write a proclamation banning Satan from her town. Her story appeared in the St. Petersburg Times in November, 2001, and recently made the AP wire when the American Civil Liberties Union announced that it would challenge the ban.
>
> There is a legal angle to the story. As the ACLU is sure to point out, the use of government offices and public funds to promote religion is a clear violation of the establishment clause of the Constitution, and potentially of the free exercise clause as well. There is also an historical angle. Risher's attempt to ban

Satan falls within a long and well-documented tradition of attempting to cleanse communities of evil. Though it has not blossomed into anything like Salem's witch trials of 1692, it seems to reflect a remarkably similar worldview. The theological angle, however, places Risher in the middle of a recurring tendency in American society, that appears to be on the rise.

A passage from Risher's proclamation reads: "Be it known from this day forward that Satan, ruler of darkness, giver of evil, destroyer of what is good and just, is not now, nor ever again will be, a part of this town of Inglis. Satan is hereby declared powerless, no longer ruling over, nor influencing, our citizens." By placing copies of the document in "hollowed-out fence posts placed at the four entrances to the town," Risher hoped to chase from her town the cause of "division, animosity, hate, confusion, ungodly acts on our youth, and discord among our friends and loved ones."

Representative image of Satan.

One cannot fault Risher's motives. . . . Who wouldn't want their community to be united, charitable, loving, of clear mind, populated by godly acting children and harmonious families, and free of drunk drivers, child molesters, and the fashion challenged?

Risher does go awry, however, and leads her community into danger on two fronts. First, by issuing such a proclamation she appears to recognize no distinction between her will and the divine will. Second, in the spirit and the letter of her work she associates evil and sin solely with Satan, and moves forward on the assumption that evil and sin are, somehow, external to our communities and to our humanity. . . .

If the problem of evil could be solved as easily as posting notices for Satan, evil would likely have ceased to be a problem long ago. What makes the problem so difficult is that good and evil are not so easily distinguished.

There is a danger in actions like those taken by Carolyn Risher that legal opposition will ignore. . . . By convincing ourselves that evil is external to us, and that we are the doers of God's will, we take a giant step toward avoiding thorough consideration of the potential for good and evil in our own actions. Does such a recognition necessarily hinder efforts to attain a more just domestic and international society? Does it, as Mayor Risher might argue, give Satan free reign? No. It merely, hopefully, leavens international, communal, and personal relationships with an awareness that now we see as through a glass darkly.[7]

Do you agree with the author's suggestion about the danger of externalizing evil? Is he right that putting evil onto an external reality or enemy runs the risk of allowing us to not examine closely our own behaviors and actions? You might be familiar with the phenomenon of the scapegoat, someone or something onto which others can shift blame and responsibility. Does "the devil" become the scapegoat in Inglis, Florida?

In spring 2002, a trial took place in Massachusetts as to whether or not a man was insane at the time he committed a mass murder at his workplace. The defendant claimed that the Archangel Michael told him to kill Hitler and six Nazi generals, and that this was what he had done when he killed his co-workers. In this case, according to the recipient of the message, the scapegoat was "angelic," not demonic. We might ask whether an angel would tell someone to commit mass murder, even of so-called Nazis. But what is the effect on human responsibility and accountability to say that either the devil or an angel is responsible for our actions? In the case in Massachusetts, the murderer was trying to excuse himself by saying that he followed the instructions of an archangel. In the case in Florida, the mayor seems to be suggesting that Satan is to be blamed for all the problems, major and minor, of the town. Why do we never hear someone claim that an angel has told them to go live in an impoverished area to help with childcare for the children of single mothers? Is it that we usually seek credit for our own good actions, yet try to avoid responsibility for actions that are not so good by placing blame on some agent beyond our control?

Another approach to the source of evil is the traditional Hindu concept of karma. Summed up simply in the idea, "what goes around comes around," karma originates in the idea that whatever befalls one in life—good or bad—is the result of prior actions, either in this lifetime or in a prior incarnation. The only way to advance, to ensure that one's experiences in life improve in the future, is to faithfully fulfill the obligations that pertain to one's particular role in this life. In the novel *The Death of Vishnu,* Manil Suri recounts the story of a man named Vishnu whose only home is the landing of an apartment building. In return for his doing odd jobs, the occupants of the apartments tolerate Vishnu's presence and provide him with some minimal means of sustenance. At the beginning of the novel, Vishnu has become very ill and appears near death. Mrs. Asrani, one of the tenants, is unsure about the obligation she has taken on regarding Vishnu:

> What to do about the cup of tea she brought Vishnu every morning? On the one hand, it was obvious that Vishnu did not have much need for tea right now. Even yesterday, he had barely stirred when she had filled his plastic cup, and she had felt a flutter of resentment at not having received her usual salaam in return. On the other hand, giving tea to a dying man was surely a very propitious thing to do. Since she had taken this daily task upon herself, it would be foolish to stop now, when at most a few more cups could possibly be required. Besides, who knew what sort of repercussions would rain down upon her if she failed to fulfill this daily ritual?
>
> Pressing the edge of her sari against her nose to keep out the smell, Mrs. Asrani descended gingerly to the landing. Using the scrap of brown paper she had brought along for the purpose, she fished out the cup from the small pile of belongings near Vishnu's head, taking care to always keep the paper between her fingers and the cup, so as not to infect herself—with whatever he had. She placed the cup on the step above the landing and poured tea from the kettle.

Ten incarnations (avatars) of the Hindu god, Vishnu.

Hating the idea of good tea being wasted, she hesitated when the cup was half full, but only for a second, filling it to its usual level to fulfill her pledge. Then she ascended the steps and surveyed her handiwork. The cup lay steaming where she had left it—but now Vishnu looked like he was stretching out across the landing to try and reach it, like a man dead in the desert, grasping for the drink that could have saved him. She thought about moving the cup to correct this, but the scrap of paper she had used now lay on the landing, and she couldn't be sure which surface had touched the cup. There was nothing she could do anymore, so she turned and climbed up the remaining steps. At the door of her flat, it occurred to her that she still didn't know if Vishnu was alive or dead. But it didn't really matter, she had done her duty in either case. Satisfied, Mrs. Asrani entered her flat and closed the door behind her.[8]

How do Mrs. Asrani's actions demonstrate the concept of karma as we have discussed it? In your own opinion, does she fulfill her duty to Vishnu?

CAN WE ALWAYS RECOGNIZE EVIL?

On September 11, 2001, television viewers around the world watched in horror as the devastation of the terrorist attacks on the World Trade Center and the Pentagon and the plane that crashed in Pennsylvania unfolded before our eyes. For many people around the world, there was no doubt that they were being brought face to face with evil. As time went on, however, questions arose as to just what varieties and sources of evil contributed to those events. Certainly, for most, evil was represented in the attacks that caused the deaths of thousands of ordinary people who were going about their day-to-day lives and in the horror of taking planeloads of civilians and turning them into missiles. Many claimed that it is evil to use religious ideology to justify hatred and violence, as the terrorists had done. While people have applied the term "evil" to the events of September 11 in these ways, others have suggested that we may also need to look deeper to find other sources of the evil.

In 1958, writers William Lederer and Eugene Burdick co-authored a novel entitled *The Ugly American*. Originally planned as a work of nonfiction, this book detailed some of the unfortunate ways in which Americans behaved and were perceived around the world. The book has sold over 7 million copies, and "ugly American" has become part of our everyday language. In December 2001 journalist Yvonne Daley interviewed Lederer, now 89 years old, about his perspectives in the wake of the September 11 attacks. Lederer is writing a nonfiction sequel to the original book, but on the day of Daley's visit had crumpled up the latest chapter and tossed it into his wastepaper basket, lamenting that there didn't seem to be any use: nothing changed anyway. "What *are* these problems that need addressing?" Daley asks.

> "Greed and power," Lederer says softly. "It's always about greed and power—material power or sexual power or religious power or ideological power. In the end, they're all the same. In 1958, the enemy was communism; today, it's terrorism and religious ideation.
>
> "It pains me to say this: Our military leaders and CIA agents and diplomats are still ignorant about the countries they're assigned to. We're still fighting poor, hungry, angry people with bombs and tanks when what they would really respond to is food and water, good roads, health care, and a little respect for their religion and culture.
>
> "I certainly don't condone the acts of September 11," he says. "They were monstrous. But the Taliban Stingers they're using against us in their pitiful defense were ones we gave them to use against the Soviet Union not that many years ago. I wrote about the same use of our weapons against us in *The Ugly American* and my other books. I'm an old man now. I can't believe I'm almost 90. I wanted to live to be 100, but now I'm so discouraged about the fate of the world that I sometimes just don't have the energy to go on, never mind write the same old thing that won't make any difference anyhow."[9]

We may never know precisely what motivated the particular individuals behind the September 11 attacks, and regardless of motivation, the acts themselves seem unequivocally evil. But what about Lederer's suggestions as to what might have made a difference? For example, is the poverty to which Lederer refers evil? And if so, is someone responsible for it? Who? Is "evil," even the evil of September 11, more complex and complicated than the overt actions of terrorists?

More than 2700 people died in the September 11, 2001, attacks. Thousands of people, many of them children, die annually around the world from malnutrition and preventable health problems. Thousands are killed on American roads each year, over half of them in accidents involving alcohol. Where does evil lie in these situations? Is it evil to refuse aid to starving populations? Is it evil to serve alcohol to someone who is already impaired and who might get behind the wheel of a car? Compare these and other examples you can think of, and assess the different levels of "evil" that you find in each.

Perhaps another way to put this question is to ask whether evil is always manifested only through specific actions of individuals or groups. In August 1993, as South Africa was beginning to emerge from the devastation of apartheid and was preparing for its first all-inclusive, democratic election, American Fulbright scholar Amy Biehl was killed by a group of black youths in one of the Black townships, Guguletu. In a fictional portrayal of some of the complexities involved in the tragedy, novelist Sindiwe Magona looks at one of the young men involved through the eyes of his mother. Of course, Magona is not the real mother of the youth; rather, as a writer of fiction, she is imagining the feelings a mother might have about a son who has perpetrated such an act. As you read this material, think about where evil lies in this narrative. Is it limited to the specific violent actions that took Amy Biehl's life?

> My son killed your daughter.
> People look at me as though I did it. The generous ones as though I made him do it. As though I could make this child do anything. Starting from when he was less than six years old, even before he lost his first tooth or went to school. Starting, if truth be known, from before he was conceived; when he, with total lack of consideration if not downright malice, seeded himself inside my womb. But no—people look at me as if I'm the one who woke up one *shushu* day and said, Boyboy, run out and see whether, somewhere out there, you can find a white girl with nothing better to do than run around Guguletu, where she does not belong.
> And hey, while you're at it, Sonnyboy, hey, if she's American, all the better! As though that were something—a badge or label—she would have worn on her face. As though he would go out there, weigh the pros and cons, and carefully choose her for her sake, for being who she truly was.
> My revilers seem to think that, with such perfect understanding between mother and son, I wouldn't have had to say one word more. Naturally, he'd've just known what it was I wanted done . . . what I wanted him to do.
> I should have such an obedient son! Why do they think he did what he did if he were such a lamb, a model child?
> Let me say out plain, I was not surprised that my son killed your daughter. That is not to say I was pleased. It is not right to kill.

But, you have to understand my son. Then you'll understand why I am not surprised he killed your daughter. Nothing my son does surprises me any more. Not after that first unbelieving shock, his implanting himself inside me; unreasonably and totally destroying the me I was . . . the me I would have become . . .

But, let me ask you something: what was she doing, vagabonding all over Guguletu, of all places, taking her foot where she had no business? Where did she think she was going? Was she blind not to see there were no white people in this place?

Yes, the more I think about this the more convinced I am that your daughter must have been the type of person who has absolutely no sense of danger when she believes in what she is doing. That was your daughter's weakness, I can see. How many young white South African women were here in Guguletu that day she was killed? Do you see them driving up and down this township as though they are going to market?

But people like your daughter have no inborn sense of fear: They so believe in their goodness, know they have hurt no one, are, indeed, helping, they never think anyone would want to hurt them.

I bet you anything, if she ever thought she might be in danger . . . she probably saw that coming from the authorities, who might either hamper and hinder her in what she was bent on doing, or in some way stop her altogether from doing it.

To people like your daughter, doing good in this world is an all-consuming, fierce and burning compulsion. I wonder if it does not blinker their perception.

And, if he had killed one of the other women who were with your daughter, d'you think there would be all this hue and cry? He'd be here now; like the hundreds of killers walking the length and breadth of Guguletu. But then he never did have any sense. No sense at all in that big head that burdens his shoulders till they stoop. Full of water it is. What a shame. For the years he has lived, hasn't he learnt anything at all? Did he not know they would surely crucify him for killing a white person?

And your daughter; did she not go to school? Did she not see that this is a place where only black people live? Add to that, where was her natural sense of unease? Did she not feel awkward, a fish out of water, here? That should have been a warning to her . . . a warning to stay out. Telling her the place was not for her. It was not safe for the likes of her: Oh, why did she not stay out? Why did she not stay out?

White people live in their own areas and mind their own business—period. We live here, fight and kill each other: That is our business. You don't see big words on every page of the newspapers because one of us kills somebody, here in the townships. But with this case of Boyboy's, even the white woman I work for showed me. The story was all over the place. Pictures too.

It's been a long, hard road, my son has travelled. Now, your daughter has paid for the sins of the fathers and mothers who did not do their share of seeing that my son had a life worth living.

Why is it that the government now pays for his food, his clothes, the roof over his head? Where was the government the day my son stole my neighbour's hen; wrung its neck and cooked it—feathers and all, because there was no food in the house and I was away, minding the children of the white family I worked for? Asked to stay in for the week-end—they had their emergency . . . mine was just not being able to tell my children beforehand that they would be alone for the weekend . . . not being able to leave them enough food for the time I was away . . . not being able to phone and tell them of the change of plans. Who was on the phone, in Guguletu then? And why would the awarding of phones have started with a nobody such as I am?

Why now, when he's an outcast, does my son have a better roof over his head than ever before in his life? . . . living a better life, if chained? I do not understand why it is that the government is giving him so much now when it has given him nothing at all, all his life. God, you know my heart. I am not saying my child shouldn't be punished for his sin. But I am a mother, with a mother's heart. The cup You have given me is too bitter to swallow. The shame. The hurt of the other mother. The young woman whose tender life was cut so cruelly short.

God, please forgive my son. Forgive him this terrible, terrible sin.[10]

Try to list the manifestations and implications of evil that you discovered as you read the above. On the face of it, the young man—one of a group later convicted of the crime—has committed an unfathomable act of violence, on a young woman whose motivations and intentions were to help in whatever way she could to address some of the very problems the mother in Magona's account describes. As the mother acknowledges, her son performed an evil act, committed a terrible sin, and deserves punishment. But there are wider forms of evil at work in the society in which this young man was raised—the particularly virulent form of racism long practiced by South Africa's apartheid government; the Bantu Education Act that required black South African children to be taught only those skills necessary for the menial jobs they were expected to hold; the poverty and hopelessness that such a system generates. Are we absolutely sure that "Boyboy" is an evil person? Or is the reality of evil broader and more pervasive than any, even all, such individual actions?

For example, corporations, governments, religious groups—through the agency of their members, can take on a life of their own which makes them capable of actions that even the individuals involved might not consider appropriate in other contexts. We should look behind what we often perceive as individual actions to see if there are institutional components that need addressing. To what extent, if at all, does our awareness of the broader systemic expressions of evil change the way we think about individual actions? Should it?

The response of the murdered young woman's parents has been perhaps as astonishing as the murder itself was shocking. Amy Biehl's parents have spent much time in South Africa since their daughter's death working with the young men involved in her murder, seeing that they receive education and the possibility of a better life for themselves and their families. Can you imagine the Biehls' response to the questions about evil we have been discussing?

SOME RESPONSES TO EVIL

We have identified some acts that most persons would probably agree are evil. A question we must address before we can identify appropriate responses to evil, however, is whether we think the persons who commit evil themselves are evil or whether only their actions are evil. Are "evil" persons only those who know their acts are evil, but who go ahead and do them anyway? Are the soldiers who used babies for target practice evil, if they don't think that their actions are wrong, but, in fact, commendable? What about the soldiers who followed orders in Vietnam to kill villagers, for the pragmatic reason that they could not tell allies from enemies? Are they evil, or was this action a necessary evil consequence of war, with no culpable agent? What about the civilians who were killed in Afghanistan after the terrorist attacks on the United States, or civilian casualties in any war, however "just" the war itself may seem? Who is culpable, responsible? And is this the same as "evil"?

Depending on how you answer these questions, you might respond differently to instances of "evil" and to individuals who commit "evil" acts. In her account of her ministry with death row inmates, Sr. Helen Prejean describes how she began visiting prisoners who had been condemned to die. Initially asked if she would correspond with an inmate, Prejean becomes increasingly involved in the issues surrounding the death penalty. As she exchanges letters with condemned prisoner Patrick Sonnier, Prejean eventually wants to know more about the crimes this man has been convicted of. After reading the files that contain accounts of Sonnier and his brother posing as security officers to handcuff a young couple, rape the woman, and eventually shoot both individuals, Prejean reflects on the conflicting emotions she feels:

> The sun is setting and a shaft of orange filters through one of the tall windows. I close the folder and put my head in my hands.
> A boy and girl, their young lives budding, unfolding. Snipped.
> And their parents, condemned to wonder for the rest of their lives about their children's last tortured hours; sentenced for the rest of their days to fear for their families, their other children; startled out of their sleep at night by dreams of the terror that ripped their children from them.
> The details of the depravity stun me. It is like the spinning merry-go-round that I had once tried to climb aboard when I was a child, but it was spinning too fast and it threw me to the ground.
> You may take the documents home, Chava had said, but I do not want to take them home. I know enough. More than enough. I leave the documents on the table and walk across the dying sunlight to the door and close it behind me, the words of Jeremiah welling within me:

A voice was heard in Ramah,
sobbing and lamenting:
Rachel weeping for her children,
Refusing to be comforted
because they were no more. (31:15) . . .

Then it comes to me. The victims are dead and the killer is alive and I am befriending the killer.

Have I betrayed his victims? Do I have to take sides? I am acutely aware that my beliefs about the death penalty have never been tested by personal loss. Let Mama or my sister, Mary Ann, or my brother, Louie, be brutally murdered and then see how much compassion I have. My magnanimity is gratuitous. No one has shot my loved ones in the back of the head. If someone I love should be killed, I know I would feel rage, loss, grief, helplessness, perhaps for the rest of my life. . . .

In sorting out my feelings and beliefs, there is, however, one piece of moral ground of which I am absolutely certain: if I were to be murdered I would not want my murderer executed. . . .

I am beginning to notice something about Pat Sonnier. In each of his letters he expresses gratitude and appreciation for my care. He makes no demands. He doesn't ask for money. He does not request my phone number (inmates at Angola are allowed to make collect phone calls). He only says how glad he is to have someone to communicate with because he has been so lonely. The sheer weight of his loneliness, his abandonment, draws me. I abhor the evil he has done. But I sense something, some sheer and essential humanness, and that, perhaps, is what draws me most of all.[11]

Is Patrick Sonnier evil? How do you think Sr. Helen Prejean would answer that question? Even in Nazi Germany, some individuals like Herman Goering were nice to their children and dogs. Do good actions or impulses compensate for evil ones? Can an "evil" person do good things? Can a "good" person do evil things? Is there any such thing as an "evil" or "good" person? Your answers to these questions will shape the ways in which you identify what you consider to be appropriate responses to evil.

Most religions that have an idea of evil also have a way for people to atone or compensate for the evil they do, intentionally or unintentionally. Some suggest that the idea that we can make up for the evil acts that we do implies that we are not ourselves evil. Or does this merely suggest that although we can be evil, we can also turn away from evil?

Finally, what should we do when we are actually faced with evil? The question of evil is often a practical and immediate one. In 1964, newspapers printed the account of a young woman who was assaulted and killed in a neighborhood in New York City. Many people were at home and witnessed the attack, but "didn't want to get involved" and so did not respond to her cries for help. The story of Kitty Genovese became a nationwide indictment of the neighborhood. People around the country claimed that something like that could never happen in their neighborhood, that someone—perhaps even everyone—would go to help. Movies and TV shows were produced, based on this story. What would happen if a similar incident were to occur in your own neighborhood? Was this just an isolated incident? How do we, collectively, respond in the face of evil?

In another incident, an elderly man was beaten to death in the parking lot of a busy supermarket. Newspaper reports indicated that the person responsible for the beating was mentally ill, and that he believed he was attacking demons in some way. A number of bystanders watched, and eventually someone told the attacker to stop, which he did. It was too late, however: the victim was fatally injured. Would you have stopped and tried to help the man being beaten? Would you have tried to get help? Or would you have considered that it was none of your business? What might be some reasons for not stopping to help? Because you feared for your own safety? Because you were late for another engagement? Because you didn't want to get involved? Have you ever tried to help someone in an emergency situation—assisting at an accident site, helping an elderly person to cross the street, breaking up a fight, or reporting a suspected case of domestic violence? Why did you do what you did? Would you do it again? Did anyone appreciate your efforts? Did anyone get angry with you for "interfering"? (You might refer again to the Parable of the Good Samaritan at the end of Chapter 1.)

SOME QUESTIONS ABOUT EVIL

"Why do bad things happen to good people?" Rabbi Harold Kuschner wonders in his famous book. Within those religious traditions that posit the existence of an all-good, all-powerful deity, the existence of evil obviously poses this question: If God created everything and is all-good, then where does "evil" come from? And if God is all-powerful, then why does He/She allow evil actions? This question is discussed under the term "theodicy," which means, literally, the justice of God. Some people suggest that the free will they believe was given to humans at their very creation means that many will make choices that are bad, even evil, and that God's intervention would mean an unacceptable denial of human freedom. Within Christianity, the Genesis story of Adam and Eve in the garden is often used as a metaphor for the advent of evil, or at least disobedience. Saint Augustine and others after him developed an elaborate theory of original sin, in which all humans are said to be born flawed because of Adam and Eve's transgression. This inherent flaw means that we often do things that are against our best God-given natures. In this way, Christianity avoids the dualism that would suggest a second force with power equal to God's, an evil force. Again according to Christian belief, the life, death, and resurrection of Jesus is understood to have restored the possibility of a return to the goodness and harmony depicted in the early verses of Genesis.

Other traditions, such as Buddhism, do not speculate on the genesis of evil per se but rather focus on dealing with the suffering experienced as part of human be-ing. Still others see life as a battle between the forces of good and evil—maybe God and Satan—and our human role is to work on the right side of this conflict.

Regardless of our beliefs about the source of evil, we all encounter events and situations during our lives that are touched by a force that causes over-whelming suffering. We have to develop ways of thinking about and living with this reality so that we can deal with such circumstances, no matter what their source or explanation.

What Some Others Have Said About Evil

With or without reference to God or some divine force, the question of evil has occupied thinkers through the ages. In her book *Wickedness: A Philosophic Essay,* philosopher Mary Midgley discusses the question of evil independent of the issue of the existence of a divine being.[12] What difference does it make to approach this topic from Midgley's perspective? Is it more or less satisfactory to sidestep the question of God—of theodicy?

Midgley argues that "since we are capable of [wrongdoing] what we need is to understand it" (p. 2). Further, she argues that those who claim that the causes are external are just as confused as those who assert that the causes are internal, and that, in fact, the causes are both. She points out that all of the rec-ognized vices are the opposites of recognized virtues. If we can do good, we can do evil, and vice versa. This is the result of free will. We have these options, and we must choose. Which we choose may depend on both internal and exter-nal circumstances.

Midgley also points out that evil comes from both active and passive causes. It is easy to recognize the active causes, but the passive ones are just as real—failure to do something right, failure to object to something wrong being done.

Since we tend to identify with things we understand, we must be careful in learning about evil. Endeavoring to learn about and understand something does not mean that we accept it. But it is critical that we learn to recognize evil before it goes too far, so that we can do something about it. Midgley suggests that we "think of wickedness not primarily as a positive, definite tendency like aggres-sion, whose intrusion into human life needs a special explanation, but rather as negative, as a general kind of failure to live as we are capable of living."[13]

According to Midgley, we should recognize that the natural motives that give rise to evil are connected with power, but this should not give rise to

fatalism, because though natural, they are not inevitable. Since multiple out-
comes are possible, they will not all be equally valued by all persons all of the
time. These natural impulses are not in and of themselves evil, but can lead to
evil if we are not careful of them.

We must, says Midgley, understand the relationship among all causes,
inner and outer, and free will. If we only deal with the outer causes, whether
"influences" or "demons," we negate the idea of personal responsibility. She
claims that "[the existence of inborn tendencies to evil] only means that our
good tendencies are not complete or infallible, that we are not faultless
moral automata."[14] She closes the first chapter of her book with the following summary:

> The problem of evil is not just a problem about God, but an important and
> difficult problem about individual human psychology. We need to understand
> better the natural tendencies which make human wickedness possible. Various
> contemporary habits of mind make this hard:
>
> (1) There is a notion that both method and morals require human behaviour
> in general, and particularly wrong-doing, to be explained only by external,
> social causes. But this is a false antithesis. (i) As far as method goes, we need
> both social and individual causes. Neither makes sense alone. (ii) Morally, what
> we need is to avoid fatalism, which is an independent error, no more tied to
> thought about individuals than about societies.
>
> From this angle, however, the idea of natural sources of wrong-doing has
> been obscured because it was supposed that any such source would have to be
> a fairly specific positive tendency, such as aggression. But aggression certainly
> does not play this role, and it is hard to see what would. It is probably more
> helpful to use here the traditional notion of evil as negative, as a more general
> rejection and denial of positive capacities. The psychological task is then one of
> mapping those capacities, understanding what potential gaps and conflicts
> there are among them, spotting the areas of danger at which failure easily takes
> place and so grasping more fully the workings of rejection. (This does not have
> to involve identifying with it. The danger of identifying with a mental process
> just because we come to understand it exists, but it can be resisted.)
>
> (2) Difficulty, however, still arises about this programme today from a sus-
> picion that the whole problem is imaginary. Officially, people are sceptical now
> about the very existence of sin or wickedness. When examined, however, this
> position usually turns out to be an unreal one, resulting from exaggeration of
> reforming claims. It often means merely that different things are now
> disapproved of, e.g. repression rather than adultery. . . .
>
> The idea of evil as negative does not, of course, imply that it is weak or
> unreal, any more than darkness or cold. What it does imply is a distinct, origi-
> nal human nature with relatively specific capacities and incapacities, rather
> than total plasticity and indefiniteness. Unless evil is to be seen as a mere
> outside enemy, totally external to humanity, it seems necessary to locate some
> of its sources in the unevenness of this original equipment. But this negative
> conception has often struck enquirers as insufficiently dramatic.[15]

How do you think some of the other people you have encountered in this chapter would respond to Midgley's discussion of evil, for example, the mayor of Inglis, Florida? To what extent does Midgley's perspective fit with or contradict religious explanations you have heard or read about? How would Midgley analyze the case of Andrea Yates?

We have discussed various understandings of evil—why bad things happen—and some of the responses suggested by different cultures and traditions. One of the ways in which human societies have responded to the presence of evil is through the development of systems of ethics, the topic of our next chapter.

CHAPTER FIVE

How Should We Live?
Personal Ethics

What do you think of when you hear the term *ethics?* Does it remind you of having been in some kind of dilemma when you had to figure out what was the right thing to do? Have you ever said about somebody's action, "that's just not right"? Have you ever felt guilty about something you have done yourself that you felt or knew on some deep level wasn't "right"? There may be issues that you feel passionately about and may argue about with friends who hold a different position. Do you hold some of your own positions out of a deep sense of what's right and what's wrong? Your responses to these questions mark a starting point for our discussion of the realm of ethics in the human search for meaning.

Setting the Stage: Questions of Right and Wrong

Your own experiences, if you have thought about them in light of the questions above, probably would tell you that it's not always clear what's right and what's wrong. If you've ever been engaged in a passionate argument with someone over an issue about which you both hold firm views, you already understand a little of the complexity of ethics. The following excerpt, from a work of speculative fiction by Octavia Butler, illustrates well the complicated decisions we sometimes have to make in life. Set in the early 21st century, Butler's novel tells of a group struggling to survive after the ordinary social structures we count on to sustain order have disintegrated. Butler's character, Lauren, is trying to lead a small group of companions north toward an area where they hope to find less chaotic and violent conditions. Lauren has a condition known as hyperempathy, caused by drugs taken by her mother during pregnancy. Lauren's hyperempathy means that when anyone in her immediate vicinity suffers pain of any kind, she shares that pain, physically, in her own body. As you read this excerpt, try to determine how you might respond if you were in Lauren's position. Would you act in the same way? If you were Harry, would you have the same questions and reservations?

I heard scrambling and thrashing near me. There were grunts and sounds of blows. A fight. I could see them in the darkness—two figures struggling on the ground. The one on the bottom was Harry.

He was fighting someone over the gun, and he was losing. The muzzle was being forced toward him.

That couldn't happen. We couldn't lose the gun or Harry. I took a small granite boulder from our fire pit, set my teeth, and brought it down with all my strength on the back of the intruder's head. And I brought myself down.

It wasn't the worst pain I had ever shared, but it came close. I was worthless after delivering that one blow. I think I was unconscious for a while. . . .

I got up, swaying from the residual shock of the blow. I felt sick and dizzy, and my head hurt. . . .

I checked him. He was still alive, unconscious, not feeling any pain now. What I was feeling was my own reaction to the blow I'd struck.

"The other one's dead," Harry said. "This one . . . Well, you caved in the back of his head. I don't know why he's still alive."

"Oh, no," I whispered. "Oh hell." And then to Harry. "Give me the gun."

"Why?" he asked.

My fingers had found the blood and broken skull, soft and pulpy at the back of the stranger's head. Harry was right. He should have been dead.

"Give me the gun," I repeated, and held out a bloody hand for it. "Unless you want to do this yourself."

"You can't shoot him. You can't just . . ."

"I hope you'd find the courage to shoot me if I were like that, and out here with no medical care to be had. We shoot him, or leave him here alive. How long do you think it will take him to die?"

"Maybe he won't die." I went to my pack, struggling to navigate without throwing up. I pulled it away from the dead man, groped within it, and found my knife. It was a good knife, sharp and strong. I flicked it open and cut the unconscious man's throat with it.

Not until the flow of blood stopped did I feel safe. The man's heart had pumped his life away into the ground. He could not regain consciousness and involve me in his agony.

But, of course, I was far from safe. Perhaps the last two people from my old life were about to leave me. I had shocked and horrified them. I wouldn't blame them for leaving.

"Strip the bodies," I said. "Take what they have, then we'll put them into the scrub oaks down the hill where we gathered wood."

I searched the man I had killed, found a small amount of money in his pants pocket and a larger amount in his right sock. Matches, a packet of almonds, a packet of dried meat, and a packet of small, round, purple pills. . . .

I put the pills back in the pocket I had taken them from. Everything else, I kept. The money would help sustain us. The food might or might not be edible. I would decide that when I could see it clearly.

I looked to see what the others were doing, and was relieved to find them stripping the other body. Harry turned it over, then kept watch as Zahra went through the clothing, shoes, socks, and hair. She was even more thorough than I had been. With no hint of squeamishness, she hauled off the man's clothing and examined its greasy pockets, seams, and hems. I got the feeling she had done this before.

"Money, food, and a knife," she whispered at last. . . .

We chose a spot between two ridges, settled, and sat silent for some time. I felt set-apart. I knew I had to speak, and I was afraid that nothing I could say would help. They might leave me. In disgust, in distrust, in fear, they might decide that they couldn't travel with me any longer. Best to try to get ahead of them.

"I'm going to tell you about myself," I said. "I don't know whether it will help you to understand me, but I have to tell you. You have a right to know."

And in low whispers, I told them about my mother—my biological mother—and about my sharing.

When I finished, there was another long silence. Then Zahra spoke, and I was so startled by the sound of her soft voice that I jumped.

"So when you hit that guy," she said, "it was like you hitting yourself."

"No," I said. "I don't get the damage. Just the pain."

"But, I mean it felt like you hit yourself?"

I nodded. "Close enough. When I was little, I used to bleed along with people if I hurt them or even if I saw them hurt. I haven't done that for a few years."

"But if they're unconscious or dead, you don't feel anything."

"That's right."

"So that's why you killed that guy?"

"I killed him because he was a threat to us. To me in a special way, but to you too. What could we have done about him? Abandon him to the flies, the ants, and the dogs? You might have been willing to do that, but would Harry? Could we stay with him? For how long? To what purpose? Or would we dare to hunt up a cop and try to report seeing a guy hurt without involving ourselves. Cops are not trusting people. I think they would want to check us out, hang on to us for a while, maybe charge us with attacking the guy and killing his friend." I turned to look at Harry who had not said a word. "What would you have done?" I asked.

"I don't know," he said, his voice hard with disapproval. "I only know I wouldn't have done what you did."

"I wouldn't have asked you to do it," I said. "I didn't ask you. But, Harry, I would do it again. I might have to do it again. That's why I'm telling you this."[1]

How would you classify Lauren's action? Could you call it self-defense? What about the rationales she gives? What were the options? Would any of them have been preferable to the one Lauren chose? In light of the fact that in Butler's narrative, the "cops" she mentioned were mostly privately hired and were more likely than not to be corrupt, would you have gone the route of reporting the incident? Most people agree that "murder" is wrong; complications arise when we try to determine just what constitutes murder as opposed to other forms of the taking of life, such as in war or self-defense. Should we hold onto such principles as "the taking of human life is wrong" no matter what the circumstances, or consequences, or do we have to take such factors into account? Can we say, once and for all, that some things are just plain wrong, that certain courses of action are always right?

WHAT DO YOU THINK?
ETHICS AND PERSONAL RESPONSIBILITY

In the discussion following Lauren's actions in the last selection, Lauren says to her companions, "I wouldn't have asked you to do it." What does this say about personal responsibility? Lauren knows what she has done. She knows too what the consequences might be. Her friends might be so distressed that their trust in her is shattered. They might abandon her, no longer want to travel with her. What does it really mean to be responsible for one's actions? In the last chapter, we discussed the problem of evil, and the idea in some traditions that some external force, perhaps in the form of a demon, or Satan, at least influences us into taking actions that are wrong. Are there other forces that might pressure us into taking actions that we might, in other circumstances, consider "wrong"?

Here are two real-life cases to consider. In the first case, on December 3, 1999, two homeless persons who had been living in an abandoned warehouse in Worcester, Massachusetts, accidentally knocked over a candle in the course of an argument and started a fire. When their efforts to put out the blaze were unsuccessful, they ran from the building. The woman, Julie, seventeen years old at the time and pregnant, had some degree of mental impairment; the man, Thomas, was 36, had a history of mental illness and had been on the streets for years. Questions emerged as to whether they were capable of making better decisions, such as calling to report the fire.

Because the building was boarded up, it was some time before neighbors noticed the fire and called the fire department. Firefighters knew that homeless people had been using the building for shelter and feared that some might be trapped inside. In the course of checking the building, six firefighters lost their lives. Should the two who started the blaze be held responsible for these deaths? Initially, the courts dismissed the charges, but in March 2002 the Massachusetts Supreme Judicial Court ruled that the two parties could be charged and tried. The people of Worcester were divided over the action that should be taken.

A brawl in a college hockey game. Who is responsible?

How responsible were Julie and Thomas for the deaths of the firefighters? What is the best way to encourage people to act responsibly, to take responsibility for their actions? Can everybody do so, in all circumstances?

In the second case, questions of responsibility arise in a case involving an argument between two "hockey dads" at an ice arena. The altercation left one of the men dead from the injuries he received and the other facing a murder charge in court. The fight started when one man, Thomas Junta, became upset at the other, Michael Costin, over Costin's apparent refusal to intervene in what Junta thought was overly rough play during an informal hockey stick practice. Junta maintained that he feared for the safety of his son and the other players. The jurors found him guilty of involuntary manslaughter. How do the terms "right" and "wrong" and the concept of "responsibility for one's individual actions" apply in this situation?

> The message from the jury that found Thomas Junta guilty of involuntary manslaughter yesterday in the death of Michael Costin is that even if the burly hockey father didn't throw the first punch, he clearly overpowered the much smaller man and yet continued to pummel him, according to legal specialists.
>
> "Essentially, the jury has found him guilty of the less blameworthy form of manslaughter," said Boston lawyer Andrew Good, adding that jurors concluded that Junta didn't mean to kill Costin, but used more force than was necessary to reasonably defend himself.

"They could have rejected his claim of self-defense outright, or returned this verdict to say he used more blows than necessary to repel the attack, that at some point this person was no longer a threat and he kept hitting him," said Good. . . .

Attorney Paul V. Kelly, who won a self-defense case earlier this week involving a fight that didn't result in death, said, "The key facts are, at what point did the person cease to be in a defensive posture and become the aggressor? If a person overcame the person who attacked him and suddenly takes on the role of aggressor and throttled the person, which sounds like what happened in the Junta case, he crossed the line."

Although Junta appeared soft-spoken and composed on the witness stand, his sheer size hindered his ability to persuade the jury that he was merely defending himself, legal specialists agreed.

"I think overall he did as well as could be expected, but no matter how well your witness does you're still constrained by the overall facts that attach to every case," said another lawyer, Timothy Burke. . . . "Here, the inescapable fact is, you have a 270-pound man on foot outweighing and struggling with someone who weighs 100 pounds less and is on ice skates," Burke said. . . .

The Junta jury "had to decide which of the witnesses they found more credible regarding the number and manner of blows inflicted by Junta," Carney said. "These fights are always very fast, very scary to bystanders, and traumatic for people to recall."

Boston College law professor Phyllis Goldfarb said Junta's testimony may have drawn sympathy from the jury, but prosecution witnesses who witnessed the fatal encounter probably convinced jurors that Junta was reckless in the amount of force he used. "The seemingly disinterested witnesses who observed the fight, who said that he threw many punches and that their thought process while it was happening was that he could kill the victim, gave testimony that was very difficult to overcome," Goldfarb said.

But by taking the stand, the specialists agreed, Junta probably convinced the jury not to convict him of the more serious crime of voluntary manslaughter, which would have meant he intentionally used enough force to kill Costin.

"I thought he came across as genuinely remorseful, saddened by the consequences, and totally traumatized," Kelly said. "But I have to believe the jury felt they would be sending a terrible message to society if they let him walk out the door."[2]

Does it make a difference whether Junta *meant* to kill Costin? Does it matter that he is apparently deeply remorseful over the result of his action? The jury decided that, although there was no evidence that Junta meant to kill Costin, yet he should have known that death would be the likely result of the kind of physical force he used to subdue the much smaller man. How responsible do you think Junta is for the consequences of his actions, however unintended they might have been? Are we accountable for what we "should have known" as well as for what we actually claim to know?

Go online and look for reports of trials that are taking place now, or that have occurred recently. Use the key words "trial," "murder," "extenuating circumstances," "sentencing trials," and the like to define your search. Look particularly for those where the defense is not claiming that the defendant did not commit the crime, but rather where they are claiming "extenuating circumstances." Compare the situations you find with those of the Worcester firefighters case, and that of Junta, particularly in terms of the defenses presented that suggest that the person charged might not be "responsible" for the crime, even if he or she did commit it. Do any of these "excuses" seem valid to you? Is there a difference between explaining behavior and excusing behavior?

CULTURAL AND SOCIAL APPROACHES TO ETHICS

As you have pondered the questions about the stories above, you have undoubtedly drawn on many resources, both conscious and unconscious, that have informed your opinions about the actions of the people involved. Do we just automatically know what is right, or do we discover in the course of our lives how to act rightly in a given situation? How do we know what's right?

What is the first memory you have of dealing with questions of right and wrong? What were the circumstances? For some of you, it might have been a situation in early childhood, perhaps involving a sibling or friend. For others, it might have taken place at school, or in a playground or other setting. If you were the person doing something "wrong," how did you feel? How did you know that what you or someone else did was wrong? Where do these concepts come from? How do they become part of our individual and group consciousness and conscience?

Most of us form our earliest sense of conscience in the context of our families. Our cultural and religious traditions have everything to do with the ethics and behaviors that are expected of us and that are embraced by our social groups. Failure to live up to these norms means that we stand the risk of nonacceptance by the group. As we mature and form relationships with other groups who become increasingly important to us, some of those earlier patterns change. Sometimes such changes are a response to peer pressure, but sometimes they reflect our own life experiences, experiences that might require different responses from those of persons even a generation earlier. Think of some of the ideas that you now hold about certain issues and behaviors that might be different from the ways of thinking presented to you by your family of origin. What influences caused you to make the changes and which of those older ideas do you still embrace?

SOURCES OF OUR ETHICAL CODES

Whatever patterns of ethical behavior we are raised with, they never emerge from nowhere. Sometimes it is helpful to make a distinction between personal morals, the ways in which we live individually as moral persons, and ethics, the systems of moral codes of behavior that are part of our social reality. You are probably familiar with the next selection that comes from the Tanakh. In this passage, God gives to the people, through Moses, the law that we know as the Ten Commandments. As you read this ethical code, think about how relevant—or not—each point is in today's world.

> God spoke all these words, saying:
>
> I the LORD am your God who brought you out of the land of Egypt, the house of bondage: You shall have no other gods besides Me.
>
> You shall not make for yourself a sculptured image, or any likeness of what is in the heavens above, or on the earth below, or in the waters under the earth. You shall not bow down to them or serve them. For I the LORD your God am an impassioned God, visiting the guilt of the parents upon the children, upon the third and upon the fourth generations of those who reject Me, but showing kindness to the thousandth generation of those who love Me and keep My commandments. You shall not swear falsely by the name of the LORD your God; for the LORD will not clear one who swears falsely by His name. Remember the sabbath day and keep it holy. Six days you shall labor and do all your work, but the seventh day is a sabbath of the LORD your God: you shall not do any work—you, your son or daughter, your male or female slave, or your cattle, or the stranger who is within your settlements. For in six days the LORD made heaven and earth and sea, and all that is in them, and He rested on the seventh day; therefore the LORD blessed the sabbath day and hallowed it.
>
> Honor your father and your mother, that you may long endure on the land that the LORD your God is assigning to you.
>
> You shall not murder.
>
> You shall not commit adultery.
>
> You shall not steal.
>
> You shall not bear false witness against your neighbor.
>
> You shall not covet your neighbor's house: you shall not covet your neighbor's wife, or his male or female slave, or his ox or his ass, or anything that is your neighbor's.[3]

This particular code has been normative in the development of legal systems in most nations where Judaism or Christianity is the dominant religious tradition. Think about the extent to which the laws of the United States, for example, reflect the basic values of the Ten Commandments. Despite the fact that some of these commands seem a bit dated, reflective of a different time and place—the references to slaves, for example—there is nonetheless a certain timelessness about them, a relevance that carries across time and place. While we might interpret them differently today than did the Israelites of Moses's time, this law gives some basic rules that are similar to those that most societies have adopted as necessary to ordering their lives as communities.

Sometimes an ethical code is addressed to a whole people, sometimes to a group within a culture or community. You might have heard tales of the Samurai warriors of Japan. They were a particular group within the wider Japanese society who had a very specific role to play. The ethical code of the Samurai covered almost every aspect of their lives. In what respects do the instructions in this passage from the Code of the Samurai apply only to these specific persons in a particular time and place? Which, if any, might have something to say to us?

> Right and wrong are nothing but good and evil, for though I would not deny there is a slight difference between the terms, yet to act rightly and do good is difficult and is regarded as tiresome, whereas to act wrongly and do evil is easy and amusing, so that naturally most incline to the wrong or evil and tend to dislike the good and right. But to be thus unstable and make no distinction between right and wrong is contrary to reason, so that anyone who understands this distinction and yet does what is wrong is no proper samurai, but a raw and untaught person. And the cause of it is small capacity for self-control. Though this may not sound so bad, if we examine into its origin we find it arises from cowardice. That is why I maintain that it is essential for a samurai to refrain from wrong and cleave to what is right.[4]

The Samurai are best known for their role in battle and their willingness to not only be killed but sacrifice their lives intentionally for their lord or country and also for their eagerness to retain (or regain) their sense of honor after some kind of failure. But the ethical code by which they lived extended far beyond this rather stereotyped and simplistic image. Like most codes of ethics, the code of the Samurai was intended to apply to the whole of life.

Many of the moral codes and values of a culture or tradition are passed on informally, often in the form of story. The next selection is a parable from the Christian Scriptures. A parable is a story form that uses familiar concepts and symbols to get a deeper point across. Read the story carefully and see if you can identify the message that is being conveyed. How effective is the genre of story or parable for conveying ethical instruction? If this lesson were put in the form of a rule or law, would it be clearer? Less clear? More effective? Less effective?

> Again [Jesus] began to teach beside the sea. Such a very large crowd gathered around him that he got into a boat on the sea and sat there, while the whole crowd was beside the sea on the land. He began to teach them many things in parables, and in his teaching he said to them: "Listen! A sower went out to sow. And as he sowed, some seed fell on the path, and the birds came and ate it up. Other seed fell on rocky ground, where it did not have much soil, and it sprang up quickly, since it had no depth of soil. And when the sun rose, it was scorched; and since it had no root, it withered away. Other seed fell among thorns, and the thorns grew up and choked it, and it yielded no grain. Other seed fell into good soil and brought forth grain, growing up and increasing and yielding thirty and sixty and a hundredfold." And he said, "Let anyone with ears to hear listen!"[5]

Like most stories, this one can be interpreted in more than one way. If you were a member of the crowd listening to this itinerant teacher, what might you think he is trying to say to you? Can you think of any contemporary circumstance in which this story might have relevance? Michelle Chaflin, a student in a Religious Studies course—actually a Jewish student for whom the story is *not* a part of her own tradition—rewrote this story in contemporary terms:

> One day a teacher began a lesson to his class about ethics and morals. He was a great teacher and students from all over the entire school sat in on his classes just to hear him teach. But not all of his students were as appreciative as others for his guidance. Some students looked out the window and daydreamed about soccer practice after school. Others listened intently but were high on drugs and soon forgot the message in the teaching; for them the point never sank in. Some students listened but their parents were made rich by embezzling or getting kids addicted to cigarettes, and the children of these parents tried to do what the teacher taught but were struck down by their unethical parents. But some students, especially those who came from other classes and their own free time, did absorb the message of ethics the teacher was trying to convey. They went on to lead good lives and were fair and just with all people. And they taught others to be fair and just by example, so to increase the teacher's students by hundreds. The ethics teacher's lessons were carried on by his students.[6]

Do you think that Michelle's version of the story is easier for contemporary people to relate to than the original version? Do you think she retains the main "lesson" of the original?

Try this same exercise yourself. Find a teaching story from a religious scripture of your choice. You might choose one with which you are familiar, or look for one from a tradition other than your own. Think about the main point you think the writer was trying to convey. Now rewrite the story using contemporary symbols and metaphors in such a way that you think it would convey an important message to people in your own time and culture. Is your version clearer? Which do you prefer? Why?

Buddhism is another tradition that has a combination of specific and well-developed sets of ethical guidelines and more informal stories that convey moral messages. In this short tale, "Dhitika Ends a Sacrifice," what kind of understanding do you gain of the Buddhist view of life and responsibility? (An *arhat* is a person who has reached enlightenment.)

> There was a wealthy and powerful Brahmin named Adarpa who slaughtered one thousand goats each day as a sacrificial offering. On one special occasion he was inspired to offer ten thousand white cows to the gods.
> As the sacrifice was being prepared, the fifth Buddhist patriarch, the arhat Dhitika, suddenly appeared as if by magic before the sacrificial altar. Then no matter what the Brahmin ritualists did, they could neither kindle the sacrificial

fire nor slaughter the milling cows; even their recitation of the sacred Vedas became perfectly soundless.

A wise Brahmin saw that it was Dhitika's magical powers that were preventing the priests from performing their duty. He and his colleagues stoned the arhat, but all the rocks turned into flowers that cascaded harmlessly around him.

This caused the Brahmins, who were not fools, to gain faith in the old sage who had come among them. Dhitika said to them, "O cruel sons of religion, why are you performing such evil sacrifices? What do you hope to attain? Far better would it be to make charitable offerings and perform other virtuous acts. How can offerings of warm flesh and blood please a benevolent deity? Would it delight a loving parent to receive feast offerings of his own children's flesh?

"Aren't cows considered deities in your Brahminic faith? Then how can you slaughter them, your own avowed objects of reverence and devotion? Your ancestral creed declares it impure to eat cow meat or even to touch it. Isn't it therefore a sin and an insult to offer it to your gods? Through this path, one only harms and debases oneself and others. If you wish to develop spiritually, give up such perverse and contradictory practices!"

Then the intelligent Brahmins comprehended the folly of their ways. Renouncing animal sacrifice, they became interested in investigating and adopting the non-violent creed of the compassionate Buddha, led by Adarpa himself and the head priests. Becoming students and followers of the arhat Dhitika, they led their entire community into virtue and reverence for all that lives.[7]

The story illustrates the Four Noble Truths of Buddhism that we discovered in the last chapter, specifically that humankind suffers in life because of attachment to material things, and that the way to remove this suffering is to give up such attachments. The way to achieve this detachment is to follow the Eight-Fold path, a list of eight values that, if lived faithfully, lead the follower to Nirvana— that state of enlightenment where the individual is free of all attachments, even attachment to a sense of individual selfhood. Three parts of the Eight-Fold Path apply most directly to ethics: Right Speech, Right Action, and Right Livelihood. Right Speech means saying appropriate things, and avoiding gossip and slander. Right Action concerns doing the appropriate things when the need for action occurs. Right Livelihood has to do with how one earns a living; among other prohibitions, you must not use others, or engage in an occupation that might lead to the use of or killing of others. Rather, you must earn your living in a way that respects the whole of creation. How do those three principles apply to the story of the arhat and the sacrifice?

The parable demonstrates another important feature of Buddhist ethics. The steps of the Eight-fold Path are guidelines for *positive* acts, not merely prohibitions of negative acts. So, for example, Right Speech not only prohibits slander and gossip, it also calls for speaking out with courage to call attention to wrongful acts, and, more mundanely, speaking courteously and kindly to one another. Look at the parable for examples of the prohibition aspects of

Right Action and Right Livelihood. Then look for the positive aspects demonstrated. What understanding of Right Action and Right Livelihood do you get from this? Do these perspectives remind you of lessons from your tradition, whether cultural or religious? Some ethicists maintain that the way to be an ethical person is to develop "character," by which is meant the automatic tendency to act in a virtuous way, with "virtuous" being defined as "goodly" or "righteously." How does this parable point us toward developing character? What would it mean for you, personally, to act with character?

> *Given the three rules of morality that are contained in the Eight-fold Path, and the principles you think are conveyed in the parable "Dhitika Ends a Sacrifice," what rules to you think might emerge for ordinary people (the laity, not priests)? Make a list of ethical rules that you think might apply under each of the headings: Right Speech, Right Action, and Right Livelihood. Do any or all of the rules you came up with have relevance for your own life? Do the texts suggest principles that seem difficult, even impossible to follow?*

DO WE ALWAYS KNOW WHAT'S RIGHT?

In September 2000, three Lords Justice of the Court of Appeal in the Royal Courts of Justice in the United Kingdom were faced with a particularly challenging case. They had to decide whether or not to order the separation of conjoined twins, knowing that if they were separated, one would die and if they were not separated, both would die. Who has the right to make such a decision? An article in the *Manchester Guardian* outlines some of the dilemmas faced by persons who had to make decisions in this case. What would you have decided if you were one of the parents? The doctors? A lawyer or judge in the courts?

> A doctor arrives at the scene of an accident to discover two injured men. He immediately sees that one is so badly hurt that he is bound to die but the second could be saved. But the first man is lying on top of the second and moving him would inevitably hasten his death.
>
> What should the doctor do? Would it be right for him to move the first man even though this would accelerate his death in order to save the life of the second? Does he have the right to choose to save one life though his actions would harm a second?
>
> This is the sort of dilemma—taking in complex legal, moral and ethical issues—which the lawyers embroiled in the case of conjoined twins Jodie and Mary have been confronting as they frame arguments for and against the separation operation which would save one of the girls but kill the other.
>
> At one level, the case is a heartbreaking human story. It is impossible to imagine the torment of the girls' parents whose Roman Catholic beliefs mean that they cannot give permission for a procedure which would bring about the death of Mary, only kept alive by the oxygenated blood she receives from her sister. On another level, the case has raised a series of profound questions

which are troubling some of Britain's sharpest legal minds and most serious moral and religious thinkers.

Ultimately, the case could have implications about the way the courts and society at large look at fundamental life and death issues. . . .

The judges . . . raised the possibility that a crime might be committed if an operation took place because it would lead to Mary's death—or if it did not because this would lead to Jodie's death. If the twins remained conjoined, doctors believe both will die within six months.

Entwined in this legal argument is the most difficult moral issue. Can it ever be right for a doctor to save one life at the expense of another?

Ethicists believe the problem can be approached in two ways. A utilitarian approach is that it is better to save one life even at the cost of another. The absolutist approach—as put forward by the parents and largely backed by Catholic thinkers—is that it can never be right to sacrifice a life. . . .

While "great weight" has to be attached to [the parents'] wishes, the court has a duty to ignore them in the best interests of the child.

But Richard Nicholson, editor of the *Bulletin of Medical Ethics,* suggested that the judges in this instance simply could not make the decision. "In a situation like this when there isn't an obvious right answer, do we not need to put the onus for the decision back on to those for whom it will mean the most, those who are going to have to live with the consequences of the decision? Surely we have to give great power and credence to the parents? . . ."

And so to the inevitable question of religion. In another dramatic courtroom moment, Lord Justice Ward suggested that it could not be "God's will" that Mary survive because she had not been born with the capacity for independent life. The parents' position remains that it is not "God's will" that people terminate life.

Much of modern British criminal law . . . is based on 19th-century case law made by judges basing their conclusions on Judaeo-Christian principles.

The thorny question of whether Mary was a "viable" being has also been addressed. If she had not been connected to Jodie she would have died because she lacked a functioning heart or lungs.

The judges queried whether Mary had in fact been "born alive" given the fact that she depended on her twin for her very life breath.[8]

The parents refused the surgery, citing their love for both children and their belief in a divine command against killing. Their Roman Catholic faith was such that the taking of one life, even to save the other, was not acceptable to them, and their pastor and the local bishop supported their decision. The twin known as Mary has no heart or lungs. Was she ever meant to live? Should Jodie be forced to give up her chance at life to support Mary for the three to six months medical experts say is the life expectancy if the twins are not separated? Health care professionals took the case to court, and received an injunction to overturn the parents' objection to the surgery, on the grounds that Jodie had a right to "defend herself" against her twin. The surgery was performed, Mary died as expected, and Jodie survived. Was this the right decision? Who has the right to make such decisions? Was it "fair" to the parents to override their religious beliefs?

> *Rent (or obtain from your library) a copy of the movie* Sophie's Choice. *How does Sophie's choice compare with that of the parents of Jodie and Mary? In their current situations, can there be a single "right" or "moral" choice for Sophie or these parents?*

RIGHT, WRONG, OR A MATTER OF OPINION?

In the selections and cases that we have discussed in this chapter, you will have formed your own opinions in many instances about the particular choices that the individuals involved made, and perhaps you will have determined whether you think they were right or wrong. Can we—and should we—make judgments about the actions of others? Can we afford *not* to do so?

As we discussed above, religious and cultural groups and traditions develop over time codes of values and ethical guidelines that are intended to be normative for the community. That is, members of the community generally are expected to abide by those guidelines, to use them as norms when deciding how to act, how to live. Exceptions are often allowed, of course, both when new interpretations of old codes emerge and sometimes when new situations arise that could not have been anticipated when the original rules were developed. You are probably aware yourself of ethical rules and principles that have been held up for you to follow yet which don't seem to make sense, which in fact might go against some other fundamental principle that you have come to hold. Often we have to determine how we shall square our individual consciences with the norms held by our community or society, when these are in conflict.

In addition, there are many times when extenuating circumstances make a difference as to the way we perceive an ethical dilemma. Think back to the story of Andrea Yates and the multiple factors that might have played a part in her ultimate violent and fatal actions. If Yates was mentally ill, we might judge her differently from the way we would judge her if she had tried to get rid of her children so that she could engage in a more liberated and fun-filled lifestyle. Yet judge her we do—or at least we judge her actions. If a parent steals in order to be able to provide food, or perhaps medicine, for a needy child, we will consider this action more understandable than theft which has no such desperate motivation. Yet the mere fact that the parent has to steal the medicine or food indicates to us that something is wrong somewhere—again, we make a moral judgment.

Perhaps these examples clarify the difference between the necessary activity of *judging*, in which we participate all the time, and being *judgmental*, even self-righteous. We cannot live in the world, certainly not with others, without making judgments about right and wrong, judgments usually rooted in the tradition in which we have been raised. But judgmentalism implies that we hold our own perspectives to be absolute and all others therefore to be wrong. There is a world of difference between offering an opinion that, on the basis of our own values and beliefs, a certain action is wrong—or right—and claiming that our particular opinion is the only possible valid view. All opinions, of course, are not created equal. Those closest to a given situation, who have taken the necessary time and effort to explore all dimensions of the issue, may have a greater insight and thus a "better" opinion than those who simply read a newspaper report and accept the perspective of the journalist. If you have a serious injury or illness, you will seek out the appropriate expert rather than turning to someone who might be full of uninformed advice and opinions! Consider whether there are things you are willing to say are always right or always wrong, in any situation, for any person, in any time or place. Have you ever struggled with this question, perhaps in the context of a friend's decision that for you would be unthinkable but that (s)he finds appropriate and moral? How do you resolve such a dilemma?

With these questions in mind, read this selection by Australian singer/songwriter Judy Small, in which she reflects on the historical relationships between her own European ancestors and the indigenous Aboriginal peoples of Australia. As Small states in her notes accompanying the CD, this is "a song of respect and reconciliation for the indigenous people of Australia. After attending a forum on reconciliation, I was profoundly moved by a speaker whose message was 'if you live here and call this place home, you belong, but you also have a responsibility to work to make it a better place for all its inhabitants.'" The "dreaming" in the song refers to a specific spiritual concept embraced by Aboriginal peoples regarding their understanding of the creation and ongoing sustenance of the earth and all its inhabitants.

> When my people first came to this land they came with fire and sword
> They tried to burn the dreaming in the name of their great god
> In arrogance and ignorance they raised their bloodied flag
> But they couldn't kill the spirit in the land.
>
> You have borne the brunt of bigotry, of genocidal men
> We took away your children and yet you call me friend
> We tried to strip your dignity but you would not be bound
> I know now that I stand on sacred ground.
>
> Chorus:
>
> So we'll reach across the water and we'll reach across the land
> We'll work to heal the wounds so that our children understand
> There's no one loves this earth like the ones who lived here first
> And together we can walk this sacred ground.
>
> There's a peace about you sister that I want to understand
> You tell me that it comes out of the spirit of the land
> This land that is your mother, this land that gave you birth
> Your dreaming joins your spirit to the earth.

Contemporary aboriginal peoples maintain their traditional connection with the land.

We tried to stop you singing now we're listening to your song
You say that if we love this land this is where we belong
And it doesn't matter who we are or where we first came from
Together we can call this land our home.

And if we say we love this land and want to call it home
We have an obligation to take care
To respect this land we walk on to learn its lessons well
To understand our place and purpose here.[9]

What does the song suggest about our capacity to learn from and even to critique a culture that is different from our own? What about making judgments about events that occurred in the past? And is there a difference between making these judgments and being "judgmental"?

List two or three contemporary issues that you find yourself needing to make judgments about, but about which you have concerns about being judgmental.

CAN AND SHOULD WE ALWAYS DO WHAT'S RIGHT?

In the preceding sections, we have looked at the difficulty we sometimes have in determining just what is "right" in a given situation. But are there ever times when we *shouldn't* do what's usually considered to be "right"? Some would suggest that there are certain moral principles that we should never violate, no matter what. Others would say that we need to weigh the probable consequences of an action and make our decision based on what would lead to the best outcome. Still others propose that, while taking principles and consequences into account, we have to look primarily at any given situation and make decisions based on the present circumstances. As you read the next selection, think about how each of these perspectives might affect the judgment you would make of the situation. The excerpt is from a contemporary mystery novel by P. M. Carlson. The key characters in this selection, from the final pages of the book, are Dale, the dead man; Donna, his wife; Tina and Josie, their young daughters; Holly Schreiner, a police officer haunted by the violence she saw as an army nurse; and Maggie, Donna's friend and a self-styled detective. Dale has been found dead in his study, locked in from the inside, and with no sign of any violence or forced entry. Did he die of natural causes—perhaps related to a recent medical diagnosis of a condition in which excessive exposure to heat could be deadly? Maggie doesn't think so. We listen in here on a hypothetical, off-the-record conversation:

"So it was heatstroke," said Holly slowly. She'd seen a couple of cases in Nam: The body's cooling system failed, a high fever cooked the brain centers, leading to convulsions, coma, cardiac failure, death. . . .

Donna was looking at her fearfully. "But the blood!" she said. "Someone hit him! Someone got in and hit him—and got out—"

"No, Donna." Holly shook her head. "The door was bolted from the inside. He probably went into convulsions before he died. Often happens in heatstroke. Slammed into that lamp on the edge of the desk thrashing around."

"Convul— Oh, God!" Donna doubled over. "Oh, my God! I thought—I thought it would be a coma—very quiet, just going to sleep for his nap and—"

Whoopee. So smirking Death had played another nasty one. A mild woman, seeking a mild escape from violence, and failing.

Donna whispered, "I should have phoned sooner."

Maggie had hurried across the room and was bending toward Donna now. "You had second thoughts? That's why you tried to call him from the beach?"

"Yes. To wake him up. But he didn't answer."

Holly asked, "Why yesterday? After all these years, why then?"

Donna was still sobbing. Maggie, kneeling beside her, arm across her heaving shoulders, raised her face toward Holly's. "We're still just supposing."

"Okay."

"We're supposing he'd started to beat Josie."

"Josie? You mean he never hurt the girls before?"

Donna lifted her head, indignation mingling with her tears. "Never! I would have left!" she said in a choked voice. "But he never hurt the girls. If he was mad at them he'd hurt me. He'd say I should be able to control the kids. That I was a—a bad mother."

"I see. Then Josie took the tape with his interview on it," said Holly slowly. Damn tape. The officer who'd listened to it had reported that it was all John Denver music. None of Dale's stuff left.

Donna said, "The tape set him off. But I realized it could be anything. Josie wasn't safe anymore. He had those guns—" She straightened up at the other end of the sofa and wiped a hand across her forehead. Maggie found a Kleenex in her pocket and offered it to Donna, then sat back on the floor at her feet.

Well, Schreiner, what do you do now? Open homicide investigation. She owed it to Dale, right? She could squeeze a proper confession from Donna, probably. Get a big press play, commendations, promotions. Schreiner the supercop. And Donna? She could go up for quite a few years. Even for manslaughter, she'd be in for six, maybe. Tina and Josie would be, what, fifteen and eighteen then. Father dead, mother in jail for murder, the girls living with—who? Dale Colby's icy parents, most likely. People who had raised a violent son already.

Or suppose a jury let Donna off. Self-defense didn't strictly fit but juries were mulish sometimes. But even if they decided in Donna's favor, there would be months of legal maneuvers. And publicity. There was no acquittal in the press. Olivia Kerr and her colleagues would play it big. Schoolteacher Kills Sick Husband! Murderous Mom Roasts Dad! As for Donna's job—forget it. School boards were politically vulnerable and wouldn't risk hiring a teacher tainted by a murder charge, regardless of her legal guilt or innocence. And even if this fragile battered family got sympathetic treatment from the press, like Joanne Little, the glare of publicity was brutal. To say nothing of the trial itself. She could picture little Josie on the stand, the DA's insinuations gentle so as not to antagonize the jury: "Josie, honey, don't you think most daddies spank their children when they're bad?" The girl's cuts and bruises would be healed on the surface by then, the brutality nothing but cold abstract words to the jury. What was it Maggie had said? It's not justice if it hurts a child.

Was it justice if it betrayed the dead? How much did she owe Dale Colby?

And how did you measure violence? To save her children, a meek and terrified woman had turned a thermostat dial. A far cry from Ernie Grant's arsenal of explosives and firearms. Much as Holly ached for him, she knew Ernie was an ongoing source of violence.

Like Dale Colby.

Was Donna an ongoing source of violence?

Donna, for years, had responded to violence with peace. Exactly what a nice girl was supposed to do. She'd absorbed the violence until it had touched her child. And when she'd fought back at last, it was with a twist of a thermostat dial. Expecting a peaceful death in his sleep for a violent man. . . .

Holly said, "Donna?"

Donna twisted the Kleenex in her hand. "I know. His brain—God, convulsions too." She struggled for a moment before she continued. "I didn't know there would be convulsions. But I knew it would be real. I faced it myself, over and over. Those guns—it's like you said, just touch the trigger. I was so scared each time that he would go too far. And when the doctor said he must never get overheated—at first it was a fantasy, but I saw Dale's fear of the heat, and I knew." She raised her head, gazing around the orderly room. "My marriage was a game. Make-believe. All this time I've tried to pretend it was okay, pretend he wouldn't do it to me again. But with Josie—I saw that was real. He was out of control. He'd destroy her too. I had to do something." She looked down at her Kleenex, then, unexpectedly, square at Holly. "But I didn't know I would feel so—filthy. I just thought about the girls, but now—"

"Some situations force us to be filthy," said Maggie soberly, dark memories stirring in her blue eyes. "Because every choice violates someone."

"But if I—Will they send me to jail?"

"Maybe," said Holly. "You'd certainly have a trial. Months of it. The newspapers would hound you. Hound your girls."

Donna nodded.

What the hell, Schreiner, you went to Nam because you wanted to be a healer. Maybe, just maybe, a cop could be a healer too. She took out her notebook. "Tell you what. We have Nate Rosen's evidence that the house was too warm at three-thirty. So I'm writing down that the air conditioner malfunctioned. Doc Craine will be delighted to get a reasonable cause of death. For the rest, well, we were just supposing, weren't we?" She closed her notebook and stood up. "If I get hard evidence I'll have to move on it, of course. It's up to you, Donna. Think about your girls and decide." She started for the door.

"Please," begged Donna, "tell me what to do!"

"She's told you," Maggie said. "She said, think about the girls. You've got to make the decisions now, Donna. And live with the results."

Donna was bent over again, face in her hands.

Holly paused by the entry arch and said gently, "I can tell you one thing. You're on the other side of the great divide now. You've met killing face to face. So whatever else you decide, better put a soft rug next to your bed. You're going to fall out of it with nightmares, lady."

Donna's head, still bowed, gave a tiny nod. Holly's gaze lingered a moment, then her eyes met Maggie's in sorrow. Tentatively, Maggie raised her fingers in a V.

Holly hesitated, then returned the salute. "Peace," she said and went back out into the night.[10]

What do you see as the ethical issues in this excerpt? What would you have done if you were Donna? Holly? Maggie? What should Donna do now? Why? How does attention to principles, consequences, and specific situation affect each person's actions in this excerpt? What do you think Maggie meant when she said, "every choice violates someone"?

What would you do if your best friend confided in you that he had cheated on an exam, or had handed in a paper he'd downloaded from the Internet? Are there any circumstances that would make you conceal some of what you know? Are there circumstances that would make you reveal it?

Can you think of an example of a situation or circumstance when you might choose to do something that is ordinarily considered "wrong"? Why would you make such a choice? What are the implications of such a stand regarding ethics?

SOME QUESTIONS ABOUT ETHICS

In this chapter we have been looking at the ways in which humans relate to each other in their lives in the world and how cultural and religious traditions shape those relationships. The realm of ethics is the human attempt to put parameters around relationships in terms of how any given culture or tradition believes humans *should* relate to one another and often to the rest of the world. Throughout the chapter, we have encountered selections that raise more questions than they answer—welcome to the realm of ethics in particular and life in general! One thing that has become clear is that ethics and personal moral decision making are complex and sometimes defy easy answers and responses. The seemingly simple question of what constitutes "right" behavior or thought often does not draw unanimous agreement even within a single tradition or culture. The more complex life becomes, as illustrated at the beginning of the chapter by Lauren's struggles in Butler's *Parable of the Sower,* the more difficult it seems to be to be absolutely sure of just what one should do, how one should act.

And just how much responsibility do humans carry for their actions? We are all accustomed to reading about trials where the defendant pleads "not guilty by reason of insanity." What does this mean in terms of ethics, as opposed to a court of law? If our capacity for ethical judgment is diminished by mental illness, or other factors beyond our control, does this mean we are no longer accountable for our actions? The ability to make informed choices and to act upon them is referred to as moral agency. When our "agency" is diminished in any way, some would suggest that we cannot be held accountable to the same degree. We do not, for example, hold children responsible for their actions to the same degree that we do adults, and debates continue over whether it is acceptable to execute those who are developmentally disabled in any way. Are we responsible only if we *intend* to do harm, or also if the consequences are something we could have anticipated or expected?

Religious and cultural traditions give us guidelines for ethical behavior in many different genres and forms. From the formalized texts of the Baghavad Gita, the Tanakh, the Bible, and the Qur'an to the stories and proverbs passed on by word of mouth, the values of a tradition are transmitted across the generations. What contribution do these powerful and wise texts and stories make to contemporary communities? To what extent do they provide us with a continuing blueprint for ethical behavior in our own time and place?

The case of the conjoined twins Jodie and Mary that you read about earlier presented multiple values in conflict. We discussed briefly "virtue ethics," which suggests that the major moral task of an individual is the development of a virtuous character. There are other systems of ethics developed by philosophers over the years and that are relevant when we consider religious codes. "Teleological ethics" holds that one should make ethical decisions based upon the expected consequences; in its "utilitarian" form, this means choosing the action that will bring about the greatest good for the greatest number. "Deontological ethics," on the other hand, holds that we cannot know what the consequences of any particular action will be; thus we should make decisions on the basis of universal principles. If it is fundamentally wrong to kill, then it is always wrong to kill. More recently, "situational ethics" suggests that we cannot make ethical decisions in a vacuum and must consider the individual situation.

The case of the conjoined twins, Mary and Jodie, raised many complicated ethical issues that would be resolved differently by people coming from such diverse religious or philosophical perspectives. Some of these issues were cast in the media as a conflict between science and religious belief.

In a response to what he saw as a false dichotomy, Scottish Rabbi Tobias suggested that this particular dimension of the conflict could be enlightened by a better understanding of how religious texts and traditions inform our current decisions.

> As a rabbi, I assume I have the right to define myself as a religious person. Members of my congregation—and other congregations—presumably see themselves in the same terms. This manifests itself not in adherence to archaic and outdated practices and beliefs, but in a genuine attempt to learn about the world, using our ancestors' wisdom as a starting point.
>
> At this time of the year, a series of laws from the Book of Deuteronomy is read in synagogues. A fundamentalist approach to these laws would, of course, regard them as divine law to be obeyed without question, but that is not my position, nor that of reform or progressive Judaism.
>
> The latter approach to this religious text would see it as a collection of regulations, whose purpose was to establish a society which demonstrated justice, both individually and collectively, in the moral, political and social spheres of the existence of a group of people some 2,500 years ago. Such laws and regulations were an attempt by our ancestors to come to terms with a strange and puzzling world, and to create structures to promote justice and an understanding of the divine will.
>
> Thus it is that we read that it is forbidden to abuse a needy and destitute labourer, whether a fellow countryman or a stranger in one of the communities of your land (Deuteronomy 24:14). Thus it is that instruction is given not to subvert the rights of the stranger or the fatherless, nor to take a widow's garment in pawn (24:17). Thus it is that our ancestors are told not to gather every last sheaf, olive or grape at harvest time, but to leave some for those who are needy (24:19–21).
>
> Such laws are not the fundamentalist ravings of humans who subvert their own will and behaviour to the apparent demands of some invisible greater power. These are intelligent, sensible teachings, whose aim is to create justice— hardly the irrational perspective on the world which many supposed rationalists seem keen to assign to anything which defines itself as religious.
>
> The truth is that religion and rationalism are as entwined as—well, as conjoined twins, I suppose. . . .

Religion does not offer scientific and medical explanations and options. It does not (though some might consider it does) give pseudo-theological justification for tragic occurrences by regarding them as some kind of divine punishment for apparent previous failings. Instead, it offers a blanket of comfort, a framework within which elements of humanity that cannot be rationally defined—such as compassion and care—find expression.

And it is here that religion can speak out most clearly in a world seemingly obsessed with scientific and rational definitions—by recognising that there are elements of life which cannot be so easily quantified, that what makes us human is not our ability to rationalise and explain, but our capacity to care and support one another, to yearn for harmony and, where there is none, to hope and struggle against seemingly impossible odds to rediscover its possibility.[11]

How does Rabbi Tobias understand the role of the scriptural texts that are fundamental to his Jewish faith? And what kind of understanding of religion does he suggest leads the public to sometimes dismiss religious perspectives on difficult issues as "irrational and emotional"? Clearly the Rabbi is not dismissing the texts as irrelevant—far from it. He is suggesting that their wisdom and capacity to inform our own ethical decision making lie in fundamental principles of justice that underlie the specific rules, rules created in a specific time and place for purposes that made sense then but may not be relevant or adequate today.

WHAT SOME OTHERS HAVE SAID ABOUT ETHICS

One of the most difficult issues to address in the field of ethics is that of moral relativism. In the following selection, philosopher Mary Midgley addresses this issue. She asks us to consider whether we can and should make judgments about the rightness or wrongness of something when it is not in our own culture or religion. As you read Midgley's argument, consider how the points she makes might apply to ethical issues of which you are aware and which you know evoke different responses from different people. Does Midgley's argument make sense to you? What does she suggest will happen if we *don't* make any such judgments?

All of us are, more or less, in trouble today about trying to understand cultures strange to us. We hear constantly of alien customs. We see changes in our lifetime which would have astonished our parents. I want to discuss here one very short way of dealing with this difficulty, a drastic way which many people now theoretically favour. It consists in simply denying that we can ever understand any culture except our own well enough to make judgements about it. Those who recommend this hold that the world is sharply divided into separate societies, sealed units, each with its own system of thought. They feel that the respect and tolerance due from one system to another forbids us ever to take up a critical position to any other culture. Moral judgement, they suggest, is a kind of coinage valid only in its country of origin.

I shall call this position "moral isolationism." I shall suggest that it is certainly not forced upon us, and indeed that it makes no sense at all. People usually take it up because they think it is a respectful attitude to other cultures. In fact, however, it is not respectful. Nobody can respect what is entirely unintelligible to them. To respect someone, we have to know enough about him to make a *favourable* judgement, however general and tentative. And we do understand people in other cultures to this extent. Otherwise a great mass of our most valuable thinking would be paralysed.

To show this, I shall take a remote example, because we shall probably find it easier to think calmly about it than we should with a contemporary one, such as female circumcision in Africa or the Chinese Cultural Revolution. The principles involved will still be the same. My example is this. There is, it seems, a verb in classical Japanese which means "to try out one's new sword on a chance wayfarer." (The word is *tsujigiri*, literally "crossroads-cut.") A samurai sword had to be tried out because, if it was to work properly, it had to slice through someone at a single blow, from the shoulder to the opposite flank. Otherwise, the warrior bungled his stroke. This could injure his honour, offend his ancestors, and even let down his emperor. So tests were needed, and wayfarers had to be expended. Any wayfarer would do—provided, of course, that he was not another Samurai. Scientists will recognize a familiar problem about the rights of experimental subjects.

Now when we hear of a custom like this, we may well reflect that we simply do not understand it; and therefore are not qualified to criticize it at all, because we are not members of that culture. But we are not members of any other culture either, except our own. So we extend the principle to cover all extraneous cultures, and we seem therefore to be moral isolationists. But this is, as we shall see, an impossible position. Let us ask what it would involve.

We must ask first: Does the isolating barrier work both ways? Are people in other cultures equally unable to criticize *us*? This question struck me sharply when I read a remark in *The Guardian* by an anthropologist about a South American Indian who had been taken into a Brazilian town for an operation, which saved his life. When he came back to his village, he made several highly critical remarks about the white Brazilians' way of life. They may very well have been justified. But the interesting point was that the anthropologist called these remarks "a damning indictment of Western civilization." Now the Indian had been in that town about two weeks. Was he in a position to deliver a damning indictment? Would we ourselves be qualified to deliver such an indictment on the Samurai, provided we could spend two weeks in ancient Japan? What do we really think about this?

My own impression is that we believe that outsiders can, in principle, deliver perfectly good indictments—only, it usually takes more than two weeks to make them damning. Understanding has degrees. It is not a slapdash yes-or-no matter. Intelligent outsiders can progress in it, and in some ways will be at an advantage over the locals. But if this is so, it must clearly apply to ourselves as much as anybody else.

Our next question is this: Does the isolating barrier between cultures block praise as well as blame? If I want to say that the Samurai culture has many virtues, or to praise the South American Indians, am I prevented from doing *that* by my outside status? Now, we certainly do need to praise other societies in this way. But it is hardly possible that we could praise them effectively if we could not, in principle, criticize them. Our praise would be worthless if it rested on no definite grounds, if it did not flow from some understanding. Certainly we may need to praise things which we do not *fully* understand. We say "there's something very good here, but I can't quite make out what it is yet." This happens when we want to learn from strangers. And we can learn from strangers. But to do this we have to distinguish between those strangers who are worth learning from and those who are not. Can we then judge which is which?

This brings us to our third question: What is involved in judging? Now plainly there is no question here of sitting on a bench in a red robe and sentencing people. Judging simply means forming an opinion, and expressing it if it is called for. Is there anything wrong about this? Naturally, we ought to avoid forming— and *expressing—crude* opinions, like that of a simple-minded missionary, who might dismiss the whole Samurai culture as entirely bad, because non-Christian. But this is a different objection. The trouble with crude opinions is that they are crude, whoever forms them, not that they are formed by the wrong people. Anthropologists, after all, are outsiders quite as much as missionaries. Moral iso-lationism forbids us to form *any* opinions on these matters. Its ground for doing so is that we don't understand them. But there is much that we don't understand in our own culture too. This brings us to our last question: If we can't judge other cultures, can we really judge our own? Our efforts to do so will be much damaged if we are really deprived of our opinions about other societies, because these provide the range of comparison, the spectrum of alternatives against which we set what we want to understand. We would have to stop using the mir-ror which anthropology so helpfully holds up to us.

In short, moral isolationism would lay down a general ban on moral reasoning. Essentially, this is the programme of immoralism, and it carries a distressing logical difficulty. Immoralists like Nietzsche are actually just a rather specialized sect of moralists. They can no more afford to put moralizing out of business than smugglers can afford to abolish customs regulations. The power of moral judgement is, in fact, not a luxury, not a perverse indulgence of the self-righteous. It is a necessity. When we judge something to be bad or good, better or worse than something else, we are taking it as an example to aim at or avoid. Without opinions of this sort, we would have no framework of compari-son for our own policy, no chance of profiting by other people's insights or mis-takes. In this vacuum, we could form no judgements on our own actions.

Now it would be odd if Homo sapiens had really got himself into a position as bad as this—a position where his main evolutionary asset, his brain, was so little use to him. None of us is going to accept this sceptical diagnosis. We cannot do so, because our involvement in moral isolationism does not flow from apathy, but from a rather acute concern about human hypocrisy and other forms of wickedness. But we polarize that concern around a few selected moral truths. We are rightly angry with those who despise, oppress or steamroll other cultures. We think that doing these things is actually *wrong*. But this is itself a moral judgement. We could not condemn oppression and insolence if we thought that all our condemnations were just a trivial local quirk of our own culture. We could still less do it if we tried to stop judging altogether.

Real moral scepticism, in fact, could lead only to inaction, to our losing all interest in moral questions, most of all in those which concern other societies. When we discuss these things, it becomes instantly clear how far we are from doing this. Suppose, for instance, that I criticize the bisecting Samurai, that I say his behaviour is brutal. What will usually happen next is that someone will protest, will say that I have no right to make criticisms like that of another culture. But it is most unlikely that he will use this move to end the discussion of the subject. Instead, he will justify the Samurai. He will try to fill in the background, to make me understand the custom, by explaining the exalted ideals of discipline and devotion which produced it. He will probably talk of the lower value which the ancient Japanese placed on individual life generally. He may well suggest that this is a healthier attitude than our own obsession with security. He may add, too, that the wayfarers did not seriously mind being bisected, that in principle they accepted the whole arrangement.

Now an objector who talks like this is implying that it *is* possible to understand alien customs; that is just what he is trying to make me do. And he implies, too, that if I do succeed in understanding them, I shall do something better than giving up judging them. He expects me to change my present judgement to a truer one—namely, one that is favourable. And the standards I must use to do this cannot just be Samurai standards. They have to be ones current in my own culture. Ideals like discipline and devotion will not move anybody unless he himself accepts them. As it happens, neither discipline nor devotion is very popular in the West at present. Anyone who appeals to them may well have to do some more arguing to make *them* acceptable, before he can use them to explain the Samurai. But if he does succeed here, he will have persuaded us, not just that there was something to be said for them in ancient Japan, but that there would be here as well.

Isolating barriers simply cannot arise here. If we accept something as a serious moral truth about one culture, we can't refuse to apply it—in however different an outward form—to other cultures as well, wherever circumstance admit it. If we refuse to do this, we just are not taking the other culture seriously. This becomes clear if we look at the last argument used by my objector—that of justification by consent of the victim. It is suggested that sudden bisection is quite in order, *provided* that it takes place between consenting adults. I cannot now discuss how conclusive this justification is. What I am pointing out is simply that it can only work if we believe that *consent* can make such a transaction respectable—and this is a thoroughly modern and Western idea. It would probably never occur to a Samurai; if it did, it would surprise him very much. It is *our* standard. In applying it, too, we are likely to make another typically Western demand. We shall ask for good factual evidence that the wayfarers actually do have this rather surprising taste—that they are really willing to be bisected. In applying Western standards in this way, we are not being confused or irrelevant. We are asking the questions which arise *from where we stand,* questions which we can see the sense of. We do this because asking questions which you can't see the sense of is humbug. Certainly we can extend our questioning by imaginative effort. We can come to understand other societies better. By doing so, we may make their questions our own, or we may see that they are really forms of the questions which we are asking already. This is not impossible. It is just very hard work. The obstacles which often prevent it are simply those of ordinary ignorance, laziness and prejudice.

If there were really an isolating barrier, of course, our own culture could never have been formed. It is no sealed box, but a fertile jungle of different influences— Greek, Jewish, Roman, Norse, Celtic and so forth, into which further influences are still pouring—American, Indian, Japanese, Jamaican, you name it. The moral iso- lationist's picture of separate, unmixable cultures is quite unreal. People who talk about British history usually stress the value of this fertilizing mix, no doubt rightly. But this is not just an odd fact about Britain. Except for the very smallest and most remote, all cultures are formed out of many streams. All have the problem of digesting and assimilating things which, at the start, they do not understand. All have the choice of learning something from this challenge, or, alternatively, of refusing to learn, and fighting it mindlessly instead.

This universal predicament has been obscured by the fact that anthropolo- gists used to concentrate largely on very small and remote cultures, which did not seem to have this problem. These tiny societies, which had often forgotten their own history, made neat, self-contained subjects for study. No doubt it was valuable to emphasize their remoteness, their extreme strangeness, their inde- pendence of our cultural tradition. This emphasis was, I think, the root of moral isolationism. But, as the tribal studies themselves showed, even there the anthropologists were able to interpret what they saw and make judgements— often favourable—about the tribesmen. And the tribesmen, too, were quite equal to making judgements about the anthropologists—and about the tourists and Coca-Cola salesmen who followed them. Both sets of judgements, no doubt, were somewhat hasty, both have been refined in the light of further experience. A similar transaction between us and the Samurai might take even longer. But that is no reason at all for deeming it impossible. Morally as well as physically, there is only one world, and we all have to live in it.[12]

Where do you find yourself agreeing or disagreeing with Midgley? Some would say that you can make moral judgments about something, but this does not necessarily mean that you should be able to enforce your opinion on oth- ers. Do you think Midgley would agree with this? Others make a distinction between ethical relativism—the idea that ethics depends on personal and cul- turally defined norms so that we cannot make judgments about the morality of a group that is different from our own—and cultural pluralism—appreciation for the diversity of cultural beliefs and practices. Do you think Midgley would embrace cultural pluralism even as she rejects ethical relativism? Does she give us clues as to how we might respect other cultures with different values while at the same time not giving up our ability to make moral judgments?

CHAPTER SIX

WHAT DO WE MEAN BY JUSTICE? SEEKING THE COMMON GOOD

What is justice? Is it arresting a person suspected of a crime, then trying and punishing him or her? What is injustice? Do you think that "injustice" relates in any way to the "unfairness" we talked about in the last chapter? We discussed "fairness" and "unfairness" with regard to individual choices and actions, but can groups be "unfair," or "unjust?" What about governments and societies? Other organizations? Religious groups?

This brings us to what justice means in a religious context. Despite the fact that many religions claim that justice in society should be ensured by obedience to their rules and regulations, when we look more closely at religious traditions, we find that justice has to do with the common good of the people, not with narrow interpretations of "law and order." In fact, the people of Israel thought that Yahweh recognized that actions of justice were more effective in showing worship of Yahweh than were the offerings in the temple. Both Tanakh and Talmud make this point. Righteousness requires justice. And this concept held true for Christians as well. The beatitudes demonstrate a caring for the common good. Muslims also are familiar with this idea. *The Qur'an* states, in Surah 117, beginning at the 4th verse, "Ah, woe unto worshippers Who are heedless of their prayer, who would be seen (at worship) yet refuse small kindnesses!" And one of the bases of Islam is that of Zakat, tithing, to ensure that no one wants for those things that are needed in life.

Religions other than the Abrahamic religions also are concerned with justice. We only need to look at the writings of Thich Nhat Hanh or the Dalai Lama to see a Buddhist perspective on justice. Confucius taught that *li* (rights, ceremonies, and propriety) in the five relationships among persons—parent and child, husband and wife, older and younger brother, older friend and younger friend, emperor and subject—would automatically ensure justice. When those relationships were ignored, particularly by the emperor, injustice would result, and the mandate of heaven would be withdrawn, bringing about a change in emperors. The emperor had to fulfill his ceremonial duties, and he had to treat his subjects as he would his children.

In none of these understandings was justice perceived merely as "law and order." On the contrary, some laws grew out of religious notions of justice, and it was thought that the law could not and should not survive if it conflicted with justice.

SETTING THE STAGE: QUESTIONS OF THE COMMON GOOD

As we have seen, one major function that religions serve is to establish a system of ethics for both individuals and communities. When the religion is practiced within a larger community, its system of ethics may serve to critique and/or support the institutions of that society. You are probably aware of instances in your own community where religious ideas are put forward in support of, or in opposition to, proposed laws, policies, and practices. Some would argue that, in the United States, for example, with its constitutional separation of Church and State, to do this is an inappropriate attempt by a particular religion to influence policy that will affect everyone. Others might suggest that persons from a religious perspective have as much right as anyone else to make their own positions known. Still others believe that their particular religious orientation requires them to attempt to bring about what they perceive as a more "just" society.

Is attentiveness to our own morality enough, should we merely refrain from acting unjustly ourselves, or do we have a responsibility to correct what we see as injustice? Your response to these issues will affect the ways in which you respond to the first reading in this chapter. In her short story, "The Ones Who Walk Away from Omelas," Ursula LeGuin gives us a fictitious city where life seems idyllic. Or does it?

> With a clamor of bells that set the swallows soaring, the festival of Summer came to the city Omelas, bright-towered by the sea. The rigging of the boats in harbor sparkled with flags. In the streets between houses with red roofs and painted walls, between old moss-grown gardens and under avenues of trees, past great parks and public buildings, processions moved. Some were decorous: old people in long stiff robes of mauve and grey, grave master workmen, quiet, merry women carrying their babies and chatting as they walked. In other streets the music beat faster, a shimmering of gong and tambourine, and the people went dancing, the procession was a dance. Children dodged in and out, their high calls rising like the swallows' crossing flights over the music and the singing. All the processions wound towards the north side of the city, where on the great water-meadow called the Green Fields boys and girls, naked in the

bright air, with mud-stained feet and ankles and long, lithe arms, exercised their restive horses before the race. The horses wore no gear at all but a halter without bit. Their manes were braided with streamers of silver, gold, and green. They flared their nostrils and pranced and boasted to one another; they were vastly excited, the horse being the only animal who has adopted our ceremonies as his own. Far off to the north and west the mountains stood up half encircling Omelas on her bay. The air of morning was so clear that the snow still crowning the Eighteen Peaks burned with white-gold fire across the miles of sunlit air, under the dark blue of the sky. There was just enough wind to make the banners that marked the racecourse snap and flutter now and then. In the silence of the broad green meadows one could hear the music winding through the city streets, farther and nearer and ever approaching, a cheerful faint sweetness of the air that from time to time trembled and gathered together and broke out into the great joyous clanging of the bells.

Joyous! How is one to tell about joy? How describe the citizens of Omelas?

They were not simple folk, you see, though they were happy. But we do not say the words of cheer much any more. All smiles have become archaic. Given a description such as this one tends to make certain assumptions. Given a description such as this one tends to look next for the King, mounted on a splendid stallion and surrounded by his noble knights, or perhaps in a golden litter borne by great-muscled slaves. But there was no king. They did not use swords, or keep slaves. They were not barbarians. I do not know the rules and laws of their society, but I suspect that they were singularly few. As they did without monarchy and slavery, so they also got on without the stock exchange, the advertisement, the secret police, and the bomb. Yet I repeat that these were not simple folk, not dulcet shepherds, noble savages, bland utopians. They were not less complex than us. The trouble is that we have a bad habit, encouraged by pedants and sophisticates, of considering happiness as something rather stupid. Only pain is intellectual, only evil interesting. This is the treason of the artist: a refusal to admit the banality of evil and the terrible boredom of pain. If you can't lick 'em, join 'em. If it hurts, repeat it. But to praise despair is to condemn delight, to embrace violence is to lose hold of everything else. We have almost lost hold; we can no longer describe a happy man, nor make any celebration of joy. How can I tell you about the people of Omelas? They were not naive and happy children—though their children were, in fact, happy. They were mature, intelligent, passionate adults whose lives were not wretched. O miracle! but I wish I could describe it better. I wish I could convince you. Omelas sounds in my words like a city in a fairy tale, long ago and far away, once upon a time. Perhaps it would be best if you imagined it as your own fancy bids, assuming it will rise to the occasion, for certainly I cannot suit you all. For instance, how about technology? I think that there would be no cars or helicopters in and above the streets; this follows from the fact that the people of Omelas are happy people. Happiness is based on a just discrimination of what is necessary, what is neither necessary nor destructive, and what is destructive. In the middle category, however—that of the unnecessary but undestructive, that of comfort, luxury, exuberance etc.—they could perfectly well have central heating, subway trains, washing machines, and all kinds of marvelous devices not yet invented here, floating light-sources, fuelless power, a cure for the common cold. Or they could have none of that: it doesn't matter. As you like it. I incline to think that people from towns up and down the coast have been coming in to Omelas during the last days before the Festival on very fast little trains and double-decked trams, and that the train station of Omelas is actually the handsomest building in town, though plainer than the magnificent Farmers' Market. But even granted trains, I fear that Omelas so far strikes some of you as goody-goody. Smiles, bells, parades, horses, bleh. If so, please add an orgy. If an orgy would help, don't hesitate. Let us not, however, have temples from which issue beautiful nude priests and priestesses already half in ecstasy and ready to copulate with any man or woman, lover or stranger, who desires union with the deep godhead of the blood, although that was my first idea. But really it would be better not to have any temples in Omelas—at least, not manned temples. Religion yes, clergy no. Surely the beautiful nudes can just wander about, offering themselves like divine soufflés to the hunger of the needy and the rapture of the flesh. Let them join the processions. Let tambourines be struck above the copulations, and the glory of desire be proclaimed upon the gongs, and (a not unimportant point) let the offspring of these delightful rituals be beloved and looked after by all. One thing I know there is none of in Omelas is guilt. But what else should there be? I thought at first there were no drugs, but that is puritanical. For those who like it, the faint insistent sweetness of *drooz* may perfume the ways of the city, *drooz* which first brings a great lightness and brilliance to the mind and limbs, and then after some hours a dreamy languor, and wonderful visions at last of the very arcana and inmost secrets of the Universe, as well as exciting the pleasure of sex beyond all belief; and it is not habit-forming. For more modest tastes I think there ought to be beer. What else, what else belongs in the joyous city? The sense of victory, surely, the celebration of courage. But as we did without clergy, let us do without soldiers. The joy built upon successful slaughter is not the right kind of joy; it will not do; it is fearful and it is trivial. A boundless and generous contentment, a magnanimous triumph felt not against some outer enemy but in communion with the finest and fairest in the souls of all men everywhere and the splendor of the world's summer: this is what swells the hearts of the people of Omelas, and the victory they celebrate is that of life. I really don't think many of them need to take *drooz*.

Most of the processions have reached the Green Fields by now. A marvelous smell of cooking goes forth from the red and blue tents of the provisioners. The faces of small children are amiably sticky; in the benign grey beard of a man a couple of crumbs of rich pastry are entangled. The youths and girls have mounted their horses and are beginning to group around the starting line of the course. An old woman, small, fat, and laughing, is passing out flowers from a basket, and tall young men wear her flowers in their shining hair. A child of nine or ten sits at the edge of the crowd, alone, playing on a wooden flute. People pause to listen, and they smile, but they do not speak to him, for he never ceases playing and never sees them, his dark eyes wholly rapt in the sweet, thin magic of the tune.

He finishes, and slowly lowers his hands holding the wooden flute.

As if that little private silence were the signal, all at once a trumpet sounds from the pavilion near the starting line: imperious, melancholy, piercing. The horses rear on their slender legs, and some of them neigh in answer. Sober-faced, the young riders stroke the horses' necks and soothe them, whispering, "Quiet, quiet, there my beauty, my hope. . . . " They begin to form in rank along the starting line. The crowds along the racecourse are like a field of grass and flowers in the wind. The Festival of Summer has begun.

Do you believe? Do you accept the festival, the city, the joy? No? Then let me describe one more thing.

In a basement under one of the beautiful public buildings of Omelas, or perhaps in the cellar of one of its spacious private homes, there is a room. It has one locked door, and no window. A little light seeps in dustily between cracks in the boards, secondhand from a cobwebbed window somewhere across the cellar. In one corner of the little room a couple of mops, with stiff, clotted, foul-smelling heads, stand near a rusty bucket. The floor is dirt, a little damp to the touch, as cellar dirt usually is. The room is about three paces long and two wide: a mere broom closet or disused tool room. In the room a child is sitting. It could be a boy or a girl. It looks about six, but actually is nearly ten. It is feeble-minded. Perhaps it was born defective, or perhaps it has become imbecile through fear, malnutrition, and neglect. It picks its nose and occasion-ally fumbles vaguely with its toes or genitals as it sits hunched in the corner farthest from the bucket and the two mops. It is afraid of the mops. It finds them horrible. It shuts its eyes, but it knows the mops are still standing there; and the door is locked; and nobody will come. The door is always locked; and nobody ever comes, except that sometimes—the child has no understanding of time or interval—sometimes the door rattles terribly and opens, and a person, or several people, are there. One of them may come in and kick the child to make it stand up. The others never come close, but peer in at it with frightened, disgusted eyes. The food bowl and the water jug are hastily filled, the door is locked, the eyes disappear. The people at the door never say anything, but the child, who has not always lived in the tool room and can remember sunlight and its mother's voice, sometimes speaks. "I will be good" it says, "Please let me out. I will be good!" They never answer. The child used to scream for help at night, and cry a good deal, but now it only makes a kind of whining, "eh-haa, eh-haa," and it speaks less and less often. It is so thin there are no calves to its legs; its belly protrudes; it lives on a half-bowl of corn meal and grease a day. It is naked. Its buttocks and thighs are a mass of festered sores, as it sits in its own excrement continually.

They all know it is there, all the people of Omelas. Some of them have come to see it, others are content merely to know it is there. They all know that it has to be there. Some of them understand why, and some do not, but they all understand that their happiness, the beauty of their city, the tenderness of their friendships, the health of their children, the wisdom of their scholars, the skill of their makers, even the abundance of their harvest and weathers of their skies, depend wholly on this child's abominable misery.

This is usually explained to children when they are between eight and twelve, whenever they seem capable of understanding; and most of those who come to see the child are young people, though often enough an adult comes, or comes back, to see the child. No matter how well the matter has been explained to them, these young spectators are always shocked and sickened at the sight. They feel disgust, which they had thought themselves superior to. They feel anger, outrage, impotence, despite all the explanations. They would like to do something for the child. But there is nothing they can do. If the child were brought up into the sunlight out of that vile place, if it were cleaned and fed and comforted, that would be a good thing, indeed; but if it were done, in that day and hour all the prosperity and beauty and delight of Omelas would wither and be destroyed. Those are the terms. To exchange all the goodness and grace of every life in Omelas for that single small improvement: to throw away the happiness of thousands for the chance of the happiness of one: that would be to let guilt within the walls indeed.

The terms are strict and absolute; there may not even be a kind word spoken to the child.

Often the young people go home in tears, or in a tearless rage when they have seen the child and faced this terrible paradox. They may brood over it for weeks or years. But as time goes on they begin to realize that even if the child could be released, it would not get much good of its freedom: a little vague pleasure of warmth and food, no doubt, but little more. It is too degraded and imbecile to know any real joy. It has been afraid too long ever to be free of fear. Its habits are too uncouth for it to respond to humane treatment. Indeed, after so long it would probably be wretched without walls about it to protect it, and darkness for its eyes, and its own excrement to sit in. Their tears at the bitter injustice dry when they begin to perceive the terrible justice of reality and to accept it. Yet it is their tears and anger, the trying of their generosity and the acceptance of their helplessness which are perhaps the true source of the splendor of their lives. Theirs is no vapid, irresponsible happiness. They know that they, like the child, are not free. They know compassion. It is the existence of the child, and their knowledge of its existence, that makes possible the nobility of their architecture, the poignancy of their music, the profundity of their science. It is because of the child that they are so gentle with children. They know that if the wretched one were not there snivelling in the dark, the other one, the flute-player, could make no joyful music as the young riders line up in their beauty for the race in the sunlight of the first morning of summer.

Now do you believe in them? Are they not more credible? But there is one more thing to tell, and this is quite incredible.

At times one of the adolescent girls or boys who go to see the child does not go home to weep or rage, does not in fact go home at all. Sometimes also a man or woman much older falls silent for a day or two, and then leaves home. These people go out into the street, and walk down the street alone. They keep walking, and walk straight out of the city of Omelas, through the beautiful gates. They keep walking across the farmlands of Omelas. Each one goes alone, youth or girl, man or woman. Night falls; the traveler must pass down village streets, between the houses with yellow-lit windows, and on out into the darkness of the fields. Each alone, they go west or north, towards the mountains. They go on. They leave Omelas, they walk ahead into the darkness and they do not come back. The place they go towards is a place even less imaginable to most of us than the city of happiness. I cannot describe it at all. It is possible that it does not exist. But they seem to know where they are going, the ones who walk away from Omelas.[1]

Are you one of the ones who walk away from Omelas? If so, why do you do this? What good does it do for you, for the city, for the child? Is merely refusing to benefit from the child's misery enough?

What would you do if you stayed? Would it be your responsibility to do anything? After all, you didn't put the child in the closet. Why should you or any of the other regular citizens feel guilty, or responsible for doing anything? Would it be morally right to sacrifice the good of the entire city for the good of the child? Has the threat of the destruction of Omelas as it is ever been tested? Should it be, if it has not? What if the child is too badly traumatized by his/her captivity to become truly human again? Does that make a difference in your choice?

We do not know who demands the imprisonment of the child, only that it must be done for the good of Omelas. Is this story purely a fiction, or is it a metaphor? In other words, are there situations you can think of where the well-being of one individual or a group is sacrificed for the good of others?

We usually decide what is right on the basis of what we have learned growing up. It might be helpful to distinguish between "fairness" and "justice," and to consider whether they always lead to the same conclusions. If we think of "fairness" as pertaining to individuals and "justice" relating more to the common good, we might ask ourselves whether what is "just" is always what is "fair"—and whether it should be. The story of Omelas has us look at this conflict. Apparently, some power has made Omelas an "ideal" place to live—no hunger, no crime, great happiness. But this ideal exacts a particular price—the absolute degradation of the child. To reject the cost means to invite hunger, crime, and unhappiness into the city. Is it right that the citizens must make this choice? Does the "common good" demand that the child remain locked in the closet? Can the issue be placed in such simple, dualistic terms?

WHAT DO YOU THINK?
JUSTICE AND SOCIAL RESPONSIBILITY

In her essay collection *Small Wonder*, Barbara Kingsolver recounts a personal experience of being faced with a dilemma about whether or not to act in the face of injustice. As you read Kingsolver's account, think about what you would do in a similar situation.

I was headed home with my mind on things. I can't even say what they were. It was an afternoon not very long ago, and probably I was ticking through the routine sacrament of my day—locating every member of my family at that moment and organizing how we would all come together for dinner and what I would feed us—when my thoughts were bluntly interrupted. A woman was being attacked fifty feet away from me. My heart thumped and then seemed to stop for good and then thumped hard again as I watched what was happening. The woman was slight, probably no taller than my older daughter, but she was my age. Her attacker, a much taller man, had no weapon but was hitting her on the head and face with his fists and open hands, screaming, calling her vile names right out in the open. She ducked, in the way any animal would, to save the more fragile bones of her face. She tried to turn her back on him, but he pursued her, smacking at her relentlessly with the flat of his hand and shouting angrily that she was trash, she was nothing, she should get away from him. And she was trying, but she couldn't. I felt my body freeze as they approached. They came very close, maybe ten feet away or even less, and then they moved on past us. I say *us* because I wasn't alone here: I was in a crowd of several dozen people, all within earshot. Maybe there were closer to a hundred of us; I'm not sure. Unbelievably, most weren't even looking. And then I did my own unbelievable thing: I left. I moved forward toward my home and family and left that battered woman behind.

I did and I didn't leave her behind, because I'm still thinking and now writing about this scene, reviling my own cowardice. Reader, can you believe I did what I did? Does it seem certain that I am heartless?

Let me give some more details of the scene, not because I hope to be forgiven. I ask only that all of us try to find ourselves in this weird landscape. It was the United States of America. I was at a busy intersection, in a car. The woman had the leathery, lined face and tattered-looking hair of a person who lives her whole life outdoors beneath the sun. So did her attacker. Both of them wore the clothes that make for an instantly recognizable uniform: shirts and pants weathered by hard daily wear to a neutral color and texture. Her possessions, and his, were stuffed into two bulky backpacks that leaned against a signpost in a median dividing six lanes of city traffic. I was in the middle lane of traffic on one side. All of the other people in this crowd were also in automobiles, on either side of me, opposite me, ahead and behind, most of them with their windows rolled up, listening to the radio or talking on cell phones. From what I could tell, no one else was watching this woman get beaten up and chased across three, then six, then nine separate lanes of traffic in the intersecting streets. I considered how I could get out of my car (should I leave it idling? lock it? what?) and run toward this woman and man, shouting at him to stop, begging the other drivers to use their phones to call the police. And then, after I had turned over this scenario in my mind for eight or nine seconds, the light changed and every car but mine began to move, and I had to think instead about the honking horns, the blocked traffic, the public nuisance I was about to become, and all the people who would shake their heads at my do-gooder foolishness and inform me that I should stay away from these rough-looking characters because this was obviously a domestic dispute.

> But that could not have been true. It was not domestic. *Domestic* means "of the home," and these people had no home. That was the problem—theirs, mine, everybody's. These people were beneath or somehow outside the laws that govern civil behavior between citizens of our country. They were homeless.[2]

Is Kingsolver right that "the problem—theirs, mine, everybody's" is that the two individuals were clearly homeless? Is Kingsolver suggesting that homeless people in contemporary U.S. culture are somehow like the child in Omelas? Are there similarities between the two examples? Are there other individuals or groups, either today or historically, that might be considered "expendable" for the common good?

If we do have some responsibility for one another, to which "others" does that responsibility apply? To return to the issue of "justice" and "fairness," we might question whether it is "fair" that those of us who are employed should pay taxes to support people on welfare, to build subsidized housing, to educate other people's children, or to provide health care for people who are unemployed (or unemployable) or whose jobs do not offer benefits. Does justice (the common good) demand—morally if not legally—that we step in and help when we see someone in some kind of trouble? What happens if we don't?

Some groups are concerned about our responsibility for future generations. For example, the Iroquois people operated—and still operate in their tribal business—on a principle we might call the "seventh generation." This means that all decisions made by the group must be considered not only in light of current needs, but in terms of the effect such decisions would have for future generations. In an introduction to his interview with two members of the Six Nations of the Haudenosaunee, often known as the Iroquois, Steven McFadden refers to and quotes from their 1978 publication, *Basic Call to Consciousness*:

> Through this document, Native Americans are essentially calling for righteousness. . . . "Righteousness occurs," they write, "when the people put their minds and emotions in flow with the harmony of the universe and the intentions of the Good Mind, or Great Creator. The principles of righteousness demand that all thoughts of prejudice, privilege or superiority be swept away and that recognition be given to the reality that Creation is intended for the benefit of all equally—even the birds and the animals, the trees and insects, as well as the human beings.
>
> "In the beginning, we were told that the human beings who walk about on the Earth have been provided with all of the things necessary for life. We were instructed to carry love for one another, and to show a great respect for all the beings of this Earth. We were shown that our well-being depends on the well-being of the vegetable life, that we are close relatives of the four-legged beings. . . . We give a greeting and thanksgiving to the many supporters of our own lives—the corn, the beans, the squash, the winds, the sun."
>
> A fundamental tenet of native cosmology places people in a balanced relationship with the Earth. As the elders write in *Basic Call*, "Our philosophy

An Onon Jaga clan mother, member of a secret medicine society and keeper of the ancestor ceremonies.

teaches us to treat the natural world with great care. Our institutions, practices, and technologies were developed with a careful eye to their potential for disturbing the delicate balance we lived in."

They say that whenever we are about to create or buy something—from gene splicing to laundry soap—we should first consider the effect it will have on the next seven generations. Only when we believe our actions and creations will be life supporting over this long span of time should we proceed.

Putting it another way, these elders call upon us to respect not just the rights of other human beings, but the rights of all beings of Creation: "The people who are living on this planet need to break with the narrow concept of human liberation, and begin to see liberation as something which needs to be extended to the whole of the Natural World. What is needed is the liberation of all the things that support life—the air, the waters, the trees—all the things which support the sacred web of life."[3]

What would it mean in our own context to take seriously this principle? If we did so, which of our actions do you think we would most need to reexamine? How would decision making regarding business and political issues change?

Develop a model for a business that takes seriously this ideal of the seventh generation. Consider the acquisition of goods and/or materials, the treatment of employees, etc. Could your plan work?

CULTURAL AND SOCIAL PERSPECTIVES ON JUSTICE

Often we think of justice as something handed out in a court of law. But justice in the context of religious understandings often has implications other than merely what we are required by law to do. According to the Confucian scholar, Mencius, a sense of justice is what defines our very humanity. Mencius has a very optimistic view of human nature. As you read what he has to say about justice, ask yourself how realistic his perspective is in light of the world you know. How do you think Mencius would evaluate the world we live in today?

> Mencius said, "It is a feeling common to all mankind that they cannot bear to see others suffer. The Former Kings had such feelings, and it was this that dictated their policies. One could govern the entire world with policies dictated by such feelings, as easily as though one turned it in the palm of the hand.
>
> "I say that all men have such feelings because, on seeing a child about to fall into a well, everyone has a feeling of horror and distress. They do not have this feeling out of sympathy for the parents, or to be thought well of by friends and neighbours, or from a sense of dislike at not being thought a feeling person. Not to feel distress would be contrary to all human feeling. Just as not to feel shame and disgrace and not to defer to others and not to have a sense of right and wrong are contrary to all human feeling. This feeling of distress (at the suffering of others) is the first sign of Humanity. This feeling of shame and disgrace is the first sign of justice. This feeling of deference to others is the first sign of propriety. This sense of right and wrong is the first sign of wisdom. Men have these four innate feelings just as they have four limbs. To possess these four things, and to protest that one is incapable of fulfilling them, is to deprive oneself. To protest that the ruler is incapable of doing so is to deprive him. Since all have these four capacities within themselves, they should know how to develop and to fulfil them. They are like a fire about to burst into flame, or a spring about to gush forth from the ground. If, in fact, a ruler can fully realize them, he has all that is needed to protect the entire world. But if he does not realize them fully, he lacks what is needed to serve even his own parents."[4]

Do you find what Mencius says about "humanity" persuasive? Do you agree that it is a basic human capacity to be unable to stand seeing someone else suffer? Is the alleviation of such suffering what constitutes "justice"?

What kinds of suffering are currently obvious in your community? What activities could resolve the suffering? Who would have to get involved?

HOW DO WE KNOW WHAT'S JUST?

What religious traditions often provide for their followers is some kind of vision of what a truly just society would look like, along with some guidelines and principles to inspire followers to attempt to achieve at least an approximation of the ideal. Sometimes they will have their own highly developed code of law to which believers are supposed to subscribe. We saw some of these in the preceding chapter on ethics. One religious approach to justice is discussed in the following passages from the Tanakh, the Hebrew Scriptures.

As with many such traditions, observance of the Sabbath has its roots far back in Hebrew history. You might be familiar with the creation story in the first chapter of Genesis, the first book in the Tanakh, in which Yahweh—God— creates the world in six days and then rests on the seventh day, known as the Sabbath. This day is still very important to observant Jews, who continue this tradition. But the concept of Sabbath is more important in Hebrew religious history, and in Hebrew ideas of justice, than simply as a day off from the work and cares of daily life. Notice in this next passage that the concept of justice is extended beyond just the human members of the Hebrew people. What idea of "justice" begins to emerge as you read on in the book of Exodus? Notice too the rationale that is given for the particular kind of treatment that should be extended to those who are not members of the community.

> You shall not oppress a stranger, for you know the feelings of the stranger, having yourselves been strangers in the land of Egypt.
>
> Six years you shall sow your land and gather in its yield; but in the seventh year you shall let it rest and lie fallow. Let the needy among your people eat of it, and what they leave let the wild beasts eat. You shall do the same with your vineyards and your olive groves.
>
> Six days you shall do your work, but on the seventh day you shall cease from labor, in order that your ox and your ass may rest, and that your bondman and the stranger may be refreshed.[5]

How do these mandates relate to the idea of "Sabbath" discussed above? What is the relationship between the religious faith of the people in the God who led them out of slavery and promised to be with them always and the rules they are developing to structure their communal life? Are there areas where you think the Hebrew society was unjust according to your own beliefs about justice? Keep these questions in mind as you read on.

> Every seventh year you shall practice remission of debts. This shall be the nature of the remission: every creditor shall remit the due that he claims from his fellow; he shall not dun his fellow or kinsman, for the remission proclaimed is of the LORD. You may dun the foreigner; but you must remit whatever is due you from your kinsmen.
>
> There shall be no needy among you—since the LORD your God will bless you in the land that the LORD your God is giving you as a hereditary portion—if only you heed the LORD your God and take care to keep all this Instruction that I enjoin upon you this day. For the LORD your God will bless you as He has promised you: you will extend loans to many nations, but require none yourself; you will dominate many nations, but they will not dominate you.
>
> If, however, there is a needy person among you, one of your kinsmen in any of your settlements in the land that the LORD your God is giving you, do not

harden your heart and shut your hand against your needy kinsman. Rather, you must open your hand and lend him sufficient for whatever he needs. Beware lest you harbor the base thought, "The seventh year, the year of remission, is approaching," so that you are mean to your needy kinsman and give him nothing. He will cry out to the LORD against you, and you will incur guilt. Give to him readily and have no regrets when you do so, for in return the LORD your God will bless you in all your efforts and in all your undertakings. For there will never cease to be needy ones in your land, which is why I command you: open your hand to the poor and needy kinsman in your land. If a fellow Hebrew, man or woman, is sold to you, he shall serve you six years, and in the seventh year you shall set him free. When you set him free, do not let him go empty-handed: Furnish him out of the flock, threshing floor, and vat, with which the LORD your God has blessed you. Bear in mind that you were slaves in the land of Egypt and the LORD your God redeemed you; therefore I enjoin this commandment upon you today.

But should he say to you, "I do not want to leave you"—for he loves you and your household and is happy with you—you shall take an awl and put it through his ear into the door, and he shall become your slave in perpetuity. Do the same with your female slave. When you do set him free, do not feel aggrieved; for in the six years he has given you double the service of a hired man. Moreover, the LORD your God will bless you in all you do.[6]

Have you ever heard those who invoke the Bible to "prove" an ethical point quote these particular passages? And the challenge doesn't stop with simple rules regarding the behavior of humans toward one another:

The LORD spoke to Moses on Mount Sinai: Speak to the Israelite people and say to them:

When you enter the land that I assign to you, the land shall observe a sabbath of the LORD. Six years you may sow your field and six years you may prune your vineyard and gather in the yield. But in the seventh year the land shall have a sabbath of complete rest, a sabbath of the LORD: you shall not sow your field or prune your vineyard. You shall not reap the aftergrowth of your harvest or gather the grapes of your untrimmed vines: it shall be a year of complete rest for the land. But you may eat whatever the land during its Sabbath will produce—you, your male and female slaves, the hired and your bound laborers who live with you; and your cattle and the beasts in your land may eat all its yield. . . .

[A]nd you shall hallow the fiftieth year. You shall proclaim release throughout the land for all its inhabitants. It shall be a jubilee for you: each of you shall return to his holding and each of you shall return to his family. That fiftieth year shall be a jubilee for you: you shall not sow, neither shall you reap the aftergrowth, or harvest the untrimmed vines. For it is a jubilee. It shall be holy to you: you may only eat the growth direct from the field. . . .

If your kinsman, being in straits, comes under your authority, and you hold him as though a resident alien, let him live by your side; do not exact from him advance or accrued interest, but fear your God. . . .

If your kinsman under you continues in straits and must give himself over to you, do not subject him to the treatment of a slave. He shall remain with you as a hired or bound laborer; he shall serve with you only until the jubilee year. Then he and his children with him shall be free of your authority; he shall go back to his family and return to his ancestral holding. For they are my servants, whom I freed from the land of Egypt; they may not give themselves over into servitude. . . .

If he has not been redeemed in any of those ways, he and his children with him shall go free in the jubilee year. For it is to Me that the Israelites are servants; they are My servants, whom I freed from the land of Egypt: I the LORD your God.[7]

Are the rules regarding ownership of the land fair? What assumptions are made about the owning of slaves? Are there injustices here that you think our contemporary world has addressed? Is there justice that we could learn from? How do you think our state or federal governments, or the chief executives of major companies and corporations, would feel about some of these demands? How might today's credit card companies and the banks standing behind them react to these commandments regarding the remission of debts? Would you be willing to lend a friend money knowing that if he or she had not repaid it by the end of seven years, you would have to forgive the debt? Might there be circumstances in which you'd remit the debt prior to seven years?

It's important to note that there is no evidence that these strictures about the year of Jubilee were ever observed totally even by the Israelites, but do they make any kind of sense in the context of justice? What do you think are the basic principles behind these mandates? Could such demands ever be appropriate for larger social entities, or do they apply only to individuals, and maybe the religious groups to which they belong? How might a group that believes in these ideals challenge and critique our own contemporary society?

These same passages from the Tanakh form part of the Christian Bible. This represents in very clear form the relationship of Jesus of Nazareth and his early followers with their Jewish heritage. Indeed, not until almost a century after the death of Jesus did his followers think of themselves as anything other than a sect within Judaism. It is not surprising, then, that our next excerpt, from the Christian Gospel of Luke, reiterates many of the same themes you have just encountered. In what ways do Jesus' words challenge his followers to continue in the spirit of their Jewish forebears?

Then Jesus, filled with the power of the Spirit, returned to Galilee, and a report about him spread through all the surrounding country. He began to teach in their synagogues and was praised by everyone. When he came to Nazareth, where he had been brought up, he went to the synagogue on the sabbath day, as was his custom. He stood up to read, and the scroll of the prophet Isaiah was given to him. He unrolled the scroll and found the place where it was written: "The Spirit of the LORD is upon me, because he has anointed me to bring good news to the poor. He has sent me to proclaim release to the captives and recovery of sight to the blind, to let the oppressed go free, to proclaim the year of the LORD's favor."[8]

Liberation from injustice was and is a very important idea for the Jewish people, and this theme finds many echoes in the Christian scriptures, as well as in at least some strands of Christian history and practice. One need only listen to the speeches of Martin Luther King, Jr., or view the movie *Romero,* on the life of assassinated Salvadoran Archbishop Oscar Romero, to see the extent to which deep religious faith can lead to a commitment to work for social justice.

Can "deep religious faith" exist without this commitment to work for social justice? What specific activities or ways of living would you suggest to indicate deep religious commitment?

Of course, Judaism and Christianity are not the only religions with a history of concern for the entire community, for the common good. Traditions such as Hinduism and Buddhism are often perceived as focused solely on the individual and thus less concerned with social change, social justice. But the life of Mohandas K. Gandhi illustrates the way in which commitment to the principles of his own Hindu faith led to a life of extraordinary activism and accomplishment. As you read this next selection, note places where you think Gandhi's perspectives are similar to or different from those of Mencius, or the Jewish and Christian ideas presented above. What do you think Gandhi would have thought of these others? What might Mencius, the Hebrew people, and Jesus and his followers have thought of Gandhi's perspective?

My uniform experience has convinced me that there is no other God than Truth. And if every page of these chapters does not proclaim to the reader that the only means for the realization of Truth is non-violence, I shall deem all my labor in writing to have been in vain. And, even though my efforts in this behalf may prove fruitless, let the readers know that the vehicle, not the great principle, is at fault. After all, however sincere my strivings after *Ahimsa* [non-violence] may have been, they have still been imperfect and inadequate. The little fleeting glimpses, therefore, that I have been able to have of Truth can hardly convey an idea of the indescribable luster of Truth, a million times more intense than that of the sun we daily see with our eyes. In fact what I have caught is only the faintest glimmer of that mighty effulgence. But this much I can say with assurance, as a result of all my experiments, that a perfect vision of Truth can only follow a complete realization of *Ahimsa.*

To see the universal and all-pervading Spirit of Truth face to face one must be able to love the meanest of creation as oneself. And a man who aspires after that cannot afford to keep out of any field of life. That is why my devotion to Truth has drawn me into the field of politics; and I can say without the slightest hesitation, and yet in all humility, that those who say that religion has nothing to do with politics do not know what religion means.

Identification with everything that lives is impossible without self-purification; without self-purification the observance of the law of *Ahimsa* must remain an empty dream; God can never be realized by one who is not pure of heart. Self-purification therefore must mean purification in all the walks of life. And purification being highly infectious, purification of oneself necessarily leads to the purification of one's surroundings.

But the path of self-purification is hard and steep. To attain to perfect purity one has to become absolutely passion-free in thought, speech, and action; to rise above the opposing currents of love and hatred, attachment and repulsion. I know that I have not in me as yet that triple purity, in spite of constant ceaseless striving for it. That is why the world's praise fails to move me, indeed it very often stings me. To conquer the subtle passions seems to me to be harder far than the physical conquest of the world by the force of arms. Ever since my return to India I have had experiences of the dormant passions lying hidden within me. The knowledge of them has made me feel humiliated though not defeated. The experiences and experiments have sustained me and given me a great joy. But I know that I have still before me a difficult path to traverse. I must reduce myself to zero. So long as a man does not of his own free will put himself last among his fellow creatures, there is no salvation for him. *Ahimsa* is the farthest limit of humility.

In bidding farewell to the reader, for the time being at any rate, I ask him to join with me in prayer to the God of Truth that He may grant me the boon of *Ahimsa* in mind, word, and deed.[9]

Gandhi's life brought him into contact with many of the world's religious traditions, including Christianity, Buddhism, and Islam in addition to his own Hinduism. Indeed, he encountered his own tradition in more depth during his time studying law in London than he had done prior to that time. One of the most remarkable things about Gandhi's life was that he did not "recruit" followers, yet people did indeed follow him in the tens of thousands, particularly in his native India when he opposed the continuing violence of British rule. What do you think might account for this?

We cannot study history at all, or pick up a daily newspaper, without being aware of conflicts over the meaning of "justice," in a religious and a secular sense. One of the issues religions have to deal with is how their idea of justice relates to persons outside of the specific tradition. Notice the ways in which the Jubilee passages from the Hebrew Scriptures address this issue explicitly. What might have been Gandhi's response to conflict between adherents of different religious faiths? Gandhi ended his life convinced of his own failure, because the newly independent India was split into Hindu and Muslim states. Why do you think this was such a great source of grief to him? Why might Gandhi's commitment to *ahimsa*, nonviolence, have provoked another Indian Hindu to assassinate him?

Does justice demand nonviolence, as Gandhi and Martin Luther King, Jr., suggest? Can justice be achieved through violence?

DO WE ALWAYS KNOW WHAT'S JUST?

Gandhi and his assassin had very different ideas about what constituted justice. Yet both were faithful Hindus who took the Bhagavad Gita seriously as a foundational religious text.

You can no doubt think of many issues that concern your community, your country, or a wider global population about which people have very different ideas about what constitutes "justice." The conflict in the Middle East is a centuries-old conflict based on the issue of rights to land, to a homeland. Contemporary political tensions there and the violence itself mask complex and difficult realities that underlie the conflict. The following excerpts, while perhaps clarifying some of the reasons why tensions in the Middle East seem so intractable, illustrate the difficulty of a just solution in situations where the "common good" is difficult to define, let alone achieve. The first excerpt is from the charter written in 1948 upon the founding of the State of Israel. Following the horrific events of World War II, world opinion strongly favored the idea of a Jewish homeland, in order that Jewish people worldwide would never again be left with no place to turn as had happened during Hitler's genocidal campaign.

> The State of Israel will be open for Jewish immigration and for the Ingathering of the Exiles; it will foster the development of the country for the benefit of all its inhabitants; it will be based on freedom, justice and peace as envisaged by the prophets of Israel; it will ensure complete equality of social and political rights to all its inhabitants irrespective of religion, race or sex; it will guarantee freedom of religion, conscience, language, education and culture; it will safeguard the Holy Places of all religions; and it will be faithful to the principles of the Charter of the United Nations.
>
> The State of Israel is prepared to cooperate with the agencies and representatives of the United Nations in implementing the resolution of the General Assembly of the 29th November, 1947, and will take steps to bring about the economic union of the whole of Eretz-Israel.
>
> We appeal to the United Nations to assist the Jewish people in the building-up of its State and to receive the State of Israel into the comity of nations.
>
> We appeal—in the very midst of the onslaught launched against us now for months—to the Arab inhabitants of the State of Israel to preserve peace and participate in the upbuilding of the State on the basis of full and equal citizenship and due representation in all its provisional and permanent institutions.
>
> We extend our hand to all neighbouring states and their peoples in an offer of peace and good neighbourliness, and appeal to them to establish bonds of cooperation and mutual help with the sovereign Jewish people settled in its own land. The State of Israel is prepared to do its share in a common effort for the advancement of the entire Middle East.

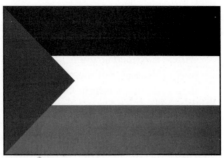

Israeli flag   Palestinian flag

We appeal to the Jewish people throughout the Diaspora to rally round the Jews of Eretz-Israel in the tasks of immigration and upbuilding and to stand by them in the great struggle for the realization of the age-old dream—the redemption of Israel.

Placing our trust in the Almighty, we affix our signatures to this proclamation at this session of the provisional council of state, on the soil of the homeland, in the city of Tel Aviv, on this Sabbath eve, the 5th day of Iyar, 5708 (14th May, 1948).[10]

How do the words in this document sound in the context of today's conflict in Israel and the occupied Palestinian lands? How do they sound in the context of the passages from Tanakh that we discussed earlier in the chapter?

The next selection is excerpted from a statement by the Palestinian Liberation Organization (PLO), Israel's chief antagonist. Compare this statement with the one you just read. Is it possible to uphold the values of both? Note that the Palestinian statement was written twenty years after the Jewish Covenant. The State of Israel had perceived itself as threatened by the presence of a Palestinian state on its border and had occupied Palestinian territories and begun the establishment of Jewish settlements there. The PLO's statement is in direct response to this action.

Article 3: The Palestinian Arab people possess the legal right to their homeland and have the right to determine their destiny after achieving the liberation of their country in accordance with their wishes and entirely of their own accord and will. . . .

Article 6: The Jews who had normally resided in Palestine until the beginning of the Zionist invasion will be considered Palestinians.

Article 7: That there is a Palestinian community and that it has material, spiritual, and historical connection with Palestine are indisputable facts. It is a national duty to bring up individual Palestinians in an Arab revolutionary manner. All means of information and education must be adopted in order to acquaint the Palestinian with his country in the most profound manner, both spiritual and material, that is possible. He must be prepared for the armed struggle and ready to sacrifice his wealth and his life in order to win back his homeland and bring about its liberation. . . .

Article 9: Armed struggle is the only way to liberate Palestine. Thus it is the overall strategy, not merely a tactical phase. The Palestinian Arab people assert their absolute determination and firm resolution to continue their armed struggle and to work for an armed popular revolution for the liberation of their country and their return to it. They also assert their right to normal life in Palestine and to exercise their right to self-determination and sovereignty over it. . . .

Article 15: The liberation of Palestine, from an Arab viewpoint, is a national (qawmi) duty and it attempts to repel the Zionist and imperialist aggression against the Arab homeland, and aims at the elimination of Zionism in Palestine. Absolute responsibility for this falls upon the Arab nation—peoples and governments—with the Arab people of Palestine in the vanguard. Accordingly, the Arab nation must mobilize all its military, human, moral, and spiritual capabilities to participate actively with the Palestinian people in the liberation of Palestine. . . .

Article 16: The liberation of Palestine, from a spiritual point of view, will provide the Holy Land with an atmosphere of safety and tranquility, which in turn will safeguard the country's religious sanctuaries and guarantee freedom of worship and of visit to all, without discrimination of race, color, language, or religion. Accordingly, the people of Palestine look to all spiritual forces in the world for support.

Article 17: The liberation of Palestine, from a human point of view, will restore to the Palestinian individual his dignity, pride, and freedom. Accordingly the Palestinian Arab people look forward to the support of all those who believe in the dignity of man and his freedom in the world. . . .

Article 19: The partition of Palestine in 1947 and the establishment of the state of Israel are entirely illegal, regardless of the passage of time, because they were contrary to the will of the Palestinian people and to their natural right in their homeland, and inconsistent with the principles embodied in the Charter of the United Nations, particularly the right to self-determination. . . .

Article 24: The Palestinian people believe in the principles of justice, freedom, sovereignty, self-determination, human dignity, and in the right of all peoples to exercise them. . . .

Article 26: The Palestine Liberation Organization, representative of the Palestinian revolutionary forces, is responsible for the Palestinian Arab people's movement in its struggle—to retrieve its homeland, liberate and return to it and exercise the right to self-determination in it—in all military, political, and financial fields and also for whatever may be required by the Palestine case on the inter-Arab and international levels. . . .

Article 28: The Palestinian Arab people assert the genuineness and independence of their national (wataniyya) revolution and reject all forms of intervention, trusteeship, and subordination.[11]

As you compare these two statements, think about where "justice" lies. Are there areas you think are inherently "unjust" in either or both statements?

What would have to change for the two groups to be able to live together peacefully? These are questions that have vexed analysts and politicians for centuries, and they highlight the complexity of achieving "justice" in a world where competing claims and needs clash.

> *Identify a group that you think lacks some basic rights or is involved in a struggle for autonomy. Create a statement on their behalf along the lines of those of Israel's and the PLO's. What specific items must be included to achieve full justice for the group?*

ARE JUSTICE AND LAW THE SAME?

In light of the questions we have asked in this chapter, do you now think that justice and law are the same thing? How do you think one of the prophets of the Hebrew people might have answered? What about an Iroquois elder? And if there is a difference between justice and law, at least within the context of religious thought, where does that difference lie?

One possible difference is suggested in the actions of people who *intentionally break* laws that they perceive are unjust. Gandhi refused to obey many of the laws imposed by the British colonial government in India when he believed that they did violence to the Indian people. During the civil rights movement Martin Luther King, Jr., and others challenged the segregation laws in force in southern states. Peace activists enter military compounds and sometimes have inflicted symbolic damage on warheads in an effort to alert people to the dangers of such weapons.

In the following excerpt, Martin Luther King, Jr., offers us a glimpse of an analysis of the situation of his day and a vision of what might be accomplished if we focused on "justice" rather than simple law. King is writing in 1967, during the Vietnam war and at a time when communism is considered the major threat to world peace. In our own time, try substituting the word "terrorism" for communism and see if King's words make sense in that context.

> These are revolutionary times. All over the globe men are revolting against old systems of exploitation and oppression and out of the wombs of a frail world new systems of justice and equality are being born. The shirtless and barefoot people of the land are rising up as never before. "The people who sat in darkness have seen a great light." We in the West must support these revolutions. It is a sad fact that, because of comfort, complacency, a morbid fear of communism, and our proneness to adjust to injustice, the Western nations that initiated so much of the revolutionary spirit of the modern world have now become the arch anti-revolutionaries. . . . Therefore, communism is a judgment against our failure to make democracy real and follow through on the revolutions that we initiated. Our only hope today lies in our ability to recapture the revolutionary spirit and go out into a sometimes hostile world

declaring eternal hostility to poverty, racism, and militarism. With this power-ful commitment we shall boldly challenge the status quo and unjust mores and thereby speed the day when "every valley shall be exalted, and every mountain and hill shall be made low, and the crooked shall be made straight and the rough places plain."

A genuine revolution of values means in the final analysis that our loyalties must become ecumenical rather than sectional. Every nation must now develop an overriding loyalty to mankind as a whole in order to preserve the best in their individual societies.

This call for a world-wide fellowship that lifts neighborly concern beyond one's tribe, race, class and nation is in reality a call for an all-embracing and unconditional love for all men. This oft misunderstood and misinterpreted con-cept . . . has now become an absolute necessity for the survival of man. When I speak of love I am not speaking of some sentimental and weak response. I am speaking of that force which all of the great religions have seen as the supreme unifying principle of life. Love is somehow the key that unlocks the door which leads to ultimate reality. This Hindu-Moslem-Christian-Jewish-Buddhist belief about ultimate reality is beautifully summed up in the first epistle of Saint John:

> Let us love one another; for love is God and everyone that loveth is born of God and knoweth God. He that loveth not knoweth not God; for God is love. If we love one another God dwelleth in us, and his love is perfected in us.

Let us hope that this spirit will become the order of the day. We can no longer afford to worship the god of hate or bow before the altar of retaliation. The oceans of history are made turbulent by the ever-rising tides of hate. History is cluttered with the wreckage of nations and individuals that pursued this self-defeating path of hate. As Arnold Toynbee says: "Love is the ultimate force that makes for the saving choice of life and good against the damning choice of death and evil. Therefore the first hope in our inventory must be the hope that love is going to have the last word."

We are now faced with the fact that tomorrow is today. We are confronted with the fierce urgency of now. In this unfolding conundrum of life and history there is such a thing as being too late. Procrastination is still the thief of time. Life often leaves us standing bare, naked and dejected with a lost opportunity. The "tide in the affairs of men" does not remain at the flood; it ebbs. We may cry out desperately for time to pause in her passage, but time is deaf to every plea and rushes on. Over the bleached bones and jumbled residue of numerous civilizations are written the pathetic words: "Too late." There is an invisible book of life that faithfully records our vigilance or our neglect. "The moving finger writes, and having writ moves on. . . . " We still have a choice today; non-violent coexistence or violent co-annihilation.

We must move past indecision to action. We must find new ways to speak for peace in Vietnam and justice throughout the developing world—a world that borders on our doors. If we do not act we shall surely be dragged down the long dark and shameful corridors of time reserved for those who possess power without compassion, might without morality, and strength without sight.

Now let us begin. Now let us rededicate ourselves to the long and bitter—but beautiful—struggle for a new world. This is the calling of the sons of God, and our brothers wait eagerly for our response. Shall we say the odds are too great? Shall we tell them the struggle is too hard? Will our message be that the forces of American life militate against their arrival as full men, and we send our deepest regrets? Or will there be another message, of longing, of hope, of solidarity with their yearnings, of commitment to their cause, whatever the cost? The choice is ours, and though we might prefer it otherwise we must choose in this crucial moment of human history.[12]

What do *you* think about the tactics King advocates in this passage? King and others speak of having a "vision" or "dream" of what justice is, what a just society might look like. What would be your dream—or vision—of a just world? What laws might you enact that would help the people living in your society move toward realizing that vision? How would you evaluate those laws in order to be sure they were in themselves "just"? These are some of the questions with which religious and secular authorities must grapple as they try to bring together their concepts of law and justice.

Either alone or with a couple of friends, discuss your own vision of what would constitute a "just" world. What particular elements would such a world have to include? How would society be structured? How would you ensure that things remained just? Is your vision, your utopia, possible? Are there elements of it that are possible? Are any of these elements already present in any culture or society you know about? What first steps could you and others take to realize some small part of your vision?

Some Questions about Justice

What can we say, then, about justice as a central concept within religious traditions? Some social ethicists have made distinctions among different kinds of justice that go beyond the distinction we have made between religious and legal justice. Christian ethicist Karen Lebacqz, in her book *Justice in an Unjust World,* suggests that the three traditional categories of justice—retributive, commutative, and distributive—are not adequate. Retributive justice can be understood as justice achieved by giving back to someone what they deserve, where the punishment must fit the crime. Commutative and distributive justice usually have to do with economic or material well-being, with commutative justice denoting fairness in exchange and distributive justice implying that the benefits and burdens of the society—material and other—should be fairly distributed. From her own faith perspective, and her understanding of the demands of justice in a religious sense, as we discussed it earlier, Lebacqz insists that we should focus more on *restorative justice,* with a view to achieving social justice—the productive participation of all persons in their society. To Lebacqz, restorative justice acknowledges the present existence of injustice in the world and attempts to restore "the bases for a genuine human community of liberty and equality."[13]

In Boston, Massachusetts, an association of various faith traditions, the Greater Boston Interfaith Organization (GBIO), has organized to give voice to members' concerns about the "common good" in the Greater Boston metropolitan area. The GBIO is particularly concerned about the issues of education and of the lack of affordable housing in an economy that saw real estate and rental prices soar in the late-20th and early 21st century. Members lobby state and local government officials, gain signatures on petitions, and generally organize their broad constituency to advocate for themselves and for others who have limited access to the resources enjoyed by some members of the society.

Similar interfaith organizations exist in many parts of the United States. Members of Jewish, Christian, Muslim, and other faiths, as well as other community groups, are motivated by their religious beliefs or by some other vision of social justice to call to accountability various institutions—financial, governmental, private investors, property owners—and to focus attention on the issues that are of most concern to their people. It is a matter of justice that all inhabitants of the city should have appropriate and affordable housing and that all children should have access to appropriate and well-funded educational programs. How do these activities reflect Lebacqz's view of justice as we discussed it above? How would our societies be different if we took her "restorative" approach? Would this be an improvement?

WHAT SOME OTHERS HAVE SAID ABOUT JUSTICE

In Chapter 1, we encountered the idea that identity may not be strictly an individual concept, but that the human self develops and acquires meaning in the context of one's community. Here, we meet African philosopher Kwame Gyekye, who discusses the Akan tribe's ideas of justice. As you read, note how ideas of a communal sense of self translate into concepts of social justice.

> On what grounds are some acts (etc.) considered good? The answer is simply that each of them is supposed (expected or known) to bring about or lead to social well-being. Within the framework of Akan social and humanistic ethics, what is morally good is generally that which promotes social welfare, solidarity, and harmony in human relationships. Moral value in the Akan system is determined in terms of its consequences for mankind and society. "Good" is thus used of actions that promote human interest. The good is identical with the welfare of the society, which is expected to include the welfare of the individual. This appears to be the meaning or definition of "good" in Akan ethics. It is clear that this definition does not at all refer to the will or commands of God [Onyame].

> Human sociality . . . is seen as a consequence of basic human nature, but it is also seen as that which makes for personal well-being and worth. Because community life is natural to man, the kind of society that permits the full realization of human capacities, needs, and aspirations should be communal. . . .
>
> Inherent in the communal enterprise is the problem of contribution and distribution. The communal enterprise tends to maximize the common good because each individual is expected to contribute to it, but obviously individuals are not equal in their capacities and talents. . . . Now, the question is: should inequality in contribution lead to inequality in distribution? Akan social thought, with its social and humanistic thrust, answers this question in the negative. It may be objected that this leads to an unfair treatment of those who have contributed more, to which one may respond that those who have contributed more must have been endowed with greater talents and capacities—natural characteristics and assets for which they were not responsible. . . . The natural assets of human beings are, . . . different and should therefore not be made the basis of unequal distribution . . .
>
> The Akan position is defensible for, irrespective of an individual's contribution to the common good, it is fair and reasonable that everyone's *basic* human needs be satisfied by the society: From each according to *whatever contribution* one can make; to each according to one's *basic* needs.[14]

Gyekye points out that in the Akan communitarian philosophy, persons understood that the basic needs of all should be met, regardless of the particular contribution each person had been able to make. If we were to entertain such a concept, what do you think we would include as "basic needs"? You might have been reminded here of some of the other passages in this chapter, such as that on "jubilee" from the Tanakh. What differences would we see in our social, political and economic structures—and in our secular systems of justice—if some of these religious ideas were to prevail?

PROGRESS . . . OR FRANKENSTEIN'S MONSTER?[1]

Suppose, as has been suggested, that there is a "violence gene." What would this do to our understanding of the concept of "evil"? Would we have to say now that evil is definitely located in the individual as well as in the act? Or are people to be excused from their acts of violence because it is in their genes? Is the effect of the gene the same in countries in which weapons are readily available as it is in those that restrict access to weapons? Are bullfighters examples of people who have the "violence gene"? How about prize fighters? Should we test children at an early age to determine whether or not they have the gene? If we test these children, what should we do about their genetic material—recruit them into the military at this early age? Or perhaps we need to do some genetic engineering to remove the "violence gene." Supposing the presence of such a gene, could its effects be either worsened or ameliorated by the influences of a person's social environment? The possibility of a genetic factor raises interesting and complex questions about our ideas of evil and personal responsibility.

Another area of modern medicine making the news has been reproductive technology—artificial insemination (AI) and in vitro fertilization (IVF), in particular. Some religions prohibit AI of any sort, while others allow it; others allow AI only if the husband is the donor. The issues around IVF are even more difficult, because of the range of possibilities. You can have a situation in which the parents are the donors; one or the other parent is not a donor; both the sperm and the ova are donated. Further, IVF makes possible surrogate motherhood, or, more accurately, a gestational mother. Because of their particular views on how reproduction should take place—as a result of natural intercourse within the institutions of marriage—both Islam and Roman

Catholicism, for example, prohibit these forms of reproduction, while Protestant Christian churches vary. Some allow any of the above possibilities while others agree with Muslims and Roman Catholics in allowing only those particular methods that cannot be in any way contrary to their teachings regarding sexuality and reproduction. As time goes on, more ethical issues will arise in this area, particularly as more genetic causes for illnesses and birth defects are determined. Think about the ethical issues that arise in the following case.

> A private infertility clinic in Toronto offers embryo screening for twenty-seven genetic disorders, including Huntington's disease, cystic fibrosis, and sickle cell disease, for couples undergoing in vitro fertilization (IVF). For an additional $500 to $2,800, parents can have their preembryos screened for one or all of these disorders prior to implantation. "Defective" preembryos are killed, usually by washing them down a sink. Dr. Perry Phillips, director of the clinic, explains, "It is the job of medicine to alleviate suffering. The body makes mistakes and, with this screening, bad, bad things can be avoided. Parents who don't want to inflict this suffering on their children no longer need to." He compares the use of genetic testing to eliminate defective embryos to the use of antibiotics to eliminate bacterial disease. "The genetically defective," he predicts, "may soon be regarded as relics of a barbarous age."[2]

When, if ever, might it be appropriate for someone to test a fetus or preembryo for genetic defects? During the past few years, we have read newspaper accounts of couples who have had a child in hopes of treating an older sibling with bone marrow transplants. In one case, the parents insisted that they would love the child even if it turned out not to be compatible with its sibling. Others have been reported to have had compatibility testing done on the fetus so that an incompatible one could be aborted. In one case, the parents donated both the sperm and ova for IVF. The resulting blastocysts were tested to determine if they, too, carried the defective gene which had afflicted their son. Only those blastocysts that matched and did not carry the gene were implanted. Which, if any, of these cases seem to you to be appropriate use of emerging technology?

Other issues will arise as genetic researchers find more areas in which genes are a contributing factor. Concerns around health-related issues will vary with what a particular family or culture thinks of as healthy; these ideas of health will be affected in part by what their particular religion, or the religion established in their country of residence, says. For example, the Roman Catholic Church allows genetic testing only for fetal abnormalities in order for the parents to prepare to care for an affected child. However, we need to learn the difference between *probability* owing to a particular gene, and certainty. For example, many women were convinced that they were definitely going to have breast cancer on the basis of genetic testing which indicated only an increased possibility.

What about genes purportedly connected with behavioral issues? We have already had an episode in which a particular gene was identified for schizophrenia; subsequently this too was found to indicate only a slightly higher possibility; it is no longer considered causative. Likewise alcoholism is sometimes seen as inevitable if the person has the alcoholism gene. These genetic causes are, in some cases, perhaps half of the story, with environmental causes also contributing to the particular abnormality. We as societies need to look at what the effect may be of ascribing a genetic cause to something which is considered a societal ill.

Currently, people do not "own" their personal genetic makeup. If their tumor or tissue is useful to researchers, the researcher who has developed a way of multiplying the tissue sample can patent it, thus preventing others from duplicating it and ensuring that the researcher will receive any future profits; the person whose tissue or tumor it was has no right to any of this future gain. This is the case even when the person has *donated* tissue or blood for something like the Human Genome Project. Is this ethical? Is it just? What do you think Karen Lebacqz would say about this property claim?

Connected to genetic testing is the issue of cloning. At present, most countries have outlawed cloning human beings for reproductive purposes. Many have passed legislation outlawing cloning of any human tissue. The whole issue of stem cell research falls in this area. This relates to the ethics of genetic testing in two ways. First, if genetic testing *in utero* shows that a fetus has a developmental problem, it could some day be possible to extract stem cells from the embryo to use to grow a replacement part, ready for transplant when the child is born. This possibility has already been suggested by a researcher in Boston. Secondly, in cases of IVF, many blastocysts are created, so that there will be opportunities for the couple to have additional children without the parents undergoing extraction of ova and sperm a second time. Blastocysts not used in the first implantation are frozen for later use. Sometimes, and the incidence of this is growing more frequent, the couple has as many children as they would like and there are left over blastocysts. What should be done? Various suggestions have been proposed: that the parents should continue to pay for the storage of their blastocysts; that other couples who want children should be able to adopt them; that they should be disposed of in whatever fashion is available; that these blastocysts should be thawed and used for various types of research, including as sources of stem cells. How would you resolve this issue?

These are just some of the questions which will arise as we travel further into the future. What do you think the various religions might decide about these sorts of issues? Given that many religions have a strong component of peace and justice, what would be their reaction to determining at an early age that a particular person had the "violence gene" and therefore perhaps should be in the military? What about the possibility of using genetic engineering to create an army of people with the "violence gene"? Would this be appropriate?

A further justice issue is involved in genetic screening and IVF generally. Roughly 85 percent of the world doesn't need to investigate these issues, because they cannot afford these kinds of procedures anyhow. Should anyone be spending thousands of dollars on these treatments when many people do not have access to even the most rudimentary levels of health care? Should we be seeking to develop "designer babies" when many babies have no home? On the other hand, should people be denied the rights and freedoms to choose these procedures in order to correct or prevent a serious abnormality in a child? How do these questions relate to Lebacqz's ideas of restorative and social justice? As we have asked repeatedly in this part of the book, do we always know what's right or just?

III

Seeking Wisdom, Seeking Truth: Experiencing Knowing

CHAPTER SEVEN

How and What Do We Know? Knowledge and Truth

In the preceding three chapters, we struggled with issues it's difficult to be sure about. What actually constitutes evil and what do we do about it when we encounter it? How do we know what's right and wrong? And how do we know what would really constitute a just society? You might wonder by now what it means to say that we "know" anything. And how do we come to know it? Of all the areas of knowing, perhaps religious "knowing" is the most disputed of all. Many people suggest that "religion" is just a matter of faith or belief, and that it doesn't have anything to do with "real" knowledge, that scientific and religious approaches to knowledge are mutually exclusive.

We turn our attention now to the particular ways in which religious faith is perceived as knowledge by those who follow a particular tradition. First, in the present chapter, we will look at some understandings of knowledge itself. In Chapter 8, we will explore some of the narratives and other forms in which religious traditions have shaped and passed on their own particular forms of knowledge. In Chapter 9, we will look at some of the bases on which claims to knowledge rest by examining some ideas of tradition, power, and authority.

Setting the Stage: Knowing and Truth

Try to identify something that you are sure you know. It might be something as specific as a "fact" that you were taught in a history or chemistry class, or something as difficult to pin down as the "fact" that someone in your life loves you. On what basis do you claim to "know" this reality, whatever it is?

What do we mean by "knowing," or "knowledge"? What do we mean by "truth"? Are they the same thing? These might seem like ridiculous questions until we begin to try to answer them. What kinds of disciplines or courses do you expect will give you knowledge, or truth? Do you expect religion to contribute to knowledge or truth? Are there particular assumptions we have to accept in order to claim any other kind of knowledge? Do we have different kinds of knowledge that rest on different kinds of assumptions?

Our first reading in this chapter is from Herman Hesse's fictionalized account of encounters between a young man, Siddhartha, and the Buddha. Although the author is European (Swiss), he seems to capture something of the simplicity and depth of a Buddhist understanding of knowledge and truth. As we have discovered already, Buddhism, like many other Eastern traditions, places great emphasis on what we can learn by paying close attention to the natural world.

Siddhartha has spent a number of years in the city, living a life of ease and prosperity, before he realizes that this is not what he seeks, this is not the way to Enlightenment. Leaving the city, he wanders somewhat aimlessly until he finds himself at the bank of a river. Distraught by the way in which he has lived the last period of his life, Siddhartha is discouraged even to the point of considering suicide. But after a sound and dreamless sleep on the river bank, Siddhartha wakes refreshed, and with a renewed sense of purpose. What new kinds of "knowledge" come to Siddhartha in this passage? And what are the sources of this new wisdom?

> I will stay by this river, Siddhartha thought. It is the same one I crossed long ago on the way to the child people. A kindly ferryman took me across then. I will go to him. My way to a new life once started at his hut. That life is now old and dead. May my new way, my new life, have its starting point there!
>
> Tenderly he gazed into the translucent greenness of the flowing water, at the crystalline lines of the mysterious designs it made. He saw pale pearls rising out of the depths and still bubbles floating on the surface with the image of the blue sky in them. The river looked at him with a thousand eyes, green ones, white ones, crystal ones, sky blue ones. How he loved this river, how it charmed him, how grateful he was to it! In his heart he heard the voice speaking, the newly awakened voice, and it said to him: "Love this river! Stay by it! Learn from it!" Oh yes, he wanted to learn from it, to listen to it. Whoever could understand this river and its mysteries, it seemed to him, would also understand many other things, many mysteries, all mysteries.
>
> Among the mysteries of the river today, however, he saw only one that gripped his soul. He saw that the river flowed and flowed, flowed ever onward, and yet was always there, was always the same yet every moment new! Oh, if one could grasp that, understand that! He did not understand or grasp it, felt only an inkling stir, a distant memory, divine voices.

Siddhartha got up. The stabs of hunger in his body had become unbearable. Driven by them, he wandered up the path on the riverbank, upriver. He listened to the current, listened to the snarling of hunger in his gut.

When he reached the place where the ferry crossed, the boat lay at the ready, and the same ferryman who had once taken the young shramana across the river stood in the boat. Siddhartha recognized him—he too had greatly aged.

"Will you take me across?" he asked.

The ferryman, astonished to see such an eminent person wandering alone and on foot, took him into the boat and pushed off.

"You have chosen a wonderful life," said the guest. "It must be wonderful to live every day on this river and ply its waters."

Smiling, the oarsman swayed back and forth. "It is wonderful, lord, as you say. But is not every life, every task, wonderful?"

"That may be. However, I envy you yours."

"Ach, you might soon get tired of it. It is not something for people in fine clothes. . . . "

When they came alongside the bank, he helped him tie up the boat at its mooring. Then the ferryman asked him to come into the hut and offered him bread and water, which Siddhartha ate with pleasure, as well as the mangos that Vasudeva offered him,

Afterward—it was getting on toward sunset—they sat down on a tree trunk on the bank, and Siddhartha told the ferryman about his origins and about his life as he had seen it pass before his eyes that day during his hour of despair. His tale lasted deep into the night.

Vasudeva listened with great attention. As he listened, he took everything in, origins and childhood, all the studying, the seeking, all the joys, all the troubles. Of the ferryman's virtues, this was one of his greatest: He knew how to listen as few people do. Though Vasudeva spoke not a word himself, the speaker felt him receiving his words into himself; quietly, openly, unhurriedly, missing nothing, not jumping ahead through impatience, attributing neither praise nor blame—just listening. Siddhartha felt what happiness can come from opening oneself to such a listener, having one's own life—one's seeking, one's suffering—enter this other's heart.

Toward the end of Siddhartha's story, as he was talking about the tree by the river, of how low he had fallen, of the sacred OM, and what deep love he had felt for the river after his sleep, the ferryman listened with attention redoubled, fully and completely given over, his eyes closed.

When Siddhartha had stopped talking and after the long silence that followed had passed, Vasudeva said: "It is as I thought. The river spoke to you. It is your friend too; it speaks to you too. That is good; that is very good. Stay with me, Siddhartha, my friend. Once I had a wife. Her bed was next to mine, but she died long ago. I have lived by myself for a long time. Live with me now. There is room and food for both of us. "Thank you," said Siddhartha. "I thank you and accept. And I also thank you, Vasudeva, for having listened to me so well! Few people know how to listen, and I never met anyone who knows how as well as you. In this, too, I will learn from you."

"You will learn that," said Vasudeva, "but not from me. The river taught me how to listen; you will learn that from the river too. The river knows everything; everything can be learned from it. Look, you have already learned from the river that it is good to aim low, to sink, to seek the bottom. The rich and prominent Siddhartha has become an oarsman's helper; this, too, was the advice of the river. You will learn the other thing from it too. . . .

I have taken many across, thousands, and for all of them my river has been nothing but an obstacle on their journey. . . . For a few among the thousands— very few, four or five of them—the river stopped being an obstacle. They heard its voice, they listened to it, and the river became sacred to them as it has to me. Let us now take our rest, Siddhartha."

Siddhartha stayed with the ferryman and learned the work of the boat. And when there was nothing to do on the ferry, he worked with Vasudeva in the rice field, gathered wood, picked fruit from the banana tree. He learned how to make an oar, repair the boat, weave baskets, and was glad about everything he learned. And the days and months passed swiftly by. But the river taught him more than Vasudeva could. He learned from it unceasingly. Above all he learned from it how to listen, how to listen with a still heart, with an expectant, open soul, without passion, without desire, without judgment, without opinion.

He and Vasudeva lived together in friendship, and from time to time they exchanged words—few words long pondered. Vasudeva was no friend of words. Siddhartha seldom succeeded in getting him to talk.

Once he asked him: "Have you also learned from the river the secret that there is no time?"

A bright smile came over Vasudeva's face. "Yes, Siddhartha," he said. "This is probably what you mean: that the river is everywhere at once—at its source, at its mouth, by the waterfall, by the ferry crossing, in the rapids, in the sea, in the mountains—everywhere at the same time, And that for it there is only the present, not the shadow called the future."

"That's it," said Siddhartha, "And when I learned that, I looked at my life, and it too was a river; and the boy Siddhartha and the man Siddhartha and the old man Siddhartha were only separated by shadows, not by anything real. Siddhartha's previous births were also not a past, and his death and return to Brahma were not a future. Nothing was, nothing will be; everything is, everything has its being and is present."

Siddhartha spoke with rapture; this revelation had brought him profound happiness. Was not all suffering time, was not all self-torment and fearfulness time? Was not all that was heavy and hostile in the world overcome and over with once one had overcome time, had been able to rid oneself of the notion of time? He had spoken with rapture. But Vasudeva only smiled at him radiantly and nodded confirmation, Silently he nodded, stroked Siddhartha's shoulder with his hand, and returned to his work.

And another time, in the rainy season when the river was swollen and rushing headlong, Siddhartha said: "Is it not true, friend, that the river has many voices, very many voices? Does it not have the voice of a king, of a warrior, of a bull, of a night bird, of a woman giving birth, of a man sighing, and a thousand other voices too?"

"That is true," nodded Vasudeva, "all creatures' voices are in its voice."

"And do you know," Siddhartha continued, "what word it speaks when you succeed in hearing all its ten thousand voices at once?"

Happiness shone in Vasudeva's face as he laughed, He leaned over to Siddhartha and whispered the sacred OM into his ear. And that is just what Siddhartha had also heard. . . .

Often the two sat in the evening on the tree trunk on the bank and listened in silence to the river, which for them was not a river but the voice of life, the voice of what is, eternal becoming. And occasionally it happened that while listening to the river both men would think of the same thing—a conversation from the day before yesterday, one of their passengers whose face and fortune had caught their interest, of death, of their childhood; and then at the same moment, when the river had said something good to them, they would look at each other, both thinking exactly the same thing, both gladdened by the same answer to the same question.[1]

Have you ever felt that you learned something profoundly true and important from a most unlikely source? Think about the insights Siddhartha has into time—past, present, future—as he and the ferryman spend their days and nights by the river. What is the importance to Siddhartha of this knowledge? Would you be satisfied with this kind of knowing, or do you think it's important to "know" in other ways as well?

WHAT DO YOU THINK? HOW DO YOU KNOW?

In the selection you just read, would you say that Siddhartha has learned something that is "true" from the river? What does it mean to say that something is true? At the beginning of this chapter, we asked you to consider some things that you know for a fact to be true. Is there something objective called the Truth, or are there various truths? Must something be scientifically verifiable to be called truth?

Scientist Chet Raymo writes a weekly newspaper column in which he often reflects on the relationship between the knowledge generated by scientific method and other forms of "truth." As you read the next selection, ask yourself just what distinction Raymo is making. Do you have to be a religious believer to think that there are other ways of knowing? Do you have to suspend religious belief to be a scientist?

"Science Finds God," screamed the cover of *Newsweek* not long ago.

"Science Sees the Light," blurted the cover of a recent *New Republic.*

The *New Republic* does not use the G-word, presumably out of deference to its more worldly audience, but its intent is the same: To tease the reader with the proposition that science has discovered a "higher meaning" among the galaxies and the DNA. These banner headlines are only a notch above the supermarket tabloids that proclaim, "NASA Scientists See the Face of Jesus on Mars." Of course, science has not found God, nor has it seen the Light. Science has nothing to say about God or the Light one way or the other. Science goes on doing what it has always done: Describing how the world works. If some folks see the hand of God in the way the world works, then well and good. Other folks may choose to see God's absence.

What the *Newsweek* and *New Republic* cover stories are all about is not a scientific breakthrough—the discovery of God's signature in creation—but rather a renewed interest in matters of knowledge and faith among the general public, including, of course, many scientists. Unfortunately, the misleading headlines reinforce a mistaken notion of science. Science is not Truth, nor should it be confused with any particular statement or group of statements about how the world works. Science is not the Big Bang, or evolution, or DNA, or chaos theory, or the Heisenberg Uncertainty Principle—all of which have been used to evoke God's presence or absence, and all of which are subject to revision if and when new data require it.

Science is a socially organized instrument for generating reliable knowledge about the world. It relies upon theoretical speculation, experiment, mathematical description, specialized languages, refereed journals, exacting citation of previous work, scientific societies, and university departments. It eschews miracles and metaphysics. What science seeks is the most concise, most elegant story of the world that explains and predicts what we see when we make exacting, reproducible, quantitative observations. The proof, of course, is in the pudding. That science provides reliable knowledge of the world is evident all around us, in the astounding technological achievements of modern civilization. Even those religious fundamentalists who regularly excoriate science rely upon the fruits of science in their electronic ministries.

What science doesn't provide is meaning. It reveals neither God nor his absence. And it is precisely this reluctance to engage in metaphysical or theological speculation that is the source of its success. The autonomy of science from the churches was hard won by the sacrifices of the Brunos and Galileos and the tenacious scrappiness of the Tyndalls and Huxleys. It is a cornerstone of our confidence in the scientific enterprise. Pick up any scientific journal and read any article. You will not be able to tell if the author is a theist or an atheist, an advocate of Intelligent Design or a believer in a universe of meaningless chance. There is no such thing as The Christian Journal of Physics or the Atheist Annals of Microbiology.

Last year, researchers Edward Larson and Larry Witham reported in *Nature* magazine a 1996 survey of the religious beliefs of scientists. They queried 1,000 biological and physical scientists and mathematicians randomly drawn from the 1995 American Men and Women of Science. About 40 percent of the scientists professed belief in God or an afterlife. Roughly 45 percent disbelieved, and 15 percent were doubters. Interestingly, these numbers have not significantly changed since a similar survey was conducted by James Leuba in 1916. Any proclamations on the part of the media that, "Science Finds God" or, "Science Sees the Light" do not reflect any measurable change of religious belief within the scientific community. What has changed is the willingness of many theistic scientists to talk about their faith. This is partly due to the efforts of the John Templeton Foundation, which for some years has been doling out generous grants to support the study of science and religion. Whatever might be the agenda of the Templeton Foundation, it is certainly no bad thing that this important topic should be discussed. According to polls, we are a people grievously torn between our way of knowing—science—and our ways of believing. For example, nearly 80 percent of us believe in miracles, and nearly half of us are open to the influence of the stars in our personal lives, both of which suggest a certain detachment from the scientific way of knowing.

Scientists are represented in all parts of the religious spectrum, from firebrand atheism to belief in a personal God who acts miraculously in the world. Like everyone else, they seek an integration of knowing and believing in their personal lives. However, the mixing up of science and religion is not a good thing for science. Science has succeeded as a provider of reliable knowledge precisely because it has kept itself separate from the eternally contentious questions of God and meaning. [2]

Is Raymo right that science must keep itself apart from questions of meaning? Do you think he would also advocate dividing science from questions of good and evil? Some would suggest that, with today's rapidly advancing technologies in the fields of medical science, for example, these questions of meaning should be paid close attention to. Again we might ask whether "truth" always depends upon a set of scientifically verifiable facts.

One area in which science and questions of meaning are converging is ecology. Ecology is increasingly a concern of many religions, including those of the First Peoples of the world. Modern technology seems to them to be heedless of the possible destruction that implementing the technology may cause. Many theologians in the major world religions also are involved in asking whether or not the ramifications of technology have been carefully enough studied. They ask if we have already forgotten the lessons of DDT, for example—a highly toxic chemical that scientists eventually realized remained in the environment for years. Recently reports have been published linking high rates of cancer in dogs to chemicals used to keep lawns lush and green. How do these same substances affect children who play on such lawns? Should religious concerns also be brought to bear on such issues? Theologians who address these questions depend on their religion and on scientific research in reaching their positions. And many scientists make common cause with the religious writers. Are both kinds of truth relevant in these areas? Can you think of additional areas in which this might be the case?

Think about someone who loves you. How do you know this? How could you devise a scientific experiment to prove that the person loves you? Of what would your experiment consist? Is it possible that the evidence you would gather could be explained by something other than love?

WHAT IS KNOWLEDGE? WHAT IS TRUTH?

We know that so-called *factual* accounts may be biased, intentionally or unintentionally, by the author's background. This does not mean we should not read such accounts—histories—of anything; rather, we must learn to read critically, no matter what we read, and recognize that the events that the text describes have been interpreted by the author. At the same time, we need to allow for the possibility that some kinds of truth may be more present in fiction than in "fact."

You may have read Antoine St. Exupery's *The Little Prince,* perhaps in grade school or high school. If so, suspend your memories of it, and your skepticism about what seems on the surface to be a children's book, and read the following excerpt from the narrative. *The Little Prince* is an imaginative story about a little boy who is spirited away from his very small planet en route to a space odyssey in which he has numerous encounters with a variety of beings. As we join the story, the Little Prince is feeling despondent because he has just encountered a large bush full of roses. On his home planet he had just one rose that he tended with great care and considered special because of her uniqueness. If there are hundreds of other roses just like her, wonders the Little Prince, what is special about *his* rose? The truth in St. Exupery's fantasy text is clear, though unexpected. Obviously the truth we encounter in a fantasy novel is not scientific. Is it then irrelevant to science, or automatically relevant to religion? Are scientific . . . and religious truths themselves limited?

> It was then that the fox appeared.
> "Good morning," said the fox.
> "Good morning," the little prince answered politely, though when he turned around he saw nothing.
> "I'm here," the voice said, "under the apple tree."
> "Who are you?" the little prince asked. "You're very pretty . . . "
> "I'm a fox," the fox said.
> "Come and play with me," the little prince proposed. "I'm feeling so sad."
> "I can't play with you," the fox said, "I'm not tamed."
> "Ah! Excuse me," said the little prince. But upon reflection, he added, "what does *tamed* mean?"
> "You're not from around here," the fox said. "What are you looking for?"
> "I'm looking for people," said the little prince. "What does *tamed* mean?"
> "People," said the fox, "have guns and they hunt. It's quite troublesome. And they also raise chickens. That's the only interesting thing about them. Are you looking for chickens?"
> "No," said the little prince, "I'm looking for friends. What does *tamed* mean?"
> "It's something that's been too often neglected. It means, 'to create ties' . . . "
> "To create ties?"
> "That's right," the fox said. "For me, you're only a little boy just like a hundred thousand other little boys. And I have no need of you. And you have no

need of me, either. For you I'm only a fox like a hundred thousand other foxes. But if you tame me, we'll need each other. You'll be the only boy in the world for me. I'll be the only fox in the world for you. . . ."

"I'm beginning to understand," the little prince said. "There's a flower . . . I think she's tamed me. . . ."

"Possibly," the fox said. "On Earth, one sees all kinds of things."

"Oh, this isn't on Earth!" the little prince said.

The fox seemed quite intrigued. "On another planet?"

"Yes."

"Are there hunters on that planet?"

"No."

"Now that's interesting. And chickens?"

"No."

"Nothing's perfect," sighed the fox. But he returned to his idea. "My life is monotonous. I hunt chickens; people hunt me. All chickens are just alike, and all men are just alike. So I'm rather bored. But if you tame me, my life will be filled with sunshine. I'll know the sound of footsteps that will be different from all the rest. Other footsteps send me back underground. Yours will call me out of my burrow like music. And then, look! You see the wheat fields over there? I don't eat bread. For me wheat is no use whatever. Wheat fields say nothing to me. Which is sad. But you have hair the color of gold. So it will be wonderful, once you've tamed me! The wheat, which is golden, will remind me of you. And I'll love the sound of the wind in the wheat. . . ."

The fox fell silent and stared at the little prince for a long while. "Please— tame me!" he said.

"I'd like to," the little prince replied. "But I haven't much time. I have friends to find and so many things to learn."

"The only things you learn are the things you tame," said the fox. "People haven't time to learn anything. They buy things ready-made in stores. But since there are no stores where you can buy friends, people no longer have friends. If you want a friend, tame me!"

"What do I have to do?" asked the little prince.

"You have to be very patient," the fox answered. "First you'll sit down a lit- tle ways away from me, over there, in the grass. I'll watch you out of the corner of my eye, and you won't say anything. Language is the source of misunderstandings. But day by day, you'll be able to sit a little closer. . . . "

The next day the little prince returned.

"It would have been better to return at the same time," the fox said. "For instance, if you come at four in the afternoon, I'll begin to be happy by three. The closer it gets to four, the happier I'll feel. By four I'll be all excited and wor- ried; I'll discover what it costs to be happy! But if you come at any old time, I'll never know when I should prepare my heart. . . . There must be rites."

"What's a *rite*?" asked the little prince.

"That's another thing that's been too often neglected," said the fox. "It's the fact that one day is different from the other days, one hour from the other hours. My hunters, for example, have a rite. They dance with the village girls on Thursdays. So Thursday's a wonderful day: I can take a stroll all the way to the vineyards. If the hunters danced whenever they chose, the days would all be just alike, and I'd have no holiday at all."

That was how the little prince tamed the fox. And when the time to leave was near:

"Ah!" the fox said. "I shall weep."

"It's your own fault," the little prince said. "I never wanted to do you any harm, but you insisted that I tame you. . ."

"Yes, of course," the fox said.

"But you're going to weep!" said the little prince.

"Yes, of course," the fox said.

"Then you get nothing out of it?"

"I get something," the fox said, "because of the color of the wheat." Then he added, "Go look at the roses again. You'll understand that yours is the only rose in all the world. Then come back to say goodbye, and I'll make you the gift of a secret."

The little prince went to look at the roses again. "You're not at all like my rose. You're nothing at all yet," he told them. "No one has tamed you, and you haven't tamed anyone. You're the way my fox was. He was just a fox like a hundred thousand others. But I've made him my friend, and now he's the only fox in all the world."

And the roses were humbled.

"You're lovely, but you're empty," he went on. "One couldn't die for you. Of course, an ordinary passerby would think my rose looked just like you. But my rose, all on her own, is more important than all of you together, since she's the one that I've watered. Since she's the one I've put under glass. Since she's the one I sheltered behind a screen. Since she's the one for whom I killed the caterpillars (except the two or three for butterflies). Since she's the one I listened to when she complained, or when she boasted, or even sometimes when she said nothing at all. Since she's *my* rose."

And he went back to meet the fox.

"Goodbye," he said.

"Goodbye," said the fox. "Here is my secret. It's quite simple: One sees clearly only with the heart. Anything essential is invisible to the eyes."

"Anything essential is invisible to the eyes," the little prince repeated, in order to remember.

"It's the time you spent on your rose that makes your rose so important."

"It's the time I spent on my rose . . . " the little prince repeated, in order to remember.

"People have forgotten this truth," the fox said. "But you mustn't forget it. You become responsible forever for what you've tamed. You're responsible for your rose. . ."

"I'm responsible for my rose . . . " the little prince repeated, in order to remember.[3]

On what basis might you—or the Little Prince—claim the truth of what you have come to know through this work of imaginative fiction? These truths cannot be tested in the laboratory; can they be tested in other ways?

In this chapter so far, we have discussed some different kinds of "truth" that people acquire, and some of the different purposes that these different dimensions of knowing might serve in our lives. If you think about your own relationship with truth, you will probably recognize at least several different kinds of knowledge or truth that you have gained over the years. In addition, you might realize that you came to this knowledge in a variety of different ways—or that some ways of learning are much more effective for you than others. For example, do you learn best by listening to someone talk, or do you need to see the material in order to really learn it? Can you learn a new skill by having someone describe to you how to do it, either orally or through a printed manual, or do you need the hands-on experience to be able to fully grasp the techniques? What is your preferred learning style? Does it depend upon the kind of information you are trying to learn? Have you sometimes found quite difficult material easier to learn because of the way or ways in which it was presented to you? Some of these differences depend upon the kind of knowledge we are trying to acquire, but nonetheless there seem to be great differences among people in terms of the ways in which we learn.

> *Suppose you want to acquire three different pieces of knowledge tomorrow: how to use a new computer program, what it would be like to spend Spring break building a Habitat house, and whether a certain special person really cares about you. Could you learn all three things in the same way? How would you expect to "know" each?*

CULTURAL AND SOCIAL APPROACHES TO KNOWING

As we have explored in the preceding chapters, our surroundings play a central role in the ways in which we develop our self-understandings and our place in the world. This is no less true when we come to the area of knowing and truth. In this next selection, we encounter two women who have volunteered for a "grandmothers' program" at their local hospital. Although a fictional account, the story of Nettie Lee and Martha is nonetheless sufficiently realistic in its details that it certainly *could* have happened. Their role will be to assist with highly vulnerable newborn infants, some abandoned at birth, others very premature and/or with an array of life-threatening conditions. Nettie Lee is poor, has little formal education and a large extended family that causes her nothing but trouble. She is already raising one grandson when her daughter Yolanda has another baby and dumps it in a porta-potty. Nettie Lee finds out what has happened by seeing the news account of the baby's discovery on television. Nettie Lee must somehow attend to the well-being of this new member of her family without exposing her daughter as the one who now might face charges of attempted murder for abandoning her baby. Then Nettie Lee sees in the newspaper an advertisement for volunteers, placed by the hospital to which the abandoned infant has been taken. This seems like an answer to Nettie Lee's prayers.

Nettie Lee's first day on the job begins with an interview with the hospital's Child Life Advocate. As you read Ms. Czajwolski's explanation of the work that Nettie Lee will do, and Nettie Lee's responses, ask yourself just how each woman has acquired the knowledge she has to do the job expected of her, and how her acquisition of such knowledge is related to her social location.

"On top of this immense workload, the nurses are expected to provide nurturing to each infant. Studies show that newborns, whether they are full-term or premature, will wither and fail to thrive if they are deprived of human touch. In fact, some studies show that older babies who received regular full-body massage several times each day had an increase in nerve myelination and in the production of growth hormone." Her eyes returned to Nettie Lee's face. "I'm sorry. I guess I was rambling on. It's just that I really feel the grandmother job is so important. But you do know what I mean about the babies needing touch?"

"Mmm-hmm. I know just what you talking about. When a baby don't get the love it needs, it wants to curl up and die."

"That's right. That's *exactly* right, Nettie Lee." Ms. Czajwolski paused, then gassed up again. "So it is the volunteer grandmothers' job to supply the preemies' nurturing needs that our staff is simply too encumbered to address." Her eyes rested on Nettie Lee's ring, watched her twist it around her finger. "Do you have any questions?"

She watched Ms. Czajwolski lift her eyes from her ring to her face. "Yeah, I guess so." This was the part she knew was coming, when the woman would try to judge her intelligence by the way she talked or the way she phrased her questions. "I was kind of wondering about the efficiency of holding the babies. I mean, how efficient do you think it's going to be?"

"Efficient?"

Nettie Lee didn't like the puzzled look on Ms. Czajwolski's face. She wasn't doing so well at impressing her. She was screwing up. Damn. Yolanda had her so she couldn't even think straight. "The holding, I mean. Because I know there's a right way and a wrong way to hold a baby. You got to let the baby know you're in charge, you're *strong,* but you still got a soft heart for them, all at the same time. They can feel it in your touch. The know when somebody don't care, or when they can cry and fuss for no reason and get away with it. Sometimes I think they smarter than we are." Ms. Czajwolski cracked a smile. "Good. I know babies. I know how to make them feel safe. And I'm a grandmother myself, too. I had on-the-job training. I'm efficient. And I just love babies. Don't matter if they mine or somebody else's, I love them all."

Ms. Czajwolski began to speak. The small office was getting hot. There was a curtainless window in the corner behind the desk. A radiator under it blew a hot draft that weakly tufted Ms. Czajwolski's hair. From the window, Nettie Lee could see the yellow brick edge of the hospital's east wing. It rose up eight floors, the top windows glaring in the mid-morning sun. At one window, somewhere about the fourth or fifth floor, a little boy in pajamas leaned flat-palmed onto a pane of glass, then pressed his entire face, white as the moon, into the window. Nettie Lee sat Motionless, wanting air. Several seconds passed before Ms. Czajwolski's words seemed meant for her again.

" . . . of course." The woman finished her sentence, letting her smile grow into a question that needed attending to.

"Yeah," Nettie Lee agreed, uneasily. "Of course."

"Good!" Ms. Czajwolski breathed deeply and placed her hands together, almost in a handclap. "I'm glad we can agree about that. We need you to come in every day. That's the part the volunteers sometimes balk at."

Nettie Lee felt unsettled. "Well, I don't ballcat anything. I'll take the job." She would worry about the details later. What was important now was her granddaughter.

Later in the morning, Ms. Czajwolski sent her to see George Johns, a registered nurse from Antigua (An-*tee*-ga, he called it). He stood at a blackboard and instructed Nettie Lee, the lone student sitting at an eight-foot folding table in the fourth-floor conference room inside the neonatal nursery. Her training was brief. Mr. Johns wore an island-flowered shirt; a picture ID badge pulled down the pocket of his lab coat. In the picture his smooth brown face was rounder, his hair longer. Seemed like everybody who worked here used to have longer hair. Nettie Lee thought his lilting accent strange, comforting. His voice reminded her of the man who ran the corner grocery where she did her weekday shopping: musical in range but crisp as an apple in pronunciation.

Mr. Johns chalked five principles on the board for Nettie Lee to remember, then pointed to them with a ballpoint pen he pulled from his breast pocket. The Five Don'ts: Don't disconnect any equipment connected to the baby. Don't remove the baby from the Isolette unless the nurse says it's okay. Don't give any medication, that's not your job. Don't talk about the babies in front of Mom or Dad. Don't become personally involved with the babies.

"Those are just the rules to keep yourself out of trouble," Mr. Johns said, placing his pen back in his pocket. He dusted his hands on his lab coat. "Now for the rules that will cause you trouble." He smiled at Nettie Lee. "Most important thing to remember: You can love these babies too much. What do I mean by this?" He did not pause for Nettie Lee's answer. "I mean that a premature baby is neurologically fragile. There are individual variations, of course, but—and this is a very important point—they are immature neurologically, just recently pushed from a womb they would prefer to inhabit, and they cannot handle stress *at all*. Now, what do I mean by stress? I mean there will be no handling of these babies that is not extremely gentle and well-considered. For instance," He walked to a file cabinet piled high with papers, on which a dusty breast pump sat, opened the bottom drawer, and pulled out a plastic baby wearing a stocking cap on its head, diapered in a tiny Pampers. "When you are told it is okay to remove the baby from the Isolette, place your palm under his bottom like so—see this?—and slip your fingers under his head for support. Then with your other hand—remember: always two hands, though you will be tempted to pick them up with one, especially if you have large hands, and I see that you do—see this? With my other hand, I add extra support under the thighs." He held the doll toward Nettie Lee. "You see? Okay. Now you try, ma'am."

Nettie Lee gingerly held the doll's head on the edge of her fingertips, her palm steady under the diaper.

"That's it," Mr. Johns praised. "You are doing quite well."

"Mmm-hmm. This comes like second nature to me." Was this as big as the babies got? This little doll couldn't have been more than twelve, maybe thirteen inches long.

"Now as you are holding the baby, remember his weak neurological system. Do not provide more stimulation than the little one can handle. What do I mean by stimulation?" This time he waited.

"You mean not to bounce him up and down and kitchy-coo him."

"Yes, I mean that and more. For example, some of the little ones cannot take more than one type of interaction at a time. So, although you may want to pick up, talk to, and stroke or even sing to a certain preemie, you'll find he can only tolerate one of these things. You must observe the baby closely to determine what his limits are, then respect those limits. We've even had babies who could not tolerate being fed and held at the same time. One preemie was especially difficult. Only if the nurse laid the infant in the Isolette, turned her head away to prevent eye contact, and did not speak a single word would this child suck the bottle."

"Well, if they so little, am I hurting or helping them by doing things?"

"Oh, you are most definitely helping them. You need only make sure you do it in the proper manner and do not carry it too far."[4]

The three characters we meet in this excerpt—Nettie Lee, Ms. Czajwolski and George Johns—all have a particular kind of knowledge that they bring to the care of the premature infants. Without the kind of formal education that Ms. Czajwolski and George Johns have had, Nettie Lee nonetheless goes on to become a highly successful "grandmother," giving nurturance and comfort to the infants in the intensive care unit. How have all of these persons come to the knowledge they have about the care of infants? Would you attribute equal importance to each kind of knowledge? Who would you most want to have holding you, or your baby?

HOW DO WE KNOW WHAT WE KNOW?

We return here to the story of the Little Prince, and to scientist Chet Raymo. This time, Raymo is specifically analyzing St. Exupery's story, from his own perspective as a scientist. What point do you think Raymo is trying to make in this column?

"I believe that for his escape he took advantage of the migration of a flock of wild birds."

Many people will recognize this caption from the frontispiece drawing of Antoine de Saint-Exupery's "The Little Prince." The drawing shows the little prince being lifted from his planet—an asteroid, actually—by a harness attached to 11 birds of indeterminate species.

"Eleven birds." "Indeterminate species." Oh dear. I am falling into the trap that Saint-Exupery's book is a caution against. I am counting and categorizing when what is called for is childlike acceptance and wonder.

I am being a grown-up.

"Grown-ups never understand anything by themselves, and it is tiresome for children to be always and forever explaining things to them . . . " wrote Saint-Exupery. In the context, it is not difficult to understand his sentiment. As he wrote and drew his book at a rented house on Long Island, N.Y., through the summer and autumn of 1942, grown-ups were slaughtering one another with a terrible ferocity in his native France, and around the world.

Saint-Exupery was a pilot and a writer. He flew often over North Africa at a time when solo flight involved great risks. "The Little Prince" tells of a pilot who has crashed in the Sahara Desert who meets a mysterious boy from another place. The book has nothing good to say about scientists, lumping them in with kings, businessmen and other grown-ups who have little sense of what is truly important.

Almost immediately the book became a classic, and has remained popular with children and grown-ups. To celebrate the half-century that has passed since its publication in 1943, Harcourt Brace and Company has issued a handsome boxed edition containing many of Saint- Exupery's unpublished preliminary sketches.

The golden-haired little prince lives on a tiny planet, scarcely larger than himself, which scientists—as scientists are wont to do—have designated Asteroid B-612. To the little prince, it is simply "my star" and he lives there with a haughty but much loved rose. The most charming drawings in the book are those of the little prince on his minuscule planet, digging out the sprouts of troublesome plants, cleaning his three volcanoes (two active, one extinct), and caring for his rose.

And. Of course. I cannot resist being a grown-up. After all, I was trained as a scientist. It is my business to make calculations, to weigh, measure and evaluate.

For example, a bit of basic physics shows that the little prince's planet is totally unfeasible as a habitat.

Asteroid B-12 appears to be about 10 feet in diameter. If we assume an average density about the same as that of Earth—5.5 grams per cubic centimeter—then the little prince would weigh less than a thousandth of an ounce.

He would float in the breezes like a thistle seed.

Except there wouldn't be any breezes. The little prince's planet would not have enough gravity to hold an atmosphere. Any molecules of gas that emerged from his two active volcanoes would drift off into space.

But his planet could not be volcanically active. The volume of a sphere is proportional to the cube of the radius, while the surface area depends on the square of the radius. As a sphere gets larger, its volume increases faster than its area, and therefore a larger planet will have more internal heat and less surface area, relatively speaking, for the heat to escape. Four billion years after the formation of the solar system, the Earth still sputters with volcanoes. But the little prince's asteroid is a million times smaller than Earth, and would have long since cooled to cold rigidity even if it were molten at its beginning,

Which it would not have been. The solar system formed when gravity pulled together gas and dust from a vast nebula. This clumping process generates heat. But the little prince's planet contains so little material that the amount of heat would have been insignificant. Not nearly enough to melt anything,

Nor would his planet have been spherical, unless it melted, which it didn't.

In short. This whole business of Asteroid B-612 is a sham. Physically and astronomically impossible.

Consider that flight of birds that the little prince uses for his escape: Completely unnecessary. The upward speed that an object must have to overcome the gravitational pull of a planet is called the escape velocity. The escape velocity of Earth is 22,000 miles per hour, which is the speed a rocket must acquire to leave the Earth. The escape velocity for Asteroid B-612 is about five-thousandths of a mile per hour. The little prince could leave his planet by making a little jump.

In fact, if he had any spring to his step at all he would have a hard time staying home. He would need to tether himself to his planet the way an astronaut is tethered to a space ship.

And what about the rose? It needs air, water, soil. There can be no . . .

Whoa! I'm taking this grown-up business too far. I should stop my calculations and listen to Saint-Exupery: The proof that the little prince existed on a planet scarcely larger than himself is that he was charming, that he laughed and that he had a rose.

If anyone has a rose, implies Saint-Exupery, that is proof enough that he exists.[5]

What St. Exupery's novel does, suggests Raymo, is challenge our view that only through the medium of scientific inquiry can we claim to know anything. Another way of describing this is to ask whether "truth" is always dependent upon scientifically or historically verifiable facts. If so, then a story such as *The Little Prince* has nothing to contribute to truth. What do you "know" that has come to you, or at least been confirmed and affirmed, through some artistic medium, whether literature, painting, music, theater and so forth? Think back to the first piece by Raymo. Since *The Little Prince* clearly does not show "how the world goes" we must ask if it tells us "why" the world goes. Or does it convey a different sort of knowing altogether?

WHAT DOES RELIGION HAVE TO DO WITH KNOWING?

We are all probably familiar with some of the long-drawn-out disputes about such issues as evolution and creation that seem to put religion and science on opposing sides of an impassable divide. You might be familiar with the famous "Scopes Trial" which took place in 1925 in Tennessee. The defendant, Scopes,

William Jennings Bryan makes his first speech during the Scopes Trial in 1925.

Clarence Darrow responds for the defense.

was on trial for suggesting in his classroom that Darwin might have been right; that human beings might have evolved from other animals. Often nicknamed "the monkey trial," because it was the suggestion that humans might be descended from the apes that drew the most wrath from certain religious groups, the case drew worldwide attention as Clarence Darrow, the attorney for Scopes, and William Jennings Bryan, the prosecuting attorney, battled each other over issues of truth and freedom of speech. Thirty years later, when the issue was still (and still is, unfortunately) very much relevant in the United States, Jerome Lawrence and Robert E. Lee wrote a play, *Inherit the Wind*, based on the issues raised in the original trial and on the clash between two powerful legal figures. At the heart of the play are questions about knowledge and truth.

Before the trial begins, prosecutor Brady signals his intention to put Rachel on the stand. Rachel is a friend and teaching colleague of defendant Bert Cates; she is also the daughter of the town preacher who is leading the movement against Cates. Meeker is the jail keeper and Drummond is the defense attorney. When Cates hears about Rachel's possible testimony, he is appalled:

RACHEL
(Looking down)
They want me to testify against Bert.

CATES

(*Stunned*)

You can't!

MEEKER

I don't mean to rush you, Bert; but we gotta close up the shop.
(CATES is *genuinely panicked.*)

CATES

Rache, some of the things I've talked to you about are things you just say to your own heart. (*He starts to go with* MEEKER, *then turns back*) If you get up on the stand and say those things out loud—(*He shakes his head*) Don't you understand? The words I've said to you—softly, in the dark—just trying to figure out what the stars are for, or what might be on the back side of the moon—

MEEKER

Bert—

CATES

They were questions, Rache. I was just asking questions. If you repeat those things on the witness stand, Brady'll make 'em sound like answers. And they'll crucify me!
(CATES *and* MEEKER go *off. The lights are slowly dimming.* DRUMMOND *puts on his coat, sizing up* RACHEL *as he does so.* RACHEL, *torn, is almost unconscious of his presence or of her surroundings . . . .*)

RACHEL

(*Distraught*) Is it true? Is Bert wicked?

DRUMMOND

(*With simple conviction*)
Bert Cates is a good man. Maybe even a great one. And it takes strength for a woman to love such a man. Especially when he's a pariah in the community.

RACHEL

I'm only confusing Bert. And he's confused enough as it is.

DRUMMOND

The man who has everything figured out is probably a fool. College examinations notwithstanding, it takes a very smart fella to say "I don't know the answer!"
(DRUMMOND *puts on his hat, touches the brim of it as a gesture of good-bye and goes slowly off.*)
Curtain.[6]

Why is Cates so distressed at the thought of Rachel testifying? Does his attorney Drummond's last comment to Rachel make sense to you? Does it make sense of Cates's anxiety about what Rachel's testimony will sound like to a courtroom full of people already convinced he is a profound sinner, if not the devil incarnate? What does this brief exchange say about "truth" and knowledge?

During the trial, prosecutor Brady questions Howard, a student, about just what he learned in Cates's classroom.

SCENE II

The courtroom, two days later. It is bright midday, and the trial is in full swing. The JUDGE is on the bench; the jury, lawyers, officials and spectators crowd the courtroom. HOWARD, the thirteen-year-old boy, is on the witness stand. He is wretched in a starched collar and Sunday suit. The weather is as relentlessly hot as before. BRADY is examining the boy, who is a witness for the prosecution.

BRADY

Go on, Howard. Tell them what else Mr. Cates told you in the classroom.

HOWARD

Well, he said at first the earth was too hot for any life. Then it cooled off a mite, and cells and things begun to live.

BRADY

Cells?

HOWARD

Little bugs like, in the water. After that, the little bugs got to be bigger bugs, and sprouted legs and crawled up on the land.

BRADY

How long did this take, according to Mr. Cates?

HOWARD

Couple million years. Maybe longer. Then comes the fishes and the reptiles and the mammals. Man's a mammal.

BRADY

Along with the dogs and the cattle in the field: did he say that?

HOWARD

Yes, sir.
(DRUMMOND *is about to protest against prompting the witness; then he decides it isn't worth the trouble.*)

BRADY

Now, Howard, how did man come out of this slimy mess of bugs and serpents, according to your—"Professor"?

HOWARD

Man was sort of evoluted.
(BRADY *slaps his thigh*).

BRADY

Did you hear that, my friends? "Old World Monkeys"! According to Mr. Cates, you and I aren't even descended from good American monkeys! *(There is laughter)* Howard, listen carefully. In all this talk of bugs and "Evil-ution," . . . of slime and ooze, did Mr. Cates ever make any reference to God?

HOWARD

Not as I remember.

BRADY

Or the miracle He achieved in seven days as described in the beautiful Book of Genesis?

HOWARD

No, sir.
(BRADY *stretches out his arms in an all-embracing gesture.*)

BRADY

Ladies and gentlemen—

DRUMMOND

Objection! I ask that the court remind the learned counsel that this is not a Chautauqua tent. He is supposed to be submitting evidence to a jury. There are no ladies on the jury.

BRADY

Your Honor, I have no intention of making a speech. There is no need. I am sure that everyone on the jury, everyone within the sound of this boy's voice, is moved by his tragic confusion. He has been taught that he wriggled up like an animal from the filth and the muck below! (*Continuing fervently, the spirit is upon him*) I say that these Bible-haters, these "Evil-utionists," are brewers of poison. And the legislature of this sovereign state has had the wisdom to demand that the peddlers of poison—in bottles or in books—clearly label the products they attempt to sell! (*There is applause.* HOWARD *gulps.* BRADY *points at the boy*) I tell you, if this law is not upheld, this boy will become one of a generation, shorn of its faith by the teachings of Godless science! But if the full penalty of the law is meted out to Bertram Cates, the faithful the whole world over, who are watching us here, and listening to our every word, will call this courtroom blessed! (*Applause. Dramatically,* BRADY *moves to his chair. Condescendingly, he waves to* DRUMMOND.)

BRADY

Your witness, sir.
(BRADY *sits.* DRUMMOND *rises, slouches toward the witness stand.*)

DRUMMOND

Well, I sure am glad Colonel Brady didn't make a speech! (*Nobody laughs. The courtroom seems to resent* DRUMMOND's *gentle ridicule of the orator. To many, there is an effrontery in* DRUMMOND's *very voice—folksy and relaxed. It's rather like a harmonica following a symphony concert.*)
Howard, I heard you say that the world used to be pretty hot.

HOWARD

That's what Mr. Cates said.

DRUMMOND

You figure it was any hotter then than it is right now?

HOWARD

Guess it musta been. Mr. Cates read it to us from a book.

DRUMMOND

Do you know what book?

HOWARD

I guess that Mr. Darwin thought it up.

DRUMMOND

(Leaning on the arm of the boy's chair)
You figure anything's wrong about that, Howard?

HOWARD

Well, I dunno—

DAVENPORT

(Leaping up, crisply)
Objection, Your Honor. The defense is asking that a thirteen-year-old boy hand down an opinion on a question of morality!

DRUMMOND

(To the JUDGE)
I am trying to establish, Your Honor, that Howard—or Colonel Brady—or Charles Darwin—or anyone in this courtroom—or *you*, sir—has the right to *think!*

JUDGE

Colonel Drummond, the right to think is not on trial here.

DRUMMOND

(Energetically)
With all respect to the bench, I hold that the right to think is very much on trial! It is fearfully in danger in the proceedings of this court!

BRADY

(Rises)
A *man* is on trial!

DRUMMOND

A thinking man! And he is threatened with fine and imprisonment because he chooses to speak what he thinks.[7]

In the play, as in the Scopes trial, the defendant was found guilty, but many people, even those with strong religious convictions, were deeply troubled by some of the issues raised. What would other people whose voices we have heard in this chapter say about these court proceedings? Chet Raymo, a reputable scientist, does not seem to need to dismiss the particular knowledge and truth conveyed by religion in order to be a serious scientific investigator.

SOME QUESTIONS ABOUT KNOWING AND TRUTH

One of the things that might have become increasingly clear to you throughout this chapter is that we are discussing different *kinds* of truth. We are not suggesting that fantasy stories like *The Little Prince* will yield the same kind of knowledge—or truth—that you will gain in a physics or biology laboratory. But for many persons, the scientific knowledge derived from laboratory or other research does not suffice on its own either. In her book *Galileo's Daughter*, author Dava Sobel wonders how the daughter of the famous scientist, who is herself a Poor Clare nun, manages to hold together her own faithful Roman Catholic belief yet still support her father in scientific explorations that the Church of the day finds contrary to that belief. Sobel suggests that "[Galileo's daughter] approved of his endeavors because she knew the depth of his faith. She accepted Galileo's conviction that God had dictated the Holy Scriptures to guide men's spirits but proffered the unraveling of the universe as a challenge to their intelligence."[8] To Galileo and to his daughter, former Vatican librarian Cesare Cardinal Baronio was right when he proposed that "the Bible was a book about how one goes to heaven—not how Heaven goes."[9] Different kinds of knowledge, then, are intended for different purposes. To Baronio, as to Galileo, religious texts are to assist believers in understanding the ways in which God works in their lives and to provide meaning and a blueprint for living good and faithful lives. Such texts are not intended to offer scientific explanations about how the universe operates. That's why humans are endowed with intelligence and creativity. For Galileo, as for many modern scientists, religious belief is in no way in conflict with their scientific investigations—the two modes of knowing fulfill quite different although complementary purposes.

> *Investigate a concept that is an object of knowledge both to science and to religion, art, or philosophy. For example, "rainbow." To get you started, find and read Elizabeth Bishop's poem, "The Fish."*

WHAT SOME OTHERS HAVE SAID ABOUT KNOWLEDGE AND TRUTH

In this final section of the chapter, we turn to a biography of prize-winning scientist Barbara McClintock. In this work, biographer Evelyn Fox Keller emphasizes the ways in which McClintock defies the usual categorizations of scientist and scientific knowing in her insistence on paying attention to ways of knowing not always considered "respectable" in the scientific arena. Keller describes just what it is that makes McClintock's approach to knowledge and knowing—particularly in her career as a biologist—so unusual.

McClintock shares with all other natural scientists the credo that nature is lawful, and the dedication to the task of articulating those laws. And she shares, with at least some, the additional awareness that reason and experiment, generally claimed to be the principal means of this pursuit, do not suffice. To quote Einstein again, " . . . only intuition, resting on sympathetic understanding, can lead to [these laws]; . . . the daily effort comes from no deliberate intention or program, but straight from the heart."

A deep reverence for nature, a capacity for union with that which is to be known—these reflect a different image of science from that of a purely rational enterprise. Yet the two images have coexisted throughout history. We are familiar with the idea that a form of mysticism—a commitment to the unity of experience, the oneness of nature, the fundamental mystery underlying the laws of nature—plays an essential role in the process of scientific discovery. Einstein called it "cosmic religiosity." In turn, the experience of creative insight reinforces these commitments, fostering a sense of the limitations of the scientific method, and an appreciation of other ways of knowing . . . In [McClintock's] mind, what we call the scientific method cannot by itself give us "real understanding." "It gives us relationships which are useful, valid, and technically marvelous; however, they are not the truth." And it is by no means the only way of acquiring knowledge.

Keller refers to Einstein's idea of "cosmic religiosity." How does this relate to Victor Frankl's "unconscious religiousness" that we discussed in Chapter 1? And how does this fit with physicist Raymo's claim that science is not about the business of attributing meaning—that this task is solely the domain of religion? How might Keller—and McClintock—respond to either of these other thinkers?

That there are valid ways of knowing other than those conventionally espoused by science is a conviction of long standing for McClintock. It derives from a lifetime of experiences that science tells us little about, experiences that she herself could no more set aside than she could discard the anomalous pattern on a single kernel of corn. Perhaps it is this fidelity to her own experience that allows her to be more open than most other scientists about her unconventional beliefs. Correspondingly, she is open to unorthodox views in others, whether she agrees with them or not. She recalls, for example, a lecture given in the late 1940s at Cold Spring Harbor by Dick Roberts, a physicist from the Carnegie Institution of Washington, on the subject of extrasensory perception. Although she herself was out of town at the time, when she heard about the hostile reaction of her colleagues, she was incensed: "If they were as ignorant of the subject as I was, they had no reason for complaining."

McClintock suggests that the inability to understand a phenomenon like ESP (extrasensory perception) does not indicate that it does not exist. You may have encountered situations where someone dismissed an idea or thought that you or another put forward because it was either outside of the realm of their own thinking, or was something they were reluctant to consider. To McClintock, this was not just an intolerant approach; it was bad science. If possibilities are dismissed out of hand, they are never adequately studied to determine whether they are indeed based in some physical reality. This attitude led McClintock into research areas that were often dismissed by her colleagues.

For years, [McClintock] has maintained an interest in ways of learning other than those used in the West, and she made a particular effort to inform herself about the Tibetan Buddhists: "I was so startled by their method of training and by its results that I figured we were limiting ourselves by using what we call the scientific method."

Two kinds of Tibetan expertise interested her especially. One was the way the "running lamas" ran. These men were described as running for hours on end without sign of fatigue. It seemed to her exactly the same kind of effortless floating she had secretly learned as a child.

She was equally impressed by the ability that some Tibetans had developed to regulate body temperature: "We are scientists, and we know nothing basically about controlling our body temperature. [But] the Tibetans learn to live with nothing but a tiny cotton jacket. They're out there cold winters and hot summers, and when they have been through the learning process, they have to take certain tests. One of the tests is to take a wet blanket, put it over them, and dry that blanket in the coldest weather. And they dry it."

How were they able to do these things? What would one need to do to acquire this sort of "knowledge"? She began to look at related phenomena that were closer to home: "Hypnosis also had potentials that were quite extraordinary." She began to believe that not only one's temperature, but one's circulation, and many other bodily processes generally thought to be autonomous, could be brought under the influence of mind. She was convinced that the potential for mental control revealed in hypnosis experiments, and practiced by the Tibetans, was something that could be learned. "You can do it, it can be taught." And she set out to teach herself. Long before the word "biofeedback" was invented, McClintock experimented with ways to control her own temperature and blood flow, until, in time, she began to feel a sense of what it took.

But these interests were not popular. "I couldn't tell other people at the time because it was against the 'scientific method.' . . . We just hadn't touched on this kind of knowledge in our medical physiology, [and it is] very, very different from the knowledge we call the only way." What we label scientific knowledge is "lots of fun. You get lots of correlations, but you don't get the truth. . . . Things are much more marvelous than the scientific method allows us to conceive."

What does McClintock mean when she says that "you get lots of correlations, but you don't get the truth"? How does this observation of McClintock's relate to the contemporary trend among most scientists to never claim that they have "proven" something? In our own time, we are more accustomed to humbler claims for science, even the most long-term and carefully controlled studies and experiments. It is interesting to note that, although McClintock was shunned for many years by much of the scientific community for her interest in such topics as Tibetan Buddhism and hypnosis, in more recent years she has received many honors from scientific societies and institutions, including, in 1983, a Nobel prize.

> Our own method could tell us about some things, but not about others—for instance, she reflects, not about "the kinds of things that made it possible for me to be creative in an unknown way. *Why* do you know? Why were you so sure of something when you couldn't tell anyone else? You weren't sure in a boastful way; you were sure in what I call a completely internal way. . . . What you had to do was put it into their frame. Wherever it came in your frame, you had to work to put it into their frame. So you work with so-called scientific methods to put it into their frame *after* you know. Well, [the question is] *how* you know it. I had the idea that the Tibetans understood this *how* you know . . . " But among biologists, these interests are not common. McClintock is right to see them, and herself, as oddities. And here, as elsewhere, she takes pride in being different. She is proud to call herself a "mystic."

> Above all, she is proud of her ability to draw on these other ways of knowing in her work as a scientist. It is that which, to her, makes the life of science such a deeply satisfying one—even, at times, ecstatic. "What is ecstasy? I don't understand ecstasy, but I enjoy it. When I have it. Rare ecstasy."

> Somehow, she doesn't know how, she has always had an "exceedingly strong feeling" for the oneness of things: "Basically, everything is one. There is no way in which you draw a line between things. What we [normally] do is to make these subdivisions, but they're not real. Our educational system is full of subdivisions that are artificial, that shouldn't be there. I think maybe poets— although I don't read poetry—have some understanding of this." The ultimate descriptive task, for both artists and scientists, is to "ensoul" what one sees, to attribute to it the life one shares with it; one learns by identification. . . .

> From reading the text of nature, McClintock reaps the kind of understanding and fulfillment that others acquire from personal intimacy. In short, her "feeling for the organism" is the mainspring of her creativity. It both promotes and is promoted by her access to the profound connectivity of all biological forms—of the cell, of the organism, of the ecosystem.

> The flip side of the coin is her conviction that, without an awareness of the oneness of things, science can give us at most only nature-in-pieces; more often it gives us only pieces of nature. In McClintock's view, too restricted a reliance on scientific methodology invariably leads us into difficulty. "We've been spoiling the environment just dreadfully and thinking we were fine, because we were using the techniques of science. Then it turns into technology, and it's slapping us back because we didn't think it through. We were making assumptions we had no right to make. From the point of view of how the whole thing actually worked, we knew how part of it worked. . . . We didn't even inquire, didn't even see how the rest was going on. All these other things were happening and we didn't see it."[10]

Does McClintock's approach to her science offer new ways of approaching the tensions that are often seen to exist between "scientific" and "religious" knowledge? How might McClintock respond to the Scopes trial or to contemporary debates about the teaching of evolution or creation in schools?

For scientists like McClintock and Raymo, the religion/science conflict is a false and unnecessary dilemma. Today in the United States, many medical schools include training for potential physicians in some of the emerging data on spirituality and healing. People of faith enter the scientific disciplines in about the same numbers as anyone else. Increasingly, we see more of the kind of openness McClintock urged in approaching areas that once would have been seen as beyond the purview of science. Much of the tension between religious and scientific knowing occurs because of particular ways of interpreting the foundational texts and beliefs of a religious tradition. This is the issue to which we turn in Chapter 8.

CHAPTER EIGHT

INTERPRETING THE CANON: COMMUNICATING SACRED TRUTH

What do you think of when you hear the word "sacred"? In particular, what does it mean to you when applied to "truth," as we discussed this concept in the last chapter? Are those truths we hold "sacred" the ones that are verified through scientific inquiry, or are they more likely to be the kind of truth that doesn't lend itself to this kind of investigation? You will give different answers to these questions depending on your own perspectives. Some would hold that scientifically supported facts are the only things we can hold as "true"; some would go so far as to call such information "sacred." Others believe that there are other realms of truth and knowledge, and that it is here that "sacred" reality is known and experienced. Still others do not find it helpful or necessary to make such definite distinctions between the two. We will leave the question of how different religious traditions define and understand the "sacred" for the final part of this book. In the present chapter we will explore some of the ways in which peoples historically and today have tried to communicate that which they hold most "sacred" to one another and across ages and geographical distance.

SETTING THE STAGE: FACTS, TRUTH, AND WISDOM

Throughout this book we have been concerned with the kind of questions that seem to be of deepest concern to humans in their search for a meaningful life. The responses to those questions, filtered through religious and other cultural traditions, are what enable people to live together in communities, to survive difficult challenges and great hardship, and to deal with the ordinary and extraordinary experiences and events that are part of living. As we saw in the last chapter, different people use very different means to approach these questions of ultimate meaning. Our next set of readings comes from quite diverse sources. We begin with a mythic tale from Australia's Aborigine people. Does this short excerpt from the Karraur Tribe's creation story convey any degree of "truth"? What function might such a story play in the tribe's search for meaning?

> Once the earth was completely dark and silent; nothing moved on its barren surface. Inside a deep cave below the Nullabor Plain slept a beautiful woman, the Sun. The Great Father Spirit gently woke her and told her to emerge from her cave and stir the universe into life. The Sun Mother opened her eyes and darkness disappeared as her rays spread over the land; she took a breath and the atmosphere changed; the air gently vibrated as a small breeze blew.
>
> The Sun Mother then went on a long journey; from north to south and from east to west she crossed the barren land. The earth held the seed potencies of all things, and wherever the Sun's gentle rays touched the earth, there grasses, shrubs, and trees grew until the land was covered in vegetation. In each of the deep caverns in the earth, the Sun found living creatures which, like herself, had been slumbering for untold ages. She stirred the insects into life in all their forms and told them to spread through the grasses and trees, then she woke the snakes, lizards, and other reptiles, and they slithered out of their deep hole. As the snakes moved through and along the earth they formed rivers and they themselves became creators, like the Sun. Behind the snakes mighty rivers flowed, teeming with all kinds of fish and water life. Then she called for the animals, the marsupials, and the many other creatures to awake and make their homes on the earth. The Sun Mother then told all the creatures that the days would from time to time change from wet to dry and from cold to hot, and so she made the seasons. One day while all the animals, insects, and other creatures were watching, the Sun traveled far in the sky to the west and, as the sky shone red, she sank from view and darkness spread across the land once more. The creatures were alarmed and huddled together in fear. Some time later, the sky began to glow on the horizon to the east and the Sun rose smiling into the sky again. The Sun Mother thus provided a period of rest for all her creatures by making this journey each day.[1]

Historically, people have been intrigued by questions of origins. How did the world come to be? What was the origin of life in all its many forms? What is the significance of life? You might be more familiar with the next account, from the book of Genesis in the Hebrew Scriptures.

> When God began to create heaven and earth—the earth being unformed and void, with darkness over the surface of the deep and a wind from God sweeping over the water—God said, "Let there be light"; and there was light. God saw that the light was good, and God separated the light from the darkness. God called the light Day, and the darkness He called Night. And there was evening and there was morning, a first day.
>
> God said, "Let there be an expanse in the midst of the water, that it may separate water from water." God made the expanse, and it separated the water

which was below the expanse from the water which was above the expanse. And it was so. God called the expanse Sky. And there was evening and there was morning, a second day.

God said, "Let the water below the sky be gathered into one area, that the dry land may appear." And it was so. God called the dry land Earth, and the gathering of waters He called Seas. And God saw that this was good. And God said, "Let the earth sprout vegetation: seed-bearing plants, fruit trees of every kind on earth that bear fruit with the seed in it." And it was so. The earth brought forth vegetation: seed-bearing plants of every kind, and trees of every kind bearing fruit with the seed in it. And God saw that this was good. And there was evening and there was morning, a third day.

God said, "Let there be lights in the expanse of the sky to separate day from night; they shall serve as signs for the set times—the days and the years; and they shall serve as lights in the expanse of the sky to shine upon the earth." And it was so. God made the two great lights, the greater light to dominate the day and the lesser light to dominate the night, and the stars. And God set them in the expanse of the sky to shine upon the earth, to dominate the day and the night, and to separate light from darkness. And God saw that this was good. And there was evening and there was morning, a fourth day.[2]

Make a list of the similarities and differences in these two accounts. Consider what they deal with, how the environment of the story's hearers is important, and whether elements like time, emotion, and characters, used in all stories, enter the picture.

Why do you think these stories continue to have power for their listeners? Do these stories conflict with what you know of scientific explanations for the seasons and for night and day? In an address to The American Academy of Arts and Sciences, physicist Victor Weisskopf outlines current scientific theory regarding the Big Bang, and raises interesting questions regarding multiple kinds of truth. What do you think Weisskopf would think about suggestions that scientific explanations must be wrong if they contradict "The Bible," as some religious believers would say? What would he say about the claims made by some scientists that religion is mere superstition and has no place in the life of the serious investigator?

It must be emphasized again that [the Big Bang and other scientific theories] are unproven hypotheses. They may turn out to be pure fantasies, but the ideas are impressively grandiose.

The origin of the universe is not only of scientific interest. It always was the subject of mythology, art, and religion. Such approaches are complementary to scientific ones. Most familiarly, the Old Testament describes the beginning of the world with the creation of light on the first day. It seemed contradictory that the sun, our terrestrial source of light, was only created on day four, but it turns out to be in line with current scientific thought, according to which the early universe was full of various kinds of radiation long before the sun appeared.

Those first days have been depicted in various forms, in pictures and poetry, but to me, Franz Josef Haydn's oratorio *The Creation* is the most remarkable rendition of the Big Bang. At the beginning we hear a choir of angels singing mysteriously and softly, "And God Said Let There Be Light." And at the words "And There Was Light" the entire choir and the orchestra explode into a blazing C major chord. There is no more beautiful and impressive presentation of the beginning of everything.[3]

Weisskopf is clear that even the wonderful theories of contemporary science are just that: theories. But he is also clear that one need not have advanced degrees and experience in physics to know the grandeur of creation and experience and express that reality in multiple ways. Could you say that the stories from the Aboriginal and Hebrew peoples are in some way a metaphor for the Big Bang? How do you think Weisskopf might respond to this suggestion? How does this touch on what we might call the "communication of sacred reality"?

Listen to the beginning of the Haydn oratorio to which Weisskopf refers. Does it have the same effect on you that it does on Weisskopf? Can you think of other pieces of music or other art that likewise convey this meaning? Are there other ways in which you have experienced what Weisskopf is talking about? For instance, you might have heard Gustav Holst's "The Planets," or you may be familiar with the creation story in C. S. Lewis's The Narnia Chronicles.

WHAT DO YOU THINK? PASSING ON SACRED TRUTH

In every culture and religion, there are multiple ways of passing on the information, symbols, rituals, and traditions that are of most importance to the community. Think about those elements within your own culture or family background that have been passed on to you. Which of them, if any, would you say fall into the category of "sacred truth"? What makes a particular truth "sacred" rather than simply important, even significant? As we will see in Chapter 10, people have very different ideas about what makes something "sacred," and how to define the term. For now, begin to develop your own definition, based upon your own experience.

Those of you who have any familiarity with Christian tradition will recognize the Lord's Prayer, the most well-known and beloved of all Christian prayers. This prayer is recited by individuals during almost all Christian worship services, and it is often the first prayer learned by a child in a Christian family. Below, we offer three English language versions of this prayer, one traditional and the others more contemporary interpretations. This prayer is used so often that most Christians can recite the traditional version without thinking about it at all—almost like a habit. What difference does it make to change the language and interpretation of such a prayer? What is lost and what is gained? Does it make it more significant, less significant, or simply different?

Traditional Version:

Our Father, who art in heaven
Hallowed be thy name
Thy kingdom come,
thy will be done,
On earth as it is in heaven.
Give us this day our daily bread
And forgive us our trespasses
As we forgive those who trespass
against us.
Lead us not into temptation
But deliver us from evil
For thine is the kingdom, the power,
and the glory,
For ever and ever. Amen

Revised Version:

Our Father in heaven,
hallowed be your name,
your kingdom come,
your will be done,
on earth as in heaven.
Give us today our daily bread.
Forgive us our sins
as we forgive those who sin
against us.
Save us from the time of trial
and deliver us from evil
For the kingdom, the power, and
the glory are yours
now and forever. Amen

Contemporary Version:

Eternal Spirit,
Earth-maker, Pain-bearer, Life-giver,
Source of all that is and that shall be,
Father and Mother of us all,
Loving God, in whom is heaven:
The hallowing of your name echo through the universe!
The way of your justice be followed by the peoples of the world!
Your heavenly will be done by all created beings!

time for them, but in the end he pretended to give in, because they were such nice birds. "I'll sing for you, " he told the ducks, "but you must help me. "

"We'll do what you want. Tell us the rules."

"Well, you must form three rows. In the front row, all you fat ones, get in there. In the second row go all those who are neither fat nor thin—the in-betweens. The poor scrawny ones go in the third row, way down there. And you have to act out the song, do what the words tell you. Now the words to my first song are 'Close your eyes and dance!'"

The ducks all lined up with their eyes shut, flapping their wings, the fat ones up front. Iktome took a big club from underneath his coat. "Sing along as loud as you can, " he ordered, "and keep your eyes shut. Whoever peeks will get blind." He told them to sing so that their voices would drown out the "thump, thump" of his club when he hit them over the head.

He knocked them down one by one and was already half done when one of those low-down, skinny ducks in the back row opened its eyes and saw what Iktome was up to.

"Hey, wake up!" it hollered. "That Iktome is killing us all!" The ducks that were left opened their eyes and took off.

Iktome didn't mind. He already had more fat ducks than he could eat.

Iktome is like some of those bull-shipping politicians who make us close our eyes and sing and dance for them while they knock us on the head. Democratic ducks, Republican ducks, it makes no difference. The fat, stupid ones are the first in the pot. It's always the skinny, no-account, low-class duck in the back that doesn't hold still. That's a good Indian who keeps his eyes open. Iktome is an evil schemer, Grandpa told me, but luckily he's so greedy that most of the time he outsmarts himself.[5]

This is a "mythic" story, one that contains elements that our experience tells us can't really happen, fantastic events such as a talking spider large and strong enough to club to death a number of ducks. What, if anything, does this myth say that might be "true"?

The stories to which we have access today are mostly those that have, at some time, been recorded in written form. Whether we are most familiar with a particular culture's set of tales, or with the religious texts of some tradition, the stories that form the basis of our communal past probably had their origins in the kind of storytelling referred to by Lame Deer.

Now we turn to a rather different kind of story, told in the Taoist *Chuang-tzu.* How is this story different from those related above? Are there ways in which it is similar? Would you call it a legend, a myth, or something else?

When Chuang Tzu went to Khu, he saw an empty skull, bleached but still retaining its shape. Tapping it with his horse-switch, he asked it, "Did you, Sir, in your greed of life, fail in the lessons of reason, and come to this? Or did you do so, in the service of a perishing state, by the punishment of the axe? Or was it through your evil conduct, reflecting disgrace on your parents and on your wife and children? Or was it through your hard endurance of cold and hunger? Or was it that you had completed your term of life?"

Having given expression to these questions, he took up the skull, and made a pillow of it when he went to sleep. At midnight the skull appeared to him in a dream and said, "What you said to me was after the fashion of an orator. All your words were about the entanglements of men in their lifetime. There are none of those things after death. Would you like to hear me, Sir, tell you about death?" "I should," said Chuang Tzu, and the skull resumed: "In death there are not the distinctions of ruler above and minister below. There are none of the phenomena of the four seasons. Tranquil and at ease, our years are those of heaven and earth. No king in his court has greater enjoyment than we have." Chuang Tzu did not believe it, and said, "If I could get the Ruler of our Destiny to restore your body to life with its bones and flesh and skin, and to give you back your father and mother, your wife and children, and all your village acquaintances, would you wish me to do so?" The skull stared intently at him, knitted its brows, and said, "How should I cast away the enjoyment of my royal court, and undertake again the toils of life among mankind?"[6]

In the telling of this story, the author uses ordinary rather than fantastic events to make a point. You might not consider the finding of a skull "ordinary," but it was probably not uncommon in Chuang-tzu's time. Stories that use everyday contemporary themes and objects to convey a deeper message are sometimes referred to as parables. When we are considering narratives that have been passed down through hundreds, even thousands of years, there is seldom a way to verify the factual accuracy of most of the events or people described. To what extent, if at all, do these last two stories depend upon such factual verification to convey their truths?

> a. Write or tell and record a story of a momentous event that has happened in your lifetime, as you might tell it to your grandchildren. What elements will be most important to remember? What form will your story take so that it will best capture these significant components? How will you tell it so that it is sure to be remembered?
>
> Or:
>
> b. Create a teaching story that you might tell to your children or grandchildren, to get across something that you consider to be a very important point that they will need to know to get along well in their lives.

You have no doubt encountered a great number of words in your life that have been intended to communicate truth of one kind or another to you. Some of these words might have been in the form of stories: myths, legends, parables, biographies, histories. But what other forms can words take to pass along information, beliefs, truth? What form best enables us to communicate those concepts that are hardest to express because they are not as concrete, as easy to grasp as the more clearly definable realities of our lives? To some extent, all of the stories we have encountered use the language of metaphor. But religious and other traditions are not only concerned with describing realities that transcend our current material existence.

The following reading is from a collection of Swahili sayings. These sayings are usually communicated orally and are common to many tribal groups in East Africa who speak the Swahili language. Which of these sayings, or proverbs, sound familiar to you? Which seem quite different from anything you have heard before? Are there any that you can't understand at all in terms of what is being communicated?

> He who laughs at a scar has not received a wound.
> He who ridicules the good will be overtaken by evil.
> A fool is a person too, don't say he is a cow.
> A man's greatness and respect come from himself.
> He who does not trust others cannot be trusted.
> It is useless for me to recognize him who does not recognize me.
> Help him who helps you.
> Please him who does not please you.
> He who does not harm you, do no harm to him.
> Love your enemy.
> It is better to build bridges than walls.
> A boat doesn't go forward if each one is rowing his own way.
> Unity is strength, division is weakness.
> People were told "Come and live together"; they were not told "Come and compete with one another."
> Avarice is the root of all evil.
> If you can't build a hut, build a shack.
> You do not have the strength to defeat elephant.
> If you bake fish, you cannot pluck a chicken.
> There is no rainy season without mosquitoes.
> He who wants everything loses everything.
> He who chooses is never satisfied.
> The environment is the beginning of success.
> A person saved by God is not crooked.
> Payment on earth is the reckoning of the hereafter.
> The world is nothing, depend not on it.
> The world is a mixture of good and evil.[7]

Does the fact that some of these proverbs seem to contradict each other detract from the wisdom in the sayings?

Think of some of the sayings or proverbs that come from your own tradition. If you don't know any, ask your parents or grandparents. Do any of them seem to teach the same lesson as any of the Swahili proverbs? Are there proverbs or other wise sayings in your culture that you don't think would be easily understood by people outside the culture? Are there sayings in your culture that seem to contradict each other? Why do you think this is so?

Take a copy of Bartlett's *or the* Oxford Dictionary of Quotations *and see how many of these proverbs you could match in the Western tradition. Work with some of your classmates. Then look at the remaining proverbs. Do they each seem universal even though we don't have a matching proverb in the West, or are they special perceptions of the Swahili? Has the gist of any of these been preserved in African American tradition, e.g., as song?*

Many of the excerpts you have read in this section have come from ancient traditions and texts, handed down orally or in written form over generations. Is this the only expression of sacred truth? As you read the next selection, from a poem by 20th century poet Denise Levertov, consider whether Levertov's words—and those of other poets whose work you have encountered—have the power to communicate profound truths. Levertov comes out of the Christian tradition, in which one of the metaphors commonly used for Jesus, believed by Christians to be the Son of God, is "Lamb of God." If you have read or heard other references to this metaphor, does Levertov's poetic reflection raise any new questions or possibilities for you? What kind of understanding of God do you think Levertov is trying to suggest here?

vi **Agnus Dei** (Lamb of God)
Given that lambs
are infant sheep, that sheep
are afraid and foolish, and lack
the means of self-protection, having
neither rage nor claws,
venom nor cunning,
what then
is this 'Lamb of God'?
This pretty creature, vigorous
to nuzzle at milky dugs,
woolbearer, bleater,
leaper in air for delight of being, who finds in astonishment
four legs to land on, the grass
all it knows of the world?
 With whom we would like to play,
whom we'd lead with ribbons, but may not bring
into our houses because
it would soil the floor with its droppings?

What terror lies concealed
in strangest words, O *lamb*
of God that taketh away

the Sins of the World: an innocence
                    smelling of ignorance,
                    born in bloody snowdrifts,
                    licked by forebearing
dogs more intelligent than its entire flock put together?
                    God then,
          encompassing all things, is
          defenseless? Omnipotence
          has been tossed away, reduced
          to a wisp of damp wool?
                    And we,
          frightened, bored, wanting
only to sleep till catastrophe
has raged, clashed, seethed and gone by without us,
                    wanting then
to awaken in quietude without remembrance of agony,
                    we who in shamefaced private hope
          had looked to be plucked from fire and given
          a bliss we deserved for having imagined it,
                    is it implied that *we*
          must protect this perversely weak
          animal, whose muzzle's nudgings
          suppose there is milk to be found in us?
          Must hold to our icy hearts
          a shivering God?

So be it.
          Come, rag of pungent
          quiverings,
                    dim star.
                              Let's try
          if something human still can shield you,
                    spark
          of remote light.[8]

What does Levertov do with the "lamb" metaphor? Do you think this is the kind of understanding that was in the minds of those who first used this image? Are there other ways to interpret this metaphor?

CONVEYING SACRED TRUTH THROUGH SCRIPTURE

What comes to your mind when you hear the word "scripture"? While we have suggested above that sacred truth is passed on—communicated—in many different media and forms, the "scriptures"—sacred texts—of some religious traditions hold a particular power and authority. We have already encountered excerpts from some of these texts, in the forms of stories, rules and laws, and so forth. How, if at all, is Sacred Scripture different from the other forms of truth-bearing communications we have read in this chapter?

In almost every case, the stories and other materials that comprise the sacred texts of any tradition have been handed on orally, often for hundreds, if not thousands, of years, before they are recorded in written form. Then they were edited, revised, and rearranged over another long period of time before they were accepted in the form in which we know them today. Many of the stories, such as that of Noah and the flood in the Jewish, Christian, and Muslim sacred texts, have striking similarities with much older stories from the Babylonians. As peoples moved and encountered different traditions, elements of those traditions were incorporated into the culture and adapted to fit with the existing belief system. The oral transmission of stories made it much easier, of course, to adapt and change the tradition, to make it accessible and relevant to new generations who might be facing a radically different context and situation. On the other hand, oral transmission meant running the risk of losing the stories if those charged with their protection and communication died or were otherwise unable to complete their duties.

At some point in time, those traditions with written scriptures made decisions about just which of the multiple stories and other wisdom codes of the people should be protected and kept for all time as part of the "canon" of the tradition. This idea of a canon is not peculiar to religions. What is your own major field of study? What writings or other materials comprise the "canon" for your discipline? For example, whether or not you like or agree with Freud, you are not a well-prepared psychologist if you are not familiar with his basic writings; similarly, you are not a scientist if you have never heard of Einstein or Newton. In these latter examples, of course, the canon is constantly changing and being updated as new information and resources are added—and some obsolete texts removed. For many religious traditions, the canon is "closed," such as the Jewish Torah, the Christian Bible, and the Muslim Qur'an. While new writings about the tradition will continue throughout time, they will not be added to the sacred text itself. Buddhism and Taoism, on the other hand, do not have closed canons and the possibility exists for further material to be added.

> *What do you see as the advantages of a closed text for religions? What are the disadvantages? How would you revise the canon of your own religious tradition today? For example, if you are Jewish or Christian, would you include the whole of Genesis or only parts of it? If you were starting from scratch, in the early 21st Century, what readings, music, movement (dance), and art would you include if you were putting together a canon for your community?*

Have you ever attended any kind of religious service, whether a regular weekly service, a wedding, a funeral, or some other event? If so, what role, if any, did scripture play in the celebration? Were texts used other than formal scripture? Was there any informal language in the service? Who read from the scripture? Were there any particular rituals or symbols surrounding the sacred texts themselves? Where were the texts placed? How were they handled? The answers to these questions give a glimpse into the role that scripture plays for the community.

We have already encountered stories in the form of myths and parables. Some of these stories are probably meant to be read as meaningful fiction— allegories. The story of the spider and the ducks is an example. But are there other kinds of stories that reveal truths, even sacred truths? Read the following excerpt from the Hindu *Bhagavad-Gita*, and ask yourself what kind of story it is. What do you think is the fundamental truth it is trying to convey?

The prince Arjuna is about to engage in battle against a rival faction to claim the right to rule India. Upon arrival at the battlefield, however, he is struck by the horror of having to go to war against those who are his kin, knowing that many will die. As Arjuna realizes the implications of the upcoming fight, he instructs his charioteer, the god Krishna, to halt in a place where he can observe the forces preparing to do battle.

> Arjuna saw them standing there: fathers, grandfathers, teachers, uncles, brothers, sons, grandsons, fathers-in-law, and friends, kinsmen on both sides, each side arrayed against the other. In despair, overwhelmed with pity, he said: "As I see my own kinsmen, gathered here, eager to fight, my legs weaken, my mouth dries, my body trembles, my hair stands on end . . . I see evil omens, Krishna; no good can come from killing my own kinsmen in battle. I have no desire for victory or for the pleasures of kingship. What good is kingship, or happiness, or life itself when those for whose sake we desire them—teachers, fathers, sons, grandfathers, uncles, fathers-in-law, grandsons, brothers-in-law, and other kinsmen—stand here in battle ranks, ready to give up their fortunes and their lives? Though they want to kill me, I have no desire to kill them, not even for the kingship of the three worlds, let alone for that of the earth. . . .
>
> Arjuna said . . . "Tell me where my duty lies, which path I should take. I am your pupil; I beg you for your instruction. For I cannot imagine how any victory—even if I were to gain the kingship of the whole earth or of all the gods in heaven—could drive away this grief that is withering my senses."
>
> Having spoken thus to Krishna, Arjuna said: "I will not fight," and fell silent. As Arjuna sat there, downcast, between the two armies, Krishna smiled at him, then spoke these words.
>
> THE BLESSED LORD SAID:
> Although you mean well, Arjuna,
> your sorrow is sheer delusion.
> Wise men do not grieve
> for the dead or for the living.
>
> Never was there a time
> when I did not exist or you,
> or these kings; nor will there come
> a time when we cease to be.

Arjuna and his charioteer, Lord Krishna, prepare for battle.

> Just as in this body, the Self
> passes through childhood, youth,
> and old age, so after death
> it passes to another body.
>
> Physical sensations—cold
> and heat, pleasure and pain—
> are transient: they come and go;
> so bear them patiently, Arjuna.
>
> Only the man who is unmoved
> by any sensations, the wise man
> indifferent to pleasure, to pain,
> is fit for becoming deathless.
>
> Nonbeing can never be;
> being can never not be.
> Both these statements are obvious
> to those who have seen the truth.
>
> The presence that pervades the universe
> is imperishable, unchanging,
> beyond both *is* and is *not:*
> how could it ever vanish?[9]

This story from one of Hinduism's sacred texts has been one of the most influential narratives in the tradition. What different perspectives does the conversation between Arjuna and Krishna give on the reality of war, particularly war that pits kinsfolk against one another? What rationale does Krishna use in his attempt to convince Arjuna that he not only can but should engage in this battle? What messages do you think this passage might contain for contemporary Hindus—or others who might read it?

Sometimes, the "words" used by traditions to convey sacred truths are very straightforward and direct. Consider this brief passage from the book of Acts in the Christian Bible. What is the author trying to communicate to readers in this passage? What kind of writing is it?

> So those who welcomed [Peter's] message were baptized, and that day about
> three thousand persons were added.
> They devoted themselves to the apostles' teaching and fellowship, to the breaking of bread and the prayers.
> Awe came upon everyone, because many wonders and signs were being done by the apostles.
> All who believed were together and had all things in common; they would sell their possessions and goods and distribute the proceeds to all, as any had need.
> Day by day, as they spent much time together in the temple, they broke bread at home and ate their food with glad and generous hearts, praising God and having the goodwill of all the people. And day by day the LORD added to their number those who were being saved.[10]

Judaism, Christianity and Islam are religions that claim a historical identity. As we saw in Chapter 3, many of the rituals and practices in these religions are rooted in events that the community believes to have actually taken place in history. Think of such examples as the Jewish celebration of Passover and the Christian commemoration of Easter. While myth, legend and parable are present in these traditions in abundance, historical story also plays a central role. Does the passage from Acts simply recount historical activity, or might it also contain "sacred truth"?

The following passage is from the Qur'an, the holy text of Islam. Is this a teaching story, a history, a set of proverbs, or something else? Does this remind you of any other writing you are familiar with? How would you describe the kind of writing found in this selection?

> In the name of Allah, most benevolent, ever-merciful.
> O MEN, FEAR your Lord
> who created you from a single cell,
> and from it created its mate,
> and from the two of them dispersed men and women
> (male and female) in multitudes.
> So fear God in whose name you ask
> of one another (the bond of) relationships.
> God surely keeps watch over you.
> Give to the orphans their possessions,

and do not replace things of your own which are bad
with things which are good among theirs, and do not
intermix their goods with your own and make use of them,
for this is a grievous crime.
If you fear you cannot be equitable to orphan girls
(in your charge, or misuse their persons), then marry
women who are lawful for you, two, three, or four;
but if you fear you cannot treat so many with equity,
marry only one, or a maid or captive.
This is better than being iniquitous.
Give to women their dowers willingly,
but if they forego part of it themselves,
then use it to your advantage. . . .
Men have a share in what the parents and relatives
leave behind at death;
and women have a share
in what the parents and relatives leave behind.
Be it large or small
a legal share is fixed.
And when the relatives and orphans and the needy
collect at the time of the division (of property)
provide for them too,
and talk kindly to them. . . .
Those who devour the possessions
of the orphans unjustly
devour only fire,
and will surely burn in Hell.[11]

Throughout the text there are references to the ways in which the believers
should behave toward women and orphans. Remembering the cultural and
historical context in which this text was recorded, do any of these instructions
seem surprising? What do you think is the main point of this passage in terms
of sacred truth that needs to be communicated to believers across the ages? As
with many religious traditions, this founding text of Islam contains ideas that
were a revolutionary step forward in their own time and context.

CONVEYING SACRED TRUTH WITHOUT WORDS

So far in this chapter, we have been exploring a variety of verbal ways in
which truth—the truth that is most essential and central to human self-
understanding—is communicated. But are words the only ways in which to
share our most deeply held passions and convictions? Above, we suggested
that you listen to Haydn's "Creation"—the piece of music referred to by scientist Victor Weisskopf. Can something like a musical composition actually
hold and convey "truth"? And can it do so in a way that is different, perhaps
more powerful, than words?

Think of some belief that you hold to be a "sacred" truth. It might not have to do with God, but should be something that you really believe and that holds great importance for you. Is there a way of communicating that truth which doesn't use words? Could you make one up? Think of the proverb, "actions speak louder than words." Look back at the chapters on rituals and symbols for help.

Have you ever spent time in front of a particular painting or sculpture in a museum or art gallery, deeply moved or even spellbound by something you are experiencing as "communication" from the artist? In his novel *My Name Is Asher Lev*, Chaim Potok tells the story of a young Hasidic Jewish boy whose need to draw and paint is all-encompassing. Asher's mother tries to understand her son's compulsion, and acts in many ways as a buffer between Asher and his father, who travels widely in Europe helping Hasidic communities establish schools in the aftermath of repression and persecution because of their Jewish faith. Of particular concern to Asher's father is that his son paints nudes, something he thinks is surely "from the other side," and not from the divine. Asher tries to understand both his father's concerns and his own compulsion. His teacher, Jacob Kahn, acknowledges that Asher's commitment to his art will inevitably cause pain to his parents and his community. "Become a great artist. That is the only way to justify what you are doing to everyone's life," suggests Kahn. Asher reflects on these words:

> I did not understand what he meant. I did not feel I had to justify anything. I had not willfully hurt anyone. What did I have to justify? I did not want to paint in order to justify anything; I wanted to paint because I wanted to paint. I wanted to paint the same way my father wanted to travel and work for the Rebbe. My father worked for Torah. I worked for—what? How could I explain it? For beauty? No. Many of the pictures I painted were not beautiful. For what, then? For a truth I did not know how to put into words. For a truth I could only bring to life by means of color and line and texture and form.[12]

Are there ways in which Asher's work and his father's are parallel? Have you ever felt like Asher, that you are trying to communicate a truth that you "do not know how to put into words"? If so, what medium did you use to try to communicate more effectively? Did all the people around you understand what you were doing?

Asher's studies eventually take him to Europe, first to the city of Florence. Novelist Potok describes Asher's reaction to his first encounter with Michelangelo's *Pieta*—a sculpture depicting the anguish of the women after Jesus' crucifixion. Why is Asher, the Orthodox Hasidic Jew, so moved by this very Christian work of art? And why does he feel so much conflict because of his feelings?

> I went to the Piazza del Duomo often in those weeks to see the Michelangelo *Pieta* and the Vasari fresco and the Ghiberti East Doors of the baptistery. I carried

> my sketchbook and drawing pencils wherever I went, but I remember that the
> first time I saw the Michelangelo *Pieta* in the Duomo I could not draw it. It was
> the fifth day of July. I stared at its Romanesque and Gothic contours, at the
> twisted arm and bent head, at the circle formed by Jesus and the two Marys, at
> the vertical of Nicodemus—I stared at the geometry of the stone and felt the
> stone luminous with strange suffering and sorrow. I was an observant Jew, yet
> that block of stone moved through me like a cry, like the call of seagulls over
> morning surf, like—like the echoing blasts of the shofar sounded by the Rebbe.
> I do not mean to blaspheme. My frames of reference have been formed by the
> life I have lived. I do not know how a devout Christian reacts to that *Pieta*. I was
> only able to relate it to elements in my own lived past. I stared at it. I walked
> slowly around it. I do not remember how long I was there that first time. When
> I came back out into the brightness of the crowded square, I was astonished to
> discover that my eyes were wet.[13]

Does Asher's reaction to this Christian work of art mean that he has abandoned the "truths" of his Jewish heritage? Have you ever found "truth" in something very foreign to your own culture and background?

Asher continues to be drawn to the wealth of art in European museums, many of them with explicitly Christian themes. Gradually, these themes begin to creep into his own work. He paints a portrait of his mother in front of the window of the family apartment. When Asher finished the painting, he "looked a very long time at the painting and knew it was incomplete. . . . The telephone poles were only distant reminders of the brutal reality of a crucifix." The passion of all the anguish and torment that his mother had lived in trying to mediate between Asher and his father were not fully expressed. "It would have made me a whore to leave it incomplete," says Asher. So he returns to a fresh canvas.

> I stretched a canvas identical in size to the painting now on the easel. I put
> the painting against a wall and put the fresh canvas in its place. With charcoal, I
> drew the frame of the living-room window of our Brooklyn apartment. I drew
> the strip of wood that divided the window and the slanting bottom of the
> Venetian blind a few inches from the top of the window. On top—not behind
> this time, but on top—of the window I drew my mother in her housecoat, with
> her arms extended along the horizontal of the blind, her wrists tied to it with
> the cords of the blind, her legs tied at the ankles to the vertical of the inner
> frame with another section of the cord of the blind. I arched her body and
> twisted her head. I drew my father standing to her right, dressed in a hat and
> coat and carrying an attache case. I drew myself standing to her left, dressed in
> paint-spattered clothes and a fisherman's cap and holding a palette and a long
> spearlike brush. I exaggerated the size of the palette and balanced it by exaggerating the size of my father's attache case. We were looking at my mother and at
> each other. I split my mother's head into balanced segments, one looking at me,
> one looking at my father, one looking upward. The torment, the tearing anguish
> I felt in her, I put into her mouth, into the twisting curve of her head, the arching of her slight body, the clenching of her small fists, the taut downward point-

ing of her thin legs. I sprayed fixative on the charcoal and began to put on the colors, working with the same range of hues I had utilized in the previous painting—ochres, grays, alizarin, Prussian and cobalt blue—and adding tones of burnt sienna and cadmium red medium for my hair and beard. I painted swiftly in a strange nerveless frenzy of energy. For all the pain you suffered, my mama. For all the torment of your past and future years, my mama. For all the anguish this picture of pain will cause you. For the unspeakable mystery that brings good fathers and sons into the world and lets a mother watch them tear at each other's throats. For the Master of the Universe, whose suffering world I do not comprehend. For dreams of horror, for nights of waiting, for memories of death, for the love I have for you, for all the things I remember, and for all the things I should remember but have forgotten, for all these I created this painting—an observant Jew working on a crucifixion because there was no aesthetic mold in his own religious tradition into which he could pour a painting of ultimate anguish and torment.[14]

Why do you think Asher, an observant Hasidic Jew, would paint a picture using the very Christian image of the crucifixion? What "truth" does Asher seek to convey that requires this image? What does Asher mean when he says "for all the anguish and pain this will cause you," referring to his mother? Why does he *do* something that he knows will cause such pain to people he loves? And why does he then go on to include these very paintings in a show in a New York gallery? When he first sees the paintings hung, before the show opens, even he, the painter, is awed by their power:

I came to the end of the short wall and turned and caught my breath. She had placed the crucifixions on the wall opposite where I stood, before the turn to the elevator. They dominated the wall. I stared at them and felt them leap across the entire length of the gallery and clutch at me. I had not imagined them to be so powerful. I should have muted them. They could not be left so raw and powerful. I felt myself sweating. I felt the long clutching grasp of the canvases and myself sweating and saw my mother tied to the vertical and horizontal lines of the painting and saw my father and mother looking at the painting. Then I turned away, terrified before such an act of creation. Master of the Universe, I did not mean to attempt to emulate Your power, Your ability to create out of nothing. I only wanted to make a few good paintings. Master of the Universe, forgive me. Please. Forgive me. I turned my back to the paintings and closed my eyes, for I could no longer endure seeing the works of my own hands and knowing the pain those works would soon inflict upon people I loved.

I heard a soft voice behind me and turned and saw Anna Schaeffer. She wore a pale-blue satin dress and jewels. There was a diamond tiara in her silver hair. She looked regal.

"What do you think?" she asked. "Isn't it a splendid show?"[15]

The reaction of Asher's father is predictable, as is that of his Jewish community. And many Christians are incensed that this Hasidic artist would take their sacred symbol and use it in such a way. Why do people from both of these religious traditions feel somewhat betrayed by these works of art? What is it about some art that gives it this kind of power?

Are there other art forms that have the power to convey those truths that are often beyond words? Have you ever attended a performance by a mime or a dance group? What are some of the ways in which we communicate best our feelings of love to those closest to us? In very important ways, our bodies are powerful communicators of the "truth" of our feelings. Frequently, these modes of communication include words, but the words are enhanced by the action, the gesture.

> *Go to a place of worship—a church, Quaker meeting hall, synagogue, mosque, Buddhist or Hindu temple, etc.—for a service, if possible. Look carefully for ways other than the solely verbal that the people use to communicate sacred truth. With whom are they communicating? With themselves? With one another? With some kind of transcendent sacred reality? What is communicated to the "outsider"?*

ENGAGING SACRED TRUTHS

Whether we are talking about the formal scriptural canons of traditions such as Hinduism, Judaism, Buddhism or the more informal expressions found in indigenous cultures, we are approaching "truths" that ask for our particular concern and consideration. Stories, dances, works of art at the heart of the community's sense of meaning communicate to believers that which they think is of ultimate value.

While we may find stories and concepts from different traditions exciting, meaningful, even full of "truth," the reality is that we need to approach them with care. Can we ever embrace the perspectives in the same way as do the adherents of the tradition? We now introduce you to Mikk, a character in Katie Waitman's *The Merro Tree*. Mikk is a performance artist, a singer/dancer whose major work is mastery of the Songdance, the central art form that expresses the truth of the Somalite people, who are on the verge of extinction. Mikk performs the dance for the last dying Somalites and realizes at the end of his performance that he is causing great anguish to the group. Why are they so troubled? Is Mikk's performance flawed, failing to do honor to the truth of the community?

> The more he sang, the louder, more agonized the protests until he had to abandon the movement consciousness altogether. He was hurting them.
>
> "Whees-aru, I–I'm sorry. I've offended with my ineptitude."
>
> "No," the Somalite wheezed, "your performance was excellent. By far the most beautiful harmonic web any outworlder has ever created. That is why we grieve."

"I don't understand."

"You must forget our art. Never perform it again."

Mikk was dumbfounded.

"Forget . . . ?"

"Yes. As though you had never heard of us."

"But I can't do that!" Mikk cried. "I'm Vyzanian! I've spent two and a half centuries committing your songs and stories to *memory.* Do you know what that means? *Vyzanian* memory!"

The white box, although climatically controlled, nevertheless seemed to produce a terrific draft that reached up inside Mikk's tunic and gripped his belly.

"Gods above! Songdance is exquisite, so full of meaning. Why would you want me to forget it?"

"We will soon be extinct. We are already severed from the world that nourished our soul. As you said, our songdance is full of meaning. Only we truly understand that meaning and we will be gone."

"But . . ." Mikk suddenly had to arch and twist his back. The tremor in his shoulders had become a deep, searing burn. "But people can still benefit from your knowledge. Surely some memory is better than none at all. Many races have died and their art lives."

"No." A thin line of dark spittle ran out of the corner of Whees-aru's mouth. The Santman attendant floated by and wiped it away. "You do not understand. Yours is likely to remain the only nearly perfect version of our art after we are gone. Future people might confuse your songdance with our own, and we would rather vanish from universal memory than let that happen."

"What about those whose interpretations are even less pure than mine?" Mikk fought the urge to sound desperate, but his control was slipping.

"No one could possibly confuse their work with true songdance. Their way will die quickly. They do not concern us nearly as much as you do. Therefore, you must promise never to perform the ballads again."[16]

Why is the Somalite Whees-aru so adamant that Mikk should not perform the songdance again? Why is it better to have the piece performed badly than for Mikk to continue to perform his near-perfect version?

Many contemporary indigenous peoples regard the current fascination among many Westerners with indigenous religion as "theft" of their cultural practices and symbols. Without being part of the history of the group, they suggest, we cannot embrace the full meaning of the symbols we appropriate, and thus we trample on sacred ground, sometimes literally. How does this relate to the experience of Asher Lev in Chaim Potok's novel? To Mikk and the Somalite Songdance in Waitman's *Merro Tree?* What do you think about this idea of "cultural theft" or co-optation? Are there any practices or beliefs that you use or hold that originate in a culture or religion other than your own? Do such beliefs and practices hold the same importance in your life that they might in the context of their community of origin?

In Chapter 2, we suggested that the meaning of symbols is dependent upon both the context of the community for which the symbols have particular value and also the context of the observer or participant. How might the historical time and place of the author have shaped the ways in which she or he interpreted and related the stories of the time? Most religious groups who have written scriptures believe that these texts are in some way inspired by whatever sacred reality they believe in. Does this mean that there is no act of interpretation on the part of the one who receives the inspiration?

A fundamentalist approach to Sacred Scripture suggests that texts are to be read literally, and that the words contained come directly from God, without influence from the one who mediates their communication to the community to whom they are addressed. In the case of Islam, the message is believed to have been received from Allah by the prophet Mohammed, told to followers who committed the sayings to memory and passed them on, and finally written into a formal text. Christian fundamentalists insist that the Bible is the literal word of God. Those who wrote down the words of the text were, in this approach, totally transparent messengers, who merely received and passed on the words.

Other approaches suggest that the persons who hear the story, as well as those who eventually write it down, are influenced, as are other writers, by their own cultures, own time periods, own social and historical contexts. Earlier in this chapter, we included the first section of the book of Genesis, from the beginning of the Jewish Tanakh and the Christian Bible. Now read on, and notice that there are actually two accounts of creation in this text.

(1st Account): God said, "Let the waters bring forth swarms of living creatures, and birds that fly above the earth across the expanse of the sky." God created the great sea monsters, and all the living creatures of every kind that creep, which the waters brought forth in swarms, and all the winged birds of every kind. And God saw that this was good. God blessed them, saying, "Be fertile and increase, fill the waters in the seas, and let the birds increase on the earth." And there was evening and there was morning, a fifth day.

God said, "Let the earth bring forth every kind of living creature: cattle, creeping things, and wild beasts of every kind." And it was so. God made wild beasts of every kind and cattle of every kind, and all kinds of creeping things of the earth. And God saw that this was good. And God said, "Let us make man in our image, after our likeness. They shall rule the fish of the sea, the birds of the sky, the cattle, the whole earth, and all the creeping things that creep on earth." And God created man in His image, in the image of God He created him; male and female He created them. God blessed them and God said to them, "Be fertile and increase, fill the earth and master it; and rule the fish of the sea, the birds of the sky, and all the living things that creep on earth."

God said, "See, I give you every seed-bearing plant that is upon all the earth, and every tree that has seed-bearing fruit; they shall be yours for food. And to all the animals on land, to all the birds of the sky, and to everything that creeps on earth, in which there is the breath of life, [I give] all the green plants for food." And it was so. And God saw all that He had made, and found it very good. And there was evening and there was morning, the sixth day.

The heaven and the earth were finished, and all their array. On the seventh day God finished the work that He had been doing, and He ceased on the seventh day from all the work that He had done. And God blessed the seventh day and declared it holy, because on it God ceased from all the work of creation that He had done. Such is the story of heaven and earth when they were created.[17]

(2nd Account): When the LORD God made earth and heaven—when no shrub of the field was yet on earth and no grasses of the field had yet sprouted, because the LORD God had not sent rain upon the earth and there was no man to till the soil, but a flow would well up from the ground and water the whole surface of the earth—the LORD God formed man from the dust of the earth. He blew into his nostrils the breath of life, and man became a living being.

The LORD God planted a garden in Eden, in the east, and placed there the man whom He had formed. And from the ground the LORD God caused to grow every tree that was pleasing to the sight and good for food, with the tree of life in the middle of the garden, and the tree of knowledge of good and bad.

A river issues from Eden to water the garden, and it then divides and becomes four branches. The name of the first is Pishon, the one that winds through the whole land of Havilah, where the gold is. (The gold of that land is good; bdellium is there, and lapis lazuli.) The name of the second river is Gihon, the one that winds through the whole land of Cush. The name of the third river is Tigris, the one that flows east of Asshur. And the fourth river is the Euphrates.

The LORD God took the man and placed him in the garden of Eden, to till it and tend it. And the LORD God commanded the man, saying, "Of every tree of the garden you are free to eat; but as for the tree of knowledge of good and bad, you must not eat of it; for as soon as you eat of it, you shall die."

The LORD God said, "It is not good for man to be alone; I will make a fitting helper for him." And the LORD God formed out of the earth all the wild beasts and all the birds of the sky, and brought them to the man to see what he would call them; and whatever the man called each living creature, that would be its name. And the man gave names to all the cattle and to the birds of the sky and to all the wild beasts; but for Adam no fitting helper was found. So the LORD God cast a deep sleep upon the man; and, while he slept, He took one of his ribs and closed up the flesh at that spot. And the LORD God fashioned the rib that He had taken from the man into a woman; and He brought her to the man. Then the man said,

"This one at last
Is bone of my bones
And flesh of my flesh.
This one shall be called Woman,
For from man was she taken."
Hence a man leaves his father and mother and clings to his wife, so that they become one flesh.

The two of them were naked, the man and his wife, yet they felt no shame.[18]

You may be familiar with one of these stories, but did you realize that there were two creation narratives? Because scholars now believe that these two narratives represent different time periods and thus different social situations in the history of the Hebrew people, they can speculate about the reasons behind at least some of the differences between the two sections of text. What are the implications of each story for human relationships between men and women? Between humans and God? Between humans and the rest of the natural world? One scholarly proposal is that the Hebrew people's understanding of God, and of God's relationship with them, changed over time and the text reflects that change. Does this seem probable to you? In the case of Islam, Allah's revelations to Mohammed occurred over a significant period of the Prophet's life, and some contradictions in the text are said to reflect changes in the life circumstances of the community over that period of time. Is this a satisfactory conclusion?

If you have ever tried to translate a passage from one language into another, you will know that you cannot simply exchange the words of one language for those of the other and come up with a meaningful translation—one that conveys the same message as the original. To provide a good translation, you must engage in interpretation. Traditions such as Judaism and Islam attempt to deal with this issue by insisting that the text remain in its original language—Hebrew and Arabic respectively. Does this take care of issues of translation across time and culture, as well as across languages?

Even when the texts belong to our own tradition, we necessarily journey across time and culture when we read the narratives. Of course, this isn't peculiar only to religious texts: we might have similar difficulty fully understanding Shakespeare, or some other narratives that were written in a different era. But with religion, it is easy to forget, perhaps, that the texts many of us read and hear in our own time are translated many times over to provide us with something that our 21st century ears can hear and understand.

Have you ever been involved in a conversation—perhaps an argument—with someone who has quoted the Bible or Qur'an to you in an attempt to "prove" that he or she is correct and you are wrong? What are some of the factors that might lead two persons to have vastly different interpretations of the same passage of text? For example, would you read a Surah from the Qur'an, view the Pieta, or read a chapter from the Christian Bible in the same way that you would read your political science textbook? Does your sex make any difference to the way in which you might interpret the Genesis creation stories? Does your economic status affect the way in which you might read the Gospel passage where Jesus is cited as saying that it is easier for a camel to pass through the eye of a needle than for a rich person to get to heaven? Even two people reading the same passage in a textbook might have dramatically different perspectives on what they have just read. If this is so for so-called "factual" material, it is still more the case for those truths we refer to as "sacred."

> *What issues do the two different creation accounts raise in terms of how we should read and interpret sacred texts? Can you imagine any reasons for these somewhat different narratives? Browse Deuteronomy 21, 22, and 24 in your Tanakh or Bible and select some of the laws that present a particular problem in terms of literal interpretations of sacred texts.*

SOME QUESTIONS ABOUT THE COMMUNICATION OF SACRED TRUTHS

The ways by which religious communities give shape to and pass on their beliefs and traditions are multiple and varied. We are probably most familiar with the sacred texts that are usually referred to as Scripture: the Vedas of Hinduism, the Tao Te Ching of Taoism, the Jewish Tanakh, the Christian Bible, the Muslim Qur'an. In most instances, the stories that come to be included in the official canon of the tradition are told orally for many years before they are incorporated into an official collection of texts. The original texts that formed the foundation of what today we call The Bible, for example, span thousands of years, multiple cultural changes and numerous different languages. Many similar texts were lost, or they were simply excluded by the church councils that determined which books would actually be incorporated into the official canons of Christianity. While Roman Catholic and Protestant Christians hold most of the same books as canonical, there are books in the Roman Catholic Bible—The Apocryphal Books—that are not included in the Protestant Bible. (Episcopalians, however, do include the Aprocrypha as inspired teachings, though not scripture in the same sense that the Hebrew and Christian scriptures are.)

The narratives that carry cultural truth for members of the community are many and varied. Included in these various bodies of literature or oral narratives are multiple genres: myth and legend, historical narrative, parables and other teaching stories, poetry and song, lists of rules and laws. The sacred stories of a group, in short, reflect the diversity of human imagination and creativity in extraordinary ways as peoples have struggled to give voice to experiences that are beyond full human understanding and articulation.

But words are only part of the story. Recognizing the limitations of spoken or written language to capture fully complex and mysterious experiences and understandings, many religions turn to dance, music, or other forms of artistic expression through which to communicate and to celebrate sacred truth. The Shakers got their name because of the ecstatic dance that characterized their worship services. Members believed that when their whole bodies became involved in worship, when they were literally "caught up in the Spirit," they were at that moment particularly close to God. Sufis, members of the mystical branch of Islam, will go into a trancelike state that includes dancing. The icons of Orthodox Christianity, as well as the vivid images and statues of Hindu gods and goddesses, give visual expression to the sacred truths and beliefs of the people. The singing or chanting that characterizes religious celebrations in many traditions again aims to remove people from the "everydayness" of their lives into a stance of meditation, reflection, or joyous celebration.

Regardless of the ways in which a particular tradition passes on its wisdom and truth, *that* it be passed on is of great importance. Beliefs about transcendence—that which is considered sacred and beyond ordinary understanding—often, even usually, suggest that our current lives should be lived in a particular way. Sacred truths, in other words, affect how we live, what we do day by day. They are at the heart of a community's life together, binding individuals together not only in the present, but also with those who have gone before and those who are yet to come.

What Some Others Have Said about Sacred Truth

To conclude this chapter, we introduce you to literary theorist Northrop Frye with excerpts from his book *The Great Code: The Bible and Literature.* Frye's interest is in literature as having the function in communities of transmitting sacred truths. Frye suggests that there are multiple reasons for this, and his analysis of the text proceeds to propose ways in which we might better understand the biblical texts and their continuing relevance.

> Man lives, not directly or nakedly in nature like the animals, but within a mythological universe, a body of assumptions and beliefs developed from his existential concerns. Most of this is held unconsciously, which means that our imaginations may recognize elements of it, when presented in art or literature, without consciously understanding what it is that we recognize. Practically all that we can see of this body of concern is socially conditioned and culturally inherited. Below the cultural inheritance there must be a common psychological inheritance, otherwise forms of culture and imagination outside our own traditions would not be intelligible to us. But I doubt if we can reach this common inheritance directly, by-passing the distinctive qualities in our specific culture. One of the practical functions of criticism, by which I mean the conscious organizing of a cultural tradition, is, I think, to make us more aware of our mythological conditioning.

The Bible is clearly a major element in our own imaginative tradition, whatever we may think we believe about it. It insistently raises the question: Why does this huge, sprawling, tactless book sit there inscrutably in the middle of our cultural heritage like the "great Boyg" or sphinx in *Peer Gynt*, frustrating all our efforts to walk around it?[19]

Frye reflects on the fact of the very existence of the scripture as a written text rather than simply a compilation of oral stories. According to Frye, this is a remarkable characteristic that he attributes to the particular gifts of the Israelite people.

> The Israelites seem to have been a rather unhandy people, not distinguished for architecture or sculpture or even pottery; . . . In general it was the heathen kingdoms that produced the really impressive temples and palaces, while the Israelites produced a book. . . .
>
> In the Book of Jeremiah (36:20ff.) there is a superb scene in which the prophet's secretary sits in the king's palace reading from a scroll to the king a prophecy which consists mainly of denunciations of his foolish and obstinate policy of resistance to Babylonia. Every so often the infuriated monarch cuts off a piece of the scroll with a knife and throws it into the fire. This must have been a papyrus scroll: parchment, besides being out of the prophet's price range, would have been tough enough to spoil the king's gesture. The king's palace totally disappeared in a few years, whereas the Book of Jeremiah, entrusted to the most fragile and combustible material produced in the ancient world, remains in reasonably good shape. The supremacy of the verbal over the monumental has something about it of the supremacy of life over death. Any individual form of life can be wiped out by the smallest breath of accident, but life as a whole has a power of survival greater than any collection of stones.[20]

What do you think of Frye's assertion as to the permanence of texts over stones? In particular, he seems to be suggesting that it is of infinitely greater importance that the texts survive. What relevance does this assertion have for our discussion of the communication of sacred truth? Frye goes on to talk about different understandings of authorship itself, particularly in terms of the ways in which the biblical texts were probably initially formed and later edited and translated.

> There is a body of writings, apart from the Apocrypha and dating mostly from the last century or so before Christ, which are called Pseudepigrapha, meaning "false writings," because some of them, such as the Book of Enoch, are ascribed to venerated figures who assuredly did not write them. Most of the generally accepted data of Biblical scholarship are connected with demonstrating that many if not most books of the Bible are pseudepigrapha in the same sense.
>
> This fact seldom affects the text of the Bible, only the captions it has been traditionally festooned with. Nevertheless even a century ago many people were rather scandalized to hear that Moses could not have written any part of the Pentateuch, that David and Solomon did not write the Psalms and the

Wisdom literature, that "the Book of Isaiah" is not a book by Isaiah but a collection of oracles extending over several centuries; that the Book of Daniel turns into Aramaic halfway through, and could no more be written by a contemporary of Nebuchadnezzar than a book that turned from Latin into Italian could be Julius Caesar's; that it is unlikely that any of the twelve disciples mentioned in the Gospels wrote any part of the New Testament, and that some of Paul's most typical and personal letters may not be wholly his.

A great deal of learning and ingenuity is still employed in resisting these conclusions. . . . The anxieties in such arguments are based on modern assumptions about bookmaking and writing which are irrelevant to the Bible. The assertion that Jesus' beloved disciple John wrote the Gospel of John, the three epistles of John, and perhaps the book of Revelation as well, even if it turned out to be true, would still not be a defense of the "authenticity" of these works. Similarly with the conception of "inspiration" often invoked in this connection, that is, a semi-trancelike state in which an author is a kind of sanctified tape recorder writing from the immediate dictation of what appears to be an external source. This again, we see, is an author-centered conception, which grew up in later times after it was assumed that revelation had ceased. But the Bible is not what people whose taste in style differs from mine would call an "authored" book at all: authorship is of too little importance in the composition of the Bible for such conceptions as "inspiration" to have any real function. The word "author" is used only for convenience, and should really be kept in quotation marks. . . .

One point is clear: if the Bible is to be regarded as "inspired" in any sense, sacred or secular, the editing and conflating and redacting and splicing and glossing and expurgating processes all have to be taken as inspired too. There is no way of distinguishing the voice of God from the voice of the Deuteronomic redactor [editor].[21]

What do you think Frye means when he asserts that the concept of "authorship" is somewhat irrelevant in the context of discussing the Bible? And why do you think people are so resistant to ideas such as those that assert that Moses could not have written the Pentateuch? Because of our modern ideas of individual authorship, says Frye, we find it extraordinarily difficult to entertain the idea that any other form of writing could hold authenticity and integrity:

We are so possessed by the modern notion that all the qualities we admire in literature come from the individuality of an author that it is hard to realize that this relentless smashing of individuality could produce greater vividness and originality rather than less. But so it seems to be. . . .

Whatever the truth about the antiquity of writing as compared to the oral tradition—a question considerably fogged up in recent times—an oral tradition is normally anonymous, and a fully developed writing tradition tends toward identified authorship. Pseudonymous authorship, which we find both inside and outside the Bible, is a halfway stage between the two, and is even more difficult for the modern mind to understand. It is in a sense more primitive than either, and descends from the primitive habit of regarding everything sacred as secret, to be communicated only orally. In this process the "author" is the first person who delivered the secret, and he is a legendary figure lost in the mists of time. Occult literature is closely related to this tradition. In occult writing there normally is, or is assumed to be, a long oral tradition preceding, which does not commit itself to writing until the tradition has begun to break down. . . .

Eventually pseudonymous identification begins to clash with the ethos of a developed writing culture, which says that pseudonymous authorship must be either purely imaginative or else fraudulent.

Tertullian, writing around 200 A.D., tells us of a priest who wrote a fraudulent book about Paul, and says that when his authorship was discovered he was degraded from his office. His superiors must have felt, quite reasonably as it seems to us, that, even though his book was not written in the first person, anyone who suggests he is the Apostle Paul when he is not the Apostle Paul is a liar, and the truth is not in him. But the unlucky priest thought he was doing honor to Paul by associating his book with him. I say "unlucky" advisedly, because the second Epistle of Peter in the New Testament, perhaps not so far removed from him in time, says that it was written by Simon Peter the Apostle of the LORD, and not many New Testament scholars would accept that statement. . . . II Peter is probably best described, in terms of the ethos of a writing culture, as a pious fraud. But to infer that it should not be in the canon because it is pseudonymous would indicate a very undeveloped historical imagination, besides starting a process that logically could not stop until most of the Bible had been thrown out with it. . . .[22]

What are the implications of Frye's claim that rejection of "pseudonymous" writings as fatally flawed would mean that most of the Bible would have to be thrown out? And what connections has Frye made here between his particular understanding of the development of the current biblical texts and the oral traditions from which they arise? (Frye is ignoring the transmission complication. Obviously, texts on stone are still texts.) Frye continues by exploring the ways in which contemporary translations reflect the particular culture and assumptions of the day:

Modern translations assume a culture of rapid and silent individual reading, hence they usually render at least the prose in as continuous a rhythm as possible, with the verse numbers, which in such a context have become something of a nuisance, spattered down the side. The implication is that the AV [Authorized Version—also known as the King James] has stressed one aspect of the Biblical rhythm only, perhaps to the point of exaggeration. But the aspect it stresses is of great importance nonetheless. The clue to the immense literary success of the AV is the clause on its title page: "appointed to be read in churches." The ear of the AV translators for the rhythm of the spoken word, though there are many lapses, was very acute, and it is a sobering thought that it is sensitivity to one's own language, not scholarly knowledge of the original, that makes a translation permanent. A translator with a tin ear, including a translator of the Bible, is continually mistranslating, whatever his scholarly knowledge. . . . The AV renders *Yahweh Tzabaoth* "the LORD of Hosts"; the American Revised Version (1901) renders it "Jehovah of Hosts," which is a greatly inferior translation. Anyone who doubts this has only to try it out on his eardrum.[23]

Finally, Frye sums up some of the major themes that he develops in his book, locating the biblical texts once more in the context of their time and place.

Such resonance would be impossible without, first, an original context, and, second, a power of expanding away from that context. The unity of context that we have been exploring in the Bible, then, is there as a foundation for its real structure. The Bible includes an immense variety of material, and the unifying forces that hold it together cannot be the rigid forces of doctrinal consistency or logic, which would soon collapse under cultural stress, but the more flexible ones of imaginative unity, which is founded on metaphor. Metaphor . . . is an identity of various things, not the sham unity of uniformity in which all details are alike. . . .

Literally, the Bible is a gigantic myth, a narrative extending over the whole of time from creation to apocalypse, unified by a body of recurring imagery that "freezes" into a single metaphor cluster, the metaphors all being identified with the body of the Messiah, the man who is all men, the totality of *logoi* who is one Logos, the grain of sand that is the world. We also traced a sequence of manifestations of this reality, each one a stage more explicit than its predecessor. First is the creation, not the natural environment with its alienating chaos but the ordered structure that the mind perceives in it. Next comes the revolutionary vision of human life as a casting off of tyranny and exploitation. Next is the ceremonial, moral, judicial code that keeps a society together. Next is the wisdom or sense of integrated continuous life which grows out of this, and next the prophecy or imaginative vision of man as somewhere between his original and his ultimate identity. Gospel and apocalypse speak of a present that no longer finds its meaning in the future, as in the New Testament's view of the Old Testament, but is a present moment around which past and future revolve.

This sequence is connected with one of the most striking features of the Bible: its capacity for self-re-creation. . . . The dialectical expansion from one "level" of understanding to another seems to be built into the Bible's own structure, which creates an awareness of itself by the reader, growing in time as he reads, to an extent to which I can think of no parallel elsewhere. Nor can we trace the Bible back to a time when it was not doing this. . . . The wise woman appeals to the primitive impulse of consciousness to connect with reality which is often released by the simplest modes of language, such as metaphor. But, being wise, she knows that a transformation of consciousness and a transformation of language can never be separated.[24]

Frye is clear throughout his writing that he is referring to the Christian Bible. Do you think his insights would have relevance for the reading of other texts? We have seen that "sacred" texts can be verbal or nonverbal, can even deal with matters not directly religious, such as the founding of a nation or the identity of a clan or family. Frye makes us understand that every such text, including the Christian Bible, is affected by the times and places of its creation, transmission, and experience, and that it reveals its "sacredness" or special cultural power partly by its ability to be recreated for new cultural conditions. In particular, it is interesting to note what contribution his ideas might make to our next topic: the interaction of traditions, power, and authority.

CHAPTER NINE

WHO SAYS SO? TRADITIONS, AUTHORITY, AND POWER

In the preceding chapters, we have encountered stories, and multiple symbols, rituals, and activities that form a central part of the self-identity—the truth—of religious and other cultural groups. How do these become part of a group's tradition, then to be passed on over hundreds of years and countless generations? Who has the power to define what counts as "sacred" truth? On what authority does a group make its truth claims? These are some of the questions that concern us now.

SETTING THE STAGE: TRADITIONS, AUTHORITY, AND POWER

What does it mean to say that something is "traditional"? Clearly, traditions are not exclusively the property of religions. How do you like to celebrate your birthday? What other traditions are important in your family? Are there cultural traditions in which you participate? Are there certain traditions that you observe that you see as almost essential to your well-being, your emotional satisfaction, your sense of belonging? Could you say that these traditions have a certain kind of power? What gives them this kind of power? Who or what gives them authority to shape and give meaning to your life? On a very personal level, we have all experienced, to some extent, this relationship between tradition, power, and authority.

Most people have participated in some tradition that requires particular objects—a tree, fireworks, special food. Describe such a tradition that you observe in your family or school. How long has this been a tradition, with or without your participation? What parts must be included for the tradition to be properly observed? How does it affect you—and other participants—when some part is missing? Have you and your family (or school) ever deliberately done it differently? How did that affect you?

Religious traditions are not only established by authority, but exercise it. The following excerpt outlines testimony given in a court case in which members of a religious cult are charged with murder following the discovery of the body of a 2-year-old child who is believed to have starved to death. The witness is a sister of the accused, and a former sect member. In what ways does power come into play in this article? Is tradition a factor? What are the various kinds of authority that are being exercised in this selection? Who exercises them?

Several months before prosecutors say Samuel Robidoux starved to death "in the bosom of his family," members of the Attleboro religious group headed by the baby's father and grandfather dropped everything, threw away their money and jewelry, and left for Maine late one night.

The sect's three dozen or so members didn't take any food. They didn't take cash. And even though several of the children were still infants, they left behind diapers, too. God would provide everything, they believed.

But more than two days later, after they'd abandoned some of their cars because they had run out of gas and slept on the side of the road waiting for God to tell them what to do as the children vomited from hunger, the group returned to Massachusetts.

Their prophecy of a feast to be delivered never materialized, testified Nicole Kidson, the sister of Jacques Robidoux, 29, who is on trial for first-degree murder in his son's death.

To Roland Robidoux—Jacques's and Nicole's father and the founder of the group—they had all failed. "We'd been willing to give up everything but we hadn't been willing to give up our children," said Kidson, 35, who went on the Maine excursion. "We had caved because of them."

For several hours yesterday, Kidson gave jurors a window into life within the sect she left in late 1998—a few months before Samuel died—because its teachings had become too rigid.

Prosecutors say that in the spring of 1999 the group followed a bizarre prophecy to deprive Samuel, who was almost a year old, of solid food. They allege that even as the boy cried incessantly and withered to skin and bones because his pregnant mother wasn't producing enough breast milk, his father insisted they continue with the diet of breast milk only, knowing that his son was on the verge of death.

"This is a murder case. This is not a case about religion," Assistant Bristol District Attorney Walter J. Shea told jurors. "This is not a case about someone's choice of lifestyle. This is a case about the very short life and the very slow, excruciating death of a baby."

Robidoux's lawyer, Francis M. O'Boy, yesterday delayed his opening statement until after prosecutors finish their case. But O'Boy has said he'll argue that no one meant for Samuel to die and that the baby might have died of disease, not starvation.

Throughout yesterday, O'Boy tried to show that Jacques Robidoux's father, Roland, was the real leader of the group and held a tight grip on its members. Kidson, the first witness in the trial, testified that when she was a girl in Attleboro her family had belonged to the Worldwide Church of God and didn't believe in modern medicine. Later they developed their own brand of religion.

It all began as a weekly family Bible study, a time for singing and praying on the Sabbath, and for talking about the Lord's work over dinner. Roland Robidoux, a mason and chimney sweep, was the group's "elder" and led the sessions, she said.

Another family, headed by Roger Daneau, joined the study sessions, too. A core part of the group's philosophy was that God spoke to some of them through prayer about how to live, and members were expected to follow those "leadings" in order to achieve salvation, Kidson said.

The prophecies became increasingly extreme. Women could not wear pants. Members were to discard all books but the Bible. No more dentist appointments were allowed. "Glasses had to go, too," she said.

Those who didn't follow the teachings were shunned, said Kidson, who sometimes questioned the mandates and who says she and her husband and four children were eventually "put out" of the group in late 1998 because she bought a new pair of eyeglasses.

In 1997 or 1998, Jacques became the second "elder" in the group, said Kidson, who described her brother as "a very good father." With the increased standing came responsibility. "More was expected of him in terms of being right before God," Kidson said. "Jacques was under tremendous pressure to be the perfect elder. He had to be the perfect example."

Whole families of the sect, in which the husbands had final say in everything, moved in together in Attleboro and Seekonk, where they home-schooled their children and usually breast-fed them until at least age 1, Kidson testified.

The group adopted a philosophy about "Satan's seven counterfeit systems," Kidson said. Among other things, members were to avoid organized education, the arts, the medical system, government, and the authorities. Some closed their bank accounts and began using only cash.

In early 1999, prosecutors say, Michelle Mingo—Jacques Robidoux's sister—told the group she'd had a vision that Jacques and his wife, Karen, should only feed Samuel breast milk even though he had already started eating solid food.

Apparently, prosecutors say, she was not producing enough milk to sustain Samuel because she was pregnant again.

Jacques Robidoux had told members that they were to treat Mingo's prophecies as if they were coming from the apostle Paul, said Kidson.

In the late summer of 1999—after hearing from another former group member—Kidson alerted Maine authorities that she was concerned about children in the group, which again had left Massachusetts.

The next year authorities found the remains of Samuel and his infant cousin buried in a Maine state park. The infant's father, David Corneau—who is married to Jacques Robidoux's sister Rebecca—led authorities to the bodies.

Karen Robidoux, Samuel's mother, faces second-degree murder charges in his death, and Michelle Mingo awaits trial on a charge of accessory before the fact of assault and battery on a child.[1]

History is full of stories of leaders of religious groups who have convinced their followers that the message they communicate is from God, and that they thus have a particular kind of power which must be heeded. How do we distinguish between those who might have a valid and valuable message and those who are in some way and for whatever reason using and abusing power?

WHAT DO YOU THINK? EXPERIENCES OF TRADITIONS, AUTHORITY, AND POWER

What is the first thing that happens at a football or basketball game? Even before the players take the field or court, the national anthem is played. With the introductory notes, everyone stands. It's tradition. What are some of the other traditions around the playing of the national anthem at various events? And why does this particular tradition have so much power?

We are particularly accustomed to the first verse of the anthem. Most of us in the United States learned these words as small children and no longer have to think about them when we sing them:

Oh, say can you see, by the dawn's early light,
What so proudly we hailed at the twilight's last gleaming?
Whose broad stripes and bright stars, through the perilous fight,
O'er the ramparts we watched, were so gallantly streaming?
And the rockets' red glare, the bombs bursting in air,
Gave proof through the night that our flag was still there.
O say, does that star-spangled banner yet wave
O'er the land of the free and the home of the brave?

National anthems, like other traditions, have significant historical importance. And also like other traditions, this importance often centers on stories that are considered formative in the self-identity of the nation or community. Now, read the remaining lyrics to the United States National Anthem. These words may not be nearly as familiar to you, but as you read, think about how these added verses contribute to the meaning of the whole.

On the shore, dimly seen through the mists of the deep,
Where the foe's haughty host in dread silence reposes,
What is that which the breeze, o'er the towering steep,
As it fitfully blows, now conceals, now discloses?
Now it catches the gleam of the morning's first beam,
In full glory reflected now shines on the stream:
'Tis the star-spangled banner! O long may it wave
O'er the land of the free and the home of the brave.

And where is that band who so vauntingly swore
That the havoc of war and the battle's confusion
A home and a country should leave us no more?
Their blood has wiped out their foul footstep's pollution.
No refuge could save the hireling and slave
From the terror of flight, or the gloom of the grave:
And the star-spangled banner in triumph doth wave
O'er the land of the free and the home of the brave.

Oh! thus be it ever, when freemen shall stand
Between their loved homes and the war's desolation!
Blest with victory and peace, may the heaven-rescued land
Praise the Power that hath made and preserved us a nation.
Then conquer we must, when our cause it is just,
And this be our motto: "In God is our trust."
And the star-spangled banner forever shall wave
O'er the land of the free and the home of the brave!

How many of the verses did you know? Are there some you had never heard? The verses tell the story of the Battle of Fort McHenry, during the War of 1812, from a decidedly partisan perspective. Francis Scott Key, the author of the lyrics, had gone to the English fleet, to the ship, *Surprise*, to negotiate the release of a doctor whom the English held prisoner. The English admiral agreed, but said that both the doctor and Key would have to wait until after the attack on Fort McHenry. Key and the doctor remained on board the ship until the morning, after the firing had stopped. Key expected to see that the fort had struck its colors, but, instead, the flag still flew. Key wrote the poem on the back of an envelope while he was being rowed to shore. Just as seeing the flag was a traditional rallying point for troops in battle, the singing of the anthem has become a rallying point, or reminder, that the country was created by revolution and was defended against the English during the War of 1812. In what ways does knowing some of the history behind the National Anthem—or any other tradition—enhance the power of the tradition?

The music of the anthem also has an interesting history. Earlier, in 1806, Key had written a poem about the defeat of the Barbary pirates entitled "When the Warrior Returns," and adapted the poem to the melody that he later used for The Star-Spangled Banner. The melody was originally written by, apparently, a group of members of the Anacreontic Society, a group that met at the Crown and Anchor Tavern and "was dedicated to wit, harmony, and the god of wine." Their name came from Anacreon, a 5th century BCE poet in Greece. Does it make a difference to how you feel about the United States National Anthem to know that the tune was originally written for an English drinking song? Why?

The two sets of lyrics that accompany the melody both tell a story. Key's words recount his exuberance on finding the flag still flying after the night-long bombardment. Each song serves to establish a tradition. The Anacreontic Song's tradition was only for the members of the Society and their heirs and tells a fantastical story of the god's invitation to humans to enjoy the good things of life. The Star-Spangled Banner, however, tells a very different kind of story and is a tradition that almost all citizens of the United States honor.

Do a web search for "Anacreontic" and locate a site that gives you the words of the song. Compare and contrast these song lyrics with those of The Star-Spangled Banner. List other songs you know that have more than one set of lyrics.

CULTURAL AND SOCIAL PERSPECTIVES ON TRADITIONS, AUTHORITY, AND POWER

Think back to your response to the question at the beginning of this chapter: how do you celebrate your birthday? Would you call your particular mode of celebration a "tradition"? What does it mean to say that something is "traditional"? The word comes from the Latin root *traditio*—to pass on, hand down. Are the stories and other forms of sacred truth that we encountered in the last chapter "tradition" in this sense? Does a tradition have to be old, passed down through many generations? Can you create new traditions? By yourself? And what is the difference, if any, between tradition and habit, or custom?

What function does tradition play in communities and for individuals? You might be familiar with the musical "Fiddler on the Roof," which recounts the story of an Orthodox Jewish community under persecution in Czarist Russia. As the musical opens, Tevye, the lead character, explains how the community and its members retain their sense of purpose and dignity in the face of poverty and hardship:

> And how do we keep our balance? That I can tell you in a word—Tradition! . . .
> Because of our traditions, we've kept our balance for many, many years. Here in Anatevka we have traditions for everything—how to eat, how to sleep, how to wear clothes. For instance, we always keep our heads covered and always wear a little prayer shawl. This shows our constant devotion to God. You may ask, how did this tradition start? I'll tell you—I don't know! But it's a tradition. Because of our traditions, everyone knows who he is and what God expects him to do.[3]

Without our traditions, life would be as precarious as—a Fiddler on the Roof!

For Orthodox Jewish communities such as Tevye's, tradition forms a central part of their religious authority. How would you respond to Tevye's claim that the community retains its well-being only by holding to its traditions? The opening song goes on to outline the proper roles for each member of the family, including the parents' obligation to consult with the village matchmaker to find suitable husbands and wives for their daughters and sons. But times are changing, even in Anatevka, and Tevye will be challenged by his own daughters' desires to choose their own husbands. To what extent do traditions strengthen a community, give its members a sense of belonging and stability? When does tradition become a problem? What are the traditions in your own family or culture that you hope will always be kept?

We have seen examples of the power of traditions over the groups that hold them; if Tevye is right, traditions can also give power to individuals as part of a group. But what comes to your mind when you hear the word "power"? Is it a positive or negative thing? Who or what has power? Do you have power? If so, in what ways do you perceive yourself as having power? Are there ways or situations in which you feel powerless? In what areas of your life would you like to have more power? What limits or enhances your own feelings of power?

Sometimes it is helpful to think about power in two different ways: "power over" and "power from within." What does it mean to have power over someone or something? How do you feel about exercising power over another, or having another exercising power over you? And what does it mean to have "power within"? Another term for this might be empowerment. When have you felt empowered? What enabled this to happen? How was it different from the exercise of "power over"?

The meanings of power in society and in the lives of individuals are complex and can be changed. Can a man who died in 1981, and of whom many people have not even heard, exercise power today? Belmont, Massachusetts, filmmaker Arleigh Prelow is making a documentary about Howard Thurman, a preacher and thinker whose work on nonviolence influenced Dr. Martin Luther King Jr. and other civil rights activists. Thurman died in 1981. In the excerpt below, Prelow is interviewed by *Boston Globe* columnist Rich Barlow. Consider the many ways in which Thurman challenged traditional understandings of power in his time. What kinds of power did he exemplify? Can he continue to have power more than twenty years after his death? What challenges does he pose for us today?

Q. *What will the movie feel like?*
A. It will have a lot of archival footage. It's structured thematically. We'll start off with a childhood story of Thurman when his father died. Thurman goes to the funeral with his grandmother and mother. The minister preaches Thurman's father [is going] to hell because he wasn't a member of the church. Thurman says, "Mama, I will never have anything to do with the church." That was his vow at 7 years old. We're following how this man uses that experience to transform what a church community is to one that's more inclusive.
Q. *Why a film about him?*
A. His profound influence on people of different nations, different races, different faiths. The Fellowship Church was a part of that journey. He thought this was a statement of what Christianity was all about: If people came together to experience God, then a unity would occur. Being at B[oston] U[niversity] was an extension of that. He figured if he could touch the students, they would go to their place of origin and bring this message of a genuine worship experience, how uniting that experience is. For an African-American leader to have that experience outside the black church, where most of our leaders are put, and to have a universal influence, was a strong story and statement.
Q. *He was a Baptist?*
A. He was ordained a Baptist minister, but by the time of Fellowship Church, he convinced the membership to drop all ties with any denomination. That was a bold move, particularly in the '40s. He didn't want to be a token experiment of one denomination. He felt sometimes the tag "Christian" threw you into a superficial way of looking at the faith. So he called it the religion of Jesus—what Jesus taught professed how he lived. "Christian," when he was growing up, was exclusionary.

Q. *What was it about his personality that was so compelling?*

A. He was deep. He wasn't a hoop-and-holler, the stereotype you hear of black preachers. I was able to hear him. This happened to be almost six months before he passed. There's something that evoked that you were in the spirit when he would speak. You just felt another presence. It was like taking you on a journey, and it was a journey he was going through. It wasn't "I'm greater than thou." Lots of pauses, where he looks up into the air and kind of thinks through things and uses his hands with great gesture.

Q. *Why is he especially relevant after Sept. 11?*

A. He grew up in a time of terror in the Deep South, when you just didn't have any sense of where it was coming from. I was really feeling that in the air after Sept. 11, and now you get these alerts—it might happen any place, any time. How do you continue to live? Thurman lived it.

Q. *How do you think Thurman would have felt about our response to Sept. 11?*

A. I don't know. He knows that in war, nobody wins. World War II, he was faced with that, in working with people at home. He was never telling soldiers don't go to fight. But he was always trying to build up things in people so that it wouldn't have to happen. The love example of Christ was what he was trying to rally people for.

Q. *Did he march with Dr. King?*

A. People were kind of saying, where was he, he wasn't on the front lines. He was hurt. He did attend the March on Washington. [But] his main concern was, he always said, the march inside. He saw it as a spiritual revolution. At Rochester Divinity School, his mentor there said, "Don't devote yourself to the race question. Devote yourself to the universal issues of mankind." Thurman said they're both the same, what segregation meant to both the oppressor and the [oppressed], what kind of damage that does to the soul.

Q. *What was groundbreaking about his deanship at BU's Marsh Chapel?*

A. He was the first African-American dean at a predominantly white university. Being on television, being on radio—he was broadcast every week, delivering meditations—even with that, people would come to his office expecting to see a white person. The race question was very essential in his life. There wasn't a cross there, [in his chapel] either. That came from his experiences growing up in the South. The cross just brought back memories of the Klan and the misuse of it. He was sensitive to not stopping at symbols and doctrine, but going to the heart of your faith.[4]

How does Thurman experience the "power" in his religious tradition? Why do you think he found it necessary to found his own church group? What was the power of the labels for Thurman?

We asked you above what the "power" of tradition was in those practices that you find meaningful and important, that you would not want to change or eliminate from your life. Do those traditions come from an experience of "power over" or "power within"? Perhaps they are a combination of the two. Many of us, for example, were taken to religious services by parents, grandparents, or other caregivers when we were children. We may or may not have wanted to go, but it was often not in our own "power" to make that decision. Temporarily, at least—during the years of our childhood—others have power over us. As we move toward adulthood, we gradually assume the power to make our own determinations about just how we will or will not continue the traditions that were given us as children.

WHO OR WHAT HAS POWER?

We mentioned above the power that our early caregivers exercise over us, usually in the service of protecting us and communicating to us the values and knowledge of the community to which we belong. Where else does power lie? Does it lie only in those persons who have some kind of authority to influence our behavior? What other persons beyond your immediate family would you say have—or had—power over you? And did the power they exercised help you to move toward your own sense of empowerment?

The following passage is from martyred Salvadoran Archbishop Oscar Romero, who became an outspoken advocate for the terrorized and exploited people of his nation who lived under a repressive and violent regime. Romero had a weekly radio broadcast which was listened to by thousands of Salvadorans and which was perceived as a threat by the authorities. What is Romero suggesting that is so comforting to the poor and exploited people of his nation—and so threatening to the authorities?

> One of the signs of the present time is the idea of participation, the right that all persons have to participate in the construction of their own common good. For this reason, one of the most dangerous abuses of the present time is repression, the attitude that says, "Only we can govern, no one else; get rid of them."
>
> Everyone can contribute much that is good, and in that way trust is achieved. The common good will not be attained by excluding people. We can't enrich the common good of our country by driving out those we don't care for. We have to try to bring out all that is good in each person and try to develop an atmosphere of trust, not with physical force, as though dealing with irrational beings, but with a moral force that draws out the good that is in everyone, especially in concerned young people.
>
> Thus, with all contributing their own interior life, their own responsibility, their own way of being, all can build the beautiful structure of the common good, the good that we construct together and that creates conditions of kindness, of trust, of freedom, of peace.
>
> Then we can, all of us together, build the republic—the *res publica,* the public concern—what belongs to all of us and what we all have the duty of building.[5]

Archbishop Oscar Romero had some kind of power. Would you say that a "Mr." Oscar Romero would have had the same power? What about Archbishop X— anyone in the role of archbishop? Are there any similarities in the use of power by Romero and that by Robidoux? How is Romero's power different from that of the military and political leaders of his nation? Representatives from this group believed that they had to assassinate Romero; why, if his power was different from theirs? Do church leaders always exercise their power in the way that Romero does? Should they? Do institutions like the church, the government, the military, and economic entities exercise power beyond that of the individuals involved in them? How responsible are the individuals for the power their organizations exert?

Sometimes we use another term for persons who can influence the behavior or attitudes of others; we say they have *authority*. Is this the same as saying that they have power? Where does authority come from? Are there different kinds of authority? Who has authority in your life? When do you acknowledge another's authority? Do you respond differently to different kinds of authority? Can anything other than an individual human person have authority? Who decides whether authority is legitimate? You may have seen the old bumper sticker that reads, "Question Authority." Should we question authority? Always? Ever? Should we ever disobey authority?

The *Oxford English Dictionary* provides many varying definitions for the word "authority," but two of them are particularly interesting and relevant for our current discussion. One defines authority in the way we often think of when we hear the term: the power to enforce obedience. When we think of "authority" as the kind of power, for example, exerted over a nation by its government, over small children by their parents, over prison inmates by wardens, we get a sense of what is meant by "power to enforce obedience." The second definition is that authority is the power to inspire belief. What difference does it make to look at authority in this way? Are these two definitions mutually exclusive? Do these definitions parallel, in any way, the two kinds of power we discussed above: power over and power within? In particular, if you have had any dealings with one or more religious traditions, which of these kinds of authority did you experience as more present?

The White Rose is an autobiographical piece by young people who were part of a traditional German family during the time when Hitler was actively promoting the ideas that would lead to the Holocaust and the Second World War. As you read this excerpt, ask yourself what early signs the writers missed, and why Hitler initially seemed to make good sense to these ordinary German people. Are any of his ideas, as they are outlined in this reading, attractive to you? Which insight would have been the "red flag" that would have signaled to you that something was wrong? What was the attraction of Hitler's ideas that led so many to follow him for so long, even in the face of mounting events that we might think would have alerted people to the danger?

> One morning I heard a girl tell another on the steps of the school, "Now Hitler has taken over the government." The radio and newspapers promised, "Now there will be better times in Germany. Hitler is at the helm."

For the first time politics had come into our lives. Hans was fifteen at the time, Sophie was twelve. We heard much oratory about the fatherland, comradeship, unity of the *Volk,* and love of country. This was impressive, and we listened closely when we heard such talk in school and on the street. For we loved our land dearly—the woods, the river, the old gray stone fences running along the steep slopes between orchards and vineyards. We sniffed the odor of moss, damp earth, and sweet apples whenever we thought of our homeland. Every inch of it was familiar and dear. Our fatherland—what was it but the extended home of all those who shared a language and belonged to one people. We loved it, though we couldn't say why. After all, up to now we hadn't talked very much about it. But now these things were being written across the sky in flaming letters. And Hitler—so we heard on all sides—Hitler would help this fatherland to achieve greatness, fortune, and prosperity. He would see to it that everyone had work and bread. He would not rest until every German was independent, free, and happy in his fatherland. We found this good, and we were willing to do all we could to contribute to the common effort. But there was something else that drew us with mysterious power and swept us along: the closed ranks of marching youth with banners waving, eyes fixed straight ahead, keeping time to drumbeat and song. Was not this sense of fellowship overpowering? It is not surprising that all of us, Hans and Sophie and the others, joined the Hitler Youth. . . .

One night, as we lay under the wide starry sky after a long cycling tour, a friend—a fifteen-year-old girl—said quite suddenly and out of the blue, "Everything would be fine, but this thing about the Jews is something I just can't swallow." The troop leader assured us that Hitler knew what he was doing and that for the sake of the greater good we would have to accept certain difficult and incomprehensible things. . . .

Finally the open break came. Some time before, Hans had been promoted to the rank of . . . troop leader. He and his boys had sewn a handsome banner, bearing in its design a great mythical beast. This flag was something special; it was dedicated to the Führer, and the boys had pledged their loyalty to the banner because it was the symbol of their fellowship. One evening, however, when they had come into formation with their banner and stood in review before a higher-echelon leader, the unheard-of happened. The leader suddenly and without warning ordered the little flagbearer, a cheerful twelve-year-old, to hand over the banner.

"You don't need a banner of your own. Use the one prescribed for everyone." . . .

The order to hand over the banner was repeated. The boy stood rigid, and Hans knew how he felt and that he would refuse. When the order was given for the third time, in a threatening voice, Hans noticed that the flag was trembling. At that he lost control. He quietly stepped from his place in the ranks and slapped the cadre leader. That put an end to Hans' career as [troop leader]. . . .

The spark of tormenting doubt which was kindled in Hans spread to the rest of us. In those days we heard a story about a young teacher who had unaccountably disappeared. He had been ordered to stand before an SA squad, and each man was ordered to pass by the teacher and to spit in his face. After that incident no one saw him again. He had disappeared into a concentration camp. "What did he do?" we asked his mother in bewilderment. "Nothing. Nothing," she cried out in despair. "He just wasn't a Nazi, it was impossible for him to belong. *That* was his crime."[6]

The White Rose was written by the surviving sister of Hans and Sophie Scholl, both of whom were executed by the Nazis for their participation in the resistance movement that attempted to demonstrate the wrongness of Hitler's policies and practices. What kind of power, or authority, do persons have who offer such resistance? Did their power and authority die with them? What criteria do we use to determine the just use of power and authority as opposed to power and authority used unjustly? Is it always clear? Is it acceptable to break laws, go against the government of one's country even, to challenge the wrong use of power? Can you think of situations in which you would condone such a challenge? Should Martin Luther King Jr. have broken the Jim Crow laws in the South to make his point against racism? King, like Oscar Romero, suggested that there was tremendous power in nonviolence. Do you agree?

In religious traditions, the leaders or founders of the traditions often didn't immediately have their authority recognized by those who were close by, and they never used authority in the sense of the power to force obedience. Gandhi, Moses, Jesus, Confucius, the Buddha, and Mohammed all fall into this category. Why was their authority not always recognized, often even by their closest friends and followers? Some still don't give them "authority." What is the relationship between power and authority anyway? Are they the same thing or how are they different? Is one dependent on the other?

> Create a "family tree" showing the persons who had influence on you—or power over or with you—when you were growing up. Go up as many levels as necessary, including people who had influence on the people who had influence on you. Include any people on whom you had influence. What kinds of power relationships did you have with the individuals you list? What kinds of power or influence did they have on or with each other? Use different colors, directional arrows, or any other signs you think of to illustrate different kinds and directions of power.

WHO OR WHAT HAS AUTHORITY?

The next reading comes from the autobiography of an elderly black midwife who practiced her art for many years in Alabama. We pick up Onnie Lee Logan's narrative at the point where she discusses the limits being placed on the practice of midwifery by the civil authorities. Doctors object to the midwives because the midwives have not had the education that the doctors have had, and the midwives are impinging on the doctors' income. Throughout her life and practice, Logan has had to battle with rules and regulations, and the medical establishment—for example, the requirement that for a woman to have a home birth, she must get a slip from a doctor. The state stops issuing licenses to midwives, stating that, after midwives die or retire, no new licenses will be given. Finally, in 1984, they refuse to renew Logan's license. Yet Logan continues to deliver babies, and she insists that she indeed has authority to do so. She says:

> If they hadn't've taken my license this year I would have loved to carry two mo' years if my health would allow. But if it starts failin or I start gettin weak from age they wouldn't have to pull me off. I'd come off. I don't think they did me justice by not givin me my license as long as I feel as well as I am, although I'm an old lady. They're not gonna stop me from doin the gift that God give me to do. The Lord hadn't quite give me the answer but all I'm sayin is that God don't aim for me with the experience He give me and the talent He gave me, He don't aim for me to let man, white nor black, kill it unless my health failed on me. He certainly has used these hands alot and as long as my health and strength will allow me, I aim for these hands to be used again. I don't want no man stoppin these hands from doin what says the Lord. I don't need a permit to deliver no babies. If God tell me not to do it I won't do it.[7]

From where does Logan claim to receive her authority? What different kinds of authority do different persons have in Logan's narrative? Which kind of authority do you think is most important in the context of the story?

In the preceding chapter we discussed religious stories and sacred scripture. What does it mean to say that a particular scripture—the Tanakh, the Bible, the Qur'an—has authority for members of the religion? Does the Imam, the Rabbi, the priest, or minister have authority? How do the powers of the state and the medical profession in Onnie Lee Logan's experience compare with these religious authorities?

Do you have any authority in your religion or culture? The word "authority" comes from the same root as the word "author." What is an author? We generally think of "author" only in terms of someone who writes books or articles. What would it mean to "author" your life? If we thought of "authority" as "authoring," would we understand it differently? Which if any of the examples we've encountered in this chapter would fit into this kind of definition? Would it bear any relation to the career of Onnie Lee Logan?

We have suggested in this chapter that both power and authority can be understood in many different ways, some of them not at all like the ways in which we usually understand the terms. Do people within a given tradition sometimes understand these terms differently?

Conflicts between worldviews, particularly those rooted in religious traditions and beliefs, are notoriously difficult to resolve. Check out today's edition of your local newspaper on the Web and list the conflicts that are mentioned that are occurring in the world in your own time. How many of them have their roots in religion? To what extent are these tensions over who or what has authority?

SOME QUESTIONS ABOUT TRADITIONS, AUTHORITY, AND POWER

Most of us are in the "habit" of eating several times a day. We might even have particular "customs" in our families or cultures of eating certain foods on particular occasions. But what makes any of these ordinary events into "tradition"? This question relates to our earlier discussion of symbols and rituals. What makes something a symbol rather than a simple sign? And when is something a ritual rather than simply a habit we perform regularly? In Chapters 2 and 3 we suggested that the difference lies at least partly in the level of meaning we give to the object or event. A symbol, for example, carries meaning that goes beyond the simple object depicted, meaning that can only be interpreted by someone familiar with the "tradition" from which the symbol comes. Similarly, an ordinary event becomes a ritual when it is invested with meaning beyond the simple actions performed. Muslims performing their required prayer ritual or Christians receiving the Eucharist understand what they are doing very differently from the way in which an outside observer might describe the actions. Not long after September 11, when someone saw a group of Muslim men laying out their prayer mats in a quiet corner of a discount store, this bystander alerted store personnel, who in turn called police. The onlookers' interpretation of events was clearly very different from that of the participants.

Tradition carries a meaning beyond the obvious. Rituals generally are in the realm of tradition, even those rituals that we have developed ourselves, but tradition includes much more than ritual. It involves the whole body of beliefs, literature, art, history that enable people to retain a sense of their identity and purpose. Although sometimes tradition, symbols, or ritual can become meaningless, can lose power, when followed mindlessly, or when certain elements are no longer meaningful for a contemporary community. Without living traditions, we lose our sense of connectedness with the past, our sense of belonging to some community larger than ourselves. So traditions are always a very powerful influence on our lives. We respond to their authority.

We often are tempted to think of "power and authority" only as wielded by persons in positions from which they are able to control the behavior of others. However, there are many other ways in which we might experience these phenomena in our lives. When parents invite a two-year-old to choose which of two outfits he will wear, or trust their newly licensed teenager to take out the family car, they are suggesting by their actions that their children are able to exercise a certain power—and authority—of their own in particular areas of their lives. The course of maturing from infancy to adulthood is ideally a process of exercising increasing degrees of authority and power over our own lives. Does such a process relate in any way to our relationship with the institutions of our society, particularly, in the context of this book, our religious traditions? If you were raised in a faith community, do you now understand your own religious tradition and its authority—power—in your life the same way as you did when you were five years old . . . ten . . . fifteen? What has changed? Has your experience of such authorities been one of inspiration—the power to inspire belief—or of coercion—the power to enforce obedience? Is one of these always good and the other always bad? Think about the young people whose story is told in *The White Rose.* Clearly, in many ways, Hitler had the power to inspire belief in those who heard him, as do many leaders of religious cults. Is it always wrong to enforce obedience? A parent who grabs a child and physically removes her from danger is "enforcing obedience," as is the police officer who apprehends a drunk motorist. Are they wrong to do so?

Let's go back to the bumper sticker that asks us to "Question Authority." Should we question any and all authority? Is it disloyal to your culture, your religion, your country, to ask questions of the "authorities"—even to suggest that they might not have all the answers, or at least all the *right* answers? What criteria should we use to determine just how much authority to give to leaders, whether they are religious, political, business, or any other kind of leaders? Most important, how do we recognize the abuse of power? What should be our response when we sense that power is being used wrongly?

Power is a difficult and volatile concept to deal with, one that defies easy definition. Yet power is a prevalent reality in our world, from our immediate circle of family and friends, all the way up to global economic strategies and our relationships with the transcendent reality we have been referring to as "the Sacred."

WHAT SOME OTHERS HAVE SAID ABOUT TRADITIONS, AUTHORITY, AND POWER

In our conclusion to this chapter, we turn to sociologist of religion Meredith McGuire for her analysis of some of the ways in which power and authority function in both the leadership and the membership of religious groups. McGuire is speaking particularly about the capacity of religions and their adherents to be forces for social change. There are many different kinds of leadership, just as there are many different kinds of power and authority. Note in particular the distinction that McGuire makes between the two kinds of prophets and between the prophets and other kinds of leaders.

> Social change often requires an effective leader who can express desired change, motivate followers to action, and direct their actions into some larger movement for change. Religion has historically been a major source of such leaders largely because religious claims form a potent basis of authority. The prototype of the change-oriented religious leader is the *prophet,* whose social role is especially significant.

A prophet is someone who confronts the powers that be and the established ways of doing things, claiming to be taken seriously on religious authority. There are two types of prophetic roles. One is the *exemplary prophet,* whose challenge to the status quo consists of living a kind of life that exemplifies a dramatically different set of meanings and values. The Buddha is a good example of this kind of prophet, whose very way of life is his message. The other type is the *emissary prophet,* who confronts the established powers as one who is sent by God to proclaim a message. Most of the Old Testament prophets were of this type. The emissary prophet has historically been an important source of change because the message proclaimed offered a new religious idea (i.e., ethic) and a different basis of authority. The prophetic message was often one of judgment and criticism. Whether the message called the people back to a previous way of life or directed them to some new way, it nevertheless called for *change.*

What do you think of McGuire's claim that many significant leaders come from religious traditions because "religious claims form a potent basis of authority"? Why is this so? How does this relate to individuals such as Martin Luther King, Jr. and Mohandas Gandhi? As you read on, consider whether all "prophets" are religious.

The role of the prophet is the opposite of the priestly role. A *priest* is any religious functionary whose role is to administer the established religion—to celebrate the traditional rituals, practices, and beliefs. Most clergy and church officials perform priestly roles. The basis of priestly authority is priests' location in the religious organization as representatives of that establishment, and their actions mediate between its traditions and the people. The prophet, by contrast, challenges the established way of doing things, not only by messages of criticism but also by claiming an authority outside the established authority. Thus, the role of the prophet is essentially a force for change in society.

[Max] Weber proposed that *charisma* was the authority basis of leaders such as prophets. . . . The authority of the charismatic leader rests on the acceptance of his or her claim by a group of followers and on the followers' sense of duty to carry out the normative pattern or order proclaimed by the leader. Thus, the charismatic leader is a source of both new ideas and new obligations.

The charismatic leader says, in effect, "It is written . . . , but I say unto you . . ." By word or deed, the charismatic leader challenges the existing normative pattern, conveying to the followers a sense of crisis, then offering a solution to the crisis—a new normative order. Charismatic leaders may arise either outside or within the institutional framework. Charismatic authority is *extraordinary.* It breaks away from everyday bases of authority such as that of officials or hereditary rulers. Thus, in certain periods and social settings, charismatic authority is highly revolutionary. . . .

Pure charismatic authority is, however, unstable. It exists only in *originating* the normative pattern and the group that follows it. By the process of *routinization,* charismatic authority is transformed into a routine or everyday form of authority based on tradition or official capacity, and the new religious group comes to serve the "interests" of its members. Although this routinization usually compromises the ideals of the original message, it is a necessary process for the translation of the ideal into practice. Routinization frequently dilutes the "pure" ideals and sometimes results in a comparatively static organizational form; however, it is also the process by which charisma comes to have its actual impact on history.

The history of the Christian churches is a series of charismatic innovations, routinization, and stable organization, followed by new appearances of charisma. Saint Francis of Assisi was a charismatic leader, an exemplary prophet whose message was also one of judgment—that Christian life must return to its pristine ideals of poverty, community, and simplicity. The early stages of the Franciscan movement were a serious threat to the established church and the sociopolitical order with which the church was intertwined. . . . [Its] subsequent routinization made it no longer a serious threat to the church. Nevertheless, the Franciscan ideals had great impact and were periodically raised as a critical standard against the complacency of the church and the order itself.

Similar cycles of charismatic innovation and routinization into organizational stability have occurred in other religious groups (and, indeed, in nonreligious institutions, such as political groups). The Mormons moved from a highly charismatic form of authority under Joseph Smith and Brigham Young to a stable, routinized form under church officials called "bishops" (many of whom are laymen). Similarly, Black Muslims have undergone several phases of charisma and routinization, each time altering the group's ideology, tactics, and form of organization. . . .[8]

What does McGuire mean by "routinization"? And how would you define charismatic leadership? Why does she suggest that charismatic leadership by itself is not enough to sustain the group over time? Think of examples, historical or contemporary, that you think fit her definitions of such leadership. What about Romero, King, and Robidoux?

Whether the religious group is a small band following a charismatic leader, a growing religious movement, or a staid and established religious organization, it is a potential force for social change. This potential exists because religion—especially the religious community—is a source of power, which is a fundamental category in the sociology of religion. The same power can be and usually is, however, used to support the status quo. Religion is not only an experience of power but often also results in the sense of being empowered. Thus, the followers of the charismatic leader may experience a sense of power in their relationship with the leader and with fellow believers that enables them to apply the new order to their social world.

This sense of power, especially when identified with the leadership of a charismatic figure, can give a developing religious movement great dynamism. . . .[9]

According to McGuire, then, the early charismatic beginnings of a religious movement must later be institutionalized in such a way as to establish it within its cultural and social context. In what ways does McGuire suggest that this process both ensures the religion's continued existence *and* means that it adapts to the status quo?

McGuire then goes on to discuss the ways in which religion is or is not considered a legitimate authority within its social context. As you read on, apply her insights to your own culture or society. To what extent does your own context support or refute her ideas?

Legitimacy . . . refers to the basis of authority of individuals, groups, or institutions by which they can expect their pronouncements to be taken seriously. Legitimacy is not an inherent quality of individuals, groups, or institutions but is based on the *acceptance* of their claims by others. If an individual proclaims "it is absolutely imperative for Americans to reduce their consumption of gas and oil by 15 percent," on what basis does this person claim to be taken seriously? Such a statement by the president of the United States would be based on a different source of legitimacy than the same statement by a spokesperson for the Union of Concerned Scientists, the editor of *Newsweek,* the National Council of Churches, or, for that matter, a Chicago elevator operator.

The location of religion in contemporary society reflects societal changes in the bases of legitimacy. Relatively stable societies typically have stable sources of legitimacy. The key criterion in such societies is usually traditional authority such as the inherited authority of the patriarch or king; institutional differentiation often produces a different kind of authority: the authority of the holder of a specialized role or "office." Claims to be taken seriously are based not on who one is but on what position one holds. The authority of a judge, for example, is based on the role for that office rather than the person.

Religion legitimates authority indirectly in traditional societies by its pervasive interrelationship with all aspects of society. Myth and ritual support the seriousness of all spheres of life. The chief, priest, or matriarch can speak with authority because their roles correspond to or reflect the authority of divine beings. Historic religions legitimate authority more directly. . . . Such historic religions as Christianity, Islam, and Judaism have similarly given authority to pronouncements on education, science, economic policy, law, family life, sport, art, and music. Whether directly or indirectly invoked, the images and symbols of the sacred are a source of legitimacy. The taken-for-granted quality of religion as a source of legitimacy characterizes all of these earlier societal situations. . . .

Early differentiation of religious from political institutions meant that religious institutions could come into conflict with political institutions. The potential to legitimate implies the corollary ability to delegitimate power, whether in the context of government, courts, workplace, or family. Historically, the churches could authoritatively evaluate whether the state was engaged in a "just" war and could authoritatively criticize business practices they judged as "usurious" (i.e., charging unfair interest rates on loans). In contemporary society, by contrast, religious institutions must actively compete with other sources of legitimacy. Personal, social, and political authority are more uncertain.

This competition for legitimacy can be seen in a number of issues in recent years. Civil disobedience over civil rights, abortion, sanctuary for political refugees, and the wars in Vietnam and Central America was often based on a different source of authority than that of the prevailing legal or political ones. Civil disobedience often claimed religion or higher human values as the basis for conflict with civil authorities. Sometimes court events involve a clash of several different sources of legitimacy. In one court case, claims were made from legal, medical, parental, and religious bases of authority. A young person had been comatose for months and "as good as dead" in the commonsense view. Her body was kept alive by technological intervention, and eventually her parents sought legal permission to terminate the "extraordinary" measures of keeping her body alive. No single authority held uncontested legitimacy.[10]

McGuire's analysis is primarily concerned with power and authority as they apply to groups within their larger social context. She does not question whether or not religious groups exert power and authority; her concern is with how that power and authority are wielded. How much of McGuire's argument is rooted in the fact that she lives in the United States, where there is a constitutional separation of church and state coupled with the freedom of persons to subscribe to any religion—or to no religion at all? Would she argue differently, do you think, in a theocracy? Would the balance of power and authority be different?

Assuming that McGuire is right that religions have a particularly strong basis for the authority they wield, at least for their adherents, we turn next to an exploration of the ultimate power upon which religious traditions base their claims.

NEW CANONS,
NEW AUTHORITIES?

In this part of the book, we have been concerned with traditional modes of knowing, particularly as they pertain to the kind of knowledge that relates to sacred truths. We turn now to a passage that challenges some of our notions of "scripture" and "canon" and invites us to think in new ways about the very real and rich differences that exist within religious traditions. Steven Charleston, Episcopal bishop, is also a citizen of the Choctaw nation of Oklahoma. In his essay, "The Old Testament of Native America," Charleston raises provocative questions about the ways in which Christians from various backgrounds view the biblical canon. As you read, consider too how Charleston's proposal challenges traditional views of power and authority.

My own awareness of a Native American Old Testament began to grow while I was sitting in an introductory Old Testament class during my first year of seminary. The professor described what was unique about the religious worldview of ancient Israel. He said that Israel, unlike its neighbors, had a special understanding of the relationship between God and humanity. This was the covenant between a single God and a particular People. It involved the promise of a homeland. It was sustained by the personal involvement of God in history. It was communicated through the prophets and the Law. It made Israel a nation. It brought them together as a People.

It was the most simple, important, understanding of the Old Testament that we share as Christians. And yet, during that lecture, I couldn't help but make a list of comparisons in my mind. Each time the professor mentioned some aspect of the Old Testament story that was "unique" to early Israel, I was reminded of my own Tradition and People. To help you understand what I mean, I will repeat that list in abbreviated form:

1. God is one.
2. God created all that exists.
3. God is a God of human history.
4. God is a God of all time and space.
5. God is a God of all People.
6. God establishes a covenant relationship with the People.
7. God gives the People a "promised land."
8. The People are stewards of this land for God.
9. God gives the People a Law or way of life.
10. The People worship God in sacred spaces.
11. God raises up prophets and charismatic leaders.
12. God speaks through dreams and visions.
13. The People maintain a seasonal cycle of worship.
14. The People believe God will deliver them from their suffering.
15. God can become incarnate on earth.

These fifteen items for comparison each merit more discussion, but the point I wish to make is simply that the religious worldviews of ancient Israel and ancient Native America have much in common. This is not to say that their understandings were identical. There are many variations on the theme not only between the two communities, but within them as well. What is striking, however, is that for many key concepts the two traditions run parallel. Like Israel, Native America believed in the oneness of God; it saw God as the Creator of all existence; it knew that God was active and alive in the history of humanity; it remembered that the land had been given to the people in trust from God. Native People accepted the revelation from God as it was given to them through prophets and charismatic leaders; they recognized sacred ground and holy places in their worship; they maintained a seasonal liturgical calendar; they had a highly developed belief in the incarnational presence of God and expected that presence to be revealed in times of strife or disaster. Is it strange, therefore, that Native Americans would consider themselves to be in a covenant relationship to their Creator or that they would think of themselves as a People "chosen" by God? Take the names which the People used for themselves in their own languages and you get a clear sense of this: in the tribal languages, the many nations of Native America announced their identity as "The People" or "The Human Beings." Moreover, they tied this identity to the land given to them by God. It was this land-based covenant that gave them their identity as "The People," as the community special to a loving God.

Often in Christian history the term "Old Testament" has been used in an almost derogatory way, implying that the "New Testament" supersedes the "Old" and is thus superior to it. Is this the way Charleston understands the term? Many contemporary scholars use the term "Hebrew scriptures" instead to denote the common history shared by Jews and Christians as well as the Jewishness of Jesus. In what ways does this latter understanding enable us to entertain Charleston's suggestion that there might be other "old testaments"?

Comparisons, of course, and especially sketchy ones, don't "prove" any claim to an Old Testament for Native America. I don't intend for them to. Their function is only to illustrate the depth of the Native Tradition itself. Talking about an Old Testament which emerges from the genius of Native America is not a wild leap into the unknown. There are sound theological reasons for taking the Native heritage seriously. It embodies the collective memory of an encounter with God that should cause any theologian to stop and think. As with Israel, this memory was transmitted through all of those channels that make up any Old Testament: through stories, histories, poetry, music, sacraments, liturgies, prophecies, proverbs, visions, and laws. The mighty acts of God in North America were witnessed and remembered. They were interpreted and passed on. Taken all together, they constitute an original, unique, and profound covenant between God and humanity.

If this is true then we are confronted with a problem. Suppose that we do allow Native People to claim an "Old Testament" status for their Tradition. Then what do we do with "the" Old Testament? What is the relationship between the two? What is the relationship to the "New" Testament?

An immediate answer is that we will have to be more concise when we speak of the original covenant with ancient Israel. We won't be able to use that word *the* in quite the same way. As Christians, we're going to have to make some elbow room at the table for other "old testaments." Not only from Native America, but from Africa, Asia, and Latin America as well. That's another door that is opening up in Christianity, and I doubt that anyone is going to be able to close it again. The fact is, Christians must permit the same right for other peoples that they have claimed for themselves. God was as present among the tribes of Africa as God was present among the tribes of America, as God was present among the tribes of Israel. Consequently, we must be cautious about saying that God was "unique" to any one people; God was in a special relationship to different tribes or in a particular relationship with them, but never in an exclusive relationship that shut out the rest of humanity.

Earlier in Chapter 8 we discussed the concept of "canon"—that set of writings that a particular tradition holds as sacred in some way, as central to the beliefs of the people. The Christian canon—the Bible—has been considered closed since it was gathered into its current form. What challenge is Charleston proposing to the whole idea of a closed canon?

This understanding broadens our dialogue about the connections between old testaments. It allows us to say that while there was nothing "unique" about God's relationship to either Native America or ancient Israel, there are elements to both that were special or particular. Obviously, for Christians, the concern focuses on christology. As a theologian of Native America, I can feel comfortable (not to mention orthodox) in saying that it was into the Old Testament People of Israel that God chose to become incarnate. Consequently, the story of this community becomes of primary importance to me. I need to honor, as well as understand, the Old Testament of Israel as the traditional culture into which God came as a person.

In this way, the Old Testament of the Hebrew People remains central to my faith as a Christian and vital to my reading of the Christian scriptures.

At the same time, I can stand on my own Old Testament Tradition and let it speak to me just as clearly about the person, nature, and purpose of the Christ. I maintain that this Christ fulfills both Old Testaments. In the Pauline sense, I can assert that while as a man Jesus was a Jew, as the risen Christ, he is a Navajo. Or a Kiowa. Or a Choctaw. Or any other tribe. The Christ does not violate my own Old Testament. The coming of the Christ does not erase the memory banks of Native America or force me to throw away centuries of God's revealing acts among my People. But let me be careful about this: I am not glossing over the Old Testament of Native America with the Western whitewash of a theology that gives out a few quick platitudes about the "Christ of all cultures." When I speak of a fulfillment of Native America's Old Testament, I mean just that: a Christ that emerges from within the Native Tradition itself; that speaks of, by, and for that Tradition; that participates in that Tradition; that lives in that Tradition. Grounded in the Old Testament of Native America, it is the right of Native People to claim fulfillment of Christ in their own way and in their own language. I am not looking simply to paint the statues brown and keep the Western cultural prejudices intact. I am announcing the privilege of my own People to interpret the Christian canon in the light of Israel's experience, but also in the light of their own experience. Whether this interpretation is compatible with Western opinions is open for discussion.

Christians believe that in the person of Jesus, God became incarnate—embodied—within humanity. Clearly, if God was to become human it had to be in a particular human body, in this case a Jewish man, at a particular time and in a particular place. But Christians also believe in the resurrection of Jesus and his continuing presence as the Christ, a presence that transcends those human particularities and makes the Spirit of Jesus available and accessible to all. How does Charleston bring his Christianity into his commitment to his Native American tradition? Can you imagine a similar discussion in the context of other traditions, for example African or Asian?

The Old Testament *of* Native America, therefore, does not replace the Old Testament of Israel. It stands beside it. The Native People's claim to truth is not a competition with other traditions. The answer to the question about the relationship between the two Old Testaments is this: they do not cancel one another out (any more than they are cancelled out by the New Testament); rather, they complement each other. I firmly believe that if the Christian faith is ever to take root in the soil of Native America, both testaments will be needed. Native People can read through the New Testament from both perspectives and see the gospel far more clearly for themselves. In turn, the gospel can speak to the Tradition with far more clarity. And here's a critical point: when we talk about the "fulfillment" of the Old Testament by Christ, we are describing the dual role of Christ in both confirming and correcting a People's memory. There was much in the memory of Israel that Jesus confirmed; there was also a great deal that he sought to correct. The same applies to the Old Testament memory of Native America. There is much that the Christ confirms and much that stands corrected. No Old Testament has a monopoly on perfection. The two traditions stand side-by-side under the fulfillment of Christ. As Native People begin to actively use their own Old Testament in reading the Christian scriptures they will find strengths that were missing from the experience of Israel, just as they will find weaknesses that need to be changed.

In the end, the naming of an Old Testament of Native America should not be a cause for alarm among any group or People. It is not a threat, but a hope. Our knowledge of God will not be diminished by this act of a People to regain their memory, but enhanced. The testimony of Israel will remain central to all Christians, Western and Native alike. The Tradition of Native People will be as changed by the gospel of Christ as it changes our understanding of that gospel. Native People will discover that they can read and understand both the Old and New Testaments of the Bible with a much clearer vision. Suddenly, they will start to make sense. Not the sense of the West perhaps, the imported versions of truth handed down from a community that fears it has lost its own Old Testament, but the common sense of any People that remembers, that recounts, that reasons, that reveals, and that responds. The "old" and the "new" will merge. They will enter deeply into the Kivas and Lodges of Native America and come back out stronger than we ever dreamed possible.[1]

What implications does Charleston's proposal have for the idea of a closed canon of scripture? And what about "tradition"? Can you imagine talking about an "Old Testament" rather than the "Old Testament"—and talking about them in the plural? In what ways would Charleston's suggestions challenge or support our usual ideas of passing on—communicating—sacred truth? What gives him the "authority" to even entertain such an idea? Does he have the "power" to enact his suggestions?

IV

Seeking Ultimacy, Seeking Hope: Experiencing the Sacred

CHAPTER TEN

IS THE SENSORY WORLD ALL THERE IS? UNDERSTANDINGS OF THE SACRED

Throughout this text, we have suggested that religion is one way in which people, individually and in communities, search for meaning in their lives. In Part One, we discussed ways in which religion, for some people, helps to establish a sense of identity, through a sense of belonging to a community in which shared symbols and ritual activity help to maintain stability and security. In Part Two, we considered ways in which religious communities help people deal with questions of evil and suffering and live out their lives together through the development of codes of ethics, including visions of a just society. In Part Three, we were concerned with the ways in which religious traditions pass on their stories and how authority and tradition function to both enable and inhibit our search for meaning. Now, our attention turns to just what it is about religion that motivates people so strongly—concepts of the Sacred.

What do you think of when you hear the terms "holy," "sacred," "God"? Whether or not you believe in some kind of supernatural being, or in any reality beyond the material world, you probably have some idea what people mean by such concepts and what it is that does or does not compel your own belief. Do "sacred" subjects make you feel comforted, strong, confused, indifferent, even angry? What characteristics do you (or others) attribute to "sacred" reality? If the sacred is something that you believe in or something that you reject, does this satisfy you?

In the preceding chapters, we have referred often to some dimension of "the sacred" as related to the subjects under discussion. Let's explore now what people of various religious faiths mean when they invoke this idea of something beyond what we can experience with our material senses.

Setting the Stage: The Sacred

One of the most common Western names for the sacred is "God." While different traditions, and different people within those traditions, may sometimes call that "God" by other names, the generic term is one with which most of us are familiar, at least those of us who were raised or who live in Western societies. The traditions that believe in some form of sacred being who can be thought of in personalized terms are referred to as "theistic." But just naming oneself a believer (or disbeliever) in "God" doesn't say much about exactly what it is that one believes or doesn't believe in. In the first reading in this chapter, two women are discussing their beliefs in this God. The selection comes from Alice Walker's book, *The Color Purple,* and includes a conversation between Celie, a young woman who has been sexually abused by her stepfather and trampled by life in general, and Shug, a cabaret singer. In Shug, Celie finds a friend with whom she can discuss some of the things that trouble her, including her disappointment with the God who seems to have never done anything for her. Walker's narrative takes the form of letters written by Celie, initially to God, and then to her sister Nettie, when Celie's disillusionment about God is such that she no longer can count on God to care about her concerns. Have you ever questioned the ideas of God that you grew up with, or that other people seem to find comforting or compelling? Do any of your questions sound a bit like those of Celie's and Shug's?

Dear Nettie,

I don't write to God no more, I write to you.

What happen to God? ast Shug.

Who that? I say.

She look at me serious.

Big a devil as you is, I say, you not worried bout no God, surely.

She say, Wait a minute. Hold on just a minute here. Just because I don't harass it like some peoples us know don't mean I ain't got religion.

What God do for me? I ast.

She say, Celie! Like she shock. He gave you life, good health, and a good woman that love you to death.

Yeah, I say, and he give me a lynched daddy, a crazy mama, a lowdown dog of a step pa and a sister I probably won't ever see again. Anyhow, I say, the God I been praying and writing to is a man. And act just like all the other mens I know. Trifling, forgitful and lowdown.

She say, Miss Celie, You better hush. God might hear you.

Let 'im hear me, I say. If he ever listened to poor colored women the world would be a different place, I can tell you.

She talk and she talk, trying to budge me way from blasphemy. But I blaspheme much as I want to.

All my life I never care what people thought bout nothing I did, I say. But deep in my heart I care about God. What he going to think. And come to find out, he don't think. Just sit up there glorying in being deaf, I reckon. But it ain't easy, trying to do without God. Even if you know he ain't there, trying to do without him is a strain.

I is a sinner, say Shug. Cause I was born. I don't deny it. But once you find out what's out there waiting for us, what else can you be?

Sinners have more good times, I say.

You know why? she ast.

Cause you ain't all the time worrying bout God, I say.

Naw, that ain't it, she say. Us worry bout God a lot. But once us feel loved by God, us do the best us can to please him with what us like.

You telling me God love you, and you ain't never done nothing for him? I mean, not go to church, sing in the choir, feed the preacher and all like that?

But if God love me, Celie, I don't have to do all that. Unless I want to. There's a lot of other things I can do that I speck God likes.

Like what? I ast.

Oh, she say. I can lay back and just admire stuff. Be happy. Have a good time.

Well, this sound like blasphemy sure nuff.

She say, Celie, tell the truth, have you ever found God in church? I never did. I just found a bunch of folks hoping for him to show. Any God I ever felt in church I brought in with me. And I think all the other folks did too. They come to church to *share* God, not find God.

Some folks didn't have him to share, I said. They the ones didn't speak to me while I was there struggling with my big belly and Mr. ———————— children.

Right, she say.

Then she say: Tell me what your God look like, Celie.

Aw naw, I say. I'm too shame. Nobody ever ast me this before, so I'm sort of took by surprise. Besides, when I think about it, it don't seem quite right. But it all I got. I decide to stick up for him, just to see what Shug say.

Okay, I say. He big and old and tall and graybearded and white. He wear white robes and go barefooted.

Blue eyes? she ast.

Sort of bluish-gray. Cool. Big though. White lashes, I say.

She laugh.

Why you laugh? I ast. I don't think it so funny. What you expect him to look like, Mr ————————?

That wouldn't be no improvement, she say. Then she tell me this old white man is the same God she used to see when she prayed. If you wait to find God in church, Celie, she say, that's who is bound to show up, cause that's where he live.

How come? I ast.

Cause that's the one that's in the white folks' white bible.

Shug! I say. God wrote the bible, white folks had nothing to do with it.

How come he look just like them, then? she say. Only bigger? And a heap more hair. How come the bible just like everything else they make, all

"Did you ever find God in a church?" asks Shug.

Woopi Goldberg as Celie in the movie version of *The Color Purple.*

about them doing one thing and another, and all the colored folks doing is gitting cursed?

I never thought bout that.

Nettie say somewhere in the bible it say Jesus' hair was like lamb's wool, I say.

Well, say Shug, if he came to any of these churches we talking bout he'd have to have it conked before anybody paid him any attention. The last thing niggers want to think about they God is that his hair kinky.

That's the truth, I say.

Ain't no way to read the bible and not think God white, she say. Then she sigh. When I found out I thought God was white, and a man, I lost interest. You mad cause he don't seem to listen to your prayers. Humph! Do the mayor listen to anything colored say? Ask Sofia, she say.

But I don't have to ast Sofia. I know white people never listen to colored, period. If they do, they only listen long enough to be able to tell you what to do.

Here's the thing, say Shug. The thing I believe. God is inside you and inside everybody else. You come into the world with God. But only them that search for it inside find it. And sometimes it just manifest itself even if you not looking, or don't know what you looking for. Trouble do it for most folks, I think. Sorrow, lord. Feeling like shit.

It? I ast.

Yeah, It. God ain't a he or a she, but a It.

But what do it look like? I ast.

Don't look like nothing, she say. It ain't a picture show. It ain't something you can look at apart from anything else, including yourself. I believe God is everything, say Shug. Everything that is or ever was or ever will be. And when you can feel that, and be happy to feel that, you've found It.

Shug a beautiful something, let me tell you. She frown a little, look out cross the yard, lean back in her chair, look like a big rose.

She say, My first step from the old white man was trees. Then air. Then birds. Then other people. But one day when I was sitting quiet and feeling like a motherless child, which I was, it come to me: that feeling of being part of everything, not separate at all. I knew that if I cut a tree, my arm would bleed. And I laughed and I cried and I run all around the house. I knew just what it was. In fact, when it happen, you can't miss it. It sort of like you know what, she say, grinning and rubbing high up on my thigh.

Shug! I say.

Oh, she say. God love all them feelings. That's some of the best stuff God did. And when you know God loves 'em you enjoys 'em a lot more. You can just relax, go with everything that's going, and praise God by liking what you like.

God don't think it dirty? I ast.

Naw, she say. God made it. Listen, God love everything you love—and a mess of stuff you don't. But more than anything else, God love admiration.

You saying God vain? I ast.

Naw, she say. Not vain, just wanting to share a good thing. I think it pisses God off if you walk by the color purple in a field somewhere and don't notice it.

What it do when it pissed off? I ast.

Oh, It make something else. People think pleasing God is all God care about. But any fool living in the world can see it always trying to please us back.

Yeah? I say.

Yeah, she say. It always making little surprises and springing them on us when us least expect.

You mean it want to be loved, just like the bible say.

Yes, Celie, she say. Everything want to be loved. Us sing and dance, make faces and give flower bouquets, trying to be loved. You ever notice that trees do everything to git attention we do, except walk?

Well, us talk and talk bout God, but I'm still adrift. Trying to chase that old white man out of my head. I been so busy thinking bout him I never truly notice nothing God make. Not a blade of corn (how it do that?) not the color purple (where it come from?). Not the little wildflowers. Nothing.

Now that my eyes opening, I feels like a fool. Next to any little scrub of a bush in my yard, Mr . ——————'s evil sort of shrink. But not altogether. Still, it is like Shug say, You have to git man off your eyeball, before you can see anything a'tall.

Man corrupt everything, say Shug. He on your box of grits, in your head, and all over the radio. He try to make you think he everywhere. Soon as you think he everywhere, you think he God. But he ain't. Whenever you trying to pray, and man plop himself on the other end of it, tell him to git lost, say Shug. Conjure up flowers, wind, water, a big rock.

But this hard work, let me tell you. He been there so long, he don't want to budge. He threaten lightening, floods and earthquakes. Us fight. I hardly pray at all. Every time I conjure up a rock, I throw it.

Amen.[1]

What parts of the dialogue between Shug and Celie did you find most interesting? What do you think about Shug's assessment that Celie's God is the one in the white man's bible? What difference does it make for Shug and Celie to begin to explore different images for God? Why do you think this was such an enlightening experience for Celie, even though it is such hard work? What reaction do you think many church-goers would have to Shug's analysis of who "God" is for her?

Images of God are only a small part of any discussion of what we mean by "sacred." Eastern traditions often have a very different understanding of this sacred, or transcendent, reality. Read the following passage from the *Tao Te Ching* and compare it with the understandings of the sacred that you might have grown up with, and with those discussed by Shug and Celie. What is the major difference between the ideas in this passage and the Western ideas of "God" that you have encountered in this text and elsewhere?

> Without Limit and Perfect, there is a Becoming, beyond Heaven and Earth. It hath nor Motion nor Form; it is alone; it changeth not; it extendeth all ways; it hath no Adversary. It is like the All-Mother.
> I know not its Name, but I call it the Tao. Moreover I exert myself, and call it Vastness.
> Vastness, the Becoming! Becoming, it flieth afar. Afar, it draweth near. Vast is this Tao. Heaven is vast. Earth is vast. The Holy King is vast also. In the Universe are Four Vastnesses, and of these is the Holy King.
> Man followeth the formula of Earth; Earth followeth that of Heaven; and Heaven that of the Tao. The Formula of the Tao is its own Nature. . . .
> The Tao is immanent; it extendeth to the right hand as to the left.
> All things derive from it their being; it createth them, and all comply with it. Its work is done, and it proclaimeth it not. It is the ornament of all things, yet it claimeth not fief of them; there is nothing so small that it inhabiteth not, and informeth it.
> All things return without knowledge of the Cause thereof; there is nothing so great that it inhabiteth not, and informeth it.[2]

How does this selection compare with the conversation between Shug and Celie? Regardless of the problems Shug and Celie have encountered with their concepts of "God," nonetheless they have explicit personalized images—what we would call a theistic understanding of the Sacred. Taoism, on the other hand, is *nontheistic*—affirming of sacred reality as a pervasive force in the universe but not in a personalized form. Even the references to the Holy King and the All-Mother are only metaphors, and certainly not personalized images. For Taoism and many other Eastern understandings, talk of "the Sacred," implying a personalized image, makes little sense.

What image do you have of "sacred reality"—either what you yourself believe or what you think others believe? Why do you hold the ideas you do? What has influenced your ideas of the Sacred?

WHAT DO YOU THINK? WHO OR WHAT IS SACRED?

What or who would you say is "sacred" or "holy" in your life? You might come up with a whole list of symbols, persons, images, items, or you might find it difficult to identify anything. What does it mean to you to say that something is "holy" or "sacred"? Does a particular religious tradition motivate you to make such claims for it, or is it something else?

The following excerpt is from a one-person play, *Spoonface Steinberg*, by British playwright Lee Hall. In Hall's play, "Spoonface" is a seven-year-old autistic child who is dying of cancer. Spoonface's family are nonobservant Jews, but one of her doctors, also Jewish, responds in particularly helpful ways to some of the internal struggles encountered by this child who hears and understands a great deal more than her family realizes. After her final hospital treatments, unsuccessful in halting or even slowing her cancer, Dr. Bernstein gives Spoonface a book that her "Mam," who blames God for the family's troubles, reads to her. What understanding of God emerges for Spoonface as she absorbs the words of the book?

> And when we went home the doctor gave me this book to me—but I can't read so I had to get Mam to read it to me—and then I found all this stuff out—like you had to pray to God—and that this would help get on his good side and even if you did die then he'd look out for you afterwards—and in the book it said there was different ways you can pray—there is like when you get up and sit and say things—that is one way of praying—and then there is like you go to the synagogue and then everybody does it all together and that—and then there is this different way what was invented by these people in Poland quite a while ago—this is when everything you do is a prayer—and you have to do everything you do the best you can because it is not just normal, prayer— when you talk that's a prayer—and when you walk that's a prayer—and when you brush your teeth and when you give someone a kiss—and Mams and Dads when they go to bed that is a prayer—and when you pray that is a prayer—and when you spit, when you suck, when you laugh, when you dance, when you snore—everything you do is a prayer—'specially what you do when you meet other people because all the people in the world are in God's kingdom—and it doesn't even matter if they're Jewish—and all the animals, all the birds and bees and fishes and swans and llamas and piglets and worms and trees and buses and cars and people and that—because when the world was made, God made it out of magic sparks—everything that there is, was all made of magic sparks—and all the magic sparks went into things— deep down and everything has a spark—but it was quite a while ago since it was made and now the sparks are deep down inside and the whole point of being alive—the whole point of living is to find the spark—and when you meet someone and say hello—or if you tell them a joke or when you say that you love them or try and help someone or you see someone who is sad or injured or maybe they have lost all their money or have been battered up or

maybe they're just a bit glum or hungry or you ask the time or maybe they've missed the train—all these people, all they need is help to find the spark—and the people what invented this—the Hassids a long time ago, when they saw people that were having a chat they saw the sparks jump in the space in between them—the sparks were jumping like electricity—sparks God put there—and the sparks were put there for each other 'cos God wanted people to find them in each other—and doing this making sparks—this was to pray—and the old people a long time ago they saw the sparks and when people met and the sparks jumped right up into the air from the place they were hiding and they leapt up through the firmament and through the clouds and past the sun and they shone over the whole universe—and when people kissed there were sparks and when people held each other there were sparks and when they waved as they were going away in a car there would be sparks and they would all be prayers—they would all be prayers for the babies and the sad people with cancer—and for the kings to be good—and the experts to be clever—and all the Mams and Dads and the cleaning ladies and the milkmen—and if only you could see the spark then there was a meaning—because what was the meaning of anything?—If you were going to die, what was the meaning?—all the trees and the bushes and the famines and wars and disasters and even pencils or pens—what was the meaning of all these things?—and the meaning was if you found the spark—then it would be like electricity—and you would glow like a light and you would shine like the sparks and that was the meaning—it wasn't like an answer or a number or any such—it was glowing—it was finding the sparks inside you and setting them free.

This is what it said in this book what the doctor gave me—the doctor what's Mam was the little girl whose Mam got shot—and it meant that the meaning that everybody thought was somewhere else was right here—and all you had to do was do the sparks and become like a lightbulb—and the meaning wasn't that I was going to die but that I was still alive—and I could make everybody shine—the bus boys and the milkmen and Mrs Spud—and I thought, if I wasn't scared of when I wasn't born why would I be scared of when I wasn't existed at the other end—you can't feel the end or touch the end—'cos it was just nothing—the end of things is not the problem 'cos there was really no ends to find—that was the meaning there are no real ends— only middles, and even if I was at the end I was still in the middle—'cos it wouldn't know it was the end then—because it would be ended—so everything is in the middle—even if it was at the middle of an end—it didn't matter because I'm in it.[3]

Many of the images in this passage—such as the sparks—have their roots in Hassidic Jewish mysticism. What kind of comfort might a dying child find in ideas like these? In what ways, if any, might such concepts serve the community in addition to reassurance in times of dire distress? Would a Buddhist be able to relate in any way to Spoonface's understandings? If religion and religious ideas affect the ways in which people live in the world, what difference might it make if people approached God in this way?

What medium would work best to symbolize Spoonface Steinberg's idea of God, and particularly God's activity in the world? Do Hall's words conjure adequate images or are there other ways you think would be better? Using a medium other than descriptive prose, create an image that conveys what you think Spoonface is experiencing.

CULTURAL AND SOCIAL INFLUENCES ON THE SACRED

Both Celie and Shug, in *The Color Purple,* had been presented with images of the sacred that they pictured as an old white man with a long beard and long white robes. Spoonface, by contrast, had developed a different way of perceiving God in the world. Where do your images of the Sacred come from? Do you, like Celie, tend to think of God as an "old white man"? If you refer to God using a personal pronoun, what pronoun do you use? Because we, as humans, often find it easier to relate to something with familiar characteristics, we commonly apply everyday attributes to our conceptions of the sacred, as do peoples in other times and places.

CHANGING TIMES, CHANGING IMAGES

Images and understandings of the sacred change dramatically according to time and place. The following passage is from *The Golden Ass,* by the 2nd century CE Roman writer Apuleis. What images of the sacred emerge in this reading? What does the writer seem to be suggesting about the ways in which multiple cultures name and understand their own experiences of the sacred?

> I am the mother of the world of nature, mistress of all the elements, first-born in this realm of time. I am the loftiest of deities, queen of departed spirits, foremost of heavenly dwellers, the single embodiment of all gods and goddesses. I order with my nod the luminous heights of heaven, the healthy sea-breezes, the sad silences of the infernal dwellers. The whole world worships this single godhead under a variety of shapes and liturgies and titles. In one land the Phrygians, first-born of men, hail me as the Pessinuntian mother of the gods; elsewhere the native dwellers of Attica call me Cecropian Minerva; in other climes the wave-tossed Cypriots name me Paphian Venus; the Cretan archers, Dictynna Diana; the trilingual Sicilians, Ortygian Proserpina; the Lucinians, the ancient goddess Ceres; some call me Juno, others Bellona, others Hecate, and others still Rhamnusia. But the peoples on whom the rising sun-god shines with his first rays—eastern and western Ethiopians, and the Egyptians who flourish with their time-honoured learning—worship me with the liturgy that is my own, and call me by my true name, which is Queen Isis.[4]

In contemporary times, many scholars have suggested that images of the sacred as female, as goddess, long predate any conception of deity as a male god. Some date the earliest evidence of goddess cultures to as long ago as

25,000 years. Archeological evidence, as well as many of the myths that survive, certainly support the idea that our current images and ideas about the sacred are not the same as those held by ancient peoples. What reasons can you think of that might account for such different images of the divine? And why do you think these images have changed so much over time?

Do a Web search for "goddess." How many hits did you get? Now add some terms to refine your search. Check out two or three sites that sound most interesting to you. Are they dealing mostly with historical or contemporary approaches? What particular approach does each site take? Why do you think there is so much interest in goddess traditions in the 21st Century?

THE SACRED AND THE WORLD

In many of the traditions with which Western readers are most familiar, we have an idea of the Sacred—God—as being somehow outside the natural world which that same God created. Various traditions have different understandings of the ways in which their sacred reality interacts—or does not interact—with the world. As we have seen, many indigenous traditions see the Sacred as immersed in creation rather than outside or separate from it; even within this particular view, there is great diversity. We turn now to two texts, one a narrative from a !Kung woman, Nisa, from Africa, and the other from Sun Bear, of the Chippewa Nation. As you read Nisa's description of the ways in which her people understand their God to be relating to them, consider how this compares, for example, with the views of Shug and Celie, or Spoonface Steinberg.

My father had the power to cure people with trance medicine, with gemsbok-song trance medicine. Certain animals—gemsbok, eland, and giraffe—have trance songs named after them, songs long ago given by God. These songs were given to us to sing and to work with. That work is very important and good work; it is part of how we live.

It is the same with everything—even the animals of the bush. If a hunter is walking in the bush and God wants to, God will tell him, "There's an animal lying dead over there for you to eat." The person is just walking, but soon sees an animal lying dead in the bush. He says, "What killed this? It must have been God wanting to give me a present." Then he skins it and eats it; that's the way he lives.

But if God hadn't wanted, even if the hunter had seen many animals, his arrows would never strike them. Because if God refuses to part with an animal, the man's arrows won't be able to kill it. Even if the animal is standing close beside him, his arrows will miss every time. Finally he gives up or the animal runs away. It is only when God's heart says that a person should kill something, be it a gemsbok or a giraffe, that he will have it to eat. He'll say "What a huge giraffe! I, a person, have just killed a small something that is God's." Or it may be a big eland that his arrows strike.

That is God's way; that is how God does things and how it is for us as we
live. Because God controls everything.

God is the power that made people. He is like a person, with a person's body
and covered with beautiful clothes. He has a horse on which he puts people who
are just learning to trance and becoming healers. God will have the person in
trance ride to where he is, so God can see the new healer and talk to him.[5]

Nisa's images of God are somewhat different from those of Sun Bear, yet in
the next passage, Sun Bear suggests that our multiple images of divine being
may all point to the same reality. Sun Bear has been criticized by some of his
own people for sharing sacred teachings with a wider audience; his reasons for
taking this sometimes unpopular path are clear in his words:

"If we are going to stabilize the world through this time of Earth changes," Sun
Bear says, "then there are going to have to be some fundamental changes in the
way people think about the Earth. It's very important that they stop thinking
about the Earth as something they can just take from—and that they can
bulldoze off a hillside and take all the timber just to create a shopping center, or
something else. They have to start learning to take and do things with respect—
respect for the natural resources and energy.

"One of the programs I'm working with now is called the World Earth
Fund. I'm trying to raise funds from different places to plant trees and help
restore the balance upon the Earth, and to help humans become conscious
of taking responsibility for themselves. People have to adopt a totally new
consciousness; that's what has to happen. People have to become totally
committed to this, so that the person who is smoking a cigarette doesn't throw
the butt down on the ground, and children are learning the same thing, so that
respect for the Earth comes into their hearts and minds totally. We have to do
things with respect. There can be no more taking and living in the old way. You
can't just go out and shoot some animal for sport. You have to get to where you
know that that creature has the same right to life as you do. If you have to take
it for food, that's a different thing, but you have to learn to do it in a respectful
way. Respect everything.

"Beyond that, human consciousness has to evolve and expand. This is a
part of what I'm doing. I'm reaching out to a lot of the ancient teachings and
bringing them together, and making comparisons, and sharing with people so
that they can understand. Maybe the gods and goddesses that the ancient Egyptians were addressing are the same spirits that the native peoples of America or
elsewhere were addressing. We have different names for the spirit keepers of the
Earth. For example, Isis was goddess of the Nile and the waters, whereas we
have spirits that we call the Thunderbeings. These spirits have been around for
thousands of years, and they are probably the same, but with different names.
They have responsibility for the waters. Their work is to keep the Earth in
harmony and balance, and we are supposed to work with them. Now, people
are going to have to understand it, so that in their life path everything is in harmony. They must relate to each other and the world in a sacred manner, and no
longer be involved in the conscious and unconscious destruction of the Earth."[6]

A Chippewa Chief participates in a peace pipe ceremony.

Do you think Sun Bear is right when he says that the Egyptians might have been addressing the same spirits as the Native Americans? When Nisa uses the term "God," do you think she means what you mean when you use or hear that word? Could this be the same God addressed by Judaism, Christianity, and Islam? How do these passages compare with the one from the *Tao Te Ching?* If our images of the sacred both emerge from and influence our cultural and social customs and actions, what would change in our own time if we accepted some of the images presented in these passages? Throughout this text, we have encountered ways in which religion can function both positively and negatively in the lives of individuals and their communities. What light do these passages shed on the complexities and ambiguities of religion and images of the Sacred? How do these passages relate to the discussion of "old testament" by Steven Charleston that follows Chapter 9?

IMAGES OF THE ONE GOD

Even in the monotheistic Jewish, Christian, and Muslim religions, with their belief that there is only one God, the sacred texts and other elements of the traditions present a diversity of images and ideas about "God." The following excerpts from the Tanakh and the Christian scriptures provide a glimpse of these varied images. What does it mean that there can be so many possible images for the same reality?

An angel of the LORD appeared to [Moses] in a blazing fire out of a bush. He gazed, and there was a bush all aflame, yet the bush was not consumed. Moses said, "I must turn aside to look at this marvelous sight; why doesn't the bush burn up?" When the LORD saw that he had turned aside to look, God called to him out of the bush. "Moses! Moses!" He answered, "Here I am." And He said, "Do not come closer. Remove your sandals from your feet, for the place on which you stand is holy ground. I am," He said, "the God of your father, the God of Abraham, the God of Isaac, and the God of Jacob." And Moses hid his face, for he was afraid to look at God.[7]

"Come out," He called, "and stand on the mountain before the LORD." And lo, the LORD passed by. There was a great and mighty wind, splitting mountains and shattering rocks by the power of the LORD; but the LORD was not in the wind. After the wind—an earthquake; but the LORD was not in the earthquake. After the earthquake—fire; but the LORD was not in the fire. And after the fire—a soft murmuring sound. When Elijah heard it, he wrapped his mantle about his face and went out and stood at the entrance of the cave. Then a voice addressed him: "Why are you here, Elijah?"[8]

But they—our fathers—acted presumptuously; they stiffened their necks and did not obey Your commandments. Refusing to obey, unmindful of Your wonders that You did for them, they stiffened their necks, and in their defiance resolved to return to their slavery. But You, being a forgiving God, gracious and compassionate, long-suffering and abounding in faithfulness, did not abandon them.[9]

The LORD is a passionate, avenging God,
The LORD is vengeful and fierce in wrath.
The LORD takes vengeance on his enemies,
He rages against his foes. . . .
Why will you plot against the LORD?
He wreaks utter destruction:
No adversary opposes Him twice![10]

Do you think that I have come to bring peace to the earth? No, I tell you, but rather division! From now on five in one household will be divided, three against two and two against three; they will be divided: father against son and son against father, mother against daughter and daughter against mother, mother-in-law against her daughter-in-law and daughter-in-law against mother-in-law.'[11]

Jerusalem, Jerusalem, the city that kills the prophets and stones those who are sent to it! How often have I desired to gather your children together as a hen gathers her brood under her wings, and you were not willing![12]

There are different, possibly even contradictory images in these passages. Why did the editors of the texts—whoever they were—choose to leave these multiple different images there? Remembering that the narratives that form both the Tanakh and the Christian Bible were collected and recorded over a great space of time and place, what circumstances do you think might have encouraged development of these rather different attributes of divinity within the same belief system? Do we need more or different images today? If so, does this mean the old ones are irrelevant?

Of the world's monotheistic religions, none is more emphatic in its insistence that there is only one God than Islam. The first major principle—one of the five pillars of Islam—is that "There is one God and Mohammed is his prophet." Yet Islam, like other traditions, acknowledges that there might still be many names for this God. What do you notice about the following passage, from the Qur'an, and the preceding passages from the Jewish and Christian scriptures? What are the similarities? What are the differences?

> He is God; there is no god but He,
> the knower of the unknown and the known.
> He is the benevolent, ever-merciful.
> He is God; there is no god but He,
> the King, the Holy, the Preserver,
> Protector, Guardian, the Strong, the Powerful, Omnipotent.
> Far too exalted is God
> for what they associate with Him.
> He is God, the Creator, the Maker, the Fashioner.
> His are all the names beautiful.
> Whatever is in the heavens and the earth
> sings His praises.
> He is all-mighty and all-wise.[13]

Along with the Qur'an, Muslims acknowledge the *hadith,* collections of sayings attributed to Mohammed that did not make their way into the central sacred text. The hadith suggests that there are ninety-nine names for God, deliberately stopping short of one hundred because there must be room for God's mystery. No single name, or even collection of names, can claim to encompass the entirety of the sacred one. Do any of the names in the following passage surprise you? Which ones are familiar to you? What particular role do you think some of these names might play in a community of believers?

> It is related from Abu Hurairah that, "The Apostle of God said, 'Truly God Most High has ninety-nine names. Whoever counts them will enter paradise. He is Allah, than whom there is no other God, the Merciful, the Compassionate, the King, the Holy, the Peace, the Faithful, the Protector, the Mighty, the Compeller, the Proud, the Creator, the Maker, the Fashioner, the Forgiver, the Dominant, the Bestower, the Provider, the Opener, the Knower, the Restrainer, the Speaker, the Abaser, the Exalter, the Honorer, the Destroyer, the Hearer, the Seer, the Ruler, the Just, the Subtle, the Aware, the Clement, the Grand, the Forgiving, the Grateful, the Exalted, The Great, the Guardian, the Strengthener, the Reckoner, the Majestic, the Generous, the Watcher, the Approver, the Comprehensive, the Wise, the Loving, the Glorious, the Raiser, the Witness, the Truth, the Advocate, the Strong, the Firm, the Patron, the Laudable, the Counter, the Beginner, the Restorer, the Quickener, the Killer, the Living, the Subsisting, the Finder, the

Glorious, the One, the Eternal, the Powerful, the Prevailing, the Bringer-forward, the Deferrer, the First, the Last, the Evident, the Hidden, the Governor, the Exalted, the Righteous, the Accepter of Repentance, the Avenger, the Pardoner, the Kind, the Ruler of the Kingdom, the Lord of majesty and liberality, the Equitable, the Collector, the Independent, the Enricher, the Giver, the Withholder, the Distresser, the Profiter, the Light, the Guide, the Incomparable, the Enduring, the Inheritor, the Director, the Patient.'"[14]

Think of some names for God—either your own names or some you think Celie and Shug might come up with. How is a name different from a manifestation (e.g., the burning bush, the still small voice, an angel)? What sort of power is in a name such that some prefer not to say or write it?

In Judaism, Islam, and particularly in some branches of Protestant Christianity, verbal descriptions of the qualities of the divine are enough. Although Shug and Celie have developed visual images of what they think God looks like, such pictorial representations are strictly forbidden in Islam. And following the Protestant Reformation, many churches in Europe were stripped of icons, paintings, statues and other objects that the Reformers feared had come to be worshipped in and of themselves. Far better to avoid such representations, they believed, than to entertain the possibility that persons would be led to idol worship and distracted from the grandeur and ultimate mystery of God. Other traditions, however, rely heavily on visual and other sensory representations to indicate various attributes of divinity. We have seen how for many indigenous traditions the natural world itself embodies divinity. In Eastern traditions, such as Taoism and Buddhism, the divine cannot be named or even described in words, or in other media. Statues of the Buddha, for instance, are in no way symbols of divinity except inasmuch as they represent the one believed to have provided the ultimate model for achieving enlightenment.

Hinduism provides an interesting and complex contrast. The rich visual imagery used to depict the Hindu gods and goddesses is very different from the stark simplicity of an Islamic mosque or a Reformed Christian church. The term "Hinduism" covers a vast array of different practices and beliefs, loosely linked through a general belief in a central divinity—Brahman—that is manifest in many different forms. *Moksha*—release from the cycle of birth, death and reincarnation—can be achieved by devotion to any particular form of the sacred: Vishnu, Shiva, Krishna, Agni. A pantheon of gods and goddesses represent multiple aspects of divinity, including love, anger, war, and so forth.

In Native American traditions, as in many other indigenous traditions, nothing is outside the realm of the sacred. Yet even in such traditions, certain items and objects are considered to have special significance—to hold sacred power in a particular way. If we think back to the passage we read about Lame Deer's vision quest, at the beginning of Chapter 1, what items could we say had particular sacred significance to Lame Deer and his people? And what gives these items this sacred power?

If you belong to a religious tradition, what items are considered in your tradition to hold particular power or sacred significance? Are there sacred texts? If so, in what ways are these texts treated differently from other books? Does the importance, the particular status, of texts and other items, mean that the community thinks of these items as "God," or as whatever idea of the sacred they hold? Why do these things evoke a particular power and significance in your tradition? If you are not part of a religious group, what items in your family or culture hold particular importance? Are there some that you would say symbolize some degree of ultimate meaning for you and for others in your community?

> *Locate several websites that reflect the culture and traditions of indigenous peoples from different parts of the world. Some possibilities would be Australian Aborigines, the African Yoruba or Ibo, or the New Zealand Maori. To what extent do the images shown reflect the geographic and other features of the daily life of the people? How do these relate to the people's understanding of the sacred?*

THE SACRED AND DAILY LIFE

As we discovered in our earlier discussion, symbols that convey ultimate or sacred meaning are usually closely related to the material objects that are most important to the life and survival of the community—either in contemporary times or in the time when the tradition was developed. Our next selection is from Toni Morrison's novel *Beloved*. Set during the days of slavery, Morrison's narrative tells the story of a community that, although living in a northern state, has been and continues to be ominously touched by the consequences of that violent institution. In the passage that follows, the community has gathered in a clearing in the woods to hear Baby Suggs, holy, preach. Now Baby Suggs has no official religious status, no ordination as a minister, no particular religion to which she is attached. What then gives her the power to address her community? Where does power lie for this particular group as they listen to this elder among them share her words of wisdom? In particular, what are the images and metaphors Baby Suggs uses that are particularly powerful for the community to which she speaks? Why does she choose these terms and symbols rather than some of the others that might be available?

> It was in front of . . . 124 [the house in Ohio] that Sethe climbed off a wagon, her newborn tied to her chest, and felt for the first time the wide arms of her mother-in-law, who had made it to Cincinnati. Who decided that, because slave life had "busted her legs, back, head, eyes, hands, kidneys, womb and tongue," she had nothing left to make a living with but her heart—which she put to work at once. Accepting no title of honor before her name, but allowing a small caress after it, she became an unchurched preacher, one who visited pulpits and

The mothers of the church at a revival meeting in Harlem.

opened her great heart to those who could use it. In winter and fall she carried it to AMEs and Baptists, Holinesses and Sanctifieds, the Church of the Redeemer and the Redeemed. Uncalled, unrobed, unanointed, she let her great heart beat in their presence. When warm weather came, Baby Suggs, holy, followed by every black man, woman and child who could make it through, took her great heart to the Clearing—a wide-open place cut deep in the woods nobody knew for what at the end of a path known only to deer and whoever cleared the land in the first place. In the heat of every Saturday afternoon, she sat in the clearing while the people waited among the trees.

After situating herself on a huge flat-sided rock, Baby Suggs bowed her head and prayed silently. The company watched her from the trees. They knew she was ready when she put her stick down. Then she shouted, "Let the children come!" and they ran from the trees toward her.

"Let your mothers hear you laugh," she told them, and the woods rang. The adults looked on and could not help smiling.

Then "Let the grown men come," she shouted. They stepped out one by one from among the ringing trees.

"Let your wives and your children see you dance," she told them, and groundlife shuddered under their feet.

Finally she called the women to her. "Cry," she told them. "For the living and the dead. Just cry." And without covering their eyes the women let loose. It started that way: laughing children, dancing men, crying women and then it got mixed up. Women stopped crying and danced; men sat down and cried; children danced, women laughed, children cried until, exhausted and riven, all and each lay about the Clearing damp and gasping for breath. In the silence that followed, Baby Suggs, holy, offered up to them her great big heart. She did not tell them to clean up their lives or to go and sin no more. She did not tell them they were the blessed of the earth, its inheriting meek or its glorybound pure. She told them that the only grace they could have was the grace they could imagine. That if they could not see it, they would not have it. "Here," she said, "in this here place, we flesh; flesh that weeps, laughs; flesh that dances on bare feet in grass. Love it. Love it hard. Yonder they do not love your flesh. They despise it. They don't love your eyes; they'd just as soon pick em out. No more do they love the skin on your back. Yonder they flay it. And O my people they do not love your hands. Those they only use, tie, bind, chop off and leave empty. Love your hands! Love them. Raise them up and kiss them. Touch others with them, pat them together, stroke them on your face 'cause they don't love that either. *You* got to love it, *you!* And no, they ain't in love with your mouth. Yonder, out there, they will see it broken and break it again. What you say out of it they will not heed. What you scream from it they do not hear. What you put into it to nourish your body they will snatch away and give you leavins instead. No, they don't love your mouth. *You* got to love it. This is flesh I'm talking about here. Flesh that needs to be loved. Feet that need to rest and to dance; backs that need support; shoulders that need arms, strong arms I'm telling you. And O my people, out yonder, hear me, they do not love your neck unnoosed and straight. So love your neck; put a hand on it, grace it, stroke it and hold it up. And all your inside parts that they'd just as soon slop for hogs, you got to love them. The dark, dark liver—love it, love it, and the beat and beating heart, love that too. More than eyes or feet.

"More than lungs that have yet to draw free air. More than your life-holding womb and your life-giving private parts, hear me now, love your heart. For this is the prize." Saying no more, she stood up then and danced with her twisted hip the rest of what her heart had to say while the others opened their mouths and gave her the music. Long notes held until the four-part harmony was perfect enough for their deeply loved flesh.[15]

This probably doesn't sound like any religious worship service that you've ever attended. What are the implications for Baby Suggs's community of her telling them to see their very bodily selves as "holy"? Would you call the actions of the people involved "sacred" or "holy"? Is the clearing a sacred space or are sacred places only the temples, synagogues, mosques, and churches that have been specifically created for the purpose of worship?

In many religions, there is a tradition of sacred music, and often visual arts, either representational or symbolic, that is intended to direct the thoughts and spirits of believers toward the sacred reality that is central to the life of the community. For some groups, dance and other movements that involve the whole body are a part of the process of worshipping the sacred or divine. In Islam, as in many other traditions, music and dance are not a part of the regular service; indeed, dancing and even listening to music are forbidden in some situations, for example, in the context of other forbidden activities such as consuming alcohol. But for the Sufis, a mystical order within Islam, music and dance are considered a central means of placing oneself always and fully in the presence of Allah. Why would the same activity be forbidden in some circumstances and sacred in others?

> *Do a Web search using the phrase "sacred dance." Explore some of the sites that come up. Now add the term "Sufi" to your search. Just what does dance signify within this tradition?*

Some Questions about the Sacred

Ideas about the Sacred are many and varied. Even within the monotheistic traditions, there are widely divergent and numerous images and understandings of whatever the particular tradition calls "God." By their very number, religious texts and traditions seem to be implying that the mysterious transcendent reality they experience at the heart of their faith cannot be adequately named or imaged in human terms—or by human endeavors. Thus Islam will talk about the ninety-nine names for Allah, but insist that the hundredth be left open for mystery; Judaism and Christianity use multiple images incorporating qualities and aspects from humans and also from the other-than-human creation. Many women in the 21st century insist that the tradition of imaging the deity in mostly masculine terms is inadequate at best and at worst has encouraged and supported the idea that women are unable to fully image the divine. People from multiple racial and ethnic communities question visual depictions and statuary that suggest that divinity "images" the white Western dominating culture. Polytheistic traditions have the potential for avoiding these problems by assigning particular attributes to different gods and goddesses, although many have a concept of a central powerful deity to whom all the others are somewhat subservient.

Nontheistic traditions do not image the sacred in human or other concrete material terms at all. To followers of these traditions, speaking of the sacred in terms of "god" doesn't make sense. We saw in the selection from the *Tao Te Ching* that although the very poetry of the text evokes certain images, none of these is intended to name divinity. On the contrary, once persons believe that they have captured or named the Tao, they can be sure, in this tradition, that they are seriously off the mark.

Several of these very different ways of understanding "the Sacred" may make sense to you. You may feel that it is strange to be attracted to more than one such understanding, but that is because we often feel—or are told—that different understandings of "the Sacred" are mutually exclusive. Generally, the images or ideas we have about "the Sacred" reflect what is of greatest value to us as individuals and as communities.

WHAT SOME OTHERS HAVE SAID ABOUT THE SACRED

In this chapter, we have introduced you to many diverse understandings of the reality that is often referred to as "the Sacred," the Divine, God. In this final section, we present excerpts from two essays that form part of a "round-table" discussion by several feminist scholars of religion. The women and men involved in the conversation are interested particularly in whether images of a Goddess—which have become very popular among many contemporary communities of women (and some men)—really serve humankind any better than do images of the patriarchal God. The first selection is from Catherine Madsen's essay, "If God Is God She Is Not Nice," the essay to which the other participants are responding.

> I have just returned from another conference on women and spirituality and my ears are full of phrases like "imaging God" and "God the Mother" and "the feminine attributes of the Divine." I am surprised to find that this leaves me feeling disaffected from all religion, orthodox or feminist, God-centered or Goddess-centered. I have the feeling that I am being lied to, or that some of the women in search of the feminine divine are somehow lying to themselves, or that there is a lie somewhere in this approach to thinking about God. . . .
>
> Throughout the conference I heard only about God the Mother as nurturer, healer, caretaker, peacemaker, as though no other attributes were permitted God once she was fitted with a female pronoun. Rather than expanding the idea of God to include women's knowledge—the knowledge of unending responsibility, of the ambiguity and necessity of relationships, of being surrounded by people yet at the same time far from help—these definitions narrow God's role to the traditional feminine virtues: as though the Goddess were God's wife and our mother and her job was to clean up after all of us, and console us too.
>
> Many of the women who offered such definitions seemed to come from mainstream Christian churches; some were nuns. They had been raised in a religious tradition which pronounced that God was good without any argument, and that the believer's chief task was to bend her will to his. Now that they have understood how damaging this is to the believer (and, in particular ways, to the female believer), they can no longer accept their churches' definition of God; they cannot bend their will to a God who seems to desire the suppression of their bodies and the suffocation of their minds. But their answer to this is to try to discover a God they *can* bend their will to. Having been told that God is good, and discovered that "he" is not, they still hope that "she" may be. They are unwilling, or afraid, or perhaps it has simply not occurred to them, to match their will against God's. They are still in search of a God they can approve of.

Women have, as Madsen points out, often been alienated by constant language and images of God as male; people of different racial and ethnic groups sometimes resist the attributes of a God that have emerged in a cultural context very different from their own; people whose livelihood is eked out in a geographical location where the weather and general conditions are hostile to human habitation might find it hard to relate to images of a kind creator-God who provides a world of beauty and nourishment. But Madsen's major problem is less with particular images of the sacred than it is with a general approach to God. What problem does Madsen see with this endeavor to find an image "to which women can bend their will"? She goes on to suggest that "comfort" is not all that we need or should expect from God. Simply creating images of God that fulfill some of these needs might not be the solution.

> It is certainly true that the revelation of how deep the opposition to female authority runs in patriarchal religion has left many women profoundly in need of comfort. But it has left them in even greater need of truth. To project the attributes one trusts and approves of onto a Goddess, in order that one may still have something to worship after the betrayals of the Father God, is to underestimate what is possible in the relationship between God and the individual soul. It is to maintain a dependent and docile relationship to God, and to assert that gender is the factor which makes dependency on the Father God intolerable and dependency on the Goddess permissible. It is also (for some women) a kind of insurance that one's God will never get out of hand, never appear unbearably different from oneself. It can be a kind of evasion of one's own authority.
>
> But why is it necessary (and how is it possible?) to have a God one trusts and approves of? I say this not as someone who has known only the Father God, but as someone who has known the world: its droughts and floods, its extremes of climate, its strange combination of tender bounty and indifference, and the uneasiness of human society with its descents into savagery. However certain one may be that one is loved by some presence in the universe—and it is possible, at moments, to be very certain of that—that same presence will kill us all in turn, will visit our lovers with sudden devastating illness, will freeze our crops, will age our friends, and will never for one moment stand between us and any person who wishes us harm. Does the Goddess so care for us, if she is not moved by our pain? Does she nurture us when she blasts our fields with unrelenting sun? Did she, in some secret laboratory of vulnerable flesh, work out the mutations of the AIDS virus?
>
> Did she who made the Lamb make thee?
>
> The image of a nurturing Goddess involves us in the same difficulty as the image of a good God. There is no escape. We may remove all barriers to women's participation in religion, all sense that femaleness is contaminating. We may refute the notion of God as a punishing presence, always remote and forbidding. But, those obstacles gone, we come face to face with the essential dilemma, the vertigo, the horror of all ethical theism: we are more ethical than God. Given the power to make a world, we would never have made this one.

Madsen seems to be raising the same question of theodicy that we encountered in Chapter 4, in our discussion of evil. How do we come to an understanding of God that does not leave us disappointed in Her or Him for letting us down? For letting bad things happen and not intervening? Do you agree with Madsen's assessment of the problem?

To establish a Goddess in place of the Father God accomplishes nothing if we try to make her good. To substitute feminine virtues for masculine powers is impossible, either in divine or in human terms; in the world, virtues and powers are entirely mixed, so that no good act takes place (even nurturance, even comfort) without its undercurrent of danger; and no evil act takes place but through the intermediary of the body, the physical reality we love. If we are made in the divine image, *that* is what we are up against: the inseparability of good and evil. If we long to separate them anyway—if we have eaten the fruit of some tree, which makes us restlessly conscious that we are "as gods" and would rather not be—we are on our own: we are doomed to try to alter God's image, to refine it and discipline it and reshape it, and not with God's benign encouragement but even against God's will. We must try to become what we wish God was.

Is it so strengthening to have an image of God who nurtures us? How much more strengthening to have an image of God we can stand up to: whom we can argue with, whom we can exhort, to whose face we can insist upon justice and nurturance and wisdom and every great thing we want to be capable of. How much more strengthening to strive with God. The story of Jacob and the angel may look to women's eyes like just another masculine tussle in the dust, but it contains this truth: that it will not destroy us to strive with God, that we can wrestle and prevail, that even against God's will we can exact a blessing.

Or let us have no image of God at all, and learn to trust each other.[16]

Madsen is clearly speaking from the Western perspective of a somewhat personalized image of God. What do you think she means when she says that "we must try to become what we wish God was"? Is she right? Does this help us at all with the issue of God images? Do we need images at all, or can we do away with them, as Madsen suggests? Do you think that Madsen would agree with those who suggest that God did not say that we would not suffer and struggle, only that God would be with us in that struggle? One group member, Anne Klein, responds to Madsen from her own perspective as a scholar of Eastern religions, particularly Buddhism. For Klein, the problem with Madsen's analysis lies in Madsen's Western idea of God as "other"—outside of the creatures and creation.

The chief problem with the God Madsen considers has to do with its otherness. Once an all-powerful God is construed as other, a dynamic unfolds that tends to shape religious life in a pattern remarkably and unfortunately similar to the shape of relations between genders as our culture has constructed them. I will sketch here two features of this dynamic and reflect on them from an Asian, largely Buddhist, perspective. . . .

Rendering God as other encourages a differential hierarchy in which the weaker seeks protection and nurture from the stronger and, in order to preserve this relationship, may clothe herself in a "weakness" that goes beyond healthy recognition of mortal limitation. . . . A relationship with something or someone greater than oneself does not have to fall into this pattern; one significant factor might be whether recognition of limitations or weakness hardens into defensiveness aimed at control of others and denial of self rather than knowledge of self.

Construing God as other also suggests an external source of responsibility for the world and thus an ultimate object for blame or praise. . . .

From the Kabbalists to the Gnostics, to Sufi mystics and Process theologians, Western traditions have found various ways to deemphasize the otherness of the divine and understand religious life as a journey inward. . . .

Since my own greatest familiarity is with Asian religions, however, I draw my reflections largely from them. The overall religious structure here is quite different. For example, Confucianism, Taoism, Zen and Theravada Buddhism circumvent the problem of theodicy by de-emphasizing other-worldliness in general and a governing supernatural personage in particular. In addition, Theravada, like Buddhism and Hinduism in general, does not locate the movement of the universe in any single being or source, but in an infinitely complex series of causes and conditions set in motion by the thought and actions of each and every individual sentience. . . . Whatever the difficulties entailed in karma theory, such as the lack of a first cause and the question of rebirth, it is a model of cosmic functioning that complements well a spiritual life which focuses on internal states rather than external deity, with some of these states themselves often being equated with divinity and/or primordial reality.

For example, the . . . Upanishads were understood in India to reveal, as the ultimate good news and most profound secret of the universe, that the quintessence of all things lies deep within the mind; various forms of Indo-Tibetan Buddhism share this general perspective. In the case of Tibetan tantra, for example, even the apparently externally oriented act of prostrating to an enlightened deity or Buddha is primarily understood as a gesture toward developing or discovering one's own deepest resources of spirit. . . . The ultimate is not other than ourselves; even more radically, it is not other than our *present* selves. It is something already with us, waiting to be discovered. Not all forms of Buddhism would agree; many emphasize the necessity of developing, rather than discovering, an experience of Buddha-nature. In both cases, however, the central issue is not joining with an external God/Buddha, but becoming or recognizing one oneself.

Although not without their own interesting problems, Zen, the Great Completeness and various Tibetan tantric traditions that favor the discovery model offer the clearest contrast to a conception of God or the divine as other. By refusing to bifurcate human and divine endeavor, they emphasize not only full human participation in the divine, but full divine participation in the human. Since "the human" includes the conventions of cultural particularity, it is also possible to incorporate modern understandings of the intermingled forces of religion and culture. By contrast . . . a god which is not only other than ourselves but also ubiquitously singular, forces the most difficult questions about the nature of responsibility and truth; hence in Christianity the "problem" of pluralism.

The impetus to find god internally, shared by many North American feminist religious thinkers, is even more fundamental and at least as important a contribution to contemporary religious reflection as the re-imaging of the divine as female. Though in many ways these shifts are compatible, there is the problem that *any* gender association tends to constellate attitudes and characteristics that are culturally situated as other for half of us. This can perhaps be countered by enlarging gender concepts at work in the religious sphere. Certainly, the importance of images for spiritual life and community is not in question. Rather, the ponderable issue is the extent to which we can recognize these as formed from self and culture, and still find them meaningful. . . .

Perhaps what is most pertinent is not to find an already defined God in ourselves, but simply to see those selves as clearly as possible. If in the process, as certain Hindu and Buddhist traditions would suggest, we discover some secret key to our lives and to the universe we create and inhabit, that will remain our individual secret. It will enable us to pour meaning into texts and images whose orientation or aspect, male or female, is not bound for us by narrow constructions of gender association, but broad enough to receive a meaning which, to individual experience, yields a sense of unbridled universality.[17]

The discussion between Madsen and Klein illustrates a major distinction between theistic and nontheistic religions. In both mono- and polytheistic traditions, the presence of personalized god/dess figures—whether in human or some other form—suggests divinity somewhat external to human reality. Although such traditions frequently have a belief in some form of "spirit" that dwells within humanity, *sacred* beings are often seen as acting externally on *human* beings. What are the implications of this for the different understandings of evil and suffering that we discussed earlier? Does the imperfect nature of the world around us mean that it is not "good"? Is the power of God such that we should expect divine intervention in areas of turmoil and brokenness, or are there other understandings of such power that are more helpful? Finally, are the two positions articulated by Madsen and Klein so different that they cannot be reconciled? Where do you think indigenous traditions such as those of Native Americans would fit into this picture? Is this an area where interreligious dialogue might yield greater understanding for all those involved, or is it likely simply to lead to greater confusion? Finally, what are the implications of the Western and Eastern approaches to divinity or the Sacred for our understandings of the meaning of our lives?

Write a letter to Madsen and/or Klein responding to their comments. What points, if any, do you agree with? What points, if any, do you disagree with? Come up with an alternative suggestion that you think addresses Madsen's and Klein's concerns more adequately.

CHAPTER ELEVEN

How Are We Made Whole? Healing and the Human Condition

In the preceding chapter, we discussed some of the ways in which our understandings of divine reality affect how we respond in the world. But just what is it that "sacred reality" does for believing communities? How does faith either enhance or diminish the sense of wholeness and general human flourishing? What, if anything, does it demand in return? Do our understandings of religion ever fragment human welfare and wholeness? If so, are those understandings true or false, and how can we tell? Does religion do or ask anything other than the very practical things we have discussed so far?

Setting the Stage: Living a Whole Life

What does it mean to live a "whole" life? What elements would you say are essential to such living? What elements would you choose to add to your life that might enhance your feeling of wholeness? Are there things about your life that you think detract from such a feeling? In the human "search for meaning," this quest for a sense of *wholeness* is often central. In religious traditions, what is sought is more than simply the material realities that sustain physical life. Wholeness in the religious understanding relates to our discussion of the Sacred and has a dimension of transcendence.

In her novel *The Sparrow,* Mary Doria Russell recounts the journey of a group of humans into space, to a far-flung planet from which signals have been received indicating the presence of sentient life. After a period of several years in the confines of the spacecraft, the group finally reaches orbit around the planet. For two to three weeks, the group prepares for their final descent to the surface of the planet, trying to plan for whatever they will find when they arrive. Several members of the party are Jesuit priests, some of whom, along with others such as George and Anne, are skeptical about any idea of God or transcendence at all. One of the Jesuits, Emilio Sandoz, has always regretted that he's never really had a personal experience of God—transcendence—as many others seem to have had. All of this is about to change, however, and not only for Emilio. Have you ever had an experience even remotely like that described by Russell when her characters encounter this new world for the first time?

> I would do it all again, each of them thought.
>
> And when the time came, each of them privately felt a calm ratification of those reconciliations, even as the noise and heat and buffeting built to a terrifying violence, as it seemed less and less likely that the plane would hold together, more and more likely that they'd be burned alive in the atmosphere of a planet whose name they did not know. I am where I want to be, they each thought. I am grateful to be here. In their own ways, they all gave themselves up to God's will and trusted that whatever happened now was meant to be. At least for the moment, they all fell in love with God.
>
> But Emilio Sandoz fell hardest of all, letting his fear and doubt go almost physically, his hands opening as everyone else clutched at controls or straps or armrests or someone else's hand. And when the mind-numbing scream of the engines diminished and then fell off to a silence almost as deafening, it seemed only natural that he should move into the airlock and open the hatch and step out alone, into the sunlight of stars he'd never noticed while on Earth, and fill his lungs with the exhalation of unknown plants and fall to his knees weeping with the joy of it when, after a long courtship, he felt the void fill and believed with all his heart that his love affair with God had been consummated.
>
> Those who saw his face as he pushed himself to his feet, laughing and crying, and turned back to them, incandescent, arms flung wide, recognized that they stood witness to a soul's transcendence and would remember that moment for the rest of their lives. Each of them felt some of the same dizzying exultation as they emerged from the lander, spilling from their technological womb wobbly and blinking, and felt themselves reborn in a new world.
>
> Even Anne, sensible Anne, allowed herself to enjoy the sensation and didn't spoil it by speculating aloud that it was probably plain relief at cheating death combined with a sudden drop in blood pressure to the brain, consequent to the reversal of Fat Face, Chicken Legs. None of them, not even George who had no wish to believe, was entirely exempt from transcendence.[1]

It is not long, of course, before the difficulties of day-to-day existence on this new world become an ever-present reality—the euphoria of these early moments does not last. But something has happened for each individual that they will never forget. For most of us, perhaps, moments of transcendence, or "wholeness," are not so dramatic. But might it be that those experiences we do recall, however fleeting they may have been, instill in us the desire to seek the kind of wholeness that they reflect?

Religion is a primary source for people to attempt to make sense of just what life is all about—to search for ultimate meaning. What does this have to do with "wholeness" or "healing"? Think about this question as we explore some of the ways in which religion functions in believers' lives.

WHAT DO YOU THINK?
EXPERIENCES OF WHOLENESS AND HEALING

Sometimes in times of great tragedy people who seldom think about religion find themselves turning to religious ritual, religious leaders, religious places to find consolation and healing. In the next excerpt, a Jewish father writes a letter to his children, a letter that will not be read until after the father's death. How would you feel if you were one of the sons or daughters who receive this letter after their father's death? What elements of the Jewish faith does the father invoke in an effort to comfort his family?

To my dear and beloved sons and daughters,

The purpose of this letter is to console you for when I will not be with you anymore. A person does not know when his time will be up, but the day will come (May Hashem bless me with long life) when my place at home will be empty, and you will be orphans.

My beloved, I have seen many orphans, most of whom find themselves in darkness without hope. Some are jealous, thinking, "Others have parents, but not me." Others feel that their world has tumbled down. Few are able to strengthen and brace themselves and to eventually elevate themselves after the tragedy in their lives. I therefore came to the conclusion that before one can comfort a mourner, it is essential to teach him how to deal with the situation. I hope I succeed in this endeavor, and may you understand these words so that they illuminate your lives.

The key to the mystery of life is faith in the true G-d, the Creator of the Universe! It is G-d's power that keeps the world going; even each and every blade of grass derives its sustenance from the Creator and surely each human being. This spirit of life is the essence of everything, and the most important part of a person is his spirit and soul.

I trust that I have raised you to have faith in G-d. I now encourage you to strengthen your faith and to realize that this is also the secret to the mystery of death! If life would be over for a dead person, it would be difficult to comfort a mourner. But that is not so! Although the body passes away, the person continues to exist!

Our great teacher (Rav Yeruchem Levovitz of Mir) wrote: "Death should be understood as one who moves from one city to another. This is the real truth. Your father has not died, may his memory be blessed, for he is alive.

He has merely moved. To the understanding person there is even more to say. The deceased is now even closer to you than before for now there are no separations." One who has faith is able to deal with the concept of death. The truth is that the deceased is alive! He is aware of everything, and he is close to his relatives at all times!

However, I realize that you will still be bothered by his seeming absence. Children are accustomed to seeing their parents, asking for advice and being helped. Even after they move away from home they rely on and know that they can always turn to their parents. Who can fill this void?

But, think it over, my beloved ones. If you really loved me when I was with you, and if your love was not just superficial, you can always picture me in front of your eyes. You will know what I would have said and how I would have advised you. As an example, we see what our Sages say about Yosef Hatzadik; that he withstood temptation because of the vision of his father before his eyes. Use the vision of your father to give you strength and encouragement. Keep in mind: The essence of a person is the spiritual, and that part continues to live!

Another point. All people feel an urge to come closer to mitzvos and good deeds at a time of mourning. Even those who were non-observant come to say Kaddish, they put on a *tallis* and *tefillin* and pray. What is the reason for this? There is a deep reason. Our Sages teach that there are three partners to every human being: his father, his mother and the Holy One, Blessed be He. A child is used to seeing only his father and mother. The third partner is invisible to him. However, when the physical partners leave this world, there is an inner feeling in the person that pushes him closer to the third partner.

One whose faith is strong tells this in a concrete way: "My father and mother (may) have left me but Hashem is always there."

The truth is: The physical parent was merely a messenger from the Heavenly Father. Now that the physical father's job is over the child's relationship to his Heavenly Father becomes stronger.

This is the most important message to bear in mind, for all people at any age: to strengthen one's faith, to sense Hashem's Providence, to realize how Hashem guides and leads a person daily and provides all his physical and spiritual needs. You will not lack anything if you keep your faith strong!

Through faith one will be consoled. Normally, a person is surrounded by his family, his teachers, his friends—all of them help him to maintain his life properly. However, when a relative passes away, may Hashem spare us, one of the supports has been removed.

The process of *Nichum Aveilim* to comfort the mourners is to help replace the missing support, to raise his spirits and to help him continue.

Now my beloved ones, come closer to each other, help and encourage each other; your friendship should be wholesome, faithful, amidst the love of Torah and of those who study Torah. Always be willing to learn and improve. Hashem will surely comfort you and help you continue. . . . Be strong in emunah (faith) and in Torah, build for yourselves loyal homes with the aim of fulfilling Hashem's mitzvos. Your actions shall then serve to benefit me, as our Sages say: When one's children observe the mitzvos it is considered as if the father has not passed away. This is my advice and last request of you.

My Beloved Ones: Have faith and your faith will be fulfilled, and may your lives be successful forever!

With love,
Your father[2]

Would a letter like this, either before or after your father's (or other loved one's) death, bring you comfort and consolation? The writer predicts the feelings his sons and daughters will experience after his death and attempts to address them. What elements of this letter would you find helpful? What would you add or omit?

Like Judaism, Christianity has a set of rituals the purpose of which is to comfort and console those left behind. The one who has died is not in need of further assistance; rather, the ritual actions are for those mourning, to help restore to them a sense of wholeness and to enable them to move on with their lives. In what specific ways do you think believers in this community would be consoled by the particular words in this selection from a Christian prayer book? (At "N," the person praying fills in the deceased's name.)

Merciful and compassionate God,
we bring you our grief in the loss of N and ask for courage to bear it.
We bring you our thanks
for all you give us in those we love;
and we bring you our prayers for peace of heart in the knowledge of your mercy and love. In Christ Jesus. Amen. . . .
We commend N to God,
as *s/he* journeys beyond our sight.
God of all consolation,
in your unending love and mercy you turn the darkness of death into the dawn of new life.
Your Son, our Lord Jesus Christ, by dying for us, conquered death, and by rising again, restored life.
May we not be afraid of death but desire to be with Christ, and after our life on earth, to be with those we love,
where every tear is wiped away and all things are made new. We ask this through Jesus Christ. Amen. [3]

If you have had the experience of losing someone close to you, you will know what was particularly helpful for you in bringing a sense of consolation, a feeling that life would continue, even in the midst of your grieving. We spoke in an earlier chapter of the power of ritual to accomplish some of this. What difference does it make to believe in something/someone transcendent? What is helpful if one does not have such belief?

> *Plan your own funeral or memorial service. How would you like to be remembered? What elements need to be included to truly reflect who you are? What elements do you want to include that will be of most comfort to your family and friends?*

CULTURAL AND SOCIAL DIMENSIONS OF WHOLENESS AND HEALING

We tend to think that fragmentation is not a good thing, especially for a human. The way we address the problem of brokenness is through healing. The result of that healing is wholeness. Fragmentation and brokenness can take many forms, and likewise wholeness and healing can take many forms. While these are phenomena in human life in general, we are concerned here with the ways they are experienced in the context of religious traditions.

LIBERATING PEACE

What does it mean to experience "peace"? Does that "peace" have anything to do with "wholeness"? We turn now to a selection from a novel by Jewish writer Tova Mirvis. In *The Ladies Auxiliary*, Batsheva and her daughter Ayala have come to live in a small Orthodox Jewish community in Memphis. Batsheva converted to Judaism when she married. She has been recently widowed, and her husband's family was once part of this very community. Everyone is very curious about Batsheva—it is unusual for new people to move into the community under any circumstances, and it is clear that Batsheva is "different" in many ways from other members of the community. Early in her stay, the rabbi's wife, Mimi, invites Batsheva and Ayala to share the Shabbat meal with her family. Before the men arrive home from shul, a number of women gather and engage in conversation. Finally, Mrs. Levy, another guest, can keep her curiosity under control no longer:

> "If you don't mind my asking," Mrs. Levy began, "what made you decide to convert?"
>
> There, the question was out and asking it had been easier than she anticipated. No lightning bolts had descended from heaven, no astonished gasps had filled the room. Even Batsheva didn't act like the question was that surprising. In fact, she smiled at Mrs. Levy, happy to have a chance to talk about it.
>
> "I was always pulled toward Judaism, like God was calling to me," Batsheva said.
>
> "Really," Mrs. Levy commented. She had never felt God calling out to her, and in fact, she distinctly remembered learning that He no longer called out to people so directly in this day and age.
>
> "I was walking in the city on a Friday afternoon and I passed by a shul, although at the time I didn't know what it was. The doors were open and I

walked in. I had never seen anything like it. The room was alive. The people were singing and clapping and swaying back and forth. I also started swaying to the singing. I didn't know the words. I couldn't even understand them because they were in Hebrew. But I didn't care. Maybe they had been buried in me all along, maybe they were a part of my experience from some other time or place."

"That doesn't sound like any shul I've ever been in. Are you sure it was Orthodox?" Becky asked. "From what I hear, in New York those shuls all look the same from the outside." Becky had never been in a non-Orthodox shul, but she did have a third cousin who was Conservative and this, she believed, gave her a certain authority on the subject.

Mrs. Levy cut her off. "Go on, Batsheva. What happened next?"

"A woman came over to me and reached for my arm. We swayed back and forth together. The words had ended and the tune was sung over and over. It no longer sounded like individuals singing. All the voices had melted into one. When the next prayer began, the woman took my hand and led me to a seat at the front of the women's section next to her. She handed me a siddur and I followed along in English. Soon everyone started dancing and I was swept into a circle of women. I felt like I had been doing this my whole life. Right then, I knew that I had found what I was always missing."

"You were always missing something?" Mrs. Levy inquired, to clarify.

"Before I converted, I felt this giant hole in my life, like hunger, only deeper in my body."

"But how could you be sure you wanted to be Jewish?" Mrs. Levy said. She couldn't understand why anyone would voluntarily take on so many commandments. She had enough trouble remembering all of them and she had been born into it.

"It just felt right. I knew a Jewish family when I was young. The mother would light candles on Friday night and I started going over to watch. She lit one for each of her children and she asked if I wanted her to light one for me too. I loved seeing my candle burn next to theirs. Years later, when I ended up at this shul, everything fell into place. I have to believe that there was always a hand guiding me toward Judaism."

Hearing this, Mrs. Levy felt a renewed sense that Orthodoxy was indeed correct. If someone like Batsheva wanted to be Orthodox, there was surely something to it. Not that she doubted it (or at least she didn't ever really and truly doubt it), but it was nice to have outside validation. Whenever Mrs. Levy heard about people who left Orthodoxy, she felt a pang of insecurity. Did they know something she didn't? Were they smarter than she was? Did they now look at Orthodox Jews as silly, backward, superstitious? But with Batsheva choosing it on her own, she could breathe a little easier. She gave Batsheva a genuine smile. Maybe this newcomer would fit in better than she had anticipated.

"But let's get back to your story," Mrs. Levy said, not wanting to leave any thread hanging. "What happened next?"

"When davening ended, the woman kissed me on the cheek and invited me to join them for Shabbat dinner. There were so many things I wanted to ask, but I decided to feel it and worry about all the questions later. Her living room was filled with a huge table. No places had yet been set because she never knew how many people were coming. The guests were from all over. Some were like me who had never celebrated Shabbat before and others did every week. It didn't occur to me to mention that I wasn't Jewish. No one was worried about where I was from. All that mattered was that I was there and was happy to be.

"The meal lasted for hours, and finally, after midnight, there were only five of us left. The conversation was growing more intense and I was ready for it. How does one ever feel God, one of the men was asking. How can we reach something so far from us? I caught this man's eye. That was the first time I saw Benjamin. When I left that night, he walked me home. I went back to shul the next week and introduced myself to the rabbi. We began learning together, and I converted a year later. Benjamin and I got married right afterward. By then, it felt like we had spent several lifetimes together. Even though he had grown up Orthodox, we had the same attitude toward being religious. He agreed that it was important to explore what he really felt and to always be growing in his spirituality. I had never met anyone before that I could share this with and for the first time, I was with someone who really understood me."[4]

In addition to the very clear guidelines and rules laid down for Orthodox Jews in Torah, there is some dimension to this faith that draws people, including "outsiders" like Batsheva, to embrace the tradition. What is the brokenness that Batsheva describes? How does the Orthodox faith provide healing for Batsheva? What fragmentation can you infer that Mrs. Levy feels? How does Batsheva's experience help heal Mrs. Levy's brokenness? How does her conversion to Orthodox Judaism enhance Batsheva's sense of wholeness? Why do you think she made the decision to move from her home in New York City, where there is a large Orthodox Jewish community, to the tiny, rather isolated, community in Memphis after her husband's death? You would have to read the rest of the book to find Mirvis's answer to these questions. But what do *you* think?

Many of the Eastern traditions have a strong emphasis on peace as part of what constitutes wholeness. What kind of peace is portrayed in this next excerpt from Buddhist author Thich Nhat Hanh? Is there any relationship, do you think, between Baddhiya's experience and that of Batsheva (above)? Does either of these experiences relate at all to any experience that you have ever had? (A *bhikkhu* is a monk.)

After the noon meal, the Buddha gave a Dharma talk. When he was finished, he asked bhikkhu Baddhiya to come forward before the community, which also included many lay disciples. The Buddha asked him, "Baddhiya, late last night while sitting in meditation, did you call out, 'O, happiness! O, happiness!'"

Baddhiya joined his palms and answered, "Teacher, last night I did indeed call out those very words."

"Can you tell us why?"

"Lord, when I was the governor, I lived a life of fame, power, and wealth. Everywhere I went I was flanked by four soldiers for protection. My palace was never without armed guards, day and night. Even so, there was never a moment I felt safe. I was almost constantly filled with fear and anxiety. But now I can walk and sit alone in the deep forest. I know no fear or anxiety. Instead I feel ease, peace, and joy such as I never felt before. Teacher, living the life of a bhikkhu brings me such great happiness and contentment, I am no longer afraid of anyone or of losing anything. I am as happy as a deer living freely in the forest. Last night during my meditation, this became so clear to me that I exclaimed, 'O, happiness! O, happiness!' Please forgive me for any disturbance it caused you and the other bhikkhus."

The Buddha praised Baddhiya before the entire community. "It is wonderful, Baddhiya. You have made great strides on the path of self-contentment and detachment. The peace and joy you feel is the peace and joy to which even the gods aspire."[5]

What do you think enabled Baddhiya to feel so much safer, so much more at peace, wandering in the forest, than he had in his previous life, surrounded by guards and others charged with taking care of him? How might the life of a monk, a bhikkhu, bring a wholeness that had eluded him prior to this time?

You are probably familiar with the yin yang symbol, which originates in Chinese thought and is integral to Taoism. This simple figure depicts some very complex realities that are at the heart of the Taoist understanding and philosophy of life. Taoist thought, like that of many Eastern traditions, refuses the dualism that has long been prevalent in the West. Western thought tends to see such concepts as light and darkness, good and bad, as opposites. This is not the case in Eastern thought. Rather, each dimension of a pair such as darkness and light, good and bad, is understood to contain within it an element of the other. The two concepts are complementary, not oppositional. Thus in the diagram, the dark side has within it a small white dot, and the white side contains a black dot. Such an understanding challenges the Western idea that something is *either* one thing *or* the other; rather, it is *both* this *and* that.

Reality, in this understanding, has a wholeness and unity that is different from dualistic understandings. In reading this passage from the *Tao Te Ching*, remember that the *Tao* refers to this oneness of reality—it is not a "god."

The Tao formulated the One
The One exhaled the Two
The Three were parents of all things.
All things pass from Obscurity to Manifestation, inspired harmoniously by the Breath of the Void.

Men do not like to be fatherless, virtueless, unworthy; yet rulers describe themselves by these names. Thus increase bringeth decrease to some, and decrease bringeth increase to others.

Others have taught thus: I consent to it. Violent men and strong die not by natural death. This fact is the foundation of my Law.[6]

What does it mean to say, "all things pass from Obscurity to Manifestation, inspired harmoniously by the Breath of the Void"? How does this relate to a sense of centeredness? Do you ever have the reverse experience: a day when everything you do seems to go wrong? How do you regain a sense of peace? In what ways is such a sense of peace "liberating"?

In the summer and fall of 2003, the worldwide Anglican Communion was in turmoil over the election and confirmation of The Rev. Canon V. Gene Robinson, an openly gay priest living with his long-term partner, as bishop in the diocese of New Hampshire. This turmoil seems to be ongoing. In the Episcopal Church of the United States, a diocese elects its bishop, subject to confirmation by the other dioceses. Despite the fact that this procedure was duly followed in Robinson's case, some conservative U.S. Episcopalians are objecting, as are some other Anglicans from other countries. The presiding bishop of the Episcopal Church of the United States stated that the consecration of Robinson would go on as scheduled, acknowledging a statement by the Anglican Communion that if such an act occurs "we will have reached a crucial and critical point in the life of the Anglican Communion."

The American Anglican Council, a group of conservative Episcopalians, is leading those in the United States who opposed Robinson's elevation to bishop. They threaten to leave the national church if he is consecrated. They say that their opposition is based on biblical passages that they interpret as being opposed to homosexual activity.

Robinson's supporters, also Episcopalians, say that their interpretation of those same passages is different from the AAC's, and that the Bible supports a loving committed relationship between two people.

Gene Robinson himself says, "I'm feeling really at peace, and very calm about this decision [to remain bishop elect] and about moving forward. . . . It's tough knowing what God wants, and I work with a spiritual director to determine whether it's God's voice I'm hearing, or my own ego doing a fantastic interpretation of God's voice. But one thing that helps me to believe this is God's voice is that I'm not sure anybody would choose this for the fun of it. It has been a fairly enormous burden to bear, and something that would have been easy to walk away from. . . . I am not the devil one side paints me to be, nor am I the savior the other side paints me to be. I'm just trying to hold on to who I am: Just a follower of Christ trying to discern the will of God for me. . . . While it's intense, and it's a little nerve-wracking, inside I'm pretty calm."

Of course, while Robinson's consecration may cause a different fracture in the Anglican Communion, a fracture already exists within much of Christianity in general, and many dioceses of the Anglican Communion specifically, between gay and lesbian Christians on the one hand and the pronouncements of official church bodies on the other. Those gays and lesbians who would like to remain in the religion of their choice are frequently told they must split their religious selves from their embodied selves. If they refuse, the religion condemns them.

And yet many of those who oppose Robinson do so out of what they believe Christianity calls on them to do. Who is responsible for the various fractures? What might provide peace—liberating peace—for the Anglican Communion? For the Episcopal Church? For gays and lesbians? For those who think homosexual activity is morally wrong? Can all acquire that peace?

> *Think of a time recently when you felt scattered, uncentered, unable to focus adequately on tasks you knew you had to get done. What did you do? What are your own methods of achieving at least enough focus to be able to do what you have to do? Baddhiya experiences peace and joy during his meditation. Another form of meditation is walking the labyrinth. Look up the term "labyrinth" on your Web browser and find out a little about the history of this particular method of meditation. See if you can locate a labyrinth in your area and walk it.*

ACCEPTANCE AND CHALLENGE

Sometimes we encounter challenges in our lives that are even more intense than the ones discussed above. Such a challenge is death. In our next selection, one of those involved is facing precisely that—death. Morrie, a professor at Brandeis, was diagnosed with ALS, Lou Gehrig's Disease. Rather than just wither away, Morrie uses his experience of dying to help others understand dying, and thereby, living. A former student, sportswriter Mitch Albom, begins visiting every Tuesday and taping these "lessons" with his old professor. Those tapes were the source for the long-term bestseller, *Tuesdays with Morrie.*

"Mitch, I *embrace* aging."

Embrace it?

"It's very simple. As you grow, you learn more. If you stayed at twenty-two, you'd always be as ignorant as you were at twenty-two. Aging is not just decay, you know. It's growth. It's more than the negative that you're going to die, it's also the positive that you *understand* you're going to die, and that you live a better life because of it."

Yes, I said, but if aging were so valuable, why do people always say, "Oh, if I were young again." You never hear people say, "I wish I were sixty-five."

He smiled. "You know what that reflects? Unsatisfied lives. Unfulfilled lives. Lives that haven't found meaning. Because if you've found meaning in your life, you don't want to go back. You want to go forward. You want to see more, do more. You can't wait until sixty-five.

"Listen. You should know something. All younger people should know something. If you're always battling against getting older, you're always going to be unhappy, because it will happen anyhow.

"And Mitch?"

He lowered his voice.

"The fact is, *you* are going to die eventually."

I nodded.

"It won't matter what you tell yourself."

I know.

"But hopefully," he said, "not for a long, long time."

He closed his eyes with a peaceful look, then asked me to adjust the pillows behind his head. His body needed constant adjustment to stay comfortable. It was propped in the chair with white pillows, yellow foam, and blue towels. At a quick glance, it seemed as if Morrie were being packed for shipping.

"Thank you," he whispered as I moved the pillows.

No problem, I said.

"Mitch. What are you thinking?"

I paused before answering. Okay, I said, I'm wondering how you don't envy younger, healthy people.

"Oh, I guess I do." He closed his eyes. "I envy them being able to go to the health club, or go for a swim. Or dance. Mostly for dancing. But envy comes to me, I feel it, and then I let it go. Remember what I said about detachment? Let it go. Tell yourself, 'That's envy, I'm going to separate from it now.' And walk away."

He coughed—a long, scratchy cough—and he pushed a tissue to his mouth and spit weakly into it. Sitting there, I felt so much stronger than he, ridiculously so, as if I could lift him and toss him over my shoulder like a sack of flour. I was embarrassed by this superiority, because I did not feel superior to him in any other way.

How do you keep from envying . . .

"What?"

Me?

He smiled.

"Mitch, it is impossible for the old not to envy the young. But the issue is to accept who you are and revel in that. This is your time to be in your thirties. I had my time to be in my thirties, and now is my time to be seventy-eight.

"You have to find what's good and true and beautiful in your life as it is now. Looking back makes you competitive. And, age is not a competitive issue."

He exhaled and lowered his eyes, as if to watch his breath scatter into the air.

"The truth is, part of me is every age. I'm a three-year-old, I'm a five-year-old, I'm a thirty-seven-year-old, I'm a fifty-year-old. I've been through all of them, and I know what it's like. I delight in being a child when it's appropriate to be a child. I delight in being a wise old man when it's appropriate to be a wise old man. Think of all I can be! I am every age, up to my own. Do you understand?"

I nodded.

"How can I be envious of where you are—when I've been there myself?"[7]

Several different dimensions of "acceptance" emerge in the conversation between Mitch and Morrie. Do you see any religious dimensions in the ways in which Morrie accepts the realities of aging and his own approaching death? How about Mitch? Where are the challenges and who is challenged?

Another kind of challenge is suggested in the next passage, from Shoghi Effendi of the Baha'i movement. This work was written in the mid-20th century and in it the author articulates some of the major characteristics of the Baha'i religion. If you consider the other religious traditions we have encountered, which of them do you think would be most challenged by this text? Which might accept it, wholly or in part?

> The Baha'i Faith upholds the unity of God, recognizes the unity of His Prophets, and inculcates the principle of the oneness and wholeness of the entire human race. It proclaims the necessity and the inevitability of the unification of mankind, asserts that it is gradually approaching, and claims that nothing short of the transmuting spirit of God, working through His chosen Mouthpiece in this day, can ultimately succeed in bringing it about. It, moreover, enjoins upon its followers the primary duty of an unfettered search after truth, condemns all manner of prejudice and superstition, declares the purpose of religion to be the promotion of amity and concord, proclaims its essential harmony with science, and recognizes it as the foremost agency for the pacification and the orderly progress of human society. . . .
>
> The Faith which this order serves, safeguards and promotes is essentially supernatural, supranational, entirely non-political, non-partisan, and diametrically opposed to any policy or school of thought that seeks to exalt any particular race, class or nation. It is free from any form of ecclesiasticism, has neither priesthood nor rituals, and is supported exclusively by voluntary contributions made by its avowed adherents. Though loyal to their respective governments, though imbued with the love of their own country, and anxious to promote at all times, its best interests, the followers of the Baha'i Faith, nevertheless, viewing mankind as one entity, and profoundly attached to its vital interests, will not hesitate to subordinate every particular interest, be it personal, regional or national, to the overriding interests of the generality of mankind, knowing full well that in a world of interdependent peoples and nations the advantage of the part is best to be reached by the advantage of the whole, and that no lasting result can be achieved by any of the component parts if the general interests of the entity itself are neglected.[8]

Do you see any connections between this passage and the preceding conversation between Mitch and Morrie? Are any of the same concerns addressed? Would you expect the Baha'i belief system to offer the same kind of possibility of acceptance in the face of challenges that Morrie has been able to achieve?

> *What kinds of words or activities give you courage when you need it? List some of the things that encourage you when challenged by injury, illness, disappointment, loss, and so on. Why are these particular things encouraging?*

LIBERATING COURAGE

Religion can enable believers to regain the strength and courage to go on with their lives in the face of disappointments, tragedy, and loss. And sometimes people turn to religion to give them strength to undertake difficult tasks. In what ways does Psalm 121 try to encourage the reader? What kind of assurances does it make?

> I turn my eyes to the mountains;
> > From where will my help come?
> My help comes from the LORD,
> > maker of heaven and earth.
> He will not let your foot give way;
> > your guardian will not slumber;
> See, the guardian of Israel
> > neither slumbers nor sleeps!
> The LORD is your guardian,
> > the LORD is your protection
> > at your right hand.
> By day the sun will not strike you,
> > nor the moon by night.
> The LORD will guard you from all harm;
> > He will guard your life.
> The LORD will guard your going and coming
> > now and forever.[9]

Compare these words with those of English poet George Herbert, now used in a hymn in the hymnal of the Episcopal Church in the United States.

Jesus Christ Our Lord

Come, my Way, my Truth, my Life:
such a way as gives us breath;
such a truth as ends all strife;
such a life as killeth death.

Come, my Light, my Feast, my Strength:
such a light as shows a feast;
such a feast as mends in length;
such a strength as makes his guest.

> Come, my Joy, my Love, my Heart:
> such a joy as none can move;
> such a love as none can part;
> such a heart as joys in love.[10]

How do each of these passages strengthen someone who is about to undertake a difficult or risky task? You have undoubtedly faced frightening tasks or challenges yourself. What did you say to yourself, or did someone say to you, to get you started? How did they talk to you, or talk about the task or situation, or offer aid, offer advice, or talk about the result of the proposed action?

Find some examples of "pep talks" given before or at breaks during sporting events, battles in war, or other trying times intended to encourage people. How are they similar? Do they invoke religious images or symbols?

SURVIVAL AND LIBERATION

Christianity gives us examples of the ways in which religion can do more than simply offer peace, comfort, and solace. Indeed, religion can in some instances mean the difference between survival and destruction. Under slavery, it was illegal to teach a slave to read and write in most U.S. states. The Christianity promoted by slaveowners was one that emphasized obedience to the master and general submission to whites. The Christianity developed by enslaved people themselves, however, took on a very different emphasis. It carried the promise of survival under seemingly impossible circumstances and ultimate liberation and justification, in the afterlife if not in this life. Forbidden to have meetings and to direct their own lives, slaves nonetheless found ways to express their belief that God had indeed imbued them with a human dignity denied by their masters and that if God was "Lord," the slave master was not. The next selection, from Black theologian James Cone, contains the words of two spirituals. How, according to Cone, do these spirituals convey the people's belief in their God-given dignity? Why do you think song became such an important medium of proclamation? What do the songs promise for an afterlife? How is this belief in an afterlife related to their current existence? Do you think the slavemasters would have understood the spirituals the same way the slaves did? If not, how might the masters have interpreted them? In the second spiritual, what additional meanings does the symbol of a "train" have? From what you know about the Civil Rights Movement of the 1960s, why did that symbol continue to be important?

> For black slaves, who were condemned to carve out their existence in captivity, heaven meant that the eternal God had made a decision about their humanity that could not be destroyed by white masters. Whites could drive them, beat them, and even kill them; but they believed that God nevertheless

had chosen black slaves as his own and that this election bestowed upon them a freedom to be, which could not be measured by what oppressors could do to the physical body. Whites may suppress black history and define Africans as savages, but the words of slave masters do not have to be taken seriously when the oppressed know that they have a *somebodiness* that is guaranteed by the heavenly Father who alone is the ultimate sovereign of the universe. This is what heaven meant for black slaves.

The idea of heaven provided ways for black people to affirm their humanity when other people were attempting to define them as non-persons. It enabled blacks to say yes to their right to be free by affirming God's promise to the oppressed of the freedom to be. That was what they meant when they sang about a "city called heaven."

> I am a poor pilgrim of sorrow.
> I'm in this world alone.
> No hope in this world for tomorrow.
> I'm trying to make heaven my home.
>
> Sometimes I am tossed and driven.
> Sometimes I don't know where to roam.
> I've heard of a city called heaven.
> I've started to make it my home.
>
> My mother's gone on to pure glory.
> My father's still walking in sin.
> My sisters and brothers won't own me
> Because I'm tryin' to get in . . .

These songs make clear that the future is not simply a reality to come. It is a reality that has already happened in Jesus' resurrection, and is present now in the midst of the black struggle for liberation. To accept the future of God as disclosed in the present means that we cannot be content with the present political order. God's eschatological presence arouses discontentment and makes the present subject to radical change. That was why black slaves could not "sit down." They were on the move, "tryin' to get home." They accepted the consequences of the eschatological Kingdom, and opened their minds and hearts to the movement of the future. They were bound for the Kingdom that was breaking into the already new present, and they affirmed their willingness to "git on board" that "gospel train."

> Git on board, little chillen,
> Git on board, little chillen,
> Git on board, little chillen,
> Dere's room for many a mo'.
>
> De gospel train's a-comin',
> I hear it jus' at han',
> I hear de car wheels movin',
> An' rumblin' thro de lan'.

De fare is cheap, an' all can go,
De rich an' poor are dere,
No second class a-board dis train,
No difference in de fare.

Git on board, little chillen,
Git on board, little chillen,
Git on board, little chillen,
Dere's room for many a mo'.[11]

Remembering that both spirituals are rooted in Christian tradition, how do these ideas compare with others that we have encountered throughout this text, and particularly in this chapter? Some spirituals emphasize the notion of liberation. Others, however, stress the idea of survival. Both ideas were necessary in the condition of slavery. The next selection, "You Can Tell the World," is one of the spirituals that celebrates, and enables, survival.

You can tell the world about this,
You can tell the nation about that,
Tell 'em what Jesus has done,
Tell 'em that the Comforter has come,
And He brought joy, great joy to my soul,
Well, He took my feet out the miry clay,
        yes, He did,
And He placed them on the rock to stay,
        yes, He did,
You can tell the world about this, *etc.*
Well, you know, my Lord done just what He said,
        yes, He did,
He healed the sick and He raised the dead,
        yes, He did.
You can tell the world about this, *etc.*[12]

Find some examples of Christian and Muslim rap, Jewish folksongs, etc. How might these songs enable the continuance of the group? Try writing such a song from your own perspective.

Or:

Find some songs of faith that are meant to encourage people. How do they encourage? How do they liberate or foster survival? Some examples include "We Shall Overcome," "The Battle Hymn of the Republic," "Lift Ev'ry Voice and Sing," and "The Star-Spangled Banner." (It is particularly interesting to compare the last two, the African American national anthem and the national anthem of the United States.) How does each of these songs of faith address the individual? The group?

SOME QUESTIONS ABOUT WHOLENESS AND HEALING IN LIFE

The goal of the search for meaning is *wholeness* of some kind in most, if not all, religions. Religious traditions have their own understandings of just what constitutes the human fragmentation that requires some kind of transformation to bring about that sense of wholeness. For some, the problem is more centered on the individual; for others, it has to do with the wider community, sometimes even including animals and the land itself. Each tradition also suggests particular paths that believers should follow in order to achieve transformation, wholeness, and salvation.

Sometimes the goal can be reached during the course of physical life on this earth. The Mahayana Buddhist boddhisattva achieves enlightenment but delays entry into final Nirvana, paranirvana, in order to remain on earth and assist other seekers along their way. Some Christians believe that Christ will return in the endtimes after human endeavor has created an almost-complete transformation of the current fragmented world into a more harmonious whole—the realization of God's realm on earth. Traditions—and sometimes individuals within particular traditions—vary greatly as to how much responsibility individuals have for attempting to bring about the kind of transformation that signals wholeness. Jewish thought acknowledges responsibility as co-creators with God, attempting to bring about a more just world, as do many groups within other traditions.

Religions do not, however, always bring about wholeness. Sometimes, as they are practiced by their adherents, religions instead fragment us. We are familiar with the big occasions—September 11, 2001, the Salem witch trials, the Inquisition, the Crusades, Islamic Jihad—all of which have resulted in brokenness for many. But what about the small occasions, when, perhaps, only one or two individuals are affected? Consider the times when people are ostracized in a church because they are the wrong color, or gay, or poor, or homeless. And there are times when an institutional religion takes a position without realizing some of the nuances of that position, or how it might affect persons who do not fully understand the position, or the underlying rationale. Thus, the self-immolation of Buddhist monks during the Vietnam War shocked U.S. citizens and caused some of them to question the positions and actions of their government. But it also validated the notion of self-immolation for some others who performed the act without realizing, as the monks did, that such an act could delay paranirvana, even though the monks did it in an attempt to improve the lot of the Vietnamese. Self-sacrifice by the monks was valuable in restoring self-determination to their country; the suicide of a depressed young Buddhist was unfortunate.

Whenever religions become exclusionary, they tend to fragment people. Sometimes, as the example of the Rev. Gene Robinson demonstrates, the fragmentation is to the religion itself as well as to individuals. By excluding the full participation of gays and lesbians, the conservative Episcopalians can be seen as fragmenting their church. The conservative Episcopalians see it as the fault of gays and lesbians, who exclude a particular reading of some scripture passages. They also see gays and lesbians as inherently "broken."

The Episcopalians are not the only church experiencing strife on this issue, of course. In October 2003, the highest judicial body of the United Methodist Church determined that a minister must face a clergy trial because she announced that she is a lesbian. The Presbyterians have repeatedly studied the issues of human sexuality, trying to come to consensus about appropriate positions. Orthodox Jews reject homosexuality in any form, but Reform congregations accept gay and lesbian rabbis and perform same-sex blessing ceremonies.

Just as individuals sometimes do harm when they try to do good, so do religious and other institutions. The examples extend throughout human history.

What Some Others Have Said about Wholeness

We have discussed the turmoil in the Anglican Communion over the consecration of Gene Robinson as Episcopal bishop of New Hampshire. In the last section of this chapter, we look at another aspect of the challenge to Christianity by gay and lesbian Christians. We ask questions about wholeness within the context of particular communities, a particular social location. Despite great progress in recent years, many persons are still looked upon as less than whole, healthy persons on various grounds, one of these being their sexual orientation. Anita Hill and Leo Treadway discuss this issue from their perspective as Christian ministers and participants in a program that is set up to affirm the full personhood and participation of lesbian and gay persons in their search for a spiritual home.

> Understanding gay and lesbian Christians presents a challenge for growth in faith to both clergy and laity today. Old models of working with the homosexual community began with the premise that all homosexuals needed to be cured or saved from their illness, which prompted ministry models of counseling for change to heterosexuality or sexual abstinence. Although homosexuality was removed as a diagnosis of illness in medicine and psychiatry in 1973, the notion of same-gender sexual orientation as inherently sinful has persisted in much of the religious community. . . .
>
> A conspiracy of silence about lesbians and gay men has set the tone for an inadequate or absent sociopolitical response to the needs of these individuals in church and society. Misinformation fills the void left by silence and perpetuates myths and stereotypes. Gay and lesbian people have been castigated by the church and have been the victims of violence and oppression in our society. Yet even in the face of others' denial of their common humanity and repudiation of their Christian faith, many lesbians and gay men have remained faithful people

seeking Christian community. Because of their presence and witness, the conspiracy of silence which has surrounded gay and lesbian people in Christian communities is beginning to be broken.[13]

Hill and Treadwell go on to outline the two models that have character-ized approaches to homosexuality within the psychological and religious communities. Psychology had previously used the medical model of sickness and health—homosexuality was in the manual of psychological disorders and the goal was to "cure" the person. Religion—in this instance, Christianity—used the sin and salvation model. Homosexuality is a sin and the way to sal-vation is changing one's orientation or absolute abstinence. The authors con-clude that both of these models have had devastating effects on lesbian and gay individuals. Instead, Hill and Treadwell propose a model based on health and integration.

> The old models of ministry to homosexuals were based on a system that viewed heterosexuality as the *only* and the superior sexual orientation. This heterosexist system presumed further that since there was only one true orien-tation, homosexuality was obviously a deviant and sinful choice which should be changed at any cost. Homosexuality was viewed as illness or sinfulness in need of cure or salvation.
>
> The health/integration psychological model has an underlying premise that homosexuality is not an illness, but one orientation on the scale of human sexuality, no more or less valid than heterosexuality. In this model the care-giver's focus moves away from an exclusive preoccupation with the sexual activity of gay and lesbian persons to assisting the individual to integrate a same-gender sexual orientation into one's life. The terms "gay man and lesbian woman" and "gay/lesbian persons" replace the exclusive use of the term "homosexual(s)." . . .
>
> A gay or lesbian person can integrate his or her sexual orientation into a healthy, mature life. Sexual orientation is viewed as being as inherently natural to an individual as eye and skin color. Homosexuality is not afforded any special meaning. It is seen as a fact of life; the rest is interpretation and consequence. The task of the health/integration psychological approach is to assist gay and lesbian persons in accepting themselves and integrating their sexuality into mature lifestyles. Acknowledging societal homophobia and oppression of gay and lesbian people is an integral part of the process. . . .
>
> Relief in a therapeutic experience comes when the sufferer sees the truth about [her]himself, the causes and the meaning of this suffering. Psychoanaly-sis aims to uncover and piece together the truth for the person to see, to feel, to ponder. What one wants to be true or needs to be true, what moral rules say should be true, mean nothing. Only the actual truth—unvarnished, self-evident, open to conscious and unconscious inspection—heals or can be endured. Gay and lesbian people, through coming out, are stating what they know to be true about themselves and are bringing their reality to the attention of both psychol-ogy and theology to be considered in light of their truth.

The wholeness/acceptance model presents the theological possibility of full acceptance and affirmation of gay and lesbian people. . . . This position rests on the conviction that same-sex relationships can richly express and be the vehicle of God's humanizing intentions.

Once homosexuality is considered a variation in the realm of human sexuality (no better or worse than heterosexuality), gay and lesbian life and faith experience can be taken seriously. "In the past, many gay people simply said, 'Your theory is wrong. So is your religion. Who needs it?' and left the churches. Now, more and more gay people are saying, 'Your theory does not fit our experience. Religion and the church are important to us, and we are not going to go away.'"

Coming out is a profound spiritual experience in the individual and community lives of gay and lesbian people. To name the truths about one's own reality in the world is to make the connections which end isolation, form community, and lead to an experience of liberating grace. Coming out, naming and claiming one's self even in the face of adversity and homophobia, is a freeing revelation which helps us feel God's presence in our midst. It is to know inside that even when we feel too scared or shamed to utter our own stories, God knows the story and is with us offering acceptance and a nonjudgmental listening ear.

The wholeness/acceptance model of ministry challenges Christians to follow Jesus Christ, who cared about "the most hated, discredited persons in the society in which He lived. . . . He felt their pain, knew their hunger and thirst, recognized their humanity, saw the image of God in them. In short, He loved them." In the wholeness/acceptance model gay and lesbian people, recognized as an unjustly stigmatized, ostracized group, are accepted as whole persons receiving God's grace and concern.[14]

How do you think some of the other religious traditions we have encountered throughout this book would respond to Hill and Treadway? Where would Hill and Treadway stand on the issue of Gene Robinson's consecration as bishop? In particular, does the model proposed by these authors have implications for wholeness and health beyond the issue of sexual orientation? That is, could you apply their suggestions to other individuals and groups who have been marginalized by society in general or religion in particular?

CHAPTER TWELVE

Is This All There Is?
Going beyond Death

Does religion's contribution to our human wholeness have to do only with what happens to us in this life? Is this all there is or is there more than this one life we know as a present, material reality? For as long as we have evidence of human culture, people have wondered about the "what next?" If you are a student of art or literature, you know something of the creativity that has gone into imagining life beyond physical death.

SETTING THE STAGE: LIFE'S FINAL JOURNEY

We introduce this final chapter with an excerpt from a work of fiction by May Sarton. In her novel *A Reckoning*, the main character, Laura, is diagnosed with terminal lung cancer. The story is set in the 1970s, before many of today's common cancer treatments were developed for regular use. Deciding that she does not want treatments that cannot be curative and might compromise the quality of the time she has left, Laura must decide how she wants to use that time. Sarton's narrative begins with Laura leaving the doctor's office. Try to imagine yourself in Laura's situation. What kind of reaction do you think you might have to news such as Laura has just received?

> Walking down Marlboro Street in Boston, Laura Spelman saw the low brick houses, the strong blue sky, the delicate shape of the leafless trees, even the dirty lumps of snow along the curb as so piercing in their beauty that she felt a little drunk. She now knew that she was panting not because she was overweight, but because her lungs had been attacked. "I shan't need to diet, after all." The two blocks she had to walk from Jim Goodwin's office seemed long. She stopped twice to catch her breath before she reached her little car.

Safely inside, she sat there for a few moments sorting out the jumble of feelings her interview with Dr. Goodwin had set whirling. The overwhelming one was a strange excitement, as though she were more than usually alive, awake, and in command: I am to have my own death. I can play it my own way. He said two years, but they always give you an outside figure, and my guess is at most a year. A year, one more spring, one more summer. . . . I've got to do it well. I've got to *think.* . . .

When Laura arrives home, she is greeted by Grindle, her dog, and suddenly comes face to face with some of the implications of the news she has just heard. Who will take care of Grindle and Sasha, her cat? She puts on music and sits down to think.

There were going to be some things so awful she must begin now to learn how to set them aside. One part of her being was going to have to live only in the present, as she did when Sasha jumped up and began to knead her chest. Laura pushed her off to one side where loud purrs vibrated all along her thigh. She felt herself sinking down, down into the music, the flute calling like a celestial bird with a thousand songs instead of only one in its silver throat. While she listened, she absorbed the brilliance of the light, light reflected from snow outside so that the room itself was bathed in a cool fire. Grindle gave a long sigh as he fell asleep in his corner, and Laura felt joy rising, filling her to the brim, yet not overflowing. What had become almost uncontrollable grief at the door seemed now a blessed state. It was not a state she could easily define in words. But it felt like some extraordinary dance, the dance of life itself, of atoms and molecules, that had never been as beautiful or as poignant as at this instant, a dance that must be danced more carefully and with greater fervor to the very end. . . .

Many thoughts and feelings run through Laura's head as she pours herself a drink and listens to a favorite Mozart flute concerto. Whom must she tell? How will they take the news? And what is most important to focus on in these last months?

Here the record stopped. Without music, the room where she sat became suddenly empty. . . . Only now did the full impact of Dr. Goodwin's verdict reach Laura, and she began to shake. Her hands were ice-cold. Fear had replaced the strange elation she had felt at first, and she rose and paced up and down, then leaned her forehead against the icy window for a moment. I'm not ready, she thought, I can't do it alone. But I want to do it alone, something deep down answered. And even deeper down she knew that she would have to do it alone. Dying—no one talked about it. We are not prepared. We come to it in absolute ignorance. But even as the tears splashed down on her hands, or perhaps because their flow had dissolved the awful tension of fear, Laura felt relief. After all, she told herself, we meet every great experience in ignorance . . . being born, falling in love, bearing a first child . . . always there is terror first.

In the few seconds of silence it had become clear that she was going to have to reckon with almost everything in a new way. "It is then to be a reckoning." And Laura realized that at this moment she felt closer to Mozart and Chekov than she did to her own sister. "I shall not pretend that this is not so. There isn't time. The time I have left is for the real connections. . . ."

Life had lately sometimes felt interminable, an interminable struggle—the excitement, even relief, she had experienced when Dr. Goodwin told her the truth of her condition stemmed perhaps from the fact that setting a limit gave her a sudden sense of freedom. She did not have to try so hard any longer. In a way she realized this was what she had felt during her pregnancies, that she could let life do it, for a change—and now she could let death do it. She was carrying death inside her as she had once carried life. . . .

As Laura reflects on just what those "real connections" are that she wants to honor and focus on during what time she has left, she comes to the disconcerting realization that many of them are not her family—not her deceased husband or her children, her sisters or her mother. Rather, she keeps remembering a year spent in Paris when she was a young woman and a friendship made there that has withstood the passage of time, although she and Ella have not seen each other for many years. Eventually Laura communicates news of her illness to Ella, but she does not expect to see her friend again.

As time passes, Laura becomes increasingly weak until she is bed-ridden. She knows that death is approaching.

Laura was alerted to some event happening downstairs by Grindle's excited barks and the sound of a car driving away. Mary must have been keeping the dog downstairs today, for Laura had not seen him. She opened her eyes. Daphne whispered, "I'll go down and see who it is, maybe Daisy took an earlier plane."

But Laura felt sure it was not Daisy. She was swept by a wave of agitation and wished she had the strength to get up. That she could not do, but she did manage to lift herself into a semisitting position as Daphne ran down the stairs. The front door opened and closed. She heard women's voices but could not distinguish them one from another.

Is this a dream, Laura wondered? I'm dreaming the end of a journey. It's not real. So many times in the last weeks she had heard the door open and wondered who was there, whose feet would come up the stairs in a moment. . . . Could it be death opening the door at last, death coming up the stairs? Whoever it was on the way, Laura felt an imminence and was seized by a tremor so deep she held the sheet tightly in her hands to keep them from shaking. This waiting was the longest of all, and she silently begged that it not be prolonged.

Then she heard quick, light feet on the stairs. Laura opened her eyes, but she couldn't see very well—there was a dim figure standing in the doorway.

"Darling, it's Ella."

"Oh, Snab." And then Ella was holding her cold, trembling hands, locking them into her own warmth. "Oh, Snab," Laura whispered, "I never thought you would come." . . .

She [Laura] whispered, "It's been such a long journey, but I couldn't let go—and I didn't know what I was waiting for." . . .

She didn't want to talk yet, there was fulfillment, such fulfillment simply in Ella's being there, sitting on the bed, touchable, real, not thousands of miles away, to be conjured up for comfort during the interminable nights of waiting for the dawn to come. She didn't want to talk yet, but she knew that she must summon herself back one last time. There were things she needed to say.

"You must be tired," she whispered. "Why don't you stretch out on the chaise longue. Later we'll talk." . . .

A quiet flood of happiness lifted Laura as she lay there, not that flowing tide bearing her away, but the tide at full, just before it turns. She rested there.

Was it moments or hours later when Laura opened her eyes, feeling rested, and began to talk? Her breath came in short spasms, but at least there was still breath. "Ella, can you hear me, Snab?"

"Perfectly," said Ella from the chaise longue.

The two women talk for an extended time, sharing perceptions and understandings—the "real connections," as Laura puts it. Finally, Laura's energy gives out.

The effort had been immense, and now she lay back panting.

"Rest, Snab, rest."

"I didn't cough," Laura whispered. "That's the miracle."

"Shhhh." Ella put a finger to her lips.

There was a long silence. And within it Laura knew the tide had turned and was beginning to ebb. Ella was there, not to be touched again, but strangely Laura did not want her to come closer. It was enough that she was there.

The doorbell rang. Again there were voices in the hall. Daphne, Laura thought she heard, then Daisy whispering, and a little later the guitar being softly strummed. "It's Daisy," she murmured, "to play for me."

"Do you want her to come up?" Ella asked.

"No." Then after a silence, "Only you."

There was nothing now, no silent thread to hold her back. She had only to let go, let the tide gently bear her away. She felt light, light as a leaf on a strong current. . . .

Then she was floating away. So strange, she could see Ella down there, holding her hand, but she could not feel it. She had let go.[1]

Throughout the passage, Laura's emotions run the full range of what people often describe when confronted with impending death, their own or that of someone close to them. Laura speaks of having to go through this final experience of life alone—and to a certain extent that is true. But at the end she is, of course, dependent on others for her daily care, and she comes to some important realizations about those relationships that have been the most significant throughout her life. Is this part of the "gift" of dying? Can you apply a term like "gift" to this experience?

Throughout this chapter, we will encounter individual and cultural and social responses to the reality of human mortality. Throughout, ask yourself whether thinking about these topics contributes to seeking meaning in life.

WHAT DO YOU THINK? PERSONAL UNDERSTANDINGS OF AN AFTERLIFE

Jane Dwinell is a nurse and chaplain for a hospice and a visiting nurse organization in Vermont. Over the years, Jane has spent many hours accompanying individuals and their families through the process of dying, of trying to establish meaning in this ultimate loss. In this short excerpt, Jane reflects on what she learned from one such experience:

> I learn from the dying how to live. I found out about Jennifer's imminent death even before she was born. I was working as a maternity nurse in a small hospital and was briefed by the doctors that the birth I was about to attend would be a sad one. An ultrasound done a few days before had revealed that the fetus, a female, was anencephalic. She had no brain. Her head ended just above her eyebrows. She could not live outside the womb.
>
> Before the cesarean, I talked with the parents about what they wanted. Did they want to see her? To hold her? They weren't sure. They worried about her grotesque appearance. "Cover her head," they said at last, "and show her to us."
>
> So the baby was born, and they named her Jennifer. She tried to breathe once and didn't try again. Her heart continued beating as I wrapped her in a blanket, gently covered her head, and took her to her parents. Tentatively they touched her, and as they became more comfortable there in the operating room, they held her. They uncovered her head, and they held her until her heart stopped. Remarkably, thanks to the oxygen in her system, her heart beat for nearly an hour.
>
> Jennifer taught me love and acceptance. She taught me to wonder about the nature of life and death. Had she ever really lived? When had she actually died?[2]

As in the excerpt from May Sarton's novel, it seems that Dwinell is suggesting that much can be learned about life through facing and moving through the processes of death, one's own or someone else's. What kinds of supports are necessary or desirable to assist people through experiences of death? To what extent would you say your own culture prepares people to face mortality, their own and that of persons they love?

If you were facing death—your own or that of a loved one—who would you want around you? Why? If you knew you only had six months to live, what would you do with the time you had left?

CULTURAL AND SOCIAL VISIONS OF AN AFTERLIFE

One of the common characteristics of religious traditions is that all deal in some way with what happens after we die. Many have elaborate funeral and other rituals, some of which are actually intended to help the deceased with the journey into the afterlife. Even when intended mostly for the comfort of those left behind, these practices also say something about the tradition's beliefs, and particularly about their understanding of that dimension of being that is beyond material existence.

There is great diversity among the beliefs and practices of various religious traditions, and this is nowhere more evident than in the ritual activities that surround death or approaching death and in the images of what might happen next for the person who has died. Many traditions look toward an afterlife to realize a level of justice that is never achieved in the present world; thus some kind of judgment must occur to determine what kind of reward or punishment is due each person. Yet even among these traditions, multiple ways of conceiving these rewards and punishments abound. We examine first some of the more familiar understandings of the afterlife, particularly those that include an idea of "justice," and then we turn our attention to some of the ways in which such diverse images and understandings emerge from particular social and cultural conditions and situations.

FINAL JOURNEY, FINAL JUSTICE

We spoke earlier of the kind of justice that religions often exhort their followers to seek in their present life. But what about those areas where we don't ever see justice accomplished in our lifetime? Is there ever a final accounting when those who seem to prosper while committing evil acts finally "pay" for their misdeeds? *The Egyptian Book of the Dead* offers a particularly clear account of the kind of judgment believed to occur when an individual dies. In ancient Egypt, Osiris, a god and pharaoh, ruled the underworld. After passing the judgment of Ma'at, an impartial standard of judgment, the souls of the dead were expected to testify to their fitness for being in the court of Osiris. The following selections are the words in the scroll of Ani, a religious scribe. Ani was expected to pass the judgments that awaited him, and the guidebook supplied him was to make things easier. As you read these selections, think of other writings with which you could compare these.

> Osiris, the scribe Ani, saith: "My heart my mother, my heart my mother, my heart my coming into being! May there be nothing to resist me at [my] judgment; may there be no opposition to me from the *Tchatcha;* may there be no parting of thee from me in the presence of him who keepeth the scales! Thou art my *ka* within my body [which] knitteth and strengtheneth my limbs. Mayest thou come forth to the place of happiness to which I am advancing. May the

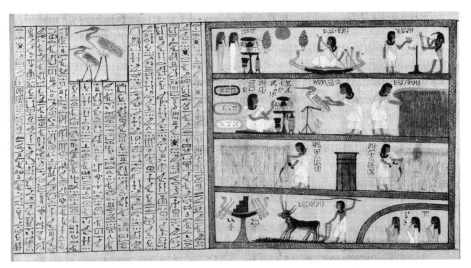

A page from one of many Egyptian "Books of the Dead," showing Maat and the god Thoth.

Shenit not cause my name to stink, and may no lies be spoken against me in the presence of the god! Good is it for thee to hear." . . .

Thoth, the righteous judge of the great company of the gods who are in the presence of the god Osiris, saith: "Hear ye this judgment. The heart of Osiris hath in very truth been weighed, and his soul hath stood as a witness for him; it hath been found true by trial in the Great Balance. There hath not been found any wickedness in him; he hath not wasted the offerings in the temples; he hath not done harm by his deeds; and he uttered no evil reports while he was upon earth."

The great company of the gods reply to Thoth dwelling in Khemennu: "That which cometh forth from thy mouth hath been ordained. Osiris, the scribe Ani, triumphant, is holy and righteous. He hath not sinned, neither hath he done evil against us. Let it not be given to the devourer Amemet to prevail over him. Meat offerings and entrance into the presence of the god Osiris shall be granted unto him, together with a homestead for ever in Sekhet-hetepu, as unto the followers of Horus."[3]

Why are so many of these declarations of innocence to the gods worded as denials? What similarities do you see between these statements and the Ten Commandments of the Torah (see Chapter 5)? The Christian scriptures? The Confucian "Silver Rule" (Don't do unto anyone what you would not want done to yourself)? Do they remind you of statements in other religions?

Another excerpt from the *Egyptian Book of the Dead* shows us a different aspect of the preparations the Egyptians made for their eventual death. While Osiris is the ruler of the underworld, there are other gods there as well. A soul must address each of them in the process of entering the court for all time.

The Negative Confession

Ani saith : "Hail, thou whose strides are long, who comest forth from Annu,
I have not done iniquity.
Hail, thou who art embraced by flame, who comest forth from Kheraba, I have
not robbed with violence.
Hail, Fentiu, who comest forth from Khemennu, I have not stolen.
Hail, Devourer of the Shade, who comest forth from Qernet, I have
done no murder; I have done no harm.
Hail, Nehau, who comest forth from Re-stau, I have not defrauded offerings.
Hail, god in the form of two lions, who comest forth from heaven, I have not
minished oblations.
Hail, thou whose eyes are of fire, who comest forth from Saut, I have not
plundered the god.
Hail, thou Flame, which comest and goest, I have spoken no lies.
Hail, Crusher of bones who comest forth from Suten-henen, I have not snatched
away food.
Hail, thou who shootest forth the Flame, who comest forth from Het-Ptah-ka,
I have not caused pain."[4]

Ani continues to address each of the gods in this way, with a specific denial.
How does this compare with the kind of "confessions of sin" that you might be
familiar with in other traditions? What do these declarations say about the
ancient Egyptian understanding of justice? What similarities do you see with
the concepts of justice that we discussed in Chapter 6?

Although religions can offer solace and the hope of better things to come
after death, there are also many concepts within religion that are less comforting. You will be familiar with some of these ideas; others might be new to you.
What function do you think each of these concepts plays in religious traditions,
in terms of positing the final achievement of justice?

IMAGES OF PARADISE

Most Western religions posit some sort of afterlife—life after death. This should
not be confused with the concept of reincarnation, which we shall discuss below.
Rather, the idea of an afterlife that is present within Christianity and Islam, for
example, concerns what sorts of rewards and/or punishments we may face, and
why we may face them. We will turn later to what happens to those deserving of
punishment. What are some ideas of heaven, or paradise, with which you are
familiar? What would be paradise for you? The first selections are from the
Qur'an. They describe the afterlife waiting for the true believers.

As for those who preserve themselves from evil
and follow the straight path,
there is attainment for them:
Orchards and vineyards,
And graceful maidens of the same age,

And flasks full and flowing.
They will hear no blasphemies there or disavowals . . .[5]

Many faces will be joyous on that day,
Well-pleased with their endeavour,
In the high empyrean,
Never hearing idle talk.
There is a stream of running water in it;
And within it are couches
placed on high,
Goblets set,
Cushions arranged,
And rich carpets spread.[6]

We can compare the Islamic passages with the next selection, a traditional African American spiritual. The people in the selections from the Qur'an above are Arabs, nomadic desert dwellers, while the African Americans in the next selection are slaves, uprooted from their native lands and subject to being sold at the slaveowner's whim or perceived need. How do these very different circumstances affect the two visions of bliss?

Oh, Glory
Ah, there's room enough in Paradise for me.
Oh, Glory! There is room enough in Paradise
To have a home in Glory!
Jesus, my all, to Heaven is gone,
To have a home in Glory;
He whom I fix my hopes upon,
To have a home in Glory!
Oh, Glory! There is room enough in Paradise
To have a home in Glory!
His track I see and I'll pursue,
To have a home in Glory!
The narrow way till Him I view;
To have a home in Glory!
Oh, Glory! There is room enough in Paradise
To have a home in Glory!

What is "heaven" according to your tradition? Are you sure? Investigate the traditions and descriptions of the destinations of the dead in your own or another tradition. Be sure to look at the sacred texts, if any. You may choose to investigate the ideas of past or present religions, for instance, Norse mythology or beliefs of indigenous people. For example, the Australian Aborigines hold that the Dreaming is just like life on earth, only the game is more plentiful. What is it about their place of origin and lifestyle that might contribute to their envisioning the Dreaming in this way? Do you have a sense of what "heaven" would be for you?

MOKSHA

Moksha, or liberation, is the view that Hindus have of a successful life and death. The goal is to no longer be reborn, to be free of samsara, the cycle of birth, death, and rebirth. The way to do this is to live your life in accord with your duties, caste, and stage of life. In this way, you will eventually reach that state where moksha is achieved.

The concept of karma is essential to understanding this belief. Connected historically—and still, in much popular practice—with the caste system, karma refers to the moral law of cause and effect. This idea is intricately connected with an understanding that one's suffering in this life is a direct result of one's prior actions, either in this life or a previous one, and one's behavior in this life will in turn influence one's status of life in future incarnations. As you read the next selection, a discussion of karma by religion scholar Huston Smith, ask yourself, how does this help Hindu believers to understand the sources of their discontent?

> The literal meaning of karma . . . is work, but as a doctrine it means, roughly, the moral law of cause and effect. The law is not foreign to the West; *"as a man sows, so shall he reap."* What India does is tighten the law to the point where it brooks no exceptions. The present condition of each interior life—how happy it is, how confused or serene, how much it sees—is an exact product of what it has wanted and done in the past. Equally, one's present thoughts and decisions determine one's future experiences. Each act that is directed upon the world reacts on oneself, delivering a chisel blow that sculpts one's destiny.
>
> This notion of a completely moral universe commits the Hindu to complete personal responsibility. . . . Karma decrees that every decision must have its inexorable consequences, but the decisions themselves are freely arrived at. . . . The course that a soul follows is charted by its wants and deeds at each stage of its journey.[7]

In addition to the law of karma, one's ignorance can prevent attainment of moksha. If one is not aware of the fact that his or her self—atman—is contained in the All-Self—Brahman—then he or she is doomed to reincarnation. In the next selection, a father is talking to his son, instructing him in the truth of his atman, his self.

> "As the bees make honey by gathering juices from many flowering plants and trees, and as these juices reduced to one honey do not know from what flowers they severally come, similarly, my son, all creatures, when they are merged in that one Existence, whether in dreamless sleep or in death, know nothing of their past or present state, because of the ignorance enveloping them—know not that they are merged in him and that from him they came.
>
> "Whatever these creatures are, whether a lion, or a tiger, or a boar, or a worm, or a gnat, or a mosquito, that they remain after they come back from dreamless sleep.

"All these have their self in him alone. He is the truth. He is the subtle essence of all. He is the Self. And that, Svetaketu, THAT ART THOU. . . .

"When a man is fatally ill, his relations gather round him and ask, 'Do you know me? Do you know me?' Now until his speech is merged in his mind, his mind in his breath, his breath in his vital heat, his vital heat in the Supreme Being, he knows them. But when his speech is merged in his mind, his mind in his breath, his breath in his vital heat, his vital heat in the Supreme Being, then he does not know them.

"That which is the subtle essence—in that have all beings their existence. That is the truth. That is the Self. And that, O Svetaketu, THAT ART THOU." [8]

What do you think Svetaketu is being told about his individual self in this passage? How does this concept differ from the idea of "heaven" discussed above?

NIRVANA

In Mahayana Buddhism, a Bodhisattva who has achieved enlightenment helps others to *nirvana*. In Theravada Buddhism, an arhat is one who reaches enlightenment, but in Theravada Buddhism the understanding is that each person must reach enlightenment on his own. (Theravada Buddhism thinks that women must be reincarnate as men before they can reach Nirvana. Mahayana Buddhism holds the view that sex is an irrelevant criterion, just as caste is.)

One may take a variety of paths to reach Nirvana, which is described only as bliss. The Buddha, when asked what Nirvana was like, responded that the question was irrelevant. He said that it was like a man who had been shot with a poison arrow who, before allowing the arrow to be removed and the wound treated, wanted to know the castes of the shooter, the doctor, and the maker of the poison. Just as treating the injury seems to be what is of primary concern, so should be the following of the eight-fold path, thereby ending suffering. So living by the eightfold path, which leads to enlightenment, leads to bliss—Nirvana, the cessation of samsara.

How similar do you think this Buddhist idea of nirvana is to the Hindu concept of moksha? Use the Web to research some of the similarities and differences. Do these concepts appeal to you? Why or why not?

PURGATORY

This is a term peculiar to Roman Catholic Christianity, and purgatory functions in something the same way as does the *samsara* cycle in Hinduism, by providing a chance beyond this life to finally achieve fulfillment. You are not reborn into this world because purgatory is a place beyond death in which the sinner has time to repent of sins committed in his or her past life and thus move on to the eternal bliss of heaven. In a way, this is a comforting notion, because the soul has a chance to atone for its sins. In *The Divine Comedy*, Dante Allighieri,

the 13th/14th century Italian poet and philosopher, portrays his own view
of purgatory.

So praying godspeed for themselves and us,
those souls were crawling by under such burdens
as we at times may dream of Laden thus,
unequally tormented, weary, bent,
they circled the First Cornice round and round,
purging away the world's foul sediment.
If they forever speak our good above,
what can be done for their good here below
by those whose will is rooted in God's love?
Surely, we should help those souls grow clear
of time's deep stain, that each at last may issue
spotless and weightless to his starry sphere.
"Ah, so may Justice and pity soon remove
the load you bear, that you may spread your wings,
and rise rejoicing to the Perfect Love— . . .
"Your way is to the right, along with ours.
If you will come with us, you will discover
A pass within a living person's powers. . . .
I had bowed low, better to know his state,
when one among them—not he who was speaking—
twisted around beneath his crushing weight,
saw me, knew me, and cried out. And so
he kept his eyes upon me with great effort
as I moved with those souls, my head bowed low.
"Aren't you Od'risi?" I said. "He who was known
as the honor of Agobbio, and of that art
Parisians call *illumination?*"
"Brother," he said, "what pages truly shine
are Franco Bolognese's. The real honor
is all his now, and only partly mine.
While I was living, I know very well,
I never would have granted him first place,
so great was my heart's yearning to excel.
Here pride is paid for. Nor would I have been
among these souls, had I not turned to God
while I still had in me the power to sin.
O gifted men, vainglorious for first place,
how short a time the laurel crown stays green
unless the age that follows lacks all grace!
Once Cimabue thought to hold the field
in painting, and now Giotto has the cry
so that the other's fame, grown dim, must yield.
So from one Guido has another shorn
poetic glory, and perhaps the man

who will un-nest both is already born.
A breath of wind is all there is to fame
here upon earth: it blows this way and that,
and when it changes quarter it changes name.
Though loosed from flesh in old age, will you have
in, say, a thousand years, more reputation
than if you went from child's play to the grave?"[9]

What do you think of Dante's description of purgatory? If you were to have an image of such a place, would it resemble Dante's in any way? Is purgatory a place of punishment or hope? How might this material have functioned in Dante's time as a guide for people contemplating their own mortality? Could it function in such a way today?

Although different from the Christian concept of purgatory, the transition period Buddhists believe in gives the person time to achieve nirvana rather than having to go again through the cycle of rebirth. In the version of Buddhism practiced in Tibet, the monks use a book, *The Tibetan Book of the Dead*, on which to meditate during their lifetimes. The focus of the book is on dying and the experiences of a soul after death. The understanding shown by the authors of the book suggests an excellent view of human psychology; while attaining Nirvana is always possible, the likelihood of one reaching it becomes more remote with each stage. To reach Nirvana, one must recognize the Buddha nature in him or herself. The trials and tribulations in the various Bardos, or places of the afterlife, are to be recognized as projections of one's psyche, not realities. At any time, you may recognize the Buddha nature in yourself and escape from further judgment. Most people fail to recognize themselves, however, and are therefore destined to be reborn. Remember that rebirth is not a goal for the Buddhist, but rather a recognition that the lifetime just finished was not completed in a way that allowed for Nirvana. After finishing your time in each of the three bardos, you will be aware of your own conception, at which time all memories cease.

The monks also use the book as a guide to help others who have died to reach Nirvana. A monk is called upon to read this book to a person who is dying, filling in his/her name in the appropriate places. Since the voyage through the Bardos is thought to take forty-nine days, the mourning and instruction to the deceased also continues for this period of time.

The next passage is from this Tibetan guidebook for the dead. Rather than being an imaginative work of fiction like Dante's *Divine Comedy*, this guide is used by Tibetan Buddhist monks to assist the dying on their way to their next life, whether a new incarnation or attaining Nirvana. The monks study the book as a way of both living and dying, and at the time of their death, their survivors read the book to them, to remind them of the passages they will see as they die. Nevertheless, what similarities do you see between Dante's work and the Tibetan Buddhist one?

Now that the process of so-called dying is upon you, frame your mind thus.

"Though the time of dying has descended upon me, I should rely upon this process of dying and generate a spirit imbued solely with the aspiration for enlightenment, that is, love and compassion. I must achieve perfect Buddhahood for the sake of all beings who are as extensive a number as space."

You should generate this attitude but in particular you should also think this: "I must recognize the radiant light of dying as the embodiment of reality and within that state achieve the supreme accomplishment, the spiritual structure of being.

"I shall then act for the benefit of all beings.

"Though I may not achieve this I shall at least recognize the dying phase for what it is and make manifest the embodiment of the spiritual structure of being that is conjoined with the dying phase. I shall then work for the benefit of all beings who are as extensive in number as boundless space, appearing in whatever form is needed to train any being."

Without letting this fervent wish slip from your mind you should now recollect the application of the instructions previously given that are familiar to you. . . .

After respiration has ceased, the guide should instruct him as follows:

Listen, (Name). The pure radiance of reality has dawned and is now present for you. Recognize it. This present aspect of your awareness that is pure and unformed, this very unformed purity devoid of any substance, attributes or colors, is reality, the All-good Mother.

Yet this unformed awareness of yours is not just a blank emptiness, for your awareness is also free from all limitations, it is sparkling, radiant, and vibrant. This is the primordial mind, enlightenment, the All-good Father.

These two aspects of your awareness; unformed emptiness and radiant vibrancy are indivisible in their presence. They form the embodiment of reality as enlightenment.

The indivisible radiance and emptiness of your awareness is present as a mass of luminosity. Herein there is no birth or death, for this is the awakened state of unchanging light.

To know just this is enough.

Knowing this pure aspect of your awareness is to know yourself as an enlightened being; for you thus to behold your own awareness is to establish yourself in the realized mind state of enlightenment.[10]

How would you feel if you were a dying monk listening to these passages being read to you by your brother monks? What do you think the experience would be like for the readers? How might knowledge of these instructions during your lifetime help you to live a better life?

HELL

According to some traditions, of course, there are those who will never attain the bliss of paradise, or even the temporary trials of purgatory. Hell may appeal to our sense of justice about recompense for injustices in this world, but it is not comforting to think of hell as a destination for oneself. For the damned, hell is the final and eternal destination. What images does the word "hell" conjure in your mind? The term is a common one in contemporary usage to describe any situation that is truly terrible, and we are probably familiar with many artistic depictions of hell. We return to Dante, whose own religious background is Christian. As you read these excerpts from Dante's descriptions of Hell, consider these questions. How does Dante "experience" death, and what medium does he use to tell others what the afterlife is to be like? Have you ever encountered similar descriptions of the afterlife? If so, were these descriptions in some religious material, or were they in a movie or TV show?

> "This is the place I told you to expect.
> Here you shall pass among the fallen people,
> souls who have lost the good of intellect."
> So saying, he put forth his hand to me,
> and with a gentle and encouraging smile
> he led me through the gate of mystery.
> Here sighs and cries and wails coiled and recoiled
> on the starless air, spilling my soul to tears.
> A confusion of tongues and monstrous accents toiled
> in pain and anger. Voices hoarse and shrill
> and sounds of blows, all intermingled, raised
> tumult and pandemonium that still
> whirls on the air forever dirty with it
> as if a whirlwind sucked at sand. And I,
> holding my head in horror, cried: "Sweet Spirit,
> what souls are these who run through this black haze?"
> and he to me: "These are the nearly soulless
> whose lives concluded neither blame nor praise.
> They are mixed here with that despicable corps
> of angels who were neither for God nor Satan,
> but only for themselves. The High Creator
> scourged them from Heaven for its perfect beauty,
> and Hell will not receive them since the wicked
> might feel some glory over them." And I:
> "Master, what gnaws at them so hideously
> their lamentation stuns the very air?"
> "They have no hope of death," he answered me,
> "and in their blind and unattaining state
> their miserable lives have sunk so low
> that they must envy every other fate.
> No word of them survives their living season.
> Mercy and Justice deny them even a name.
> Let us not speak of them: look, and pass on." . . .
> These wretches never born and never dead
> ran naked in a swarm of wasps and hornets
> that goaded them the more the more they fled,

and made their faces stream with bloody gouts
of pus and tears that dribbled to their feet
to be swallowed there by loathsome worms and maggots.
Then looking onward I made out a throng
assembled on the beach of a wide river,
whereupon I turned to him: "Master, I long
to know what souls these are, and what strange usage
makes them as eager to cross as they seem to be
in this infected light." At which the Sage:
"All this shall be made known to you when we stand
on the joyless beach of Acheron." . . .
There, steering toward us in an ancient ferry
came an old man with a white bush of hair,
bellowing: "Woe to you depraved souls! Bury
here and forever all hope of Paradise:
I come to lead you to the other shore,
into eternal dark, into fire and ice.
And you who are living yet, I say begone
from these who are dead." But when he saw me stand
against his violence he began again:
"By other windings and by other steerage
shall you cross to that other shore. Not here! Not here!
A lighter craft than mine must give you passage."
And my Guide to him: "Charon, bite back your spleen:
this has been willed where what is willed must be,
and is not yours to ask what it may mean."
The steersman of that marsh of ruined souls,
who wore a wheel of flame around each eye,
stifled the rage that shook his woolly jowls.
But those unmanned and naked spirits there
turned pale with fear and their teeth began to chatter
at sound of his crude bellow.[11]

What are the major differences in approach between this description from Dante's "Inferno" and Dante's description of purgatory (earlier)? What function do you think this kind of concept and image might play in the life of a believing Christian? Do you think this kind of image would help people to achieve wholeness? Should it be fear of Hell that impels a Christian to live morally, or should it be love of God, according to what you have read earlier?

FINAL WAYS OF JUSTICE: WHY SO MANY?

As we have discovered throughout this book, many factors determine the ways in which persons seek and find meaning in their lives. Culture and other dimensions of social location have a profound effect even on beliefs and understandings of the sacred, as well as other elements of religious traditions. To what extent does this also apply to beliefs about death and what comes after it?

DIFFERENT SOCIAL LOCATIONS

No matter what your role or position in your society, you cannot and will not avoid death. However, the dimensions of personal and social identity that we have considered throughout this book have a profound effect on how you individually will approach the idea of death—your own and that of friends and loved ones. The next two selections—on the Samurai and an African American spiritual—are examples of this. Why would Samurai have a model that called them to be always prepared to die? Although Samurai were highly respected warriors, they did not expect to inherit the family wealth or position (that belonged to the eldest surviving son), and thus they were expendable. But if Samurai died a noble death, they became honorable *kami* (spirits):

> The Way of the Samurai is found in death. When it comes to either/or, there is only the quick choice of death. It is not particularly difficult. Be determined and advance. . . .
>
> We all want to live. And in large part we make our logic according to what we like. . . . To die without gaining one's aim is a dog's death and fanaticism. But there is no shame in this. This is the substance of the Way of the Samurai. If by setting one's heart right every morning and evening, one is able to live as though his body were already dead, he gains freedom in the Way. His whole life will be without blame, and he will succeed in his calling.[12]

If you have accepted death, if you treat your body as if it were already dead, you can take risks in defense of the emperor and country that you might hesitate to take if you were concerned with living. You are resigned to death. This helps you live better and gives you an expectation of an honorable life after death.

American slaves were also seen as expendable and faced cruelties that resulted in early death. How did ideas and beliefs such as those expressed in this traditional spiritual help African American enslaved people to reclaim a sense of value and dignity in the face of the horrors and indignities of slavery? They could only dream of freedom, they expected to be slaves till they died, but they could be calm facing their circumstances secure in the belief that the Son of God was also killed by his captors yet prevailed, even to the point of overcoming death.

> They crucified my Lord
> And He never said a mumblin' word.
> Can't you hear the hammer ringin'? Surely He died on Calvary.
> They pierced Him in the side
> And He never said a mumblin' word.
> His blood came streamin' down, Lord,
> And He never said a mumblin' word, Not a word.
> He hung His head and died,
> And He never said a mumblin' word, Not a word.

The slaves could face their lot in life without complaint and despair because Jesus could. But there is another promise in spirituals—that of peace in heaven. The next selection, another traditional spiritual, expresses such calmness in the face of whatever life brings, because the healing (balm) is in Gilead (heaven). Again, why and how might slaves have found validation and hope in songs like this?

> There is a balm in Gilead
> To make the wounded whole.
> There is a balm in Gilead
> To heal the sin-sick soul.
> Sometimes I feel discouraged,
> And think my work's in vain,
> But then the Holy Spirit
> Revives my soul again.
> Oh, there is a balm in Gilead, *etc.*
> If you cannot sing like Angels,
> If you cannot preach like Paul,
> Go home and tell your neighbor:
> "He died to save us all."
> Oh, there is a balm in Gilead, *etc.*

How do the different life situations of the Samurai and the African American slaves lead to their own particular attitudes toward death and the afterlife? Do you think the eldest sons in the families from whom the Samurai came would approach life and death in the same way? What about the slaveholders who were also "Christian"? Of course, these dimensions of social status were and are not the only things that affect our beliefs and attitudes.

DIFFERENT ENTITLEMENTS

As we saw above, the social locations of people within a culture have a profound effect on the ways in which they relate to death and the afterlife. Jonathan Edwards, an 18th century Protestant minister in New England, believed in a God who knew before individuals were born who would be damned and who was to be saved. In Edwards's time, the only persons who could hold office or vote in church affairs were white male property owners, many of whom were confident that they were among those destined for salvation. On the contrary, said Edwards, only God can know who will be saved; no one can rest on a sense of entitlement.

> There is no want of *power* in God to cast wicked men into hell at any
> moment. Men's hands cannot be strong when God rises up. The strongest have
> no power to resist him, nor can any deliver out of his hands. . . . There is no
> fortress that is any defense from the power of God. Though hand join in hand,
> and vast multitudes of God's enemies combine and associate themselves, they

are easily broken in pieces. They are as great heaps of light chaff before the whirlwind; or large quantities of dry stubble before devouring flames. We find it easy to tread and crush a worm that we see crawling on the earth; so it is easy for us to cut or singe a slender thread that any thing hangs by: thus easy is it for God, when he pleases, to cast his enemies down to hell. What are we, that we should think to stand before him, at whose rebuke the earth trembles, and before whom the rocks are thrown down?

They *deserve* to be cast into hell; so that divine justice never stands in the way, it makes no objection against God's using his power at any moment to destroy them. Yea, on the contrary, justice calls aloud for an infinite punishment of their sins. Divine justice says of the tree that brings forth such grapes of Sodom, "Cut it down, why cumbereth it the ground?" Luke xiii. 7. The sword of divine justice is every moment brandished over their heads, and it is nothing but the hand of arbitrary mercy, and God's mere will, that holds it back.

They are already under a sentence of *condemnation* to hell. They do not only justly deserve to be cast down thither, but the sentence of the law of God, that eternal and immutable rule of righteousness that God has fixed between him and mankind, is gone out against them, and stands against them; so that they are bound over already to hell. John iii. 18. "He that believeth not is condemned already." So that every unconverted man properly belongs to hell; that is his place; from thence he is, John viii. 23. "Ye are from beneath." And thither he is bound; it is the place that justice, and God's word, and the sentence of his unchangeable law assign to him.

They are now the objects of that very same anger and wrath of God, that is expressed in the torments of hell. And the reason why they do not go down to hell at each moment, is not because God, in whose power they are, is not then very angry with them; as he is with many miserable creatures now tormented in hell, who there feel and bear the fierceness of his wrath. Yea, God is a great deal more angry with great numbers that are now on earth: yea, doubtless, with many that are now in this congregation, who it may be are at ease, than he is with many of those who are now in the flames of hell.

So that it is not because God is unmindful of their wickedness, and does not resent it, that he does not let loose his hand and cut them off. God is not altogether such an one as themselves, though they may imagine him to be so. The wrath of God burns against them, their damnation does not slumber; the pit is prepared, the fire is made ready, the furnace is now hot, ready to receive them; the flames do now rage and glow. The glittering sword is whet, and held over them, and the pit hath opened its mouth under them.[13]

If you were a member of Jonathan Edwards's congregation, how would you feel after this sermon? (The whole sermon, entitled "Sinners in the Hand of an Angry God," is a much longer harangue.) While many in his congregation undoubtedly thought that they were among the saved, others were not as confident. How do you think they would feel?

The next selection, a traditional African American spiritual, conveys a quite different notion of God. This God is gentle, loving and patient. What do you think brought about these two very different notions of the Christian God? The spirituals were songs of survival and liberation. This is a song of survival. This God cares for the whole world. He cares for the natural world, plants, animals, and planets. And most specifically, God cares for the human—all humans. In additional verses to this spiritual, God has "the little bitsy baby" in His hand, as well as "you and me, brother, you and me sister, right in His hand." This song envisions a God who cares about what happens to slaves as well as—perhaps more so than—what happens to the free.

> He's got the whole world in His hand,
> He's got the whole world in His hand,
> He's got the whole world in His hand,
> He's got the whole world in His hand.
> He's got the woods and the waters in His hand,
> He's got the woods and the waters in His hand,
> He's got the woods and the waters in His hand,
> He's got the whole world in His hand.
> He's got the birds and the bees right in His hand,
> He's got the birds and the bees right in His hand,
> He's got the birds and the bees right in His hand,
> He's got the whole world in His hand.
> He's got the sun and the moon right in His hand,
> He's got the sun and the moon right in His hand,
> He's got the sun and the moon right in His Hand,
> He's got the whole world in His hand.
> He's got you and me right in His hand,
> He's got you and me right in His hand,
> He's got everybody in His hand,
> He's got the whole world in His hand.

How do you think such a song would provide encouragement to slaves when they were in dire straits? Were the slaves more "entitled" to comfort than those to whom Edwards addressed his sermon? Do you think Edwards would have preached the same sermon to a congregation of slaves?

UNDERSTANDINGS OF THE SELF

As we discussed in the first chapter, religions vary a great deal in terms of how they understand the individual self. This has vast implications for the different interpretations of death and the afterlife. For example, consider the view of the human self that is illustrated in this passage from the Qur'an:

> WHEN THE SKY is cleft asunder,
> And hearkens to its Lord and is dutiful,
> When the earth is stretched out taut
> And throws out whatever it contains
> and is empty,

And hearkens to its Lord and is dutiful,
O man, you have to strive and go on striving
towards your Lord,
then will you meet Him.
And he who is given his ledger
in his right hand
Will have an easy reckoning,
And will return to his people full of joy.
But he who is given his ledger
from behind his back
Will pray for death,
But will be roasted in the fire.[14]

In this passage, the whole focus is on the individual. Although within Islam there is clearly a mandate for consideration of others in the community, as made clear in the demand for the giving of alms and for caring for those in need, nonetheless Islam is one of those traditions rooted in a somewhat individualistic idea of the person.

By contrast, we might consider some aspects of Buddhist beliefs of the self. Gaining enlightenment, in the Buddhist understanding, means acknowledging the transitory nature of selfhood and the inherent interconnection of all life. In the next passage, the young Siddhartha Gautama is brought face to face with levels of suffering that he has never before encountered. As a young man, Siddhartha, the Buddha, lived the privileged life of an upper class prince, being educated and groomed to eventually take over the rule of his father's lands and palace. As far as we know, his was a life sheltered to a great extent from the suffering that pervaded his culture beyond the walls of his own luxurious home. One day, while on an outing with his wife Yasodhara and their infant son, Siddhartha encounters a different side of life: (Channa is the coachman.)

Pleasant sunlight streamed down upon tender green leaves. Birds sang on the blossoming branches of ashok and rose-apple trees. Channa let the horses trot at a leisurely pace. Country folk, recognizing Siddhartha and Yasodhara, stood and waved in greeting. When they approached the banks of the Banganga River, Channa pulled on the reins and brought the carriage to a sudden halt. Blocking the road before them was a man who had collapsed. His arms and legs were pulled in towards his chest and his whole body shook. Moans escaped from his half-open mouth. Siddhartha jumped down, followed by Channa. The man lying in the road looked less than thirty years old. Siddhartha picked up his hand and said to Channa, "It looks as though he's come down with a bad flu, don't you think? Let's massage him and see if it helps."

Channa shook his head. "Your highness, these aren't the symptoms of a bad flu. I'm afraid he's contracted something far worse—this is a disease for which there is no known cure."

"Are you sure?" Siddhartha gazed at the man. "Couldn't we take him to the royal physician?"

"Your highness, even the royal physician can't cure this disease. I've heard this disease is highly infectious. If we take him in our carriage, he might infect your wife and son, and even yourself. Please, your highness, for your own safety, let go of his hand."

But Siddhartha did not release the man's hand—he looked at it and then at his own. Siddhartha had always enjoyed good health, but now looking at the dying man no older than himself, all he had taken for granted suddenly vanished. From the riverbank came cries of mourning. He looked up to see a funeral taking place. There was the funeral pyre. The sound of chanting intertwined with the grief-stricken cries and the crackling of fire as the funeral pyre was lit.

Looking again at the man, Siddhartha saw that he had stopped breathing. His glassy eyes stared upwards. Siddhartha released his hand and quietly closed the eyes. When Siddhartha stood up, Yasodhara was standing close behind him. How long she had been there, he did not know.

She spoke softly, "Please, my husband, go and wash your lands in the river. Channa, you do the same. Then we will drive into the next village and notify the authorities so they can take care of the body."

Afterwards, no one had the heart to continue their spring outing. Siddhartha asked Channa to turn around, and on the way back no one spoke a word.[15]

In Thich Nhat Hanh's account, this event marks a turning point for Siddhartha. His pleasant harmonious life is radically changed as he encounters the distress that exists beyond the palace walls. Shortly after this afternoon outing, he leaves the confines of the palace to take up the life of a monk. What does this action suggest about Siddhartha and his beliefs about individual personhood and death and the afterlife? Does this understanding of the personal self in relation to all creation help to explain the actions of the Bodhisattvas in Mahayana Buddhism? These persons achieve enlightenment but delay their own entry into paranirvana so as to help others achieve that goal.

Many indigenous traditions believe in interdependence not only among humans but also with all of creation. Because of their lived interdependence with nature, the afterlife is often believed to be much like this life. The only difference may be an increase in the amount of game, plants, and/or water. Again, the cultural and social context of the people influences to a great extent their beliefs about death and the afterlife.

SOME QUESTIONS ABOUT GOING BEYOND DEATH

For many religions, the quest for wholeness continues beyond physical death. This can involve both individual and communal transformation. Images of changing oppression into justice, sinners into the saved, the ignorant into the enlightened, dissonance into harmonious relationships—all indicate belief in the ongoing possibility of change, of movement toward wholeness. Sometimes, this involves paying penalties for misdeeds, for example through the Catholic belief in purgatory or the Buddhist or Hindu samsara. Whatever the specific beliefs of the religion, each attempts to provide a way for believers to move toward ultimate meaning: wholeness of being.

Many religions give us images of terrifying punishments or eternal bliss for individuals, depending on our behavior while alive. Many of these same religions, however, stress doing justice in the society to truly do the divine will, whatever name is given the divinity, leader, or concept, or even if there is no name at all. It is this justice issue that is so very basic to many religions. Why do you suppose that the reward/punishment aspect of religion came to be so important in the popular teaching of the religions, when their founding members spent much more time emphasizing right relationships in society? Even Tibetan Buddhism, whose instruction holds out the promise of Nirvana for one who recognizes the Buddha nature in her/himself, has images of terrifying figures—the wrathful Buddhas—inhabiting the Bardos. What is it about homo sapiens that makes so needful the ideas of reward and punishment? Could we ever get to a place where we could share, rather than want more for ourselves, even more heaven?

WHAT SOME OTHERS HAVE SAID ABOUT DEATH

Despite the inevitable reality of death for all living beings, contemporary Western culture finds death difficult to discuss. Think of all the euphemisms we have. How many of the following words and phrases have you heard? "Passed away," or simply "passed"; "expired"; "bought the farm"; "croaked." What other expressions have you heard?

> *Make a list of terms for death, then label each as to the attitude, the "defense" against death each represents, such as softening ("fell asleep"), transitory ("passed"), joking ("croaked"). Consider also the official terms, such as "terminated" or "pronounced dead."*

In our final selection in this chapter, we turn to Donald Heinz, author of a book called *The Last Passage*. Heinz suggests that we have lost our imagination when dealing with death, and because of this, we are not well equipped to acknowledge death as a part of life. As you read this selection from Heinz's book, consider whether or not you agree with his analysis of the contemporary Western approach to death. What might be a more helpful way to deal with this "final passage"?

In the Middle Ages "the dead were a community that lived close by and shared space with the living." Is this the mission of cemeteries? [A small garden cemetery] fills my head with musings about the world of the dead, but I do not feel uneasy, and certainly not morbid. I am wondering about my connections to these dead, imagining some common world we both might inhabit, even now. I am curious whether their dreams and failures and the color of their daily lives were much like mine. The distance between the contemporary pensive observer and those long dead may not be as great as we are determined to believe.

One can keep one's cemetery even closer to home. In Appalachia women created quilts with cloth coffins sewn on the borders, one for each member of the family. When someone died, the coffin with that name was unstitched from the border and resewn in the cemetery at the center of the quilt. Such a continuing and graceful interaction between the two worlds of the living and the dead is a long way from the twentieth-century attempt to outwit death by freezing the dead until they could be thawed, revived, and cured.

Dead are we all, and dying. "In the midst of earthly life / Snares of death surround us; Who shall help us in the strife / Lest the Foe confound us," a forgotten hymn by Martin Luther reminded us. Whatever our situation, death comes to press its claims upon us, to demand its due. We may enlarge death by the size of our wonder. We cannot extinguish it by strenuous denial. Against it we sometimes hurl epithets. Befriending it, we name it beautiful and natural. We may drive it off our daytime horizon and imagine we have escaped its power. But at night, death is "the secret agent dogging every alley way of my dreams."

From the fear of death comes conscience. From efforts to avoid its violence comes law. We may, like Marx, erect against its inexorability an inexorable historical movement. We may answer it with radical assertions of self or by bending others to our will, as romantic fascism does. But it waits inescapably to confront us, as Captain Ahab came to know of the great whale in Herman Melville's *Moby Dick*. History becomes the record of what we do with death. Schopenhauer called death the muse of philosophy. Death demands meaningful reply. With our culture we shape it, even construct it, but never fully answer it. It is always only represented, never experienced and reported on. When we try to represent it, is it a presence or an absence, a terror or a sleep? Shakespeare wrote:

> Cry woe, destruction, ruin, loss, decay;
> The worst is death, and death will have his day.

But in "When Lilacs Last in the Dooryard Bloomed" Walt Whitman offered an alternative reading:

> Come lovely and soothing death,
> Undulate round the world, serenely arriving, arriving In the day, in the night, to
> all, to each, Sooner or later, delicate death.

We fill the craters that are the wounds of death with outpourings of the heart. Religion blossoms. We are ground down by death, and we rise to visions beyond it. Which is it? Falling leaves and hurricane, friend of the old and assassin of the young, tamed and wondrous, wall and window, slayer of dreams and whisper of another world. We struggle to name the whirlwind, as everywhere around us lies its gentle and terrifying debris.

For Socrates, death is something alien, beyond which he expects to return to himself, situated in immortality. For the tragic hero death is familiar, personal, inherent. His life unfolds from death, which is not life's end but life's form—as tragic existence. Death is somehow both self and limiting Other. . . .

Today we are jerked back and forth between the living and the dead because we no longer succeed in imagining a world both inhabit. Sometimes the dead reach out from their world and intrusively force us to do their bidding. Sometimes the living manipulate the dead to enlist them for work on our side.

In death the bodies of kings have been put through their paces—organs were disbursed to multiple resting places—to serve the body politic. The journey of their remains became public theater, a miniature reproduction of death and life in the cosmos and the kingdom. Or is it the other way around, the body politic serving the king! Did the requirements of the pyramids as receptacles for kings' bodies call for a social system that made such grand ventures possible! (Do we fight wars to ward off presidential mortality?) The king's body and the body politic were sometimes at odds. Charles I of England was beheaded in order to reenliven the body politic. The funeral that followed his execution provided a social inversion: The body natural disappeared so the body politic could again become visible. Sometimes certain death does uncertain life's bidding. In the Sudan, kings were secretly suffocated at the first sign of the lessening of their powers, because that suggested *social* decay. . . .

The presence of death, sometimes benign, sometimes sharply questioning, beckons us to tasks—unfinished mourning and new creations. When we ignore death, it haunts us in various disguises. Even the appearance of the moon can invite unfinished grief work. All our watchings have filled it with tears. Death sometimes spills out of repressed consciousness and leaves its stains in unwelcome places, red blood on a white wedding dress. . . .

All mausoleums are named after the great tomb built by Queen Artemisia for her husband, Mausolos, at Halicarnassas in the fourth century B.C. By contrast, the twentieth century is the first in history in which humans dispose of the dead as unceremoniously as possible. Will mortality irresistibly break out in unwitting self-disposals, aboveground but beneath consciousness?

Individuals and social systems collaborate in their response to death, producing over time a culture of death, a death system, which is the network of symbols, rituals, and meanings by which a society mediates and expresses what death is—or what they want it to be. A close look at death systems reveals death to be a cultural product that can be made and remade. . . .

Death systems can be high-tech (cryonics) or low-tech. In America before the twentieth century, death occasioned the following homely scenario: A board was placed between two kitchen chairs and draped with a sheet. The body was laid out on it and washed. A forked stick between the breastbone and chin, fastened with string around the neck, closed the mouth. Coins closed the eyelids. In warm weather, a large block of ice was placed in a tub beneath the board and smaller chunks encircled the body.

In ancient China the death of an important person called for an entire retinue to be buried alive with him, but ceramic figures came to substitute for the living sacrifices—worthy art indeed. Until modern American military expenditures, Egypt saw the greatest percentage of gross national product devoted to death. Because death radically unsettles us, every death system is a pattern of responses intended to restore balance in the cultural system.

> A death system is a complex of cultural performances. In such performances, if we enter them imaginatively, we can see individuals and society at work, constructing meanings, revealing their values, acting out, not always fully consciously, what they think they are about. Some death systems are dense with symbols and replete with elaborate rituals, demanding the investment of great time and meaning in response to death. As a cultural construction, death remains irreversible but not immutable! [16]

Death has often been called the great equalizer—one of the few experiences that all humans share. Yet Heinz claims that death is a "cultural construction." What does he mean by this? To what extent, if at all, do our death rituals demonstrate awareness of our common humanity, and to what extent are they designed to celebrate individual uniqueness? To what extent is this influenced by our culture? Advances in medical science mean that the actual physical experience of death, at least for those persons who have access to advanced systems of health care, is dramatically different from what it might have been a generation or two ago. In what ways do you think that death will change in your lifetime? As physical death itself changes, so too will our ways of memorializing death change. Nevertheless, religious traditions remain at the center of and provide continuity for the ways in which human communities perform their end-of-life rituals, because religions express our quest for wholeness, in death as in life.

┌ **DIVERSION FOUR** ┐

Life, Death,
and the Sacred

Often, contemporary medical science and religious ideas about life and death do not seem to have much to do with each other; indeed, they may be seen as mutually exclusive. While a medical team may be doing everything possible to extend a person's life, a religious perspective may suggest that it is time to allow the person to let go and to die peacefully. Living wills, health care proxies, and other documents that make known a person's wishes about these last days and hours of life have become increasingly important as a way to maintain a level of choice even if one is no longer conscious and able to respond.

Recent trends, however, suggest that these two institutions—the medical establishment and religious traditions—might not be as far apart as has been thought. The hospice movement provides care for the terminally ill that acknowledges that "cure" is no longer possible and that the role of health care providers is now to ease the last months, weeks, or days of the dying person. Across the United States, as well as in other parts of the world, institutes and conferences attended by medical personnel, chaplains, and so forth proclaim the importance for wellness of paying attention to the spiritual dimensions of life, particularly during times of illness and crisis. As our final selection suggests, there are many ways other than conventional medical intervention—or conventional religious ministry—to assist people in their healing processes. How might Therese Schroeder-Sheker, the harpist in this selection, be said to provide "healing"? Does this apply only to family members and friends, or does it apply also to the dying person?

Therese Schroeder-Sheker is at her best when most of us are at our worst: In the company of the dying, she gains strength and is able to pass courage back. She learned of her gift in 1972 during an encounter with a man she calls an angel, explaining, "An angel gives you something that changes your life, and he changed my life." She was, at the time, a classical harpist embarking on her professional career while moonlighting in [a] Denver nursing home. Mr. Lattimore, the most ornery patient on the floor, was dying of emphysema. "I went into his room and I could hear the death rattle," Therese remembers. "He was thrashing. It was frightening for both of us. I offered my hand. Rather than push me away, as he always had, he grabbed it. He was afraid, and more than that, he needed presence. He needed a witness." She cradled Mr. Lattimore and started to sing. "I sang my way through the Mass of the Angels and the Salve Regina. We began to breathe together. I sang Gregorian chants. Long after his heart ceased to beat, I held him. Walking home that night, I thought of three words—musical, sacramental and midwifery. Death is birthing into another realm. If a woman in labor is frightened, she fights her contractions. But if she's learned breathing—to go with it—there is less agony."

Therese acted on her epiphany immediately. As she continued to study music and, subsequently, to teach at Regis University, she developed a method-ology and performed more vigils. She learned of similar work done in medieval France, and studied the music and instructions laid down by monks for achiev-ing a "blessed death." By the mid-1980s, Therese was teaching a course in death vigils and participating in more and more of them, sometimes aided by her stu-dents. She gave her efforts a name: The Chalice of Repose Project. "A chalice is an empty vessel that can be filled with spirit," she says. "And repose means a place where we experience deep, intimate rest."

Music as therapy was nothing new: Traumatized soldiers returning from World War II were soothed with music in hospitals, and today there are more than 5,000 certified music therapists in the U.S. But from the start, the Chalice Project was about music for the dying. Therese considers herself a music-thanatologist—from the Greek Thanatos, meaning death—and says, "Ours is a contemplative practice with clinical applications." She can seem esoteric, but stresses the science of her methods. Even with some unconscious patients, she says, "we can change heart rate and respiration. The entire skin surface serves as an extension of the ear."

Once Therese had organized her teachings and procedures for the vigils, she became an evangelist for music-thanatology, telling hospitals everywhere about its benefits. In April 1990 she gave a talk at St. Patrick Hospital in Missoula, a town of 50,000 in western Montana. Lawrence White, the hospital's president, recalls, "Therese did this presentation, and doctors were crying. You don't see that in this business. You can spend years studying, and out of the blue you encounter knowledge that is foreign but absolutely pertinent." White told Therese her mission could have a home at St. Pat.

In Missoula she met with some unease. "I was a skeptic," says Dr. Stephen Speckart, a 25-year veteran oncologist. "I wondered if this woman was a mys-tic. I thought, Aren't we proceeding a little quickly here?" Today, Speckart is the medical director of the Chalice Project. "I have seen nothing as effective as this. We can now reduce pain medications for the dying by a significant amount."

The vigils aren't meant just as painkillers, of course. "We try to work with the patient's pain," says Therese, "but also give the family a way to share. Sometimes they're the ones who need rest, or need to let go."

The Chalice of Repose Project has its detractors, among them ex-students who tired of Therese's philosophy or had problems with the program's focus. One complained in the local press last year that he thought he was joining a program based on Middle Ages infirmary song, but "I never saw any of that music in the year I was in the Chalice program." Despite criticisms, most folks in Missoula have taken Chalice to their hearts. They don't care what music is played if the result is solace. The late Michael Morris, who was a justice of the peace in town, turned to Chalice in the last stages of his cancer in 1996, saying the music "made a place for me to accept my death." That's all his fellow Missoulans needed to know.

The Chalice Project is now an institution. More than a hundred doctors have referred patients. Harpists are on duty from eight A.M. to eight P.M., 365 days a year, and teams of Chalice musicians make "mercy runs" out of town at a moment's notice. Foundations, private donors and the hospital support Chalice services—the Project has an annual budget of $600,000—and no individual seeking comfort is denied. Chalice veterans teach alongside Therese in the Project's school, where a rigorous two-year program starts with study of the ancient Gilgamesh epic, travels through a medieval Latin death ritual and on to graduation. Then the students are ready for service—in Missoula, or wherever they spread their gospel.

Today, at St. Patrick, a vigil has been prescribed, and Therese herself answers the call. She hurries down the hospital's corridors, carrying her harp like a balsa-weight cross. She arrives at the room, composes herself and enters. She learns that the ill person is, as the physicians call it, "actively dying." As she sets up quietly in the corner, she hears a plea to the patient: "You said you wouldn't leave us!" Therese is in no way immune to the emotions of the moment, but she cannot be of assistance unless she maintains a sense of calm. She puts the harp to her left shoulder, fingers the strings and starts to play. Gently. The patient glides in and out of consciousness, eyes wandering, lingering for a time on Therese's face. She is careful to keep her countenance comforting. She plays an Irish air, "The Gartan Mother's Lullaby," at a slow tempo. The music seems to guide the patient away from the realm of beeping monitors, away from this antiseptic hospital room, toward something beautiful and restful. All conversation has stopped, and then the patient's spouse says, "It's O.K., it's O.K. You can go." There is an exhalation, audible to all. The patient has died. The music continues even as a doctor notes time and cause. Nurses switch off machinery. Harp song is a backdrop for soft sobbing. The harpist has helped as best she could.[1]

Music, here, seems to have the ability to not only comfort the dying and their relatives, but also to make it possible for the relatives to "let go" of their loved one. This is frequently the source of much of the difficulty of a person's death; a dying person will often "hold on" if his or her family is begging for them to do so, long beyond what is comfortable for the patient. How does this capacity of music—and other artistic expressions—relate to our discussions of the sacred? Can music, even music that is not explicitly religious, convey a sense of the sacred? And does the listener have to be explicitly religious to be "healed"?

Would you like to have music played if you were gravely ill in the hospital (remember that music seems to help with healing as well as with dying)? In the article, the healing qualities of the music seem to come from its soothing capabilities. What sort of music would you like? Make a list of pieces of music and identify how you think each would contribute to your healing. Plan your own funeral, incorporating both healing music and comforting/significant texts, sacred and secular.

⌞ EPILOGUE ⌝

While we tested differing versions of this text in classes, students sometimes wondered, aloud or privately, when we were going to get to religion. One such student realized as she wrote her final paper that religion was what she had been learning about all along. Another apologized that his take-home quiz was so long and in some ways disjointed. As he answered the original questions, other questions occurred that he thought needed to be dealt with, or that just interested him. Another, again in the final paper, said that he felt we had come full circle; he was returning to the question of identity, but with some idea of what the religious dimension provided.

All three of these students experienced what you are experiencing now—the end of the book. And in it, nobody told you what religion is—or did they? In one sense you got an introduction to a way to live a fulfilling life: continue to question the things you are told, regardless of who is doing the telling; realize that answers you were once comfortable with may not continue to suffice. We believe that such a way of living is valuable for many reasons, but essential to the development of a personal sense of what "religion" is.

Another thing you have encountered is the notion of the academic study of religion. Yes, religion is something that many people practice at least part of the time, *and* it is an academic discipline. Approaching it as an academic discipline, you encountered all religions equally. If you were completely honest, you knew that some of your religious background kept wanting to jump into the discussion, but you also knew that learning of other religions, and religion per se, would enrich your life. Even if you are not religious, and have no intention of ever becoming religious, we hope that you recognize by now the benefit of knowing something of this subject that is of vital importance to many.

In this book you have been introduced to different religious traditions. Some of you may have or may find a religion which is a good fit, but we doubt you'll find one that is a perfect fit, particularly if you consider all the different ways people understand their own religions. So you will probably question parts of your religious tradition, even as you find comfort in it. You may well find ways in which a particular understanding leads to unspeakable abuses. Don't just wash your hands of the religion; challenge it.

We started this exploration of religion with discussions of identity, symbols, and rituals. That supplied the language to understand many of the other concepts.

We encountered together the word *evil*, which is used to symbolize those things we abhor, those things which seem less than human beings can be expected to be. Ethics gives us an understanding of how we should behave, and justice clarifies how we should be responsible for ourselves and others. Ethics and justice are the ways with which we can respond, individually and communally, to evil.

Probably the hardest thing for most of us in the West to comprehend is that reasonably there can be different standards of knowledge and truth, that the scientific method is not the only way to discern and verify truths. But many truths are verified in other ways. Intuition is highly valued by Easterners, and by many Westerners, even Western scientists. Feeling is another way of validating and verifying truth. All of these methods can, and should, be used in discerning Sacred Truth. For example, the great Roman Catholic theologian St. Thomas Aquinas used Western logic in writing his works of theology. His axioms came as a matter of belief—a combination of intuition and feeling—but the systematic theology he composed from these axiomatic statements is a model of systematic logic.

Looking at the power, authority, and tradition that are present in the various religions showed us examples of false authority and its abusive power; outdated traditions and the problems they can cause. Using the language of symbols and ritual, and the criteria of ethics and justice, we can discern which traditions, authority, and power are beneficial and which are not.

All of our exploration culminates in the various understandings of the sacred that we have discussed. After all, this is what we've been talking about all along. All these religions are about Sacred Truth. And Sacred Truth can give us a guidepost for meaning in our lives.

Wholeness, during life and as a metaphor for what comes after death, is a way of saying that a meaningful life will be a healthy life. These understandings of how to be in this life, and how to face death when it is near, are basic pieces of a meaningful life.

Many of us make a distinction between the two terms, "religion" and "spirituality." Often, what people mean is that there is a difference between practicing an institutional religion and having a dimension in one's life that goes beyond ordinary. Are these two concepts mutually exclusive? Although many people engage in profound spiritual practices without having a concrete connection to an established religion, and others may engage in religious practices more out of habit than of spiritual conviction, a deep spirituality exists at the core of the religious traditions we have encountered throughout this text.

One element that is essential to religions is community. From our discussions about identity all the way to our explorations of different concepts of what happens beyond death, we have been constantly aware of the ways in which individuals and communities are intricately connected with each other.

Often, when someone claims to be spiritual but not religious, she or he is not talking about an experience in community, but her or his own feelings, without the feedback from others. While our spiritual experiences are often intensely personal, there is a danger inherent in losing sight of the social nature of human beings.

In other fields, we recognize that we need to do the occasional "reality check;" we need to do so in religion as well. For example, a person could find spiritual meaning in a fire, but if that fire begins to burn out of control, the person needs to be able to recognize that fact, rather than merely to watch the object of his or her worship destroy many lives and property. Even solitary mystics, those in various religions who have profound experiences of an encounter with the divine, remain in community. This may not always involve physical proximity, but without a sense of connection to and interaction with their community, they would not know whether or not a particular experience was a valid mystical experience or a product of their own imagination.

In addition to a contemporary community, spiritual experiences need a connection with a history, with the richness provided by the experiences of those who have gone before. You may have heard of Jim Jones in Guiana. Jones began with noble motives; he wanted to start a church, a spiritual community that was truly integrated and welcoming of members of all races and ethnicities. But Jones and his followers became increasingly isolated from other Christian groups and from the society in general and ultimately moved as a group to the country of Guiana in South America. While the development and eventual violent end of Jones' "Peoples' Temple" requires far more complex analysis than is possible here, we can say that the mass suicide of members was in part the tragic result of disconnection from the historical Christian community.

Of course, historical religion is by no means free of its own errors. But spirituality that remains in relationship with traditional religions retains the ability to avoid the mistakes of the past and to correct some current mistakes. For example, self-flagellation used to be a practice in some Christian monastic orders. Today, most of these groups would agree that such practices do not reflect a healthy spirituality. The history of the religion, along with contemporary understandings of the human personality, has provided a corrective for the individual spirituality. Another example would be the practice of unquestioning obedience to authority. For example, the abuse of children in the Roman Catholic Church was perpetrated by those who also abused their authority. The abuses continued for as long as they did in part because the parents of the abused children—and often the children themselves—accepted the authority of the priests concerned. For the parents, this meant in many cases that they did not believe that their children were telling the truth. Many children who had been given an elevated view of the priest as an unquestioned representative of God kept secret the abuse, as they were told to do. Experience and history have led to the current questioning of blind obedience to clerical authority; this is no longer likely in the United States version of Roman Catholicism.

Yet, while we need to hold religious practices up to communal scrutiny in light of historical and contemporary experiences, the traditions of a religion are part of its strength. Whether participating in a liturgy or merely sitting in the sacred space of a religious community, a sense of why their adherents continue to follow their religion, even as they argue with portions of it, can be present to a person. This comforting—strengthening—of a person is one of the hallmarks of a religion.

Religion can strengthen a person to help with individual challenges and sorrows; it can also provide the strength and motivation that person needs to work in community to seek and do justice in the world. Religion, at its best, calls its adherents to be more than they thought they could be, to reach for ideals, to transcend in this lifetime at least some of the limitations the world places upon them. Judaism, for example, charges its followers to take on the task of recreating paradise. A Buddhist bodhisattva postpones paranirvana to assist others in their search for enlightenment. Christianity and many other traditions have had their martyrs, some of whom we have encountered in this book—Martin Luther King, Jr., Dietrich Bonhoeffer, Mohandas Gandhi, Oscar Romero—who have paid with their lives for seeking political and economic justice for others. Of course, most of us will not be called upon to surrender our lives in the cause of justice, but for many many people the courage and motivation to seek to create a better world, as part of their own search for meaning, come from religion.

Religion is one way of searching for meaning. Many, worldwide, find it a powerful and valuable source of meaning. Even those who no longer practice their religion as it is institutionalized find that religion a source of their spiritual life. Others stay more active in the religion, offering a loving critique of the religion, pointing to ways the institutional religion has become a force against the life-giving, life-affirming intent of that particular faith. Institutional religion can also be life-giving and life-affirming. In fact, the life-giving and life-affirming aspects of a religion are precisely why people try to reform the religion from within. How religion serves to give meaning to life depends on the person. Because you are that person, for your own life, we hope you have—not answers to remember or forget—but challenging questions to ask and to ponder.

⌐ ENDNOTES ⌐

CHAPTER ONE

1. John (Fire) Lame Deer and Richard Erdoes, *Lame Deer: Seeker of Visions* (New York: Pocket Books, 1972), pp. 1–7.

2. Dietrich Bonhoeffer, *The Cost of Discipleship,* trans. J. B. Leishman (New York: Scribner, 1959), p. 15.

3. Dorothee Sölle, *The Strength of the Weak: Toward a Christian Feminist Identity,* trans. Robert and Rita Kimber (Philadelphia: Westminster Press, 1984), p. 166.

4. Ibid., p. 168.

5. Ibid., p. 167.

6. Ibid., pp. 166–167.

7. D. R. Schanker, *A Criminal Appeal* (New York: Dell, 1998), p. 1.

8. Freda McDonald, "No Longer an Indian: My Story." In *Native American Religious Identity: Unforgotten Gods,* ed. Jace Weaver (Maryknoll, NY: Orbis, 1998), p. 73.

9. W. A. C. H. Dobson, trans., *Mencius* (Toronto: University of Toronto Press, 1963), pp. 114–116. Parentheses indicate material added by the translator for clarity.

10. Martin Luther King, Jr., "I See the Promised Land." In *A Testament of Hope: The Essential Writings and Speeches of Martin Luther King, Jr.,* ed. James M. Washington (New York: HarperCollins, 1986), pp. 284–286.

11. *The Upanishads,* trans. Swami Prabhavananda and Frederick Manchester (New York: Mentor, 1975), pp. 69–70.

12. Thich Nhat Hanh, *Old Path White Clouds: Walking in the Footsteps of the Buddha* (Berkeley, CA: Parallax Press, 1991), pp. 169, 172–173.

13. Chiang Yee, *The Chinese Eye: An Interpretation of Chinese Painting* (Bloomington: Indiana University Press, 1964), pp. 9–10.

14. Psalm 8, *Tanakh* (Philadelphia: Jewish Publication Society, 1985).

15. Viktor Frankl, *Man's Search for Ultimate Meaning* (Cambridge, MA: Perseus, 2000), pp. 29, 67–68.

16. Ibid., pp. 68, 70–71.

17. Ibid., pp. 84–85.

CHAPTER TWO

1. John (Fire) Lame Deer, *Lame Deer: Seeker of Visions* (New York: Pocket Books, 1972), pp. 107–117.

2. Patricia Wen, *Boston Globe,* July 28, 2000. Copyright © 2000 Globe Publishing Company.

3. Mari Evans, "Status Symbol." In *I am a Black Woman* (New York: William Morrow, 1970), pp. 68–69.

4. Spider and Jeanne Robinson, *The Star Dancers* (Riverdale, NY: Baen, 1997), pp. 203–205.

5. Jeremy Horner © Corbis 2004.

6. *Popol Vuh: The Mayan Book of the Dawn of Life,* trans. Dennis Tedlock (New York: Touchstone, 1996), pp. 145–149.

7. Simeon Potter, *Our Language.* (London: Pelican Books, 1953), p. 116.

8. Carl G. Jung, "Approaching the Unconscious." In *Man and His Symbols* (New York: Dell, 1964), pp. 3–5, 41–42.

9. Carolyn Walker Bynum, "Introduction: The Complexity of Symbols." In *Gender and Religion: On the Complexity of Symbols,* ed. C. W. Bynum, S. Harrell and P. Richman (Boston: Beacon Press, 1986), pp. 2–4.

CHAPTER THREE

1. Hassan Hathout, *Reading the Muslim Mind* (Plainfield, IN: American Trust Publications, 1995), pp. 65–68.

2. Tom F. Driver, *Liberating Rites: Understanding the Transformative Power of Ritual* (Boulder, CO: Westview Press, 1998), p. 30.

3. Rick Barrett, "Roadside Memorials Bring Both Comfort and Concern," *Milwaukee Journal Sentinel,* May 22, 2001.

4. James Baldwin. *Go Tell it on the Mountain* (New York: Dell, 1952), pp. 11, 14–15.

5. Anita Diamant. *The Red Tent* (New York: Picador, 1997), pp. 170–175.

6. Dayan Grunfeld, quoted at http://www.ou.org/chagim/shabbat/remember.htm (site located October 12, 2003).

7. Shudha Mazumdar, *Memoirs of an Indian Woman,* ed. and intro. Geraldine Forbes (Armonk, NY: M. E. Sharpe, 1989), pp. 18–23.

8. Susannah Heschel, April 2001, at http://www.miriamscup.com/Heschel_orange.htm (site located October 12, 2003).

9. Harriet Cole, *Jumping the Broom: The African-American Wedding Planner* (New York: Henry Holt, 1995), pp. 17–18.

10. Margaret Atwood, *The Handmaid's Tale* (New York: Fawcett Crest, 1995), pp. 356–360.

11. Driver, *Liberating Rites,* pp. 164–165.

DIVERSION ONE

1. A. Cohen, *Everyman's Talmud* (New York: Schocken, 1975), pp. 235–237.

2. Hilari Bell, *Navohar* (New York: Penguin, 2000), pp. 185–189.

3. Brenda Peterson, *Build Me an Ark: A Life with Animals* (New York: W. W. Norton, 2001), p. 82.

CHAPTER FOUR

1. Timothy Roche, "Andrea Yates: More to the Story," *Time,* March 18, 2002; *Boston Globe,* passim March 9–16, 2002.

2. Elie Wiesel, *Night* (New York: Bantam, 1960), p. 4.

3. Gregory E. Pence, *Classic Cases in Medical Ethics* (New York: McGraw-Hill, 1990), pp. 136–138.

4. Ric Kahn, "More than a Statistic," *Boston Globe,* February 17, 2002 (© Copyright 2002 Globe Newspaper Company).

5. Myrna Oliver, "Obituary," *Boston Globe,* February 18, 2002 (© Copyright 2002 Globe Newspaper Company).

6. Thich Nhat Hanh, *Old Path White Clouds: Walking in the Footsteps of the Buddha* (Berkley, CA: Parallax Press, 1991), pp. 146–147.

7. Jonathan Ebel, "Sightings," http://divinity.uchicago.edu/martinmartyinterim.html, Martin Marty Center at the University of Chicago Divinity School (accessed February 15, 2002).

8. Manil Suri, *The Death of Vishnu* (New York: W.W. Norton, 2001), pp. 13–14.

9. Yvonne Daley, "The Persistence of the Ugly American," *Boston Globe Magazine,* December 2, 2001, p. 22 (© Copyright 2001 Globe Newspaper Company).

10. Sindiwe Magona, *Mother to Mother* (Boston: Beacon Press, 1998), pp. 1–4.

11. Sister Helen Prejean, CSJ, *Dead Man Walking* (New York: Vintage, 1993), p. 17.

12. Mary Midgley, *Wickedness: A Philosophical Essay* (New York: Routledge and Kegan Paul, 1984).

13. Ibid., p. 7.

14. Ibid., p. 14.

15. Ibid., pp. 15–16.

CHAPTER FIVE

1. Octavia Butler, *Parable of the Sower* (New York: Four Walls Eight Windows, 1993), pp. 173–176.

2. Shelley Murphy, "Thomas Junta," *Boston Globe,* January 12, 2002, p. B7 (© 2002 Globe Newspaper Company).

3. Exodus 20:1–19, 21, *Tanakh.*

4. Yuzan Daidoji, *The Code of the Samurai,* trans. A. L. Sadler (Boston: Charles E. Tuttle, 1988), p. 30.

5. Mark 4:1–9, NRSV.

6. Michelle Chaflin, Northeastern University, Summer 2002. Used with permission.

7. Lama Surya Das, *The Snow Lion's Turquoise Mane* (San Francisco: HarperSanFrancisco, 1992), p. 78.

8. Steven Morris, "Jodie and Mary: The Point Where the Law, Ethics, Religion and Humanity Are Baffled," *The Guardian,* September 9, 2000, located at http://www.guardian.co.uk/uk_news/story/0,3604,366306,00.html.

9. "Sacred Ground," from the CD *Second Wind.* Words by Judy Small, music by Judy Small and David Bates (© 1993, Fairfield, Victoria, Australia: Crafty Maid Music).

10. P. M. Carlson, *Murder in the Dog Days* (New York: Bantam, 1991), pp. 223–226.

11. Pete Tobias, "Twin Dilemmas of God and Man," *The Guardian,* September 16, 2000, located at http://www.guardian.co.uk/comment/story/0,3604,369053,00.html.

12. Mary Midgley, "Trying Out One's New Sword." In *Heart and Mind* (New York: St. Martin's Press, 1981), pp. 69–75.

CHAPTER SIX

1. Ursula K. LeGuin, "The Ones Who Walk Away from Omelas." In *The Wind's Twelve Quarters* (New York: Harper & Row, 1975), pp. 276–284.

2. Barbara Kingsolver, "Household Words." In *Small Wonder* (New York: Harper Collins, 2002), pp. 195–197.

3. Steven McFadden, *Profiles in Wisdom: Native Elders Speak about the Earth* (Santa Fe: Bear, 1991), pp. 21–22.

4. *The Teachings of Mencius,* trans. W. A. C. H. Dobson (Toronto: University of Toronto Press, 1963), Chapter 6.

5. Exodus 23:9–12, *Tanakh.*

6. Deuteronomy 15, *Tanakh.*

7. Leviticus 25:1–7, 10–13, 35–42, 54–55, *Tanakh.*

8. Luke 4:14–19, NRSV.

9. Mohandas K. Gandhi, "Through Non-violence to God." In *Hinduism,* ed. Louis Renou (New York: George Braziller, 1962), pp. 233–236.

10. http://www.mfa.gov.il/mfa/go.asp?MFAH00hb0; document downloaded October 18, 2003.

11. http://www.mideastinfo.com/documents/pncharte.htm; document downloaded October 18, 2003.

12. Martin Luther King, Jr., "A Time to Break Silence." In *A Testament of Hope: The Essential Writings of Martin Luther King, Jr.,* ed. James M. Washington (San Francisco: HarperSanFrancisco, 1986), pp. 242–243.

13. Karen Lebacqz, *Justice in an Unjust World: Foundations for a Christian Approach to Justice* (Minneapolis: Augsburg, 1987), p. 128.

14. Kwame Gyekye, *An Essay on African Philosophical Thought: The Akan Conceptual Scheme.* New York: Cambridge University, 1987, pp. 132, 155–158.

DIVERSION TWO

1. "Frankenstein" is the name of the young scientist in Mary Shelley's novel *Frankenstein, or, The Modern Prometheus.* Intrigued by advances in the study of human anatomy and of electricity, Dr. Frankenstein puts together an adult male body from pieces of various cadavers and brings it to life electrically. He immediately loathes and abandons the monster he has created, which is visually repellent, but childlike in its needs and desires. Rejected by nearly everyone, the "monster" receives kindness and an education from an elderly scholar who is blind, but when family members see him, he is again reviled and rejected. He then turns on humanity, especially his creator, Frankenstein. The monster has no name. (Summary statement courtesy of Dr. Patricia B. Craddock.)

2. Michael Brannigan and Judith Boss, *Healthcare Ethics in a Diverse Society* (Mountain View, CA: Mayfield, 2001), p. 260.

CHAPTER SEVEN

1. Hermann Hesse, *Siddhartha,* trans. by Sherab Chödzin Kohn (Boston: Shambala, 2000), pp. 79–85.

2. Chet Raymo, "A Way of Knowing, Ways of Believing," *Boston Globe,* November 9, 1998 (© Copyright 1998 Globe Newspaper Company), p. C2.

3. Antoine de Saint-Exupery, *The Little Prince,* trans. Richard Howard (New York: Harcourt, 2000), pp. 56–64.

4. Linda Raymond, *Rocking the Babies* (New York: Penguin, 1994), pp. 12–16.

5. Chet Raymo, "Science Musings," *Boston Globe,* January 24, 1994, (© Copyright 1994 Globe Newspaper Company).

6. Jerome Lawrence and Robert E. Lee, *Inherit the Wind* (New York: Bantam, 1955), pp. 53–55.

7. Ibid., pp. 68–72.

8. Dava Sobel, *Galileo's Daughter* (New York: Walker, 1999), p. 8.

9. Ibid., p. 65.

10. Evelyn Fox Keller, *A Feeling for the Organism: The Life and Work of Barbara McClintock* (New York: W. H. Freeman, 1983), pp. 201–206.

CHAPTER EIGHT

1. Robert Lawlor, *Voices of the First Day: Awakening the Aboriginal Dreamtime* (Rochester, VT: Inner Traditions International, 1991), p. 88.

2. Genesis 1:1–19, *Tanakh.*

3. Victor Weisskopf, "The Origin of the Universe," as quoted in Gary Kessler, *Voices of Wisdom* (Belmont, CA: Wadsworth, 2001), p. 600.

4. Anglican Church in Aotearoa New Zealand and Polynesia, *A New Zealand Prayer Book* (San Francisco: HarperSanFrancisco, 1989), p. 181.

5. John (Fire) Lame Deer and Richard Erdoes, *Lame Deer: Seeker of Visions* (New York: Washington Square Press, 1972), pp. 22–25.

6. *Chuang Tzu,* Book 18, as cited in Robert E. Van Voorst, *Anthology of World Scriptures* (Belmont, CA: Wadsworth, 2003), p. 171.

7. As cited in Daniel Bonevac, Wm. Boon and Stephen Phillips, *Beyond the Western Tradition: Readings in Moral and Political Philosophy* (Mountain View, CA: Mayfield, 1992), pp. 67–68.

8. Denise Levertov, "Mass for the Day of St. Thomas Didymus." In *Candles in Babylon* (New York: New Directions Books, 1982), pp. 113–115.

9. *Bhagavad Gita,* trans. Stephen Mitchell (New York: Three Rivers Press, 2000), pp. 47–48.

10. Acts 2:41–47, NRSV.

11. *Al-Qur'an: A Contemporary Translation*, trans. Ahmed Ali (Princeton, NJ: Princeton University Press, 1993), Surah 4, 1–11.

12. Chaim Potok, *My Name Is Asher Lev* (New York: Fawcett Crest, 1972), p. 264.

13. Ibid., p. 295.

14. Ibid., pp. 312–313.

15. Ibid., p. 338.

16. Katie Waitman, *The Merro Tree* (New York: Ballantine, 1997), pp. 319–320.

17. Genesis 1:20–2:4a, *Tanakh.*

18. Genesis 2:4b–25, *Tanakh.*

19. Northrop Frye, *The Great Code: The Bible and Literature* (New York: Harcourt Brace Jovanovich, 1981), pp. xviii–xix.

20. Ibid., p. 200.

21. Ibid., pp. 202–203.

22. Ibid., pp. 204–206.

23. Ibid., p. 208.

24. Ibid., pp. 218, 224–226.

CHAPTER NINE

1. Michele Kurtz, *Boston Globe,* June 6, 2002 (© 2002 Globe Newspaper Company), p. B1.

2. http://www.v-a.com/communication/star-spangled-banner.html. Located February 15, 2004.

3. Joseph Stein, *Fiddler on the Roof,* lyrics by Sheldon Harnick (New York: Limelight, 1964), pp. 2–3.

4. Rich Barlow, "Interview with Arleigh Prelow," *Boston Globe,* August 10, 2002 (© 2002 Globe Newspaper Company), p. B3.

5. Oscar Romero, *The Violence of Love,* comp. and trans. James R. Brockman, S.J. (Farmington, PA: The Plough, 1988), p. 3.

6. Inge Scholl, *The White Rose: Munich 1942–1943* (Middletown, CT: Wesleyan University Press, 1983), pp. 5–12.

7. Onnie Lee Logan, with Katherine Clark, *Motherwit: An Alabama Midwife's Story* (New York: E. P. Dutton, 1989), pp. 168–175.

8. Meredith B. McGuire, *Religion: The Social Context* (Belmont, CA: Wadsworth, 1997), pp. 244–245.

9. Ibid., p. 246.

10. Ibid., pp. 278–279.

DIVERSION THREE

1. Steve Charleston, "The Old Testament of Native America." In *Lift Every Voice: Constructing Christian Theologies from the Underside,* ed. Susan Brooks Thistlethwaite and Mary Potter Engels (San Francisco: Harper & Row, 1990), pp. 56–60.

CHAPTER TEN

1. Alice Walker, *The Color Purple* (New York: Pocket Books, 1982), pp. 175–179.

2. Lao-tzu, *Tao Te Ching,* trans. by Ko Hsüan (Aleister Crowley) (York Beach, ME: Samuel Weiser, 1995), pp. 40, 49.

3. Lee Hall, *Spoonface Steinberg and Other Plays* (London: BBC Books, 1997), pp. 153–155.

4. Apuleius, *The Golden Ass,* trans. by P. G. Walsh (New York: Oxford University Press, 1994), pp. 220–221.

5. Marjorie Shostak, *Nisa: The Life and Words of a !Kung Woman* (New York: Random House, 1981), p. 300.

6. Steven McFadden, *Profiles in Wisdom: Native Elders Speak about the Earth* (Santa Fe: Bear, 1991), pp. 136–137.

7. Exodus 3:2–6, *Tanakh.*

8. I Kings 19:11–13, *Tanakh.*

9. Nehemiah 9:16–17, *Tanakh.*

10. Nahum, 1:1–2, 8, *Tanakh.*

11. Luke 12:51–53, NRSV.

12. Luke 34:14, NRSV.

13. Surah 59:22–24, *Al-Qur'an.*

14. W. Goldsack, "On God." In *Selections from the Muhammadan Traditions* (Madras, India: Christian Literature Society for India, 1923).

15. Toni Morrison. *Beloved* (New York: Alfred A. Knopf, 1987), pp. 87–89.

16. Catherine Madsen, "If God Is God She Is Not Nice," *Journal of Feminist Studies in Religion* 5, no. 1 (Spring 1989), pp. 103–105.

17. Anne C. Klein, response to Catherine Madsen, "If God Is God She Is Not Nice," *Journal of Feminist Studies in Religion* 5, no. 1 (Spring 1989), pp. 112–115.

CHAPTER ELEVEN

1. Mary Doria Russell, *The Sparrow* (New York: Fawcett Columbine, 1996), p. 189.

2. "A Letter of Consolation," quoted by Rav Shlomo Wolbe, Aley Shur, located at http://judaism.about.com/gi/dynamic/offsite.htm?site=http://www.shemayisrael.co.il/burial/index.htm.

3. Anglican Church in Aotearoa New Zealand and Polynesia, *A New Zealand Prayer Book* (San Francisco: HarperSan Francisco, 1989), pp. 822–823.

4. Tova Mirvis, *The Ladies Auxiliary* (New York: Ballantine, 1999), pp. 89–91.

5. Thich Nhat Hanh, *Old Path White Clouds: Following in the Footsteps of the Buddha* (Berkeley, CA: Parallax Press, 1991), pp. 254–255.

6. Lao-tzu, *Tao Te Ching,* trans. Ko Hsüan (Aleister Crowley) (York Beach, ME: Samuel Weiser, 1995), p. 60.

7. Mitch Albom, *Tuesdays with Morrie: An Old Man, A Young Man, and Life's Greatest Lesson* (New York: Doubleday, 1997), pp. 118–121.

8. Text located at www.Bahai-library.org (copyright © National Spiritual Assembly of The Baha'is in the United States, 1996).

9. Psalm 121, *Tanakh.*

10. Words by George Herbert. Hymn 487, 1982 Hymnal of the Episcopal Church of the United States.

11. James H. Cone, *The Spirituals and the Blues* (San Francisco: Harper & Row, 1972), pp. 91, 93–94.

12. Ibid., p. 234.

13. Anita C. Hill and Leo Treadway, "Rituals of Healing: Ministry with and on Behalf of Gay and Lesbian People." In *Lift Every Voice: Constructing Christian Theologies from the Underside,* ed. S. B. Thistlethwaite and M. P. Engels (San Francisco: Harper & Row, 1990), p. 234.

14. Ibid., pp. 237–238.

CHAPTER TWELVE

1. May Sarton, *A Reckoning* (New York: W. W. Norton, 1978), pp. 7–10, 248–254.

2. From *World,* the Journal of the Unitarian Universalist Association, July/August 2000, pp. 20–25.

3. *The Egyptian Book of the Dead,* trans. E. A. Wallis Budge (New York: Dover, 1967—reprint of 1895 edition), pp. 258–259.

4. Ibid., p. 347.

5. *Al-Qur'an: A Contemporary Translation,* trans. Ahmed Ali (Princeton, NJ: Princeton University Press, 1993), Surah 78.

6. Ibid., Surah 88:8–16.

7. Huston Smith, *The Illustrated World's Religions: A Guide to Our Wisdom Traditions* (San Francisco: HarperSanFrancisco, 1986), pp. 49–50.

8. *The Upanishads,* trans. Swami Prabhavananda and Frederick K. Manchester (New York: Mentor, 1975), p. 71.

9. Dante Alighieri, *The Divine Comedy of Dante Alighieri,* "The Purgatorio," trans. John Ciardi (New York: W. W. Norton, 1977), pp. 244–245.

10. *The Illustrated Tibetan Book of the Dead: A New Translation with Commentary,* trans. Stephan Hodges with Martin Boord (New York: Sterling, 1999), pp. 34–36.

11. Alighieri, *Divine Comedy,* "The Inferno," pp. 14–15.

12. *The Hagakure,* as cited in Michael C. Brannigan, *The Pulse of Wisdom: The Philosophies of India, China, and Japan* (Belmont, CA: Wadsworth, 1995), p. 344.

13. Jonathan Edwards, "Sinners in the Hands of an Angry God," at http://www.jonathanedwards.com/sermons/Warnings/sinners.htm. 10/27/03

14. *Al-Qur'an: A Contemporary Translation,* Surah 84:1–12.

15. Thich Nhat Hanh, *Old Path White Clouds: Following in the Footsteps of the Buddha* (Berkley, CA: Parallax Press, 1991), pp. 79–80.

16. Donald Heinz, *The Last Passage: Recovering a Death of our Own* (New York: Oxford University Press, 1999), pp. 32–38.

DIVERSION FOUR

1. Joshua Simon, "This Harpist's Job Is to Ease the Pain, Soothe the Soul," *Life Magazine,* December 1998, p. 108. For more information, Chalice of Repose is at 554 West Broadway, Missoula, Montana 59802. Visit its website at www.saintpatrick.org or call (406) 329-2810.

⸤ CREDITS ⸥

CHAPTER THREE

DIVERSION ONE

CHAPTER FOUR

CHAPTER EIGHT

CHAPTER NINE

DIVERSION THREE

⌈ PHOTO CREDITS ⌉

┎ Name Index ┚

꛷ SUBJECT INDEX ꛸